CRIMINAL
LAW

CRIMINAL LAW

DIANA ROE

Hodder & Stoughton

A MEMBER OF THE HODDER HEADLINE GROUP

Orders: please contact Bookpoint Ltd, 39 Milton Park, Abingdon, Oxon OX14 4TD. Telephone: (44) 01235 400414, Fax: (44) 01235 400454. Lines are open from 9.00 – 6.00, Monday to Saturday, with a 24 hour message answering service. Email address: orders@bookpoint.co.uk

A catalogue record for this title is available from The British Library

ISBN 0 340 730 595

First published 1999
Impression number   10 9 8 7 6 5 4 3 2 1
Year   2005 2004 2003 2002 2001 2000 1999

Cover artwork by Joanna Fernihough
Typeset by Wearset, Boldon, Tyne and Wear.
Printed in Great Britain for Hodder & Stoughton Educational, a division of Hodder Headline Plc, 338 Euston Road, London NW1 3BH by Scotprint, Musselburgh, Scotland.

ACKNOWLEDGEMENTS

Every writer on Criminal Law (and indeed almost every judge and practitioner), owes an enormous debt of gratitude to Professor John Smith and the late Professor Brian Hogan, for their comprehensive and definitive works on Criminal Law. It is also a pleasure to listen to Professor Smith's learned comments on the changes being effected in this area of law, as he gives his time so freely at various conferences.

The author would also like to thank the other authors of articles in the *Criminal Law Review* who have been mentioned in this book. Thanks also to the editorial team at Hodder & Stoughton Educational, particularly Clare Smith and Melanie Hall, for their help and guidance, to my students for their enthusiastic contributions, and finally to my husband Peter, for all his encouragement, practical help and total support.

The author and publisher would like to thank the following for their permission to reproduce copyright text material:

The Controller of Her Majesty's Stationery Office: pages 40–1.
© Telegraph Group Limited, London, 1998: pages 7, 61, 85, 148, 240, 157.
© Times Newspapers Limited, 25/03/98 (p. 62), 09/02/96 (p. 84), 15/10/98 (p. 208), 31/07/98 (p. 224).
The Evening Standard, pages 6, 36, 95, 133–4, 229, 253.
The Essex Chronicle, pages 115, 138–9.
The Guardian, page 38.

Every effort has been made to trace copyright holders; any omissions brought to our attention will be corrected in future printings.

TABLE OF CONTENTS

CHAPTER 15 BRINGING IT ALL TOGETHER

CHAPTER 1

INTRODUCTION TO CRIMINAL LAW

1.1 INTRODUCTION

IN THIS CHAPTER we shall be looking at certain preliminary matters relating to the study of criminal law. The elements of a crime will be looked at in Chapter 2 and then, in Chapters 3 to 9, there will be a discussion of the main criminal offences required for most examination boards. Chapters 10 and 11 deal with general defences and are followed by chapters on the various parties to a crime, a discussion of inchoate (incomplete) offences and the subject of vicarious and corporate liability. Chapter 15 endeavours to bring everything together into a comprehensive whole and to give advice on revision and examination technique.

In this first chapter, therefore, we discuss the reasons for writing this book and describe its structure. We then go on to look at the nature of criminal law and the definition of a crime. The next sections will investigate where the criminal law is to be found, give a brief description of the prosecution process and look at how criminal offences are classified. Following this, there will be a more detailed description of the criminal courts, with particular emphasis on the appeal system. The next section will look at the importance of the doctrine of binding precedent in criminal law and the reasons for citing cases. The chapter will conclude with an investigation into ways in which the criminal law is updated and reformed and the bodies involved in this process.

1.1.1 THE REASONS FOR WRITING THIS BOOK

Criminal law, which affects all our lives in one way or another, is an enthralling subject, in spite of all its imperfections, and most students beginning their A Level studies or embarking on their law degree courses will be looking forward to studying it.

Sometimes, however, this initial enthusiasm can wane as the student becomes drowned in a sea of detail and cannot see the wider position or, alternatively, cannot find the answers to the questions posed. It can be very frustrating when it seems impossible to grasp the intricate issues. At times like this, you should remind yourselves that the fault might not be yours at all! Some of the judges might also have experienced difficulties with the matter in hand, have come to different conclusions on it, and, in this way caused the confusion in that particular area of law. In other cases, the material studied seems to assume a basic knowledge of the law that you might not possess at the beginning of your studies. Conversely it might be incomplete, necessitating yet another visit to the law library to try to discover the outcome of a case or further detail. In addition, it is often difficult to discover the current state of the law or information about the reforms that are being planned.

My aim in writing this book, therefore is to try to address some of these issues and hopefully, in the process, make your life a little easier.

I aim to provide a clear explanation of the law, backed up by informed comment on the more controversial aspects of it. Reports from newspapers are included to help such discussion and show the relevance of the legal issues. 'Key facts' charts will clearly sum up the current state of the law in a particular area and indicate the cases and statutes in which the law is laid down. Problem questions and topics for discussion are included in the 'activities' section. The aim here is to persuade you to study the material in the chapter and, hopefully, get you to enjoy tackling the topics chosen, rather than regarding them as a chore. Lastly, at the end of each chapter, there is a brief summary of the material discussed.

1.1.2 WHO WILL BENEFIT FROM THIS BOOK?

The book is designed as a companion volume to Jacqueline Martin's best selling book on the English Legal System and is geared specifically for students studying criminal law as the whole or as part of their second paper in A Level Law. It is in sufficient depth to enable such students to reach the very highest grades and also to be of great value to students on law degree courses or for those studying for the Common Professional Examination. It is also clear enough to help the student with less time for study, who should be able to muster a pass grade simply by studying the key facts and the commentary sections – provided that this is accompanied by an ability to apply the law to the facts given. Hopefully, therefore, the book will assist students of all abilities and varying amounts of time.

1.2 THE NATURE AND DEFINITION OF A CRIME

One of the most important differences between civil and criminal law is that, in the latter, the State plays a major role in the proceedings. It will be noted in 1.4 that nearly all prosecutions are initiated by the State in one form or another in order to protect the public from harm. It is interesting to note, however, that there are current proposals to make it easier for a private individual to bring his own prosecution, should the State refuse to do this, but such cases remain very rare. Criminal wrongs are normally dealt with by the State for the following reasons.

First, they often concern matters that are so serious, for both the victim and for the public at large, that it is felt that they cannot just be left to the individuals concerned. Secondly, a claim for financial compensation would often be seen as totally inadequate: the victim and the public would want the perpetrator to be restrained and thereby rendered harmless. In addition, even where the matter could be dealt with by way of compensation, it would often be unfair for the victim to bear the expense of such a move. Again, with other wrongs, such as some of the minor public order offences, there may be too little interest on the part of individuals in getting the matter dealt with. The State therefore is called upon to deal with these problems. It now needs to be established which of the wrongs fall into this category.

There have been many attempts to define the meaning of a crime, most of them extremely lengthy. My own simple definition would be to describe a crime as a wrong against the State, either by commission or omission, regarded by that body as criminal and one to which a punishment has been attached. This helps to explain the nature of a crime but, it should be noted, still fails to address the issue of why it comes into this category. Many crimes are also moral wrongs, such as the crimes of murder and theft, but crime and morality do not always combine in such a definite way. A large section of the community would argue that it is morally wrong to tell lies or to commit adultery but, unless the lies are told under oath or the adultery committed in public so as to offend against public decency, the criminal law will not become involved. Conversely, illegal parking or drinking after hours, while thought to be anti-social and thoughtless acts, would not normally be regarded as moral wrongs. A study of criminal law will also show that, while certain crimes remain constant, views about other behaviour may change over the years. For example, acts classed as criminal 40 years ago are not offences today, such as suicide, which was decriminalised in 1961 and homosexual acts between consenting adults for which the law was changed in 1967. The Wolfenden Committee in 1957 decided that it was not the function of the criminal law to interfere in the private lives of citizens in order to try to impose certain standards of behaviour more than was considered necessary. It was felt that this should only be done:

> to preserve public order and decency, to protect the citizen from what is offensive or injurious, and to provide sufficient safeguards against exploitation and corruption of others, particularly those who are especially vulnerable.

The law, however, did not change until 10 years later, and even then there was still a continuing debate as to whether the age limit imposed by the State should remain as it was in order to protect the young or, instead, be lowered to give the latter more freedom of choice. This conflict is also apparent when the subject of decriminalising the taking of 'soft' drugs, such as cannabis, arises.

1.3 SOURCES OF CRIMINAL LAW

In addition to trying to identify whether a particular form of conduct should be regarded as criminal, there are also difficulties in finding the existing law. Criminal law is an uneasy mixture of common law rules, i.e. rules laid down by the judges over the years, and legislation. The latter is the law coming from Parliament in the form of Acts of Parliament and delegated legislation. Some statutes are of very ancient origin; for example, the Treason Act was passed in 1351. Before the last century, however, the law coming from Parliament was fairly limited and large areas of the criminal law were left to be developed by the judges. Much of this has subsequently been put into statutory form, such as the law of theft, which is now to be found in the Theft Act 1968. Our judges decided in the case of *Knuller v DPP 1973*, that it is not now their function to make new law so this will normally be done by Parliament. Despite this fact, large pockets of law still remain judge-made. A notable example is the crime of murder; there is no Act of Parliament to refer to, to discover the definition of this offence; instead, it has developed over the years.

Parliament has, however, has become involved in several ways. The common law definition used to state that the death had to occur within a year and a day. This ruled prevailed until 1996. The Homicide Act 1957 does not, as the name suggests, describe the crime of murder; instead it lays down three situations which, if successfully pleaded, will reduce the crime from murder to manslaughter. The Murder (Abolition of Death Penalty) Act 1965 suspended the death penalty for murder, except for treason and certain forms of piracy and a later piece of delegated legislation made this permanent. The Crime and Disorder Act 1998 has now removed the death penalty for treason and piracy. It can thus be seen that the law on murder or voluntary manslaughter is a confusing mixture of judge-made rules and statutory provisions. The law on involuntary manslaughter, discussed in Chapter 5, remains completely judge-made.

Even in cases where all the law on the subject is in statutory form, such as in theft and criminal damage, the judges may become involved with the relevant legislation if called upon to decide the meaning of a particular word or phrase in the act, should this be unclear.

Discovering the source of much of criminal law is not, therefore, an easy process. There have been increasing calls for a special criminal code to deal with this problem and update the law. This is not a new request. A draft code was put before Parliament as long ago as 1878 and, again, in the following two years but was never brought into law. A similar fate seemed to await the Draft Criminal Code drawn up in 1989, discussed later in this chapter, although it now appears that its provisions may be enacted in a gradual way.

1.4 THE PROSECUTION PROCESS AND CLASSIFICATION OF OFFENCES

1.4.1 THE DECISION TO PROSECUTE

As stated earlier in this chapter, the decision to prosecute comes from the State via the Director of Public Prosecutions, who is the head of the Crown Prosecution Service. In most cases, the police will start the investigations and until 1985 they carried on to prosecute. The Prosecution of Offences Act 1985 changed the position because it was believed that a separate body should be involved in this process. Despite this laudable aim, the CPS has had a bad press, with complaints being made about poor administration and the quality of its lawyers. The current Lord Chancellor has promised action on this. The CPS is not the only body involved in the prosecution process; officials from local authorities, such as Trading Standards Officers, and the Serious Fraud Office may also decide to start a prosecution. In addition, a private prosecution may be launched, although these are rare. With regard to serious offences under the Official Secrets Acts, the Attorney General, who is higher in the power structure than the DPP, must give permission for these to progress.

When making the decision to prosecute, regard must be given to the evidence available, which needs to be substantial and reliable, and whether it is in the public interest to do so. When there is doubt, the accused should be given the benefit of it, which inevitably means that some offenders are never brought to trial.

1.4.2 THE CLASSIFICATION OF OFFENCES

Offences are put into two broad categories, summary offences, the more minor ones and indictable offences, which are more serious. The James' Committee, however, recommended dividing cases into three: offences triable summarily, offences to be tried on indictment only and a third category of cases that could be tried either way. We need to look at these categories in turn.

Summary offences

These offences must be tried in the magistrates' court because an Act of Parliament decrees that they will be dealt with summarily. Normally three lay magistrates try the case although, in some of the larger towns a legally qualified, paid magistrate, called a stipendiary magistrate, will decide the case alone. If the defendant pleads not guilty, the magistrates act as both judge and jury, deciding the matter of guilt or innocence and fixing the sentence. Most of these offences are fairly minor, including minor traffic offences but, periodically, they are added to by Parliament and more serious ones have been included. Examples of summary offences are speeding, illegal parking, careless driving, assaulting a police officer in the execution of his duty, minor criminal damage, assault and battery, and driving or being in control of a vehicle with excess alcohol in the blood.

Indictable offences

Offences tried on indictment are the more serious or complicated ones which must be dealt with by the Crown Court. Such offences include offences laid down by the Official Secrets Act, murder, manslaughter, robbery, blackmail, arson and causing death by dangerous driving. The case will normally start in the magistrates' court, where the accused will be committed for trial in the Crown Court.

The magistrates still have an important task of deciding whether the accused will be remanded in custody or released on bail until his trial takes place. The Bail Act 1976, as amended, states that everyone has a general right to bail, unless the offence is a serious violent one, in which case the magistrates must state in open court why they are giving bail. In other cases, bail will be allowed unless there is a good reason why it should be refused, such as the likelihood of the defendant committing further offences or absconding.

Offences triable either way

As the name suggests, it is possible for such offences to be tried summarily in the magistrates' courts or, on indictment in the Crown Court. Under the Magistrates' Court Act 1980, it is for the courts to decide this matter. If it is decided that the case is more suitable for trial on indictment, then it must be dealt with in this way; the accused has no say in the matter. If, however, the magistrates decide that they do have enough power, (and a Practice Note of 1990 states that magistrates should be allowed to decide the case unless it has one or more of a list of aggravating features to it which make it more suitable for the Crown Court), the defendant may choose whether he wants this form of trial or would prefer to take his case to the Crown Court. The vast majority of offenders choose summary trial but in a dangerous driving or theft case, for example, the accused may believe, (often wrongly), that a jury trial will give a better chance of an acquittal. If the accused chooses such a trial, committal proceedings will take place and the case will be set down for trial in the Crown Court.

If the accused chooses magistrates' court trial, he must first be warned that the magistrates have the power to send him to the Crown Court, if they have found him guilty and believe that their powers are insufficient to deal with him. It should be remembered that magis-

trates only have the power to impose a fine of £5000 or less and/or a sentence of imprisonment of six months for any one offence.

Examples of triable either way offences include the ones just mentioned of theft and dangerous driving, burglary, actual bodily harm, criminal damage over £5000, indecent assault and obtaining property or services by deception.

1.5 THE SYSTEM OF CRIMINAL COURTS

1.5.1 COURTS OF FIRST INSTANCE

We have already noted these courts in the last section; they consist of the magistrates' courts and the Crown Court with its many branches. As stated, magistrates' courts, on the criminal side of the law, will deal with all the summary offences and with the triable either way offences where the defendant has chosen summary trial. The Crown Court is reserved for indictable offences and those triable either way offences where the magistrates decide that they have insufficient power to deal with them and cases where the accused opts for this form of trial. Trial in the Crown Court will be by a single judge, if the defendant pleads guilty, or by judge and jury if the defendant pleads not guilty. In the latter case, the jury of 12, who are selected at random, will decide upon the verdict, after listening to the facts and hearing advice on the points of law involved from the judge. The latter will be a circuit judge or a recorder (a part-time judge) for the less serious indictable or triable either way cases dealt with in this court. For the most serious cases, a High Court judge will officiate. This judge normally sits in the Queen's Bench Division of the High Court but makes periodical visits to the branches of the Crown Court on his circuit. He is sometimes known as the 'Red Judge', because of the colour of his robe.

Deliberations in the jury room are secret and, when they are complete, the foreman delivers the verdict in open court. Majority verdicts, of 11–1 or 10–2 are now accepted. If the defendant is acquitted, he will walk free from the court and cannot be retried for the same offence. If the jury finds the defendant guilty, the judge will do the sentencing. Most offences have a maximum sentence laid down by statute, but no minimum, giving the judge a large measure of discretion. Exceptions to this are certain forms of treason and piracy and the crime of murder, which have a fixed sentence of life imprisonment. Until 1998, the first two crimes were, theoretically, punishable by death but this position changed with the passing of the Crime and Disorder Act 1998. In addition to these crimes with a sentence fixed by law, the controversial Crime (Sentences) Act 1997 lays down a mandatory sentence of life imprisonment where the defendant is found guilty of a second, serious violent offence, as illustrated by the following article.

Two strikes put man in jail for life

A MAN jailed today for a brutal and motiveless stabbing at a London nightclub became one of the first in Britain to receive a life sentence under new "two strikes, you're out" legislation.

The attack carried out by Robert Thompson last November nearly killed his victim and was committed shortly after he was released on licence for another vicious knife attack in which he stabbed a man at a railway station, then pursued him over electrified tracks to stab him again.

The life sentence imposed by Judge Alan Hitching at Snaresbrook Crown Court was immediately welcomed by detectives. Sergeant Gary Holmes said: "Thompson is a tailor-made candidate for being dealt with in this way. He lives on violence, he just loves it. He carries knives all the time and loves to attack his victims in front of friends."

Thompson, 24, from Willesden smiled at friends in the public gallery during today's hearing. In the attack at the Rex nightclub in Stratford on a Saturday night last November he and an accomplice, who escaped, repeatedly stabbed warehouse foreman Nigel Skeete after accosting his girlfriend.

"They pursued him across the dance floor and cut him down," said sergeant Holmes. "He was stabbed eight times and extremely lucky not to die.

"It was an unprovoked display of extreme ferocity and sustained violence. Thompson is a man who has been looking to kill someone for years in my view and he needed to be put away."

It will be six and a half years before the parole board even looks at Thompson's case. His criminal record began as a teenager with convictions for carrying knives, an attack by a gang on a landlord with baseball bats in which he wielded a Stanley knife and the station attack in 1992, for which he received a five year sentence.

In that case only the skill of doctors and paramedics saved his victim. Under the 1997 Crime and Sentences Act a life sentence is now mandatory for certain categories of violent crime where a defendant receives a second conviction.

Jailing Thompson, the judge said: "We are dealing with someone who is a persistent knife carrier and who went out armed with a knife. When one looks at your record it is clear that the use and carrying of knives is a repeated feature. This is a case where mandatory life sentence has to be passed."

Thompson's own counsel, Richard Latham QC, said: "I have to concede this is a man with a series of previous convictions relating to knives. This isn't a man with psychopathic tendencies but he obviously needs to learn to manage his anger."

Taken from an article by Patrick McGowan in the *Evening Standard*, 26 June 1998

The judges would prefer not to have their discretion in sentencing fettered in this way, even in the crime of murder, in order that all the circumstances of the case may be looked at. The Lord Chief Justice has added his voice to this campaign, as the following report shows.

End mandatory life for murder, says senior judge

MANDATORY life sentences for murder should be abolished and judges should fix minimum jail terms, Lord Bingham, the Lord Chief Justice, said yesterday.

The law ignored a "cardinal principle of morality, justice and democratic government" — that prison terms for murder should reflect the nature and circumstances of crimes and be imposed in open court, he said.

In a lecture at Bramshill Police Staff College, Lord Bingham said that Lord Irvine, the Lord Chancellor, and other members of the Government had supported change when in opposition.

Lord Bingham said he knew his views had "the overwhelming support of the Queen's Bench judges", who sentence murderers.

He hoped that "a new, open-minded administration" would be willing to re-examine the issue.

The mandatory sentence was "no more than a formula", giving "no real clue" to the offender, victim, media or public of how many years were meant to be served in prison.

This was not decided by a judge in open court but behind closed doors later by the Home Secretary or, in most cases, by his subordinate ministers, with no right of appeal for the offender and no right for the Attorney General to challenge a decision as too lenient. At present, all murderers are jailed for life and the minimum

"tariff" they must serve to reflect punishment and deterrence is fixed by the Home Secretary after considering the recommendations of the trial judge, and the Lord Chief Justice.

Once this period is served, ministers decide if an offender should be released on licence, after taking into account the Parole Board's recommendation.

Lord Bingham said he wanted to see the mandatory life sentence for murder replaced by a discretionary life sentence, to be imposed in the worst cases.

As with other discretionary life sentences, which can be imposed for offences such as rape or arson, the judge would specify in open court the minimum sentence to be served before there was any prospect of release. His decision would be open to challenge on grounds of excessive severity or leniency.

After the minimum term had been served, the Parole Board, not a Home Office minister, would decide when it was safe to release the offender on licence.

He rejected the view that murder was a 'uniquely heinous" crime that could be adequately punished only by a life sentence.

Murders varied greatly in character, yet the law required the same sentence to be passed on a wife who had killed her brutal husband after years of

maltreatment as on the robber who killed in cold blood.

Lord Bingham also cited the case of Lee Clegg, the paratrooper now released and facing a retrial after being jailed for life for the murder of a passenger in a car driven through an Army roadblock in Belfast.

He said he was not suggesting that a crime had not been committed, or that punishment should not have followed, but Clegg was "a young man of good character attempting to do his duty in a predicament not of his own making and was most unlikely to reoffend".

It was "a travesty" to treat his case "as if it were in the same league of criminality as that of a contract killer or an armed robber".

With discretionary life sentences, judges would either pass a determinate sentence or a life sentence fixing the years to be served before consideration for release. Exceptionally, they might rule that an offender never be released.

Mandatory sentences had little deterrent value as many murders occurred in "sudden anger, drunken fury, obsession, desperation or miscalculation".

However, Jack Straw, the Home Secretary, said later that the present system gave the "greater protection" that people expected.

Taken from an article by Terence Shaw in the *Daily Telegraph*, 14 March 1998. © Telegraph Group Limited, London, 1998.

Parliament, on the other hand, has so far been opposed to what it perceives as the further 'watering down' of punishment for this most serious of crimes, even though one of its own Select Committees investigated the matter and sided with the judges on this point. This matter is returned to in Chapter 3.

1.5.2 THE APPEAL COURTS IN CRIMINAL LAW

It is very important to gain an understanding of this area before you go on to study the main offences and defences in criminal law. It will enable you to understand why an appeal has been made and to appreciate the status of the appeal court.

Appeals from the magistrates' courts

There are two main ways to appeal. The normal appeal route allows the defendant to appeal to the Crown Court, against the verdict or the sentence decided by the magistrates. In the Crown Court, there will be a complete rehearing of the case by a circuit judge and at least two magistrates. Only the accused is permitted to appeal by this method. The verdict may be affirmed or quashed or the sentence changed or, (perhaps more often), decreased.

The other route only concerns points of law or claims that the magistrates have acted *'ultra vires'*, i.e. outside the scope of their powers. Either the prosecution or defence may appeal by way of 'case stated', i.e. by a written statement asking for an opinion on the point of law involved, to the Divisional Court of Queen's Bench Division. Two or three judges of the court will give their view of the law, which will then be followed by the lower court. If the case has reached the Crown Court, this court, too, may make such an appeal if the parties require advice on a point of law.

There is a further appeal from the Divisional Court straight to the House of Lords.

Appeals from the Crown Court

Such appeals are made to the Court of Appeal (Criminal Division), which sits in the Royal Courts of Justice in the Strand. The main rules are to be found in the Criminal Appeal Act 1995, which simplified the existing system.

Against sentence

An appeal may be made by the accused against the sentence imposed by the Crown Court. Leave to appeal is needed from the Court of Appeal or the trial judge, and only in a quarter of all appeals to this court is such permission granted. In October 1998, an IRA bomber was successful in his appeal and had his sentence of 35 years reduced to 28 years by the Court of Appeal. Only in rare circumstances will a sentence be increased. The Criminal Justice Act 1988 gave such a right to the Attorney General, who is allowed to appeal against an unduly lenient sentence. An example can be seen in Chapter 4, when a sentence for manslaughter was increased from five years to nine years in the case of *Christie*.

Against the verdict

Only the defendant may challenge the actual verdict in a case, except in an exceptional case where the prosecution can show that the jury has been 'nobbled'. The defendant may appeal, either on a point of law, or because there are other reasons to suggest that the verdict may be 'unsafe'. It has now become easier to bring such evidence before the court. Leave is required for this. You will discover as you progress through this book that most appeals are on the grounds that the judge has misdirected the jury in some material way on the law relating to the crime in question.

The Court of Appeal may allow the appeal, dismiss it or order a retrial, as shown in the cases of *Ahluwalia* and *Thornton*, seen in Chapter 4, under voluntary manslaughter.

While the prosecution cannot overturn an acquittal, the Attorney General has power to ask the Court of Appeal to look at the point of law involved and set a precedent for the future. The original acquittal will not be touched. This process is called an Attorney General's Reference and several examples of these are shown throughout the book.

Either the prosecution or the defence may appeal from the Court of Appeal to the House of Lords if a point of law has been certified as one of general public importance. Such appeals rarely reach double figures each year , but have a very important influence on the law. Examples can be seen in Chapter 2, in the cases of *Moloney* and *Hancock and Shankland*, when the meaning of the word 'intention' in murder cases caused problems and in Chapter 7, in the case of *Gomez*, where the conflict over the meaning of the word 'appropriates' in theft had to be resolved.

It should also be noted that, following recent concern about miscarriages of justice and the report on this from the Runciman Commission, a Criminal Cases Review Commission was set up by the Criminal Appeal Act *1995* to make it easier for such cases to be investigated. This became operational in April 1997.

1.6 THE OPERATION OF THE DOCTRINE OF BINDING PRECEDENT IN CRIMINAL LAW

Most of you will be studying the rules relating to the English legal system as part of your course and will learn of the importance of the doctrine of precedent in English law. Our system differs from that in many other countries in Europe in that the decisions of some courts are binding on others in the system.

The general rule is that the decisions of the higher courts will bind the courts lower in the hierarchy. In criminal law, this means that the magistrates' courts and Crown Court are bound by the decisions of the Court of Appeal and the House of Lords, unless the case can be distinguished in some way. The Court of Appeal is bound by decisions of the House of Lords and is also generally bound by its own

earlier decisions, unless one of the three exceptions laid down in *Young v Bristol Aeroplane 1944* can be put forward. The previous decision need not be followed if there are two conflicting earlier decisions, as may happen on rare occasions, especially if there are several sittings of the court on the same day. In such a case, the current court may choose which of the earlier cases to follow. Secondly, the Court of Appeal need not follow one of its own earlier decisions should this conflict with one laid down by the House of Lords. Thirdly, it need not follow a decision made '*per incuriam*', i.e. one made by mistake, because a relevant precedent or statutory provision was not brought to the court's attention in the earlier case. The Criminal Division of the Court of Appeal also has more freedom than the Civil Division, to depart from its own earlier decisions where they are clearly thought to be wrong and the liberty of the subject is at stake. This was stated in *Taylor 1950*.

The House of Lords is the final appeal court in criminal matters unless Community law is involved. The House of Lords binds all the courts below it and, until 1966, was bound by its own earlier decisions. Lord Gardiner then issued his famous Practice Statement declaring that, while their Lordships still considered the doctrine of binding precedent to be an essential part of English law, the House of Lords from that time on would be prepared to depart from its own earlier decisions 'when it appears right to do so'. Lord Gardiner did go on to say that the House would bear in mind 'the especial need for certainty as to the criminal law', a statement that may have come back to haunt him after some later decisions of the Lords, which rendered the law anything but certain!

While the House of Lords is now permitted to overrule its own earlier decisions, it was made very clear in the Practice Statement that the lower courts were not to be given the same freedom. The Court of Appeal, therefore will be bound by the decisions of the House of Lords and, generally, by its own decisions. It is not, however, bound by decisions of the Judicial Committee of the Privy Council. This body sits to hear appeals from other countries, which still retain this court as the one for final appeals. The precedents set by the Privy Council are highly persuasive as, in many cases, the judges are the same as those who sit in the House of Lords, but they are not binding.

The operation of the doctrine of binding precedent explains why the citing, (or quoting), of cases is so important in criminal law. Certain cases lay down precedents that the later courts are then obliged to follow. The facts of the case are relatively unimportant, although often very interesting, it is the principle of law coming from the case which is vital and which will be binding on other judges. When answering problem questions, therefore, you need to be aware of the cases laying down the rules, or interpreting the ones laid down by Parliament, and show the ability to apply these rules to the facts you are given. This is exactly what the judges are doing as the new cases come before them!

Most criminal cases start with the word *Regina*, (the Latin for Queen), or '*R*' v *the defendant*. When this is the case, only the defendant's name will be shown throughout the book. If the case involves a prosecutor's name, this will be included in the citing. If the case concerns the Attorney General, the Director of Public Prosecutions or the Metropolitan Police Commissioner, the initials will indicate this. It should also be noted that, when an appeal is made, the defendant becomes known as the appellant or the respondent. For ease, however, I have continued to use the words 'defendant' or 'accused'.

1.7 WAYS OF REFORMING THE CRIMINAL LAW

The main law-making body in the latter part of the twentieth century is, of course, Parliament but, before Parliament can legislate, someone else must have made the decision that the law needs to be changed. The government of the day introduces Bills to deal with particular topics, often in relation to procedural matters

or sentencing, the Crime (Sentences) Act 1997 being an example, or in response to a particular problem, as for example, the Dangerous Dogs Act 1991 or the Protection from Harassment Act 1996. In addition, *ad hoc* Royal Commissions are sometimes set up to make recommendations on a specific topic as, for example, the Royal Commission on Criminal Justice, (known more often as the Runciman Commission, after the name of its chairman), mentioned earlier. On a longer-term basis, two other bodies have made vital contributions towards reforming the criminal law. The first one is the Criminal Law Revision Committee, a part-time body, set up in 1957, which has been instrumental in instigating several important reforms. One example of its work was its proposals for rationalising the law of theft, which led to the passing of the Theft Act 1968. In 1965, however, it was decided that a full-time body should be set up to undertake more comprehensive law reform, and the Law Commission was created. Its remit is extensive as shown in s.3 Law Commissions Act 1965, (there was a separate one for Scotland). The two Law Commissions were charged with keeping

under review all the law, ... with a view to its systematic development and reform, including in particular the codification of such law, the elimination of anomalies, the repeal of obselete and unnecessary enactments, the reduction of the number of separate enactments and generally the simplification and modernisation of the law.

The English Law Commission saw the codification of the criminal law as a pressing issue. It recognised that the current rules are an untidy mixture of judge-made rules and statutory provisions, and that even where there are Acts of Parliament, some of these are inadequate because of their age and style of language. A great deal of work, therefore, went into producing a Draft Code in 1989, along with a Bill to implement its proposals. This Code is referred to in the following chapters, in cases where other reforms have not overtaken it. Unfortunately, it is gathering dust. Parliament has shown little will to implement it. Undefeated, the Law Commission decided to try to implement changes in key areas in a more piece-meal fashion. This, too, has been largely unsuccessful and the patience of the Commissioners now seems to be coming to an end. In 1993, the Chairman, Mr Justice Brooke, launched a stinging attack on the government of the day, and declared that the failure by Parliament to implement any of the reforms was 'a disgrace'. This attack was widely reported and it looks as though it might have had some small effect. The Home Office has published its own consultation paper and draft Bill on non-fatal offences against the person, which might lead to changes in that area at least. We shall have to wait and see! Meanwhile, in the following chapters, we need to study the current law on the subject. I hope that you find it as interesting as I do!

CHAPTER 2

THE ELEMENTS OF A CRIME

2.1 INTRODUCTION

THIS CHAPTER WILL look first at the burden of proof in criminal law and then go on to discuss the elements of a crime. Lastly, it is necessary to look at certain crimes, often of a regulatory nature, for which liability can arise even though the party claims that he was not at fault in the normal sense. These are known as offences of strict liability.

The definition of a crime was considered in Chapter 1. Before the defendant can be convicted of a wrong against the State, the case has to be proved against him. In *Woolmington v DPP 1935*, the House of Lords clearly established that this has to be beyond reasonable doubt and that the onus is on the prosecution to prove this.

In the above quoted case, the defendant claimed that he had taken a gun with him to the home of the victim's mother to show his estranged wife that he planned to commit suicide if she failed to return to him. He alleged that the gun had then gone off by accident, as he was showing it to her. Despite this claim, the defendant was convicted of murder. The House of Lords allowed the appeal on the grounds that the judge had misdirected the jury and had suggested that the defendant had to prove that it was an accident, rather than the prosecution having to show that it was murder.

When trying to establish the requisite criminal liability, the prosecution will normally have to prove two things. Put briefly, the prosecutor must show that the defendant had actually committed the offence in question, and that he had done so with the mental element required by the law, i.e. with the necessary 'guilty mind'. These two elements of a crime are expressed in Latin, the term *actus reus* being used to describe the wrongful act and the words *mens rea* describing the mental element. It should be noted that not all judges like the retention of these archaic terms. Lord Diplock said that it would be preferable 'to avoid bad Latin . . . and speak about the conduct of the accused and his state of mind at the time of that conduct.' Despite his efforts, however, the terms remain in common use and need to be studied.

It will also be seen that to describe the *actus reus* as the guilty act and the *mens rea* as the guilty mind is far too simple a statement. It will be noted below that the *actus reus* can be more, or even less, than a simple act. In addition, when looking at the subject of *mens rea*, it will be noted that the defendant need not feel guilty at all to have what the law deems to be a guilty mind. He might well feel that he was morally justified to have acted as he did or not have given serious thought to his actions at all. Despite this, he may still have the necessary *mens rea*. The simple expressions of a guilty act and guilty mind do, however, provide a simple foundation on which the student can build in order to gain a wider knowledge of this area.

2.2 THE *ACTUS REUS*

The existence of the *actus reus* is essential for criminal liability. Each crime has its own *actus reus*, laid down by statute or by the judges. For example, under statute, the *actus reus* of s.18 Offences Against the Person Act 1861 occurs where a person unlawfully wounds or causes grievous bodily harm to another. The *actus reus* of theft under the Theft Act 1968 arises when a party 'appropriates property belonging to another'. At common law (i.e. where the criminal offence has been developed by the judges, rather than by Parliament) the *actus reus* of murder has been established as 'the unlawful killing of a person in being under the Queen's peace'. These definitions will be explained in detail when the relevant offences are dealt with later.

In many cases, the actions of the accused will speak for themselves and the *actus reus* will be easy to establish. For example, if the defendant was arrested outside a shop with ten CDs for which he had not paid in his hand, criminal liability might be obvious from his conduct. Sometimes, it is not so easy to decide on this and, in addition to the act itself the consequences flowing from it may need to be explored. On rare occasions, it will be seen that the actus reus of a particular crime may be present simply because the defendant is in the appropriate place and, lastly, the defendant's liability may be established by his failure to act in a given situation. These different ways of proving that the *actus reus* exists need to be looked at more fully.

2.2.1 CONDUCT

In many instances, the mere conduct of the accused may be enough to show that the *actus reus* has been committed. A classic example of this is perjury, i.e. lying under oath. Another example is the conduct of 'appropriating property belonging to another' as laid down in the crime of theft, and noted in the shoplifting situation, mentioned above.

2.2.2 A RESULT OR CONSEQUENCE

For the commission of some crimes, however, it is necessary to show more than just conduct; the result or consequence of that conduct must also be assessed. For example, in the crime of murder, an unlawful killing has to have arisen as a result of the defendant's violent act.

Similarly, under s.20 Sexual Offences Act 1956, it is an offence to take an unmarried girl out of the possession of her parent or guardian without lawful authority. Should such a consequence occur, the *actus reus* of the crime will be established.

2.2.3 A STATE OF AFFAIRS

In rare cases, the unfortunate defendant may be found guilty of a crime simply by being in a particular place when this state of affairs has been declared to be wrong. An example is the case of *Larsonneur 1933*. The defendant had gone to Ireland when her permission to be in the UK had expired. She was then deported from Ireland and brought back to England against her will by the police. She was charged and found guilty of 'being an alien to whom leave to land in the United Kingdom has been refused', which was an offence under the Aliens' Order 1920.

Despite widespread criticism of the unfairness of this decision, certain later Acts of Parliament have also adopted this strict approach. A modern example is s.4 Road Traffic Act 1988, under which it is an offence to be in charge of a motor vehicle on a road or public place while unfit to drive through drink or drugs. The *actus reus* of the offence will be present even if the defendant has decided not to drive the vehicle in question and has planned to sleep in the car instead. The state of affairs of being in charge of the vehicle is enough to establish liability under this section of the Act.

activity

Read the following extract and decide whether the *actus reus* of a crime has been committed:

> In *Winzar* v *Chief Constable of Kent 1983*, the defendant had been taken to hospital but, once there, it was discovered that he was not ill, merely drunk. He was therefore requested to leave the premises. He failed to comply with this order and was later found in a corridor of the hospital. The police were called and he was removed from the premises against his will and taken to a police car on the highway. He was charged with being found drunk in the highway.

2.2.4 AN OMISSION

The first point to note is that normally, in English law, a person will not be found to be criminally liable merely because he failed to act.

Stephen L J made this position clear back in the last century, when he stated:

> It is not a crime to cause death or bodily injury, even intentionally, by any omission.

He went on to describe the situation where a person sees another man drowning but does nothing to help him, even though if he had merely reached out his hand, the man who could not swim would have been saved. Under English law, the person failing to act has committed no crime.

There are, however, limited exceptions to this rule where the law has decided that a person should be criminally liable for failing to act. They include the following situations:

1 **Where a statute lays this down**
A limited number of statutory provisions create liability for omissions in specified circumstances. The following are examples under the Road Traffic Act 1988, as amended: (i) Failing to provide a breath specimen as required; (ii) Failing to give details, to someone entitled to receive them, after a traffic accident; (iii) Failing to report an accident as required.

It is also a statutory offence under the Children and Young Person's Act 1933 to fail to provide a child with adequate food, clothing, housing or medical help.

2 **Where there is a contractual duty to act**
There may be a specific duty to act laid down in the person's contract. For example, a lifeguard is employed to save lives, so would obviously be failing in his duty if he observed someone in difficulties but took no steps to save him from drowning. The same rule would apply to a person employed to guard a level crossing, as the defendant in *Pittwood 1902* discovered to his cost. He was a railway employee who had opened the level crossing gates to let a cart pass across the line, but had failed to shut the gates again before going off to have his lunch. A few minutes later, a passing train hit a hay-cart crossing the track and the driver of this vehicle was killed. The defendant was found guilty of 'gross and criminal negligence' after the judge made it clear that 'a man might incur criminal liability from a duty arising out of contract'.

3 **Where there is a duty imposed by law**
The judges themselves have imposed a duty to act in certain situations. The following are examples.
Where the person is guilty of misconduct in a public office
In *Dytham 1979*, a police officer was found to be criminally liable when he failed to preserve the Queen's peace and stood by while a man was kicked to death.
Where there is a special relationship between the parties
A party may be found guilty of failing to act

if there is duty imposed upon him by virtue of the special relationship between him and the victim. An early case on this subject was *Instan 1893*, where a niece failed to obtain help for her aunt, with whom she was living. The aunt had contracted gangrene in her leg and later died. The niece's conviction for manslaughter was upheld. The appeal court held that English law would be 'hopelessly deficient if the judges were unable to base liability on the common duty of care owed by one relative to another'.

Another case illustrating this is *Gibbins and Proctor 1918,* where a man and his common law wife were found guilty of murder when they failed to feed the man's child and she died from starvation. The woman was held to be liable because, while the child was not hers, she was living with the man and had accepted his money for food. In *Khan 1998*, however, it was decided that drug dealers are not under any special duty to look after their clients, so a manslaughter conviction was quashed.

Where the defendant has voluntarily accepted responsibility for the other

This offer overlaps with the duty imposed by a special relationship, mentioned above, but is wider in that the law may impose liability in any case where the victim has relied upon the defendant and the latter then fails to help.

A particularly gruesome example of this was the case of *Stone and Dobinson 1977,* although there was also criticism of the result and sympathy for the defendants, whom many felt were not mentally equipped to take on such responsibility. The sister of an elderly man, called Fanny, had come to stay with him and his woman friend. The man's sight, hearing and sense of smell were all deficient and his woman companion was of low intelligence. Fanny was said to be 'morbidly obsessed' with putting on weight and became bed-bound. She refused to eat and developed serious bedsores that became very badly infected. The couple made half-hearted attempts to obtain help for her but failed to obtain proper medical aid and

Fanny died.

The couple's conviction for manslaughter was upheld. The Court of Appeal held that they had assumed a duty to care for the sister, they knew that she was relying on them and they had failed to get her the assistance that she needed.

Where there is a dangerous situation caused by the defendant and he has failed to put this right

The House of Lords was of the opinion that the categories just mentioned did not cover all the situations where it was felt that liability should be imposed. In the case of *Miller 1983* a squatter had fallen asleep while smoking and his cigarette caused the mattress to catch fire. The flames woke him but instead of putting out the fire, Miller merely moved to another room and went back to sleep. The house was badly damaged and the defendant's conviction for arson was upheld.

The House of Lords decided that 'failing to take measures that lie within one's power to counteract a danger that one has oneself created' could, in circumstances like this, create liability.

In some instances, the courts will avoid the difficulties of trying to establish liability for omissions and impose liability in another way. An example was the case of *Fagan* v *Metropolitan Police Commissioner 1969,* where the Court of Appeal decided that a battery could not be committed by an omission. To impose liability, therefore, the idea of a continuing act was used.

The defendant had been told to stop his car and pull in to the kerb. As he did so, he accidentally drove on to the policeman's foot. When he was shouted at to remove the car, the defendant swore at the policeman, told him he could wait and switched off the ignition. He was convicted of assaulting a police constable in the execution of his duty but he appealed stating that no liability could be incurred by merely failing to act.

The Court of Appeal held differently. The judges decided that driving onto the policeman's foot and then keeping the car there was one continuous act, not an act followed by an omission. Fagan's conviction, therefore, was upheld.

2.2.5 SUGGESTED REFORM

The reform bodies appear to be very undecided on this subject. In 1980, the Criminal Law Revision Committee recommended that liability for omissions in offences against the person should be restricted to serious crimes. In 1989, however, the Law Commission took the opposite approach and suggested widening liability for omissions, proposing that some offences could be redrafted to allow for this. For example, the offences of murder and manslaughter could be redefined to include 'causing' death and the offence of criminal damage could be changed from damaging or destroying property to 'causing property to be damaged or destroyed'.

The latest recommendations are in a Law Commission Report of 1993 (No. 218). Attached to this report is the Draft Criminal Law Bill, ready to be put before Parliament. This ignores the earlier proposals of the Commission to widen liability and follows those put forward in 1980.

Clause 19 of the Bill states that a party may be liable for omissions in the range of situations already laid down by the judges, but confines liability to serious offences, such as intentional serious injury, torture, unlawful detention, kidnapping, abduction and aggravated abduction.

The Draft Criminal Law Bill, therefore, would not provide for more general liability for omissions. It does, however, recognise the '*Miller* principle', in clause 23. This clause states that a person will commit an offence where he fails to act, which may not at that stage be unlawful, but then fails to take reasonable steps to deal with the results of that act.

activity

Assess whether the *actus reus* of a crime has been established in the following situations. Give cases to support your findings:

Des was in the habit of feeding his bedridden grandmother at lunchtime, before going to his part-time job. He was promoted suddenly, necessitating far greater hours at his place of work and totally forgot his grandmother's needs. His grandmother has just died of starvation.

Terry noticed that the wheel of the car in front of him was wobbling dangerously but failed to inform the driver because he was late for an appointment and did not wish to become involved. The wheel came off the car and the driver was killed.

Ruby was staying illegally in college accommodation. She fell asleep while the bath was running and the bath water overflowed. Ruby woke up, decided that the water was now too cold and went to bed, leaving the water running in the bathroom. The resulting flood seriously damaged the lower two floors of the college building.

Jonathon, an electrician employed by the local council, went off for his tea break, leaving all the wires exposed. Chris, the supervisor was electrocuted.

The first point to note is that it may take some time before even the limited reform in the latest proposals is effected. We noted in Chapter 1 that Bills from the Law Commission often take years before they are introduced into Parliament and, even when they are, the Bill may be defeated or substantial amendments made to it during its passage through Parliament. Some legal writers, like Professor Glanville Williams, favour a restrictive approach to this subject. Glanville Williams argued that the judges 'should not create liability for omissions without statutory authority' and gave comprehensive reasons why such liability should not be increased. Other academics, including Professor Ashworth, take the opposite view and state that the reforms do not go far enough, as wider policy issues are involved.

Others also agree with this view and are dissatisfied with the current state of English law, which normally absolves a party from blame when he fails to help, even in extreme situations, such as where he stands watching, while a child drowns in a shallow pool of water. They would argue that there has been an unwelcome increase in the principle of non-involvement in the affairs of strangers, even when it is patently obvious that help is urgently needed. Harrowing reports of people ignoring cries for help from victims of muggers or rapists or closing their ears to the sounds of children being ill-treated are, unfortunately, all too common.

The question of failing to give aid in an emergency was given widespread coverage following the death of Diana, Princess of Wales. Tales of the unsavoury behaviour of the paparazzi, who took pictures of the dead and dying instead of calling for help, horrified many people. Failing to provide aid in certain situations is an offence under French law but it highlighted the problem in this country and accelerated calls for reform. One suggestion might be the creation of a new offence of 'failing to help in an emergency situation'. Such a provision would need to be phrased very carefully but this should not be beyond the powers of the draftsmen. On the other hand, it could be argued that there are already too many criminal offences and that a cautious approach should be taken towards creating further liability. Education in good citizenship might be an alternative route.

- The *actus reus* comprises all the elements of a crime except the mental element
- The *actus reus* may consist of conduct, (as in appropriating property in theft), a result or consequence, (i.e. a death in murder), or a state of affairs, (*Larsonneur 1933, Winzar 1983*).
- Generally, there is no liability for omissions, although there are limited exceptions, as where a statute imposes liablity, (e.g. Road Traffic Act 1988), a contract of employment, (*Pittwood 1902*), or a public duty, (*Dytham 1979*). Liability is also imposed where there is a special relationship between the parties, (*Instan 1893, Gibbins and Proctor 1918*), where one party voluntary accepts liability, (*Stone and Dobinson 1977*) or where there is a dangerous situation which the person creating the danger fails to put right, (*Miller 1983*).
- If liability cannot be imposed in this way, the courts may be prepared to say that there is a continuing act (*Fagan* v *MPC 1969*)

FIGURE 2.1 *Key facts chart on the* actus reus

2.3 THE *MENS REA* OF A CRIME

In addition to proving to proving that the *actus reus* exists, in most cases it will also be necessary to show that the defendant has committed the offence with the relevant *mens rea*, i.e. the degree of blameworthiness required by the offence in question. It will be noted towards the end of this chapter, however, that some offences, usually those of a regulatory nature, do not require fault to be proved. These are offences of strict liability.

The latter crimes are increasing but are still in the minority. In the case of other offences, some form of *mens rea* will have to be established before guilt can be shown. The mens rea for each offence will be laid down in the relevant statute, or, in the case of common law offences will have been formulated by the judges developing the crime in question, as will be seen as you travel through this book.

2.3.1 THE DIFFERENT DEGREES OF MENS REA

In relation to the most serious criminal offences, the prosecution will need to prove a high degree of blameworthiness. The defendant will only be found guilty if it is shown that he intended to commit the crime in question. This form of *mens rea* is necessary before the offence of murder is established. The person accused will only be convicted if the jury is convinced that he intended to kill or cause grievous bodily harm. Such a high degree of *mens rea* is also necessary to establish guilt under s.18 Offences Against the Person Act 1861. The accused can only be convicted for this most serious non-fatal offence against the person if he maliciously wounds another or causes grievous bodily harm, 'with intent to do some grievous bodily harm'. Intention is also needed for the crime of theft. The defendant will not be guilty of this offence unless it is shown that he appropriated property belonging to another, 'with the

intention of permanently depriving the other of it'.

Other crimes do not necessarily require such a high degree of fault. They can be committed intentionally or recklessly. The other non-fatal offences against the person that we shall be studying in Chapter 6 all come into this category. These are the offences of assault, battery, assault occasioning actual bodily harm and malicious wounding or grievous bodily harm under s.20 Offences Against the Person Act; other crimes are rape and criminal damage.

In a small number of cases, it is enough to establish mere negligence. This is comparatively common in civil law, which has laid down a duty not to be negligent in a wide variety of situations. In criminal law, however, the defendant will not normally be liable for careless acts, even where these cause harm to another person. There are, however, notable exceptions to this general rule, where criminal liability has been imposed. One example is driving without due care or attention. A much more serious offence that can be committed negligently is manslaughter although, as will be seen in Chapter 5 on involuntary manslaughter, the negligence in such a case must be 'gross'. It is now necessary to look at these three states of mind in more detail, before studying crimes of strict liability.

2.3.2 INTENTION

We noted earlier that liability for crimes like murder and theft can only be established if the jury is satisfied that the defendant intended to commit the offence. Unfortunately for law students, there is no definition of the word 'intention' and it is normally left to the jury to decide whether such a state of mind exists.

What has been made clear by the courts is that the word 'intention' is not to be equated with the word 'desire' or the word 'motive'. On occasion, we might have the desire to inflict a minor injury on a person who has upset us in some way or even to rob a bank if faced with grave financial problems. Provided that these remain as mere thoughts, we cannot be brought before a court, however strong the desire may be. It was clearly stated in *Cunliffe* v *Goodman 1950* that intention is a state of affairs 'that a person does more than merely contemplate'.

Intention must also not be confused with motive. The motive for committing the crime in question may be a good one but if the intention is present, the *mens rea* will have been established and the defendant will have to hope that his motive is taken into account at the sentencing process. In *Chandler* v *DPP 1964*, the defendant was very much opposed to the use of nuclear weapons and had been involved in a 'sit in' at a military base with the purpose of preventing aircraft containing such missiles from taking off. He was charged with breaking into a prohibited place with a purpose prejudicial to the safety and interests of the state but argued that he did not have the appropriate *mens rea* for this offence. He claimed that his purpose was to save the State from the dangers of nuclear weapons.

The case reached the House of Lords, where it was established that the defendant's motive was irrelevant. The immediate purpose of the offender was to break into the airfield and cause an obstruction.

In the earlier case of *Steane 1947* the courts had appeared to be more prepared to consider the motive of the defendant. The latter had appealed against a conviction for doing acts with the intention of assisting the enemy during the Second World War. He had broadcast favourable propaganda for the Nazi regime but argued that he had only done this after being beaten and after threats that he and his family would be sent to a concentration camp if he refused to help. His conviction was quashed, despite the fact that his immediate purpose had been to help the enemy. Lord Goddard was obviously sympathetic and compared the defendant's action to those of prisoners of war who are also forced to do unpleasant acts to assist the captors.

Despite this case, which has not been expressly overruled, the current approach is to separate motive and intention and to use other methods, such as the defence of duress, or a reduced sentence to ensure that the special circumstances are taken into account. It should be noted that the case of *Chandler* reached the highest appeal court, whereas *Steane* was decided by what was then the Court of Criminal Appeal.

Direct and oblique intent

In many cases it will not be too difficult for the jury to decide on the intention of the accused; it will be clear from the circumstances. This is referred to in law as a 'direct intent'. If a person with a grudge against humanity were to place a bomb in the Millenium Dome on the opening day in order to blow up all the people inside, his purpose will be plain and the jury would have little difficulty in deciding upon his guilt. It is another form of intent, known, in law, as 'oblique intent' that has caused the problems in this area of law. In a different version of the scenario mentioned above, the planter of the bomb may have wished, instead, to destroy the Dome because its shape offended him. He may not have given any thought to the visitors inside it. It would then have to be decided whether he had the *mens rea* for murder. He would argue that his intention and purpose was merely to destroy property, not to kill the people inside. If this view was accepted and the offender merely charged with this lesser crime, it would rightly cause outrage. The public would claim that he must have known that deaths would result in such circumstances. The word 'intention', therefore, has been widened to cover situations where the defendant's purpose was different to what is being claimed by the prosecutors. What remains a problem is how to decide on the degree of help the jury needs when faced with a case of oblique intent and what form such a direction from the judge should take. The views of the judges have changed over the years, resulting in great confusion to all. The problem is best described by looking at six cases where the defendants were charged with murder but have tried to claim that they did not intend to commit such a crime.

DPP v *Smith 1961*

In *DPP* v *Smith 1961*, the defendant had been ordered to leave his car, which contained stolen goods. Instead, he accelerated sharply and drove off at 60 miles per hour with the policeman clinging to the vehicle. The officer was thrown off and into the path of an incoming car and later died from his injuries. Smith was charged with murder and convicted. His appeal against this, on the grounds that he had not intended to cause the death, reached the House of Lords.

The House of Lords upheld the conviction, deciding that the defendant had the necessary intention for murder if an ordinary responsible man, in similar circumstances, would have contemplated the end result. At this stage, therefore, an objective test had been laid down for establishing intention in murder cases, a view that was strongly criticised by academics and later led to intervention from the newly formed Law Commission. On the advice of this body, s.8 Criminal Justice Act 1967 was enacted.

S.8 states that the jury is not bound in law to infer that the defendant intended or foresaw a result of his actions just because it was a natural and probable consequence of them. It should, instead, make the decision about whether he did have such an intention or foresight by looking at all the evidence and drawing the proper conclusions from that.

It can be seen therefore, that others are not allowed to tell the jury what it must do in such a situation. The jurors must, instead look at the matter in a subjective way and decide what the actual defendant intended or foresaw, not look at the matter from the viewpoint of the reasonable man, as suggested in *Smith*.

In the case of *Hyam* v *DPP 1975*, the House of Lords, on a three to two majority, decided that the defendant had the *mens rea* for murder if, at the time the killing took place, he knew that it was highly probable that his actions would cause death or grievous bodily harm. (It will be seen later, that, as in *Smith*, this decision has attracted a great deal of criticism.)

The defendant had become very jealous when another woman had taken her place in the affections of her man friend. In the early hours of the morning, therefore, she had poured petrol through this woman's letterbox and set fire to it. In the resulting blaze, two children died.

Hyam argued that she had only intended to frighten the other woman and her case reached the House of Lords, which rejected her appeal.

The judges varied in their reasons for dismissing the appeal and two gave the impression that intention was established if it was shown that the defendant foresaw the result as highly probable. Lord Hailsham did not subscribe to this view and his words were picked up by judges of the Court of Appeal in two non-fatal injury cases, that of *Mohan 1976* and *Belfon 1976*. These judges decided that mere foresight that death or personal injury was highly probable was not the same as having the intention to cause the act in question. Instead, it was merely evidence for the jury to look at, when deciding whether an intention was present. This view of the law is the one that has prevailed, as will be seen from later cases.

The question of what constitutes intention resurfaced in the case of *Moloney 1985*. The defendant had been drinking late at night with his stepfather after the Ruby Wedding anniversary celebration of his grandparents. Evidence showed that the parties were on good terms when the others left but, later, a disagreement had broken out over which of them could load a shotgun in the fastest time. The stepson won this argument and then claimed that his stepfather had dared him to pull the trigger. He did so and the stepfather was killed. Moloney was convicted of murder but the House of Lords changed the verdict to manslaughter.

Lord Bridge delivered the main judgment. He made it clear that it was the jury's task to decide on the matter of intention. He stated:

> The golden rule should be that, when directing a jury on the mental element necessary in a crime of specific intent, the judge should avoid any elaboration or paraphrase of what it meant by intent, and leave it to the jury's good sense to decide whether the accused acted with the

necessary intent, unless the judge is convinced that . . . some further explanation or elaboration is strictly necessary to avoid misunderstanding.

He went on to say that he thought that such cases would be very rare, even where the death is more indirect.

This part of his judgment was approved of in later cases but problems arose over the form the direction to the jury should take when those 'rare occurrences' arose. He said that the jury should be asked to decide on two matters:

First, was death or really serious injury in a murder case . . . a natural consequence of the defendant's act? Secondly, did the defendant foresee that consequence as being a natural consequence of his act? The jury should then be told that if they answer yes to both questions it is a proper inference for them to draw that he intended that consequence.

These 'Moloney guidelines' as they came to be called were themselves called into question in the case of *Hancock and Shankland 1986*. The case concerned two striking miners who had been angered when another miner had gone back to work. They had pushed a heavy concrete block and post from a bridge onto the motorway in front of the taxi and police escort taking the miner to work. The taxi driver was killed. The trial judge diligently recited the *Moloney* guidelines to the jury and the defendants were convicted of murder. The Court of Appeal quashed the conviction and this was confirmed by the House of Lords.

The Court of Appeal had argued that the *Moloney* guidelines were deficient. They seemed to imply that any natural consequence would be enough to incur liability; there was no definition of this, although in other parts of Lord Bridge's judgment, he had stated that the probability of such a consequence arising 'must be little short of overwhelming'.

In the House of Lords, Lord Scarman agreed

with the view of the Court of Appeal and stated that the *Moloney* guidelines were 'unsafe and misleading'. He declined to put others in their place, even though the Lord Chief Justice in the Court of Appeal had suggested rather lengthy ones! He did go on to reiterate, however, that it was the jurors who should decide whether the intention to kill existed, after looking at all the evidence in the case.

This case established, therefore, that the *Moloney* guidelines should no longer be used. Both the appeal courts also stressed that even where there is a belief that the defendant must have known that the consequences of his act were virtually certain, this is not the same as saying that he has such an intention. The members of the jury must still decide on this point, after hearing that they are entitled to infer this if they wish to do so after looking at all the evidence.

The matter came up again in the case of *Nedrick 1986*, a case with very similar facts to *Hyam*, mentioned earlier. The defendant again poured petrol through a letterbox and set it alight and the death of an innocent child resulted. The jury convicted Nedrick of murder. The trial at first instance was heard before the case of *Moloney* reached the House of Lords and, was, of course, also before the modifications made in *Hancock and Shankland*. The judge had therefore directed the jury in a way that followed the House of Lords' decision in *Hyam*. The appeal against the conviction for murder was accepted because of this misdirection occasioned by the changes in the law.

Lord Lane decided that the correct direction to the jurors should now be to tell them that:

if they are satisfied that at the material time the defendant recognised that death or serious injury would be virtually certain, (barring some unforeseen intervention) to result from his voluntary act, then that is a fact from which they may find it easy to infer that he intended to kill or do serious bodily harm, even though he may not have had any desire to achieve that result.

This seems to have clarified the matter to some extent, although it is debatable whether a jury, (or a student!), would understand this if not clarified further. The cases, however, continue to confuse the issue. In *Walker and Hayles 1990*, an attempted murder case, the conviction was upheld, even though it was claimed that the judge had misdirected the jurors on the lines that they could also infer the necessary intention if the defendant foresaw the consequences of his act as being 'highly probable'. The Court of Appeal stated that

> once one departs from absolute certainty, there is bound to be a question of degree. We do not regard the difference of degree, if there is one, between a very high degree of probability on the one hand and virtual certainty on the other as being sufficient to render what the recorder said a misdirection.

The court did, however, go on to state that it would prefer the words 'virtually certain' to be used.

In the case of *Woollin 1996*, similar arguments were advanced but, once again, the appeal was rejected. The defendant was alleged to have violently shaken his three-month-old baby and then thrown him across the room in the direction of his pram four or five feet away. Wollin had admitted in later interviews that the baby had hit the floor hard but 'did not think it would kill him', although he accepted that there was a risk of injury.

The trial judge had told the jurors that they might infer intention 'if they were satisfied that when the defendant threw the child he appreciated that there was a substantial risk that he would cause serious harm to it' and the defence claimed in the appeal that such a direction 'might therefore have served to confuse or mislead the jury as to the degree of foresight required'.

The Court of Appeal referred back to Lord Scarman's judgment in *Hancock and Shankland* and said that he did not suggest that the jury could only be directed that they could only infer intention in respect of those consequences of the defendant's actions which were classed as 'virtual certainties'. Instead, he drew attention to s.8 Criminal Justice Act 1967, and said that, where there is also other evidence, the judge should also remind the jury that 'the probability, however high, of a consequence is only a factor, though it may in some cases be a very significant factor, to be considered with all the other evidence'.

The Court of Appeal, in the present case, said that there was such other evidence and decided that there was no misdirection. It adopted with approval the words used in *Walker and Hayles* which stated: 'It may be that that could have been better expressed. Few summings up are perfect. But the message is clear enough'. The Court of Appeal also agreed with the decision in that case that, while it was preferable to use the words 'virtually certain', as suggested in *Nedrick*, it was not a misdirection if they were not used in a case like this, provided that it was made clear to the jurors that the decision on the matter was theirs.

▼ COMMENT

It can be seen that a great deal of time and public money has been spent to arrive back at the position stated by Lord Scarman in *Hancock*, over ten years ago. It is also apparent that even this is an unsatisfactory half-way house. It might be preferable just to quote s.8 to the jury or to put pressure on Parliament to legislate on the meaning of the word 'intention'. The present state of the law causes confusion to juries, law students and the judges themselves!

activity

1 Peter and Harry belonged to an archery club. They were 'fooling around' after a big match and decided to act out the William Tell story. Peter put an apple on his head and Harry took aim. Unfortunately, a passing motorcyclist distracted Harry, his aim wavered and he shot Peter through the heart and killed him.

Advise the judge and jury how they should approach the subject of deciding whether Harry had an intention to kill.

2 In essay form or in group discussion, assess the truth of the following statement: 'Foresight of consequences as being virtually certain is not the same as intention'.

Suggested reform of intention

There have been three reports on this, a Law Commission report in 1989, the accompanying Draft Criminal Code, a report from the Select Committee of the House of Lords on Murder and Life Imprisonment, which echoed the views of the Commission and, finally the definition of intention in the Law Commission's report 'Legislating the Criminal Code: Offences Against the Person and General Principles' (Law Com. No. 218 1993). The latter only applies to non-fatal offences but it is assumed that the same definition would be used for fatal offences. This states that a person is classed as acting 'intentionally' when 'it is his purpose to cause it, or, although it is not his purpose to cause that result, he knows it would occur in the ordinary course of events if he were to succeed in his purpose of causing some other result'.

KEY FACTS

- The *mens rea* of an offence usually consists of intention or recklessness, although in a small percentage of crimes, negligence will suffice. Manslaughter is one such crime if the negligence is gross
- In specified crimes, liability might be strict
- The word intention is not defined but is not to be equated with the words 'desire', (*Cunliffe* v *Goodman 1950*) or 'motive', (*Chandler* v *DPP 1964*), nor with the word 'foresight', *Moloney 1986*, *Hancock and Shankland 1986*, *Nedrick 1986*, *Walker* v *Hayles 1990* and *Woollin 1998*)
- S.8 Criminal Justice Act 1967 is designed to help the jury and tells them that the test is a subjective one
- In most cases, the jury should decide whether the defendant had the intention to commit the crime; this will be the case where the intention is a direct one. Only in a few cases where the defendant is claiming that it was not his purpose to kill or seriously injure the victim or cause him other harm, is a direction from the judge advisable, (*Moloney 1986*). These are cases of oblique intent
- In such cases, the jury should be directed according to the guidelines in *Nedrick 1986*, that if they decide that the defendant 'recognised that death or serious harm would be virtually certain ... to result from his voluntary act, then that is evidence that the defendant intended to kill or to do serious harm, even though he may not have had any desire to achieve that result'
- It will not, however, normally be a misdirection if other words like 'highly probable' are used (*Walker and Hayles 1990*) or apppreciating 'that there was substantial risk', (*Woollin 1997*), although the use of the *Nedrick* wording was to be preferred

FIGURE 2.2 *Key facts chart on* mens rea *and intention*

▼ **COMMENT**

It is submitted that it would be a great advance to have a statutory definition of murder, although it has to be said that it is the judges, rather than the juries, who have the problems! The definition is very clearly expressed but might result in fewer convictions for murder than under the current law and more for manslaughter. This might not be a bad thing, provided that the judges use the whole range of sentences and even impose life imprisonment where the facts seem to warrant it.

2.3.3 RECKLESSNESS

The preceding part of this chapter showed how difficult it can be in some cases to prove that the defendant intended to commit the crime in question. For many offences, therefore, it is not necessary to show such a high degree of blame-worthiness; it is sufficient to prove that the accused has been reckless as to whether the crime was committed.

Unfortunately for the law student, however, having just grappled with the complexities of the meaning of intention, it will now be discovered that there is similar uncertainty over the meaning of the word 'reckless' and that two meanings are currently in use for different types of crime. We therefore need to examine how such a situation came about.

Before we investigate the two different meanings of the word 'reckless', it is important to note that in all cases where this type of *mens rea* needs to be shown, it is essential to establish that the defendant took an unjustifiable risk. Not all risks come into this category. For example, a surgeon may perform a delicate operation on a patient, which only has a 50:50 chance of success but is one which may well give him a much better quality of life if it succeeds. There is obvious social utility in allowing the doctor to proceed without the fear of criminal

liability if the operation is a failure.

Some actions have no such utility. The throwing of a firework into a crowd of people would be such a case; the offender would be taking an unjustifiable risk that someone in the crowd might be harmed and it would be felt right for such a person to face criminal charges if that happened.

The two types of recklessness

Confusion has arisen over the meaning of the word 'reckless' because of the different opinions as to the degree of recklessness to be shown. Some would argue that a defendant should only be liable if he alone had foreseen that he was taking an unjustifiable risk, whereas others are of the belief that he should be liable if he ought to have foreseen such a risk. The latter is a more objective view under which it would be easier to establish guilt. These two types of recklessness are known respectively as Cunningham and Caldwell recklessness.

Cunningham recklessness

Before the case of *MPC* v *Caldwell 1982*, the judges had decided that the more subjective approach was the one to be used, i.e. before the defendant could be said to be liable, he must have been aware of the risk he was running.

This was established in the case of *Cunningham 1957*. It was stated that this type of recklessness had to be shown in any case where the old-fashioned word 'malicious' was used. The offence of malicious wounding is an example and another is shown in the case of *Cunningham* itself, i.e. the crime of 'maliciously administering a noxious thing so as to endanger life', contrary to s.3 Offences Against the Person Act 1861.

The defendant stole money from a gas meter and in so doing, tore the meter from the wall and left the gas pipes exposed. Gas then seeped through the porous walls into the basement of the house next door and affected a woman living there. Cunningham was convicted but made a successful appeal. It was held that the judge had misdirected the jury by telling them that the word 'malicious' simply meant 'wicked', instead of giving it its more precise legal meaning.

The appeal court stated that when the word 'malicious' was used in a statute, it was necessary to establish that the defendant either intended to cause the harm in question or should have foreseen that such an event would occur. On this test, Cunningham could only be convicted if he knew of the risk from the gas but, nevertheless, went on to take it. It was not enough that he ought to have foreseen such a risk; the test was subjective. This ruling was therefore held to apply to all cases that had the word 'malicious' in the offence and in *Parmenter 1991*, a conviction for malicious wounding was quashed because such a direction had not been given.

For several years, this test was also felt to be of a more general application, even in newer statutes where the word 'reckless' was used, as in the case of the Criminal Damage Act 1971. In this statute, the word 'reckless' replaces the word 'malicious' in the preceding act which was the Malicious Damage Act 1861. Before the Criminal Damage Act had been passed, the Law Commission had considered the mental element in this offence and had decided that the law was satisfactory in this respect, although it was admitted that it needed to be expressed more clearly. This was effected by using the words 'intentionally' and 'recklessly', instead of the word 'maliciously'. No definition of recklessness was provided in the Act, so it was therefore believed that the law remained substantially the same, despite the change in wording, i.e. it was believed that the *Cunningham* test continued to apply.

This view was followed in the case of *Stephenson 1979*. A conviction for criminal damage was quashed because the trial judge had stated that the defendant could be found guilty if he 'closed his mind to the obvious fact of risk from his act', a test which was more objective in approach.

The defendant was a schizophrenic and had decided to sleep in a haystack. He lit a fire to keep himself warm and caused £300 worth of damage. Such a result would obviously have been foreseen by an ordinary 'reasonable' man, but the Court of Appeal quashed the conviction. Lord Lane was emphatic that the test was subjective: 'we wish to make it clear that the test remains subjective, that the knowledge or appreciation of risk of some damage must have entered the defendant's mind even though he may have suppressed it'.

Caldwell recklessness

This then was the position until the cases of *Caldwell* and *Lawrence*, in *1982*. The two cases were decided by the House of Lords on the same day and, together, they introduced a high degree of uncertainty into this area of law.

In *MPC* v *Caldwell 1982*, the defendant had been engaged to work for the proprietor of a residential hotel but had been dismissed and nursed a grievance against the owner. When he was very drunk, Caldwell broke a window in the hotel and started a fire on the ground floor. Fortunately, this was discovered and put out quite quickly and no serious harm was done, either in the form of personal injury to the ten people residing in the hotel, or in the form of property damage.

Caldwell was prepared to admit to the lesser charge of criminal damage but fiercely resisted the more serious charge of causing criminal damage with intent to endanger life or being reckless as to whether life would be endangered. Despite this, the jury found him guilty and he was sentenced to three years imprisonment.

The case eventually reached the House of Lords where Lord Diplock gave the main speech and changed the law on recklessness, at least for the crime of criminal damage. Diplock argued:

> that the only person who knows what the accused's mental processes were at the time of committing the crime is the accused himself and probably not even he can recall them accurately when the rage or excitement under which he acted has passed or he has sobered up if he were under the influence of drink at the end of the relevant time.

He therefore believed that the test for reckless-ness should be widened to encompass a wider range of situations. He decided that a person is reckless under the Criminal Damage Act 1971 if:

1 He does an act which in fact creates an obvious risk that property will be destroyed or damaged, and
2 when he does the act he either has not given any thought to the possibility of there being any such risk or has recognised that there was some risk involved and has nonetheless gone on to do it.

Caldwell's appeal therefore was dismissed and a wider test of recklessness had emerged on a three to two majority. Lord Edmund Davies and Lord Wilberforce dissented on this point but upheld the conviction.

It should be noted, however, that Cunning-ham recklessness had not disappeared in this new test; it is included in the second half of point two, i.e. the defendant has recognised that there may be some risk involved but has nonetheless gone on to take it. It is the other part of the test which has the effect of widening liability substantially. It includes situations where there is a risk, which would have been obvious to a reasonable man, but the defendant in question has not given any thought to it.

Lord Diplock believed that such an exten-sion of liability was both necessary and justifi-able, because of the difficulties of trying to gauge the state of the defendant's mind. He argued that *Cunningham* style recklessness had developed for a special purpose, i.e. to deal with statutes containing the word 'malicious', which seemed to indicate some foreseeability on the part of the defendant. The Criminal Damage Act, on the other hand, had substituted the word 'reckless', so he argued that the same approach was not necessary. He also stated that it was not helpful to classify types of reckless-ness into subjective and objective categories but, despite this plea, that is exactly what has happened.

Judgment in the case of *Lawrence* was also given by the House of Lords on the same day as *Caldwell* but after that decision, and by a differ-ently constituted court, although Lord Diplock was included in both sittings. In *Lawrence*, the House, in a reckless driving case, upheld the wider definition of recklessness, laid down in *Caldwell*.

A motorcyclist had collided with and killed a pedestrian and the House held that there had been an obvious and serious risk, to which Lawrence had failed to advert. His conviction, therefore, was upheld. Later cases followed this new approach. In *Reid 1992*, discussed more fully below, Lord Keith stated that: 'absence of something from a person's state of mind is as much part of his state of mind as is its pres-ence'.

Lord Diplock's attempt to clarify the law on recklessness and, arguably, to make his new test one of universal application, attracted great criticism from both judges and academics. It was said that the change in the law was regret-table (Professor Glanville Williams), that the test was 'not very helpful' (Lord Browne-Wilkinson) and was one which made the eyes of the jury 'glaze over' when it was put to them (Professor Smith).

The test, therefore, far from becoming of universal application, was attacked from the beginning and its use has been increasingly restricted. It was used, albeit in a strained way, in the case of *Pigg 1982*, an attempted rape case, but later abandoned in similar cases where it was decided that the decision in *Morgan* and the provisions in the Sexual Offences (Amend-ment) Act 1976 had made it clear that a more subjective approach had to be taken in such cases. The case of *Satnam 1983* is an example of this.

The Court of Appeal also confirmed that *Cunningham* recklessness was still necessary for offences containing the word 'malicious', as in the offence of malicious wounding. In *W (a minor)* v *Dolbey 1983*, a boy of 15 pointed an airgun belonging to his brother at a man on a farm and, when told to put it down, fired it instead, wounding the man in question. The boy argued that he thought the gun was unloaded. His conviction for unlawful wounding was quashed because the more objective test had been applied and this was held to be incorrect for this type of offence. In *Parmenter 1991*, the House of Lords also agreed that *Cunningham* recklessness was necessary for cases of assault, as will be noted in Chapter 6.

It can be seen, therefore, that *Cunningham*, rather than *Caldwell*, recklessness must be shown for rape, attempted rape and for any cases where the word 'malicious' appears in the definition of the offence. In addition, the Caldwell test no longer has any application in driving offences because reckless driving has been replaced by dangerous driving. It will be noted in Chapter 5 that reckless manslaughter, for which Caldwell recklessness would have sufficed, has also disappeared and been replaced by manslaughter by gross negligence. Gradually, therefore, the cases to which *Caldwell* recklessness might have applied are disappearing or the judges are stating that the test should not be used. We now need to investigate the situations in which it will still be relevant and these appear to be confined, at least in the areas we are studying, to offences of criminal damage. In these cases, however, the new test is strictly applied, sometimes with unjust results.

In *Elliott v C (a minor) 1983,* the defendant was only 14 and of low intelligence. She stayed out all night without sleep and entered a garden shed, where she poured white spirit over a carpet and set light to it and the whole shed was destroyed. The Divisional Court reluctantly upheld her conviction for aggravated criminal damage, because the court was bound by the precedent set in *Caldwell,* concerning the test of recklessness. Goff L J stated, however: 'I would be lacking in candour if I were to conceal my unhappiness about the conclusion which I feel compelled to reach.'

It is clear therefore that the test, when it is applied, is a strict one and its use will make more offenders liable. It has, however, been argued that there is a loophole, or lacuna as it is called, through which some offenders may escape. It would arise where it has been established that the defendant has considered the risk, but has concluded that no risk exists and has then gone ahead with his action. The defendant, if he had not decided to plead guilty, may have been able to use such a loophole in *Crossman 1986*. He had ignored the advice from others that a load of heavy machinery was not suitably secured. He argued that 'it was as safe as houses'. Unfortunately, his judgement was wrong and the load fell off the lorry and killed a pedestrian. He had, however, given thought to the risk and erroneously decided that one did not exist, so *prima facie*, would seem to come under the alleged lacuna.

The matter was aired in the case of *Chief Constable of Avon and Somerset v Shimmen 1986.* The defendant possessed skills in martial arts and was demonstrating these to his friends. He intended to land a kick falling just short of a shop window, but his skills were not as great as he imagined and he put his leg through the window. The magistrates were not prepared to convict and the prosecution appealed to the Divisional Court. This court decided that the lacuna did not apply in this case. The judges argued that he had perceived that there was at least some risk and had then gone on to take it; he had not decided that no risk at all existed.

The Court of Appeal took a similar view in the case of *Merrick 1995*, where the defendant had gained permission to remove some old electrical equipment from a house and in so doing, had left a live cable exposed for six minutes before burying it. He argued that he had believed that there was no risk. Once again, the judges preferred to take the view that he must have known that there was some risk in the period while the cable was exposed but had thought that the risk was worth taking. That, they argued, was not the same as deciding that there was no risk at all.

Eventually, the House of Lords was called on to consider this problem. In *Reid 1992*, the defendant was driving in the centre of London and tried to overtake on an inside lane. This narrowed considerably near a junction to allow for a taxi driver's hut. Reid struck this hut and his passenger was killed. He appealed against his conviction for causing death by dangerous driving. The case reached the House of Lords, which laid down three situations in a driving case where someone might not be liable under the *Caldwell/Lawrence* test:

1 Where the driver acted under an understandable or excusable mistake of fact, (as, for example, overtaking on a hill when driving a left-hand drive vehicle and being misinformed about the safety of such an act, or where a safe manoeuvre suddenly becomes unsafe because of a fuel blockage).
2 Where the driver's ability to recognise a possible risk could be affected by a condition which is not his fault, (as, for example, illness or shock).
3 Where the driver was acting under duress

Their Lordships accepted that it was not always essential to use the exact words laid down in *Caldwell/Lawrence* and that there were limited exceptions where the rule would not apply. Reckless driving has now disappeared so the exceptions will no longer be necessary for those cases. Presumably, if relevant, they will apply to cases of criminal damage. They are, however, far narrower than at first believed. A wider lacuna has not been accepted by the courts.

To sum up, since the case of *MPC* v *Caldwell 1982*, there are two types of recklessness in English law, *Cunningham* recklessness, which is required for most of the offences we shall be studying and *Caldwell* recklessness which is now limited to criminal damage. These matters will be returned to in Chapters 6 and 9. The rules are summarised in the key facts chart.

activity

In groups or individually, discuss the following statement:

❛ *The use of two tests to assess recklessness in English law has caused confusion and injustice.* ❜

COMMENT

It is regrettable that such confusion has surrounded such a very important element in so many criminal cases. One can see why Lord Diplock wished to introduce a wider test and, arguably, such a test is not too unfair in basic criminal damage cases. What gives great cause for concern, however, is the use of the test for the aggravated offences of criminal damage, where the maximum sentence is life imprisonment. The judges have shown that they are prepared to sentence up to this maximum in these cases, especially arson, and it could be seriously questioned whether an objective view of the defendant's guilt should be taken. In other cases where the maximum sentence is life, a subjective approach is taken. Another criticism is that the *Caldwell* test blurs what was formerly a clear distinction between recklessness and negligence and creates a lack of uniformity over an important concept.

Possible reform of recklessness

The Law Commission, in the Draft Code and in later Bills, favours a return to subjective recklessness.

2.3.4 NEGLIGENCE

Negligence occurs when a person acts in a way that falls below the standard expected of the reasonable person in the same situation as the accused. Such carelessness often incurs liability in civil law but, in addition, there are certain situations where a person would also be liable under the criminal law.

As discussed in the last section, the distinction between recklessness and negligence used to be clearly defined; the former was the deliberate taking of an unjustifiable risk, while the latter was inadvertent risk taking. Since the decisions in *Caldwell* and *Lawrence*, however,

- Recklessness is the taking of an unjustifiable risk
- Before 1982, *Cunningham*, or subjective recklessness, was the test to be applied in all cases, (*Cunningham 1957*). This test seeks to discover whether the defendant knew that he was taking an unjustifiable risk
- The House of Lords' decisions on the same day in *MPC* v *Caldwell* and *Lawrence 1982*, restated the law and laid down a different test in cases of criminal damage and what was then reckless driving. This said that a person is reckless if he does an act which creates an obvious risk, when he either has not given any thought to it or has thought about it and still gone on to take it
- It can be seen that, despite Lord Diplock's opinion, it is a more objective test and will make more people liable, as can be seen in *Elliot v C (a minor) 1983*
- At first, it was suggested that the test would apply to all cases, but now, with the demise of reckless driving and reckless manslaughter, it has been restricted solely to criminal damage
- The subjective, Cunningham test is used for cases of rape, (*Satnam 1983*), malicious wounding (*W (a minor)* v *Dolbey 1993*), and assault, (*Parmenter 1991*)
- The use of a possible lacuna in the *Caldwell* test has been recognised by the House of Lords but has been strictly contained, (*Reid 1992*)

FIGURE 2.3 *Key facts chart on recklessness*

the lines between the two forms of blame-worthiness have become increasingly blurred.

Negligent acts may suffice to incur liability in driving offences. In *McRone* v *Riding 1938*, the defendant was a learner driver but, nonetheless, it was decided that he could be convicted of careless driving if his standard of driving fell below that of a reasonably competent driver.

Negligence, albeit negligence of a higher degree, will also suffice for the more serious offences of dangerous driving and causing death by dangerous driving. These offences were introduced by the Road Traffic Act 1991, which substituted new sections in to the Road Traffic Act 1988, and, at the same time, abolished the offences of reckless driving and causing death by reckless driving. The new s.2A Road Traffic Act 1988 states that a person will be guilty of dangerous driving if the way he drives falls far below what would be expected of a competent and careful driver and it would be obvious to the latter that driving in that way would be dangerous. He would also be driving dangerously if it would be obvious to a competent and careful driver that driving a vehicle in

its current state would be dangerous. The test, therefore, is objective, i.e. would a competent and careful person drive in such a way.

In addition to these serious driving offences, grossly negligent behaviour that leads to the death of a person may result in a manslaughter charge. This area of law will be examined more fully in Chapter 5 on involuntary manslaughter. For the present, it should be noted that the offence of manslaughter by gross negligence has been revived and takes place where the defendant's conduct was 'so bad in all the circumstances as to amount ... to a criminal act or omission', as stated by Lord Mackay, the former Lord Chancellor in *Adomako 1994*.

2.3.5 OFFENCES OF STRICT LIABILITY

There are many offences, often of a regulatory nature, (but not necessarily so), which have been created as offences of strict liability. Most such offences have been laid down by statute, but there are limited common law examples such as public nuisance and criminal libel.

It is commonly stated that no *mens rea* is needed for such offences. This is not quite accurate; what should be stated is that *mens rea* does not have to be proved with regard to one or more of the elements of the *actus reus*. In many offences, it is obvious that *mens rea* is required. The words 'intention' or 'recklessness', laid down for many offences, signify the degree of blameworthiness required. Other crimes will only be committed if the defendant acts 'wilfully', 'knowingly' or 'dishonestly'. He cannot, therefore, be convicted if such states of mind cannot be shown to the satisfaction of the magistrates or the jury. Should the offence be one of strict liability, however, the defendant may well be held to be criminally liable without any proof of fault on his part. It is now necessary to look at some examples of strict liability and then to consider the arguments for and against their imposition where many other case examples are also included.

An early example of liability without fault is illustrated in the case of *Prince 1875*. The defendant was charged, under s.55 Offences Against the Person Act 1861, with unlawfully taking an unmarried girl under the age of 16 out of the possession and against the will of her father, mother or any other person having lawful charge of her. Prince was found guilty, despite the fact that Annie Phillips, the girl in question, looked much older than her 13 years and despite evidence that she had told Prince that she was 18 and he had believed her.

The court stressed that the relevant section did not contain the words 'knowingly' or 'maliciously', so liability arose when Prince merely committed the act.

Another early example of a strict liability offence is *Cundy* v *Le Cocq 1884*. The unfortunate publican in this case was convicted of selling intoxicating liquor to someone who was drunk, contrary to s.13 Licensing Act 1872, despite his claim that he had no knowledge that the customer was intoxicated.

On appeal, the judges were unsympathetic. It was stated that 'the object of this part of the

Act is to prevent the sale of intoxicating liquor to drunken persons and it is perfectly natural to carry that out by throwing on the publican the responsibility of determining whether the person comes within that category'.

Arguments in favour of retaining strict liability offences

The paramount reason for the creation of such offences is to protect the public. This protection is needed in many different types of situation. The following are examples.

1   **Protection against the selling of unfit food**
    In *Callow v Tillstone 1900*, a butcher was convicted of selling meat which was held to be unfit for public consumption, despite the fact that a vet had declared that the meat to be safe. Similarly, in *Smedleys v Breed 1974*, the manufacturer's conviction for selling unfit food was upheld by the House of Lords, when four tins of peas were found to contain caterpillars! Their Lordships were unimpressed with the argument that over three million tins of uncontaminated peas had been sold. Liability in such cases is imposed to ensure that the providers of food maintain control of their checking procedures and keep standards high.

2   **Protection against pollution**
    In *Alphacell* v *Woodward 1972*, the defendant's conviction for causing polluted matter to enter a river was upheld, despite the claims that the company was unaware of any obstruction to its pumps. Lord Salmon stated that, if the offence were not one of strict liability 'a great deal of pollution would go unpunished and undeterred to the relief of many riparian factory owners. As a result many rivers which are now filthy would become filthier still and many rivers which are now clean would lose their cleanliness'. Fighting words!

3   **Protection of the countryside**
    In *Kirkland v Robinson 1987*, the Divisional Court of Queen's Bench refused to accept the defendant's claim that he was unaware he

was in possession of wild birds, contrary to the Wildlife and Countryside Act 1981. The protection of the environment was felt to be of 'outstanding social importance'.

4   **Protection from unlawful weapons**

It is believed that the holding of weapons capable of causing harm, should be strictly controlled, even if this results in the occasional injustice. In *Howells 1977*, the defendant's conviction for failing to obtain a firearms' certificate was upheld, despite the fact that he believed that his gun was an antique and therefore did not require such certification. In fact, it was discovered to be a reproduction for which a certificate was necessary. In *Bradish 1990*, the defendant argued that he was unaware that a canister in his possession contained prohibited CS gas. Once again, the conviction was upheld.

5   **Protection from illegal broadcasts**

In the case of *Blake 1997*, a conviction under the Wireless Telegraphy Act 1949 was upheld, when the defendant operated a radio station without a licence, despite his claim that he thought he was merely making demonstration tapes. The court held that the Act had been designed to deter such practices, which might otherwise interfere with emergency communications.

6   **Protection from dangerous drugs**

Strict liability is imposed in some drug offences, both to protect the public and to make it more difficult for offenders to evade liability by arguing that they did not know the drugs were in their possession. In *Warner v MPC 1969*, the defendant had taken possession of some boxes, left for him at a café. He sold perfume as a sideline and alleged that he believed that this was what the boxes contained. In fact, prohibited drugs were found in one of them. Despite his claims, the House of Lords upheld his conviction.

7   **Protection from unsafe buildings**

In *Atkinson v Sir Alfred McAlpine 1974*, a building company was convicted under the Asbestos Regulations 1969 for failing to state that it was using crocidolite, even though it was unaware of this fact. Similarly in *Gammon v AG for Hong Kong 1985* the defendants were found liable when part of the building they were helping to construct collapsed, even though the company was unaware that the plans were not being followed. The Privy Council again stressed that the main reason for enforcing liability in cases such as this was to protect the public.

In the above case, the Privy Council also went on to state that strict liability was necessary 'to encourage greater vigilance to prevent the commission of the prohibited act'. This, too, is seen as one of the main reasons for making liability strict. Manufacturers, builders, providers of food all know that they must keep to the highest standards or face possible prosecution. In addition, a successful prosecution has a powerful deterrent value, both on the offending individual or company and on others who note the conviction. In cases where the company has been convicted, the attendant bad publicity is very unwelcome so again, the organisation will be encouraged to be extra vigilant in the future.

It is also important to note that, in many cases, liability is strict but not absolute. In some situations, the defendant may be able to put forward a limited defence, such as the fact that the offence was committed by another or under duress. This helps to lesson the unfairness of the rules. The last justification for imposing such liability is a purely practical one. It would be very difficult, in many cases, to obtain a conviction if some form of *mens rea* had to be proved. It will be seen in Chapter 14 on vicarious and corporate liability, that the courts then have to resort to other methods, such as the delegation principle, in order to maintain standards.

Arguments against the imposition of strict liability

The first point to make is that it can be unjust. One of the main principles of criminal law is that a person or a company should only be liable if they are at fault in some way. In many of the cases described, the defendants were completely unaware that that an offence was being committed. For example, in *Pharmaceutical Society of Great Britain* v *Storkwain Ltd 1986*, a pharmacist's conviction for supplying drugs without a valid prescription was upheld, even though he did not know that the signature was forged. It would be fairer in such cases only to impose liability for negligent behaviour, giving the truly innocent a defence.

It could also be argued in many cases, including the ones mentioned above, that the imposition of liability would not have the effect of raising standards. The rationale behind the introduction of such legislation, therefore, is not satisfied. It could also be argued that there is no proof that the creation of such offences actually works in other cases. Instead, it might foster feelings of resentment and injustice, which might lead to a loss of respect for the law. Another argument against strict liability is that the courts often face difficulties in identifying such offences. In many statutes, it is often unclear whether or not such an offence has been created. Some guidance on this was given in the case of *Gammon* v *AG for Hong Kong 1985*, mentioned earlier. The court stated that crimes could be divided into ones which were merely regulatory and those which were 'purely criminal' in character. For the latter type of offence, there is a clear presumption that *mens rea* is required before an individual or company can be convicted. In the case of regulatory offences, there is still a presumption that *mens rea* is necessary, which would predominate unless it is felt that an issue of social concern, such as public safety, is involved. In such cases, it may then be necessary to impose liability in order to encourage greater vigilance and higher standards.

Earlier cases show that the courts are inconsistent in their attitude towards strict liability offences. In some instances they take a very harsh approach, as in *Cundy* v *Le Cocq 1884*, mentioned earlier, whereas in other similar cases, they are prepared to be more tolerant, as in *Sherras* v *De Rutzen 1895*. In this case the conviction of a publican for serving alcohol to a police officer was quashed by the Divisional Court. The officer had not worn an armband, which would have identified him as being on duty. The court felt that the presumption against strict liability should be upheld, particularly as no amount of care would have prevented the commission of the offence.

As noted earlier, in *Warner* v *MPC 1969*, the House of Lords upheld the conviction of a defendant for being in possession of drugs. In *Sweet* v *Parsley 1970*, however, the same court quashed a similar conviction and stated that where a section in an act is silent on the matter of *mens rea*, it should be presumed.

There may also be a lack of clarity in some judgments, as the courts struggle to justify the imposition of liability and, in so doing, arrive at decisions which affront notions of common sense and simple justice. The case of *Warner*, mentioned above, was the first case on strict liability to go to the House of Lords. Smith and Hogan, in the eighth edition of their book state that: 'The five speeches delivered in *Warner* differ so greatly and it is so difficult to make sense of parts of them that courts in later cases have found it impossible to extract a ratio decidendi.' The book strongly calls it 'another calamitous decision by the House'.

Such decisions may also have the opposite effect of what is intended and lead to later action by Parliament, allowing a defence in some situations, as in the Misuse of Drugs Act 1971.

Probably the most important argument against the creation of strict liability offences is that the stigma of a criminal conviction is imposed on the individual or company, sometimes for an act which he could not have foreseen or prevented. In addition, the penalties for such infringement may be very severe. Even though offences are often of a regulatory nature, with fairly minor fines, this is not always the case. In the case of *Gammon*, mentioned earlier, the maximum penalty was a $250,000 fine and imprisonment for three years.

Possible reform of strict liability

There has been a move away from the imposition of such offences by both Parliament and the judiciary, although they will continue to be important where strict liability in offences of a purely regulatory nature is still deemed to be necessary. Reform of this area is indirectly incorporated into the Draft Criminal Code. The Code, if ever enacted, would lay down a presumption that all offences require either intention, recklessness or knowledge and, if some strict liability offences are felt to be essential, then Parliament must clearly state this in the relevant provision.

KEY FACTS

- These offences are ones for which no fault has to be shown for one or more parts of the *actus reus*
- They are nearly always created by statute and are often for fairly minor infringements, although important exceptions exist
- They are laid down to protect the environment and to protect the public from unfit food, unsafe buildings, unnecessary pollution, unlawful weapons or drugs and illegal broadcasts, although equally strong arguments may be put forward for abolition of this type of liability

FIGURE 2.4 *Key facts chart on strict liability*

Discuss the following:

❝ The imposition of strict liability offences is a necessary evil in the fight to protect the public from harm ❞.

2.3.6 THE DOCTRINE OF TRANSFERRED MALICE

Before leaving the subject of *mens rea*, it should be noted at this stage that if the defendant has the *mens rea* for one offence, it may be transferred to another offence of the same type. The case of *Latimer 1886*, provides an example. The defendant, a soldier, hit a customer in a pub with his belt after an attack by that other. The belt rebounded off the first victim and hit a woman in the pub, cutting her face open in the process. The court held that the *mens rea* from the first attack could be transferred to the second offence. The position would have been different if another type of offence had been planned in the first instance as, for example, criminal damage. In such a case, the *mens rea* of that offence could not be transferred. The case of *Pembliton 1874* illustrates this in reverse. In this case, the defendant intended to throw a stone at a fighting crowd but accidentally broke a window instead. He could not be found guilty of this offence under the doctrine of transferred malice; it would have to be the subject of a separate charge.

2.4 COINCIDENCE OF THE ACTUS REUS AND MENS REA

We have noted that, normally, two elements have to be established before a crime can be committed, the *actus reus* and the requisite *mens rea*. In a small minority of cases, the courts have been willing to accept that the *actus reus* can be a continuing act, as in the case of *Fagan*, mentioned under the section on the *actus reus* in a crime. They may, instead, use the concept of a series of acts in which the *mens rea* may have been present some of the time. The case of *Thabo Meli 1954* provides an illustration of this. Further examples can be seen in the next chapter.

In this case, a gang had severely beaten the victim and, believing him to be dead, had thrown him over a cliff. At that time, he was still alive but he died later from exposure. The *mens rea* for murder had existed at the beginning of the sequence of acts and this was held to suffice. The defendants were not allowed to argue that they did not possess the appropriate *mens rea* at the time of his death. The Privy Council decided that the men should not be allowed 'to escape the penalties of the law' and found them guilty of murder. A similar view was taken in *Le Brun 1991* where the continuing act also lasted while the defendant was trying to cover up his crime.

summary

We have discovered that the *actus reus* of a crime consists of all the elements of the offence except the mental element. Usually there must be some sort of act but, on rare occasions, liability for omissions has been laid down by either Parliament or the courts.

We have seen that the *mens rea* of a crime is the mental element or the degree of fault required. We have noted that some crimes cannot be established unless an intention to commit them is proved. We have also found out that the word itself has not been defined and that it is the task of the jury to establish intention.

Other crimes can be committed intentionally or recklessly. We now know that, for most crimes, *Cunningham,* or subjective recklessness, has to be proved, although a different, more objective test was laid down in the case of *MPC* v *Caldwell* for criminal damage.

We have discovered that crimes only requiring negligence are rare, but an important example is manslaughter by gross negligence. Towards the end of this chapter, we learned that there are many examples of strict liability offences and we examined the merits and disadvantages of allowing them.

CHAPTER 3

UNLAWFUL KILLING I: MURDER

3.1 INTRODUCTION

HAVING DISCOVERED THE elements that are necessary before a crime is committed, it is now time to look at some of the most important crimes in more detail. These are known as substantive offences and in the following four chapters we shall be looking at offences against the person, starting with the most serious of these where a death results and then going on to look at non-fatal crimes, such as assault and rape.

It is very important to realise that you are not required to study every criminal offence. There are many thousands of these and it is obviously unrealistic, at this point in your studies, to expect you to have knowledge of them all. Indeed, very few barristers and solicitors would have such information; at best, they would know where to find detail on them, should this be necessary. Law courses, therefore, are selective in the choice of crimes to be studied in their syllabuses. For example, the more general courses do not usually require knowledge of drug offences, or the more minor traffic ones. This book aims to cover the offences most commonly found in A Level and undergraduate courses.

- Chapter 3, 4 and 5 examine fatal offences against the person

- Chapter Six covers non-fatal offences against the person

3.2 GENERAL INFORMATION ON HOMICIDE

Firstly, it is important to realise that killing can be either lawful or unlawful.

- Examples of lawful homicide would arise where there is an execution by lawful process or the killing of an enemy by a member of the armed forces on active military service

- Examples of unlawful homicide are murder, manslaughter, infanticide, causing death by dangerous driving and causing death by careless driving

3.2.1 THE DISTINCTION BETWEEN MURDER AND MANSLAUGHTER

Murder is the 'killing of a human being with malice aforethought'. This definition is examined in more detail below. People are said to be increasingly worried about the frequency of this crime but those who feel that it is no longer safe to walk the streets might take heart from the following article.

Manslaughter can be voluntary or involuntary:

- **Voluntary manslaughter** arises where the definition of murder appears to have been satisfied but one of three possible defences granted by statute can be pleaded, which will

London has one of lowest murder rates in the world

LONDON has one of the lowest murder rates in the world, according to a new international league table of homicides in capital cities.

Of 29 European and American cities, London ranks 24th — making it a safer place to live than Geneva, Lisbon, Stockholm, Amsterdam, Paris and Berlin.

Only Dublin, Rome, Athens and Brussels enjoy safer reputations than London. The capital's ratio of 2.1 homicides per 100,000 population is next to nothing compared with the world's most dangerous city — Washington DC — which has 69.3 per 100,000.

Washington is followed by four other US cities — Philadelphia, Dallas, Los Angeles and New York — with only Moscow, of the European capitals, joining them in the top six.

Moscow weighs in with 18.1 murders per 100,000, a clear leader as Europe's murder capital. It even beats New York, with 16.8, while Philadelphia, Dallas and Los Angeles are closely linked together on 27.4, 24.8 and 22.8 respectively. Brussels can rightly claim to be the safest place in Europe, with a murder rate of only 0.4 per 100,000. The figures were compiled by the Home Office and Home Secretary Jack Straw said today: "This research shows what a rare event homicide is in this country. I think few people would have guessed that both Lisbon and Amsterdam have murder rates more than three times higher than London.

"Moreover, despite the impact of 'zero tolerance' policies, New York City's homicide rate at 16.8 is eight times London's rate."

Mr Straw added: "These figures help show the great contribution the Metropolitan Police has made in making London a relatively safe place in which to live."

The international figures relate to killings between 1994 and 1996. In 1996 there were 681 homicides in England and Wales, rising to 711 last year — of which two-thirds of the victims were male. Suspects were charged or convicted in all but nine per cent of cases.

Research showed that the majority of killings in this country were carried out by someone known to the victim as a result of a quarrel, loss of temper or for revenge. In only four per cent of murder cases did the suspect appear to be mentally disturbed and strike without warning.

The two most vulnerable groups are babies under 12 months, who are usually killed by parents, and males aged between 16 and 49.

Taken from an article by Richard Holliday in the *Evening Standard*, 19 August 1998

---

reduce the offence from murder to manslaughter. These are diminished responsibility, provocation and the survivor of a suicide pact. As stated, this subject will be examined in Chapter 4.

- **Involuntary manslaughter** occurs where there is no malice aforethought but a death results because of an unlawful act or gross negligence. This type of manslaughter will be discussed in Chapter 5.

3.2.2 THE *ACTUS REUS* AND *MENS REA* OF THESE CRIMES

Murder and manslaughter share the same *actus reus*, which is the unlawful killing of a human being. The *mens rea* for murder and voluntary manslaughter is killing with malice aforethought. The *mens rea* for involuntary manslaughter varies, as will be noted in Chapter 5.

3.3 MURDER

Murder is a common law offence, that is a crime developed by the judges, not one laid down by statute. It is one of the oldest crimes. In most civilisations, the killing of a human being without lawful excuse is considered to be one of the most heinous acts against society and one for which the penalty should be severe. This country is no exception. In earlier times, a person convicted of murder was sentenced to death, i.e. to be hanged by the neck until dead. Once the foreman of the jury had announced that that the defendant was guilty of murder, the judge had no alternative but to don his black cap and recite the following chilling words:

It remains for me to discharge the duty which the law imposes upon the court, and without alternative, and that is to pass upon you the sentence which the law adjudges for wilful murder – that you be taken from the place where you now stand to the place whence you came; thence to a place of execution, and that you be hanged by the neck until your body be dead; and that after death your body be buried within the precincts of the gaol in which you shall have at last been confined. And may God have mercy on your soul.

The death penalty was at first suspended and then abolished altogether by the Murder (Abolition of Death Penalty) Act 1965. Now, following a conviction for murder, the judge will impose a mandatory sentence of life imprisonment.

It should be noted that, while the mandatory life sentence remains, in most cases, the accused will be released on licence after a number of years in jail. The judge can help to influence the parole board in this respect by recommending that a minimum number of years be served before the defendant is considered for such release.

COMMENT

There has been much criticism over the fact that the judges have no discretion as to the punishment to be imposed for murder. This can be unjust, because a sadistic serial killer and a mercy killer are both treated the same way and both will receive the mandatory punishment of life imprisonment. In English law, there are no degrees of murder as exist in other jurisdictions. The Criminal Law Revision Committee looked at this problem but decided not to recommend any change in the position.

In 1989, a Select Committee of the House of Lords also looked into the matter. This body did believe changes should be made but did not favour having different degrees of murder. Lord Nathan, who chaired the Committee, made the following comment:

'To divide unlawful killing into categories is going the wrong route. You should give the judges discretion for the penalty'.

Such a method also has its critics, especially among those who believe that some of the judges, when exercising their discretion, mete out sentences that are either too harsh or, more often in relation to the crime of manslaughter, considered to be too lenient. This topic will be examined further in Chapter 4. At present, it is important to note that no change in the law has yet been effected and the mandatory life sentence remains for murder (see following article).

3.3.1 THE ORIGINAL DEFINITION OF MURDER

In Coke's Institute, an early work, the famous judge and former Lord Chief Justice of England laid down his definition of murder.

Life for Billie-Jo's foster father

THE foster father of Billie-Jo Jenkins was jailed for life last night after being convicted of her "horrendous" murder with an 18-inch tent peg, on what the trial judge described as compelling evidence.

Sion Jenkins, aged 40, a deputy headmaster, was found guilty of the 13-year old's savage killing at the end of a 20-day trial. There were shouts of "you monster" and "bastard" from the schoolgirl's natural family seated in the public gallery. Two female jurors burst into tears. Billie-Jo's relatives hurled abuse and spat.

The schoolgirl's natural mother, Deborah Jenkins, sobbed quietly while her father Bill jumped to his feet and punched the air.

The judge, Mr Justice Gage, told Jenkins, of Hastings: "It was a furious attack, the motive for which only you now know. That girl was in your care as a foster child. You yourself were a deputy headmaster at the time, a man in a position of trust and authority in respect of children.

"These bare facts are sufficient to show what a horrendous crime this was ... you are a very considerable danger to the public."

Last night Jenkins's 36-year-old wife Lois described for the first time how she discovered Billie-Jo had been bludgeoned to death in her home "Sixteen months ago I returned, with two of my children, from a quiet Saturday afternoon walk on the beach, to a tragedy more horrific than any person ever expects to encounter in a lifetime.

"The loss of Billie, especially in such awful circumstances has been almost too much to bear.

"It is a terrible thing to realise that the man with whom you have lived with for 14 years, the father of your children, is capable of murdering your child. There is no reason, no explanation, for such a pointless waste of a young life."

Det Supt Jeremy Paine of Sussex police, who led the 16-month investigation, yesterday described Billie-Jo's murder as a "brutal act carried out in a moment of incomprehensible rage and violence".

Speaking outside the court Bill Jenkins, Billie-Jo's natural father, said he "felt nothing" towards the man who had murdered her. "I have been living in a daze for the last 16 months. The daze has gone now. I have no feelings."

Sussex police revealed fresh details of how Jenkins had almost completely invented his CV to become deputy headmaster of a local boys' comprehensive school in Hastings. He falsely claimed to have a degree from Kent University, a PGCE in Education and an MSc in Education Management.

Taken from an article by Luke Harding in the *Guardian*, 6 July 1998

This was said to arise where:

> a man of sound memory and the age of discretion unlawfully killed within any county of the realm any reasonable creature in *rerum natura* under the King's peace, with malice aforethought, either expressed by the party or implied by law, so that the party wounded or hurt etc. die of the wound or hurt etc. within a year and a day after the same.

Changes to the early definition

You will be glad to discover that you are not required to learn this long definition because, over the years, modifications have been made to it. The new definition is noted on page 40.

1 The term 'a man of sound memory and the age of discretion' covers both people of either sex and includes all those who are not insane or allowed some other defence. The term also applies to children between the ages of 10 and 14. Until very recently, such children were presumed not to have criminal liability unless it could be proved that they

knew that they were doing something seriously wrong. Since October 1998, this presumption has been removed and children of this age have the same liability as adults, although they will be normally be treated differently in court and when sentenced. (There will be a fuller discussion on this in Chapter 10 on general defences.)

2 The term 'any county of the realm' relates to any unlawful killings in this country, whether by a British subject or not but, under extensions created by statute, the term also includes murders committed abroad by British subjects and killings by them on British ships or aircraft.

Another very important change in Coke's definition was the removal in 1996 of what is called 'the year and a day rule'.

This ancient rule decreed that a charge of murder or manslaughter could not be brought if the victim survived for longer than a year and a day. It was first intended as a measure limiting the time period in which any prosecution for felony could be brought. By the fourteenth century, however, it came to apply solely to the crime of homicide, where it became necessary to establish that the victim of the killing had died within a year and a day following the attack.

Legal theorists believed that the rule was developed to avoid the difficulties of proving whether the injury inflicted by the accused had caused the death or whether such a death had resulted from a later illness or accident. Now that medical science makes it easier to pinpoint the reason for the mortality, there have been calls for the abolition of the rule.

In 1980, the Criminal Law Revision Committee looked at this question but rather surprisingly recommended the retention of the rule. The Committee justified its decision by arguing that, otherwise, the possibility of a murder charge could hang indefinitely over someone's head. The Committee argued that it was still possible to bring a charge of attempted murder or grievous bodily harm, both of which also carry a maximum penalty of life imprisonment.

The limitations of the rule, however, can be seen in the sad case of *Dyson 1908*. The defendant had assaulted his baby daughter on 13 November 1906 and again on 29 December 1907. She eventually died on 5 March 1908. At first instance, Dyson was convicted of manslaughter after the trial judge informed the jury that a conviction could be secured if the baby's death had resulted from either of these injuries.

On appeal, the conviction for manslaughter had to be quashed because of this misdirection by the trial judge of the 'year and a day rule'.

There was also injustice where victims of violent attacks survived for longer than a year and a day, sometimes for many years on life support machines, before eventually dying, and the offender could not be charged with murder. Further calls for the rule to be reconsidered were made.

The Law Commission reopened the debate in its Consultation Paper No. 136 1994, in which it favoured abolishing the rule, so as to follow the lead given by other jurisdictions like Australia, South Africa and closer to home, Scotland. (Students should be aware that Scotland has a separate criminal legal system to that of England and Wales.) The Commission felt that it was wrong that the existence of the rule prevented the bringing of certain prosecutions, even though it was clear that the original injury had caused the death and felt that the time was right for a change in the law. A bill was therefore drawn up by the Law Commission, and introduced into Parliament via a Private Member's Bill in December 1995. The Bill passed through all its later stages in one single day without opposition and emerged in June as the Law Reform (Year and a Day Rule) Act 1996.

activity

Read the above mentioned Act and discuss the safeguards which have been incorporated within it for the benefit of the defendant.

ELIZABETH II   c. 19

Law Reform (Year and a Day Rule) Act 1996

1996 CHAPTER 19

An Act to abolish the "year and a day rule" and, in consequence of its abolition, to impose a restriction on the institution in certain circumstances of proceedings for a fatal offence. [17th June 1996]

BE IT ENACTED by the Queen's most Excellent Majesty, by and with the advice and consent of the Lords Spiritual and Temporal, and Commons, in this present Parliament assembled, and by the authority of the same, as follows:—

1. The rule known as the "year and a day rule" (that is, the rule that, for the purposes of offences involving death and of suicide, an act or omission is conclusively presumed not to have caused a person's death if more than a year and a day elapsed before he died) is abolished for all purposes. *Abolition of "year and a day rule".*

2.—(1) Proceedings to which this section applies may only be instituted by or with the consent of the Attorney General. *Restriction on institution of proceedings for a fatal offence.*

(2) This section applies to proceedings against a person for a fatal offence if—

   (a) the injury alleged to have caused the death was sustained more than three years before the death occurred, or

   (b) the person has previously been convicted of an offence committed in circumstances alleged to be connected with the death.

(3) In subsection (2) "fatal offence" means—

   (a) murder, manslaughter, infanticide or any other offence of which one of the elements is causing a person's death, or

   (b) the offence of aiding, abetting, counselling or procuring a person's suicide.

FIGURE 3.1 *The Law Reform (Year and a Day Rule) Act 1996. Reproduced with the permission of the Controller of Her Majesty's Stationery Office.*

3.3.2 THE CURRENT DEFINITION OF MURDER

After the afore mentioned modifications are taken into account, the current definition of murder can be said to be:

> an unlawful killing of a human being under the Queen's peace with malice aforethought

The revised definition of murder now needs to be examined in more detail, particularly with regard to how the courts have interpreted the words 'unlawful', 'human being' and 'malice aforethought'.

An unlawful killing

It has already been noted that, for both murder or manslaughter to be established, the killing must be unlawful, and we have seen that it is

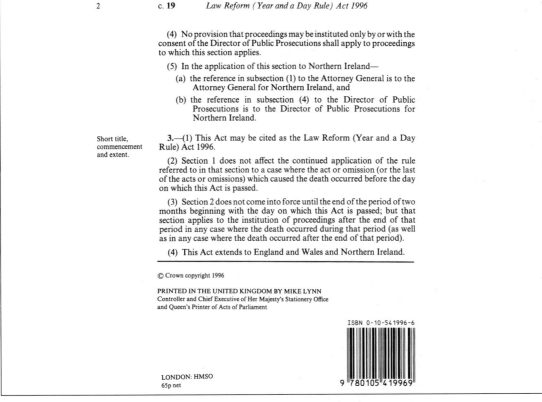

FIGURE 3.1 *continued*

possible, in rare circumstances, for a killing to be given the approval of the State and therefore be rendered lawful. If the death penalty were to be returned, a defendant convicted of murder could be lawfully killed by the process agreed upon. In other jurisdictions, various methods have been adopted, including electrocution, gassing, shooting, hanging, administering a lethal injection and even beheading.

A soldier or policeman who kills in the lawful exercise of his duty will obviously not be guilty of murder. Should he exceed the powers given to him, however, he could face criminal proceedings, as is shown in the cases of *Clegg 1995* and other soldiers in Northern Ireland who were all convicted of murder. This subject is discussed more fully in Chapter 10, where the defences of self defence and prevention of crime are explored.

For the present, it should be noted that if unreasonable force is used, these defences would fail and, if a death has occurred, a murder or manslaughter prosecution could follow.

Doctors, too, have to be careful to operate within the current state of the law and are not normally permitted to accelerate the death of a patient without the judge's permission. The doctor may wish to end the suffering of a terminally ill patient but, if he intends to kill the patient, his acts will come within the definition of murder and he could well face life imprisonment. He is accelerating the death of a human being and this is not allowed.

In *Adams 1957*, this fact was made clear to the jury by Devlin J who stated that:

> If life were cut short by weeks or months it was just as much murder as if it were cut short by years.

The judges have relaxed the strictness of this approach in very limited circumstances. One example is where the acceleration of the time of the death is minimal. Under what is called the '*de minimus* rule', a doctor would not face criminal proceedings if he gave an injection towards the very end of a patient's life, to ease his suffering, even if it was known that this might well accelerate the death by a very small degree. In the case of *Adams*, mentioned above, Devlin J did go on to qualify the statement that he made. He added:

> But that does not mean that a doctor aiding the sick or dying has to calculate in minutes or hours, or perhaps in days or weeks, the effect on a patient's life of the medicines he administers. If the first purpose of medicine – the restoration of health – can no longer be achieved, there is still much for the doctor to do, and he is entitled to do all that is proper and necessary to relieve pain and suffering even if measures he takes may incidentally shorten life.

A medical practitioner may also, in very limited circumstances, cease to provide treatment or food even though in other cases liability for gross negligence could arise, as shown in Chapter 2.

In the landmark case of *Airedale National Health Trust* v *Bland 1993*, a significant exception was made. The House of Lords decided that, provided that both doctors and parents or other close relatives agreed that it was futile to continue to treat and artificially feed a patient who was in a persistent vegetative state, the court has the power to withhold further treatment. The actual case concerned 17-year-old Tony Bland, who was crushed in the terrible Hillsborough disaster and reduced to a persistent vegetative state. He was put onto a life support system but after a period of three years there was no sign that he would recover. The

court gave permission to withhold further treatment but said that three conditions had to be satisfied before treatment and feeding could be withheld.

First, the parties involved had to come to court to obtain a declaration. Secondly, before this could be granted, a full investigation into the case had to be undertaken, and an opportunity given to the Official Solicitor to obtain independent medical opinions and all the material necessary for the court hearing. Lastly, the patient had to be in a persistent vegetative state with no hope of recovery.

The House of Lords decided that, if these steps were followed, the doctors would not then be liable for murder, even though the death was intended. Such action, or rather inaction, has thus been given the seal of approval by the courts.

Frenchay Healthcare NHS Trust v S 1994

In *Frenchay Healthcare NHS Trust* v *S 1994*, the 24-year old patient had taken an overdose in 1991, causing acute brain damage. Despite attempts to revive him, he remained in a persistent vegetative state and had to be fed through a nasogastric tube. This failed to be effective, so, in June 1993, an operation was performed, under which a gastronomy tube was fitted into his stomach.

In January 1994, this tube was no longer in its correct position, probably because of the patient's own movements, and a further operation would have been required to insert another tube. Instead, the consultant recommended that no further action should be taken, allowing the patient to die naturally. A declaration permitting this was obtained but the Official Solicitor, acting for the patient, stated that a full investigation had not been carried out. He also claimed that the evidence about the patient's medical condition was not as conclusive as that in the case of Bland.

The Court of Appeal allowed the declaration to stand. The court decided that there were bound to be some cases where a full investigation was simply not possible, (although this was not the situation here). The court also stated that it would be very reluctant to doubt the reliability and good faith of the doctor without a very good reason.

It is important to realise, however, that cases such as this, where a person can be killed in a lawful way, are very limited. Euthanasia and other related deaths are not excusable in English law.

Of a human being

In the old definition, this was said to be 'any reasonable creature in *rerum natura*'. This will usually be obvious but certain points need to be addressed.

1 **The victim must be human.** A person will not commit murder or manslaughter if he kills an animal intentionally, although he may well be liable for other offences. The term 'human' would, however, cover tragic cases where the new born baby is hardly recognisable as a human being, as can occur after the mother's exposure to radiation or drug abuse. The baby might be anercephalic, i.e. without a head or brain, although a brain stem may exist. Some would argue strongly that it should not be regarded as murder if such a child were allowed to die. Current legal and medical opinion, however, appears to favour the view that any offspring of a human mother should be protected by the law, as was indicated in *Rance* v *Mid Downs Health Authority 1991*.

2 **The courts may have to decide when life actually begins.** The killing of a child still in the womb, by either the mother herself or by another person is not homicide, although the guilty party could be convicted of abortion or child destruction, (see Chapter 5). The attacker could be liable for manslaughter and perhaps even murder if the child is born alive and then dies of the injuries, an issue that is discussed below.

For the offences of murder, manslaughter or infanticide to occur, the courts have decided that the foetus must have been expelled from the mother's womb and have an independent existence, a view affirmed by the Criminal Law Revision Committee. In *Rance v Mid-Downs Health Authority* it was stated that a baby is capable of being born alive if it can breath through its own lungs.

What appears to have been settled is that a child who is injured in the womb, then born alive and who later dies of the injuries inflicted before the birth occurred does come under the category of a human being. This would make the perpetrator of the injury liable for homicide in the form of murder or manslaughter, depending on whether or not he had the intention to injure the actual foetus. This view was stated in the early case of *West 1848* and appears to have been supported by some of the *dicta* of the House of Lords in *Attorney General's Reference (No. 3 of 1994) (1996)*.

The defendant had stabbed his girl friend in the stomach, despite the fact that he knew of her pregnancy. The unborn child was affected because the knife had penetrated the uterus and entered the abdomen of the foetus, although this fact was not discovered until later.

The woman made a good recovery but later gave birth prematurely. The baby was born alive but died four months later. The accused was found guilty of grievous bodily harm in relation to the mother but the trial judge decided that, as a matter of law, he could not be convicted of the murder or manslaughter of the baby.

The Attorney General required the opinion of the appeal courts as to whether this statement was correct. The matter eventually reached the House of Lords. Their Lordships decided that a murder charge could not be sustained if the defendant had not intended to kill or seriously injure the foetus itself. In this case, therefore, because the intention to injure the unborn child had not been proved, it was decided that the defendant did not have the necessary *mens rea* for the murder of the baby.

Despite this conclusion, Lord Hope, in his judgement expressed the view that the fact that a child is not yet born did not prevent the actus reus for both murder and manslaughter being established.

He stated:

> for the foetus life lay in the future; it could carry with it the effect of things done to it before birth which after birth might prove to be harmful

Regarding the question of the *mens rea* necessary to gain a conviction for murder in such a case, the matter was not so clearly addressed. The House of Lords failed to state categorically in this referral that the *mens rea* for murder would have existed if the foetus itself had been the subject of a serious intentional attack, although there are suggestions in Lord Hope's judgment that this might well be the case. Professor Smith, one of the leading writers on criminal law, however, does not agree with this view. He argues that the defendant, even where he intends to harm the foetus, is not intending to harm a person in being so therefore would not satisfy the *mens rea* for murder. He believes that, in such a case only a manslaughter charge is sustainable. The offender has committed an unlawful act and a death has resulted. Such crimes will be looked at in Chapter 5.

3 **The courts may also have to decide when death occurs.** The old medical view was that death occurred when the heart stopped beating and breathing ceased. In 1976, the concept of brain death was adopted by the world of medicine and a person was pronounced dead where irremediable structural brain damage was shown.

The courts have not expressly adopted this test. In *Malcherek and Steel 1981*, however, the Court of Appeal accepted that:

> there is a body of opinion in the medical profession that there is only one true test of death and this is irreversible death of the brain steam, which controls the basic functions of the body such as breathing.

Such a definition of death would protect a doctor who removed an organ from a patient in such a state to sustain the life of another. On the other hand, criminal liability would arise if the patient was in an irreversible coma but was not yet classified as brain dead.

It appears that the courts are left alone to grapple with this problem. Parliament has refrained from giving a statutory definition of death and the Criminal Law Revision Committee decided against formulating one because it believed that it would soon become outdated owing to the great strides being made in medicine.

activity

> Topsy went into a hospital ward and switched off a life support machine connected to her friend, Tim, because she could not bear to see him in this state any longer.
>
> Discuss her possible liability. Would your answer be different if a serial killer, had crept into the ward and switched off all the life support machines?

Under the Queen's peace

Most victims would come under this umbrella, including prisoners of war. The phrase would not, however, cover enemy aliens who are killed in the process of warfare.

With malice aforethought

This is a very archaic expression and has been criticised as being misleading in its present context. The word 'malice' seems to suggest that some sort of ill will must exist but this is not necessary. The expression 'malice aforethought' merely means that the accused must have the intention to cause death or grievous bodily harm. The latter was defined in *DPP* v *Smith 1961* as meaning really serious harm but in cases since then as, for example, *Saunders 1985*, it has also been stated that the word 'really' need not be added. Currently, therefore, the phrase 'malice aforethought' merely means the intention to cause death or serious injury. Before 1982, there was some doubt as to whether the intention to cause grievous bodily harm was a great enough intention for murder or whether an intention to cause death had to be proved. In *Cunningham 1982*, the House of Lords made it clear that the intention to cause serious harm was enough.

The accused had attacked his victim in a pub, hitting him many times with a chair. The victim subsequently died of the injuries inflicted. The accused appealed, stating that the judge had misdirected the jury by saying that the defendant was guilty of murder if he intended to cause serious harm.

The Court of Appeal dismissed the appeal and a further appeal was made to the House of Lords. The defendant relied on certain statements made by two of the Law Lords in the case of *Hyam 1975*, stating that the intention to cause serious harm was not sufficient to constitute the *mens rea* of murder. In that case, two other Law Lords thought that sufficient *mens rea* did exist if this was established and the other was not prepared to give a conclusive opinion.

In *Cunningham 1982* the House of Lords was unanimous in its opinion that the intention to cause grievous bodily harm constitutes enough blameworthiness to amount to malice aforethought.

The word 'malice' needs to be examined further. If a person intends to kill another human being, he is said to have express malice. If, however, he merely intends to cause serious harm he has implied malice. Before the Homicide Act 1957, a third category of malice existed, which was known as 'constructive malice'. Under this head, a person could be found guilty of murder if he killed in the furtherance of a felony (i.e. in the furtherance of a serious crime, such as rape or burglary), provided that he had the intention to commit the lesser crime. A murder charge was also possible if the defendant killed while intending to

prevent a lawful arrest (either his own or that of another person), or to escape from lawful arrest or custody. The prosecution did not need to prove that he possessed the extra *mens rea* of intending to kill or cause grievous bodily harm.

S.1 Homicide Act 1957 abolished liability for murder in these situations although the defendant would almost certainly face other charges, such as involuntary manslaughter, as discussed in Chapter 5.

3.4 POSSIBLE REFORM

The Draft Criminal Code Bill, prepared by the Law Commission in 1989, suggests that the *mens rea* of murder should be reformed. It states in Clause 54 that the mental element should only be present in cases where a person kills intending to cause death or intending to cause serious harm and being aware that it may cause death.

If this were enacted, it would narrow the liability for murder as a person could only be convicted if he caused serious harm with the knowledge that death might result. Under current law, there is no requirement that the defendant must have a foresight of death occurring; it is enough that he intends to cause grievous bodily harm.

3.5 THE CHAIN OF CAUSATION

Before we leave the subject of murder, it is important to stress that the death must have been caused by the unlawful act of the defendant. It will be seen, however, that, in some cases, the defendant might not have been directly responsible for the final act which caused the death but will still be liable for the homicide because he set in motion the chain of events which led to it. This subject of causation is also applicable to other offences but will be examined in this chapter because many of the cases on causation have involved fatal offences

KEY FACTS

- Murder is the most serious form of unlawful homicide. Less serious forms of homicide are voluntary and involuntary manslaughter and infanticide, which are dealt with in subsequent chapters
- The current definition of murder is the unlawful killing of a human being with malice aforethought, i.e. with intent to cause death, (express malice) or grievous bodily harm, (implied malice) (*Cunningham 1982*)
- Constructive malice has been abolished by s.1 Homicide Act 1957
- Certain killings can be lawful as, for example those sanctioned by the state or by the judges, (*Airedale NHS Trust v Bland 1993*), or where a full defence is possible. In other killings the charge may be reduced to manslaughter, (see Chapter 4).
- A victim is considered to be a human being when he has an existence independent of his mother. It is not certain whether he must have drawn breath, although this would be the medical view
- It appears that there could be an injury to a human being, even if this injury occurred before birth, if the baby was born alive but subsequently died (*AG's Reference [No. 3 of 1994] 1996*). It is not conclusively decided that liability for murder would arise if the accused intended to harm the foetus. It is, however, clear that the offender could be charged with involuntary manslaughter, if there had been an unlawful act against the mother, a live birth and then the subsequent death of the baby
- A victim is probably considered to be dead when he is brain dead
- The 'year and a day rule' has been abolished, Law Reform (Year and a Day Rule) Act 1996

FIGURE 3.2 *Key facts chart on murder*

against the person, in the form of murder or manslaughter.

3.5.1 ESTABLISHING THE CHAIN OF CAUSATION

There are no rules laid down by statute concerning the problems of causation; instead, various principles have been established by case law, as problem areas have come before the courts.

In most cases, it is not difficult to discover whether the defendant's conduct caused the death in question although the jury, of course, has to be convinced of this beyond reasonable doubt. In some trials, however, the defendant will be arguing that someone else caused the death, or at least contributed to it, or that the death was the victim's own fault in some way and these matters need to be explored. When ascertaining whether the defendant is the

person on whom to fix liability, the courts will look at two issues:

1 Did the conduct of the accused cause the resulting harm and, if so
2 Was the defendant also liable in law?

It will be the jury's task to look at the facts of the case but when deciding on the second question, the jurors will have to apply the legal principles explained to them by the judge. Both these issues will be examined further in the following paragraphs.

3.5.2 THE FACTUAL CAUSE OF DEATH

It should first be noted that the defendant would only be criminally liable if his conduct made a significant contribution to the death.

This was not established in the case of *White 1910*.

The accused had intended to murder his mother; he had poison in a glass ready for her but she suddenly died, instead, of heart failure. The accused was liable for attempted murder but it is clear that he had not caused her death, however much he had desired it to happen. He could not, therefore, be found guilty of murder.

The 'but for' test

When deciding on the factual cause of death, the courts use the 'but for' test, i.e. but for the act of the defendant, the death would not have occurred. It can be seen in the above case that this test was not satisfied, as the mother would have died anyway; the defendant's act had made no difference to the outcome.

A more difficult case for the jury was the early case of *Dalloway 1847*. A driver of a cart was not using his reins as he proceeded along a road. A three-year-old child then ran into the path of the cart and was killed.

It could have been argued that, but for the driver travelling along this road, the child's death would not have happened. The courts required the passing of a more stringent test, i.e. had the prosecution established that, but for the driver's negligence in failing to use his reins, the death would not have happened. As the answer was 'no', the charge could not be sustained.

3.5.3 THE LEGAL CAUSE OF DEATH

As mentioned earlier, the judge's task is to explain the legal principles to the jurors and they must then decide, after applying these principles to the facts with which they are presented, whether the prosecution has established the guilt of the accused beyond reasonable doubt.

After satisfying the test for factual causation, therefore, it still needs to be shown whether the defendant's act was a more than minimal cause of the death and that no intervening act had broken the chain of causation.

1 **The defendant's act must be more than a minimal cause of the death**
This expression may cause surprise. Many would argue that the defendant should only be liable if he makes a major contribution to the victim's death and, indeed, in earlier cases it was stated that the act of the accused had to be substantial. Cases like *Benge*, discussed below, support this.

The current view, however, is that liability might arise where the defendant has made more than a minute or negligible contribution to the death.

This point was confirmed in *Cato 1976*, a view which was later supported in the case of *Malcherek*, discussed below. It has been suggested that the word 'significant' should replace the word 'substantial', although in *Kinsey 1971*, it was not considered to be a misdirection by the trial judge when he stated that the contribution must merely be something more than 'a slight or trifling link'.

An example of a minimal contribution would be where two mountaineers were roped together and one fell over a cliff. If the other were to cut the rope to save himself from a similar fate, he would certainly be accelerating the death of the other mountaineer but this would only be by a fractional period of time. It would not be substantial enough to make him criminally liable for the other's death.

Similarly, a doctor administering painkilling drugs at the end of a patient's life might well accelerate the patient's death to a small degree but would also be protected.

The contribution must therefore be significant enough to contribute to the victim's death. In addition, nothing later must have occurred to break the chain of causation. This leads us on to the next point.

2 **A *novus actus interveniens* must not have arisen**
This means that no intervening act must have arisen to break the chain of causation leading from the defendant's act to the actual death. The defendant would be able to

escape liability if he could prove that some other act had caused the death, not his own act of violence or his own omission. In the following wide range of situations, the defendants have tried to argue such a point, nearly always unsuccessfully.

1 Where the death is not directly caused by the accused

It might seem reasonable to a layman that if the actual death had been caused by some other event, such as an act of nature or by another person's act, the first person involved in the chain should escape liability. Very often, however, this is not the position. The courts have decided that the supervening act must be something unforeseeable in order to remove the liability of the first party. If the defendant knocked the victim unconscious and then left him on the seashore near to the water's edge so that he was later drowned by the incoming tide, such an event should have been anticipated by the assailant and his liability would remain.

A more controversial situation occurred in *Pagett 1983*, where the defendant's conviction for manslaughter was upheld, even though the shot that killed the victim was fired, not by him, but by the police seeking to detain him.

The accused was being pursued by the police and had forcibly taken his pregnant girlfriend from her home to a block of flats, after injuring her mother and stepfather. He later came out of one of the flats, using his girlfriend as a human shield. He then fired his shotgun at two officers.

The policemen fired back instinctively and the girl was killed in the crossfire.

The defendant was found guilty of her manslaughter but appealed against this, arguing that the judge had misdirected the jury by stating that he had been the cause of the victim's death, not the police officers had fired the bullets.

The Court of Appeal found that there was no misdirection. Goff L J compared the situation to one where the victim acts in self preservation but his attempt fails and, instead, causes or contributes to his death, as in the case of *Pitts*, discussed below. He went on to say:

> Now one form of self preservation is self defence; for present purposes, we can see no distinction in principle between an attempt to escape the consequences of the accused's act and a response which takes the form of self defence. Furthermore, in our judgment, if a reasonable act of self defence against the act of the accused causes the death of a third party, we can see no reason in principle why the act of self defence, being an involuntary act caused by the act of the accused, should relieve the accused from criminal responsibility for the death of the third party.'

The conviction was upheld.

2 Where the victim has tried to escape and has caused himself harm

In some cases a death has occurred because the victim has tried to escape from the violent actions of the accused. Once again, the defendant will find it difficult to escape liability if he put in motion the chain of events which led to the accused having to take evasive action through fear for his safety. *A novus actus interveniens* would only arise if the reaction of the victim was considered to be something totally unexpected, or, as stated in *Roberts 1971*, discussed below, something so 'daft', when compared to how a reasonable man in the same situation might have acted.

The victim's reaction was considered to have been reasonable in *Pitts 1842*, when he jumped into a river to escape further violent assaults. The defendant was held to be responsible for his death.

In *Mackie 1973*, a manslaughter conviction was upheld when a father frightened his three-year-old son so severely that the boy fell down the stairs and was killed.

In *Roberts 1971*, an assault case, described more fully in Chapter 6, the victim jumped from a moving car to escape the sexual advances of the defendant. The Court of Appeal decided that her reaction to the threat was a reasonable one and that the defendant was responsible for her injuries.

In *DPP* v *Daley 1980*, Lord Keith stated that, in cases such as these, the prosecution had to establish that the victim was in fear of being hurt physically and this fear had caused him to try to escape and thereby meet his death. The conduct of the accused had to be unlawful and of a type which any reasonable and sober person would recognise as likely to subject the victim to at least the risk of some harm resulting from it, albeit not serious harm.

In *Williams 1992*, the defendants were luckier than most who find themselves in this position and their conviction for manslaughter was quashed because not enough direction had been given to the jury.

The prosecution claimed that the deceased had jumped from a moving car because he was in fear of being robbed. To support this contention, it was alleged that his wallet had flown into the air as he had jumped. The victim had been travelling to a festival in Glastonbury and had 'hitched' a lift from the defendants. He had jumped out five miles further on and been killed. The occupants were originally held to be liable for his death but appealed.

The Court of Appeal stressed that the conduct of the victim had to be proportionate to the threat of harm and:

> within the ambit of reasonableness and not so daft as to make his own voluntary act one which amounted to a *novus actus interveniens* and consequently broke the chain of causation.

The conviction was quashed because the trial judge had not directed the jury in this fashion. The Court of Appeal did, however, go on to state that:

> It should of course be borne in mind that a victim may in the agony of the moment do the wrong thing ... and ... may act without thought or deliberation

3 Where others, apart from the accused, are involved in the death

In some situations there may be more than one party involved in the chain of events; others may well have contributed to the outcome. Nevertheless, the party starting the action will usually retain his liability, provided that, as mentioned before, his act was a significant factor in causing the death.

In Benge 1865, a foreman plate-layer had misread a timetable so that the track had not been relaid by the time a train arrived. The defendant had also failed to put any fog signals into place and had positioned a flagman only 540 yards away, instead of the required 1000 yards. The driver of the train failed to stop and an accident occurred causing many deaths. The foreman was charged with manslaughter.

His defence tried to argue that the accident would not have occurred without the contributory negligence of the other people who were also involved.

The judge ruled that, provided that the defendant's negligence had been the main or a substantial cause of the accident, it was no defence to state that the deaths might have been avoided if the others had played their part correctly.

In Towers 1874, a young girl screamed very loudly when she was assaulted by the accused. At the time of the attack, she was holding a young baby in her arms who was so frightened by the screams that she went black in the face, had convulsions from that moment on and died four weeks later. It was decided that the girl's attacker could be charged with the manslaughter of the baby.

In *Malcherek and Steel 1981*, the two appellants had stabbed and injured their victims so severely that they had to be put on life support machines. When these machines were switched off by doctors, the defendants tried to argue that this action constituted a *novus actus interveniens*.

Their appeals failed. The Lord Chief Justice stated that where the medical treatment is given by:

> competent and careful medical practitioners, then evidence will not be admissible to show that the treatment would not have been administered in the same way by other medical practitioners.

In these two cases, there was no doubt that the original injuries inflicted by the stab wounds were still operating and were still the substantial cause of the deaths. The convictions for murder were upheld. Cases like *Cheshire* and *McKechnie,* mentioned below, are more controversial.

4 Where the victim has a pre-existing medical condition

In both criminal law and in the law of tort, there is a rule that the perpetrator of an act must 'take his victim as he finds him'. This is also known as the 'eggshell skull' rule. The courts will not allow the defendant to escape liability just because the victim is more susceptible to harm than the normal person or is unusually sensitive in some other way.

If, therefore, the victim already has a pre-existing medical condition that makes the likelihood of harm more acute, the accused cannot use this in his defence, provided that he set in motion the chain of events leading to the harm and his actions were still an operating cause of it. The following case illustrates this.

In *Hayward 1908*, the defendant had indicated that he was going to harm his wife. An argument developed and the woman ran into the road, followed by her husband who was still making threats against her. The woman then collapsed and died. She had a condition affecting her thyrus gland that

would not normally have caused problems but the unusual physical exertion and the fright caused by her husband's treatment had caused her to collapse.

The husband was held to be liable for her death because her demise had been accelerated by his actions.

5 Where the victim aggravates his condition in some way or refuses medical treatment which would help him survive

This overlaps in some measure with the above rule that the defendant must take his victim as he finds him. The defendant will not escape liability just because the victim takes an ill-advised course of action to relieve his pain or refuses to undergo the treatment suggested for his injuries, either through fear or because of religious objections.

In *Wall's Case 1802*, the Governor of Goree had inflicted an illegal flogging of 800 lashes on the deceased and was charged with his murder. He tried to argue that the victim had aggravated his condition by consuming strong alcohol to deaden the pain of the punishment. The judge refused to entertain such a notion. He stated:

> . . . there is no apology for a man if he puts another in so dangerous and hazardous a situation by his treatment of him, that some degree of unskillfulless and mistaken treatment of himself may possibly accelerate the final catastrophe.

Another early case, this time illustrating the victim's reluctance to undergo further treatment, is that of *Holland 1841*. The victim's hand had been severely cut by Holland, who had attacked him with an iron bar. Blood poisoning had then set in. The victim was advised to have his finger amputated but he refused to entertain the idea; lockjaw then set in and he died. Despite an assertion by a surgeon that the amputation would probably have saved the victim's life, the defendant was found guilty of his murder.

A more recent case illustrating the same point is *Blaue 1975*. The victim had been stabbed by the defendant, but, because of her religious beliefs as a Jehovah's Witness, she refused to have a blood transfusion which would probably have saved her life. The Court of Appeal upheld Blaue's conviction for manslaughter on the grounds of diminished responsibility, even though the Crown had conceded that the girl may well have survived if the transfusion had been permitted.

Lawton L J stated that the death was due to the bleeding into the pleural cavity caused by the penetration of the lung. This, he stated, had not been brought about by any decision made by the deceased girl but by the stab wound.

He also rejected the argument that the refusal to have a blood transfusion was unreasonable, saying 'reasonable by whose standards? Those of Jehovah's Witnesses? Humanists? Roman Catholics? Protestants of Anglo-Saxon descent? The man on the Clapham omnibus? . . .' He concluded by saying:

> It has long been the policy of the law that those who use violence on other people must take their victims as they find them. This in our judgment means the whole man, not just the physical man. It does not lie in the mouth of the assailant to say that his victim's religious beliefs which inhibited him from accepting certain kinds of treatment were unreasonable. The question for decision is what caused her death. The answer is the stab wound. The fact that the victim refused to stop this end coming about did not break the causal connection between the act and the death.

The defendant was no luckier in *McKechnie 1992*. The victim had suffered serious brain damage after an attack by the accused and, while in hospital, it was discovered that he also had a duodenal ulcer, unrelated to his injuries. The hospital decided that it would be dangerous to operate on this because of his other injuries. A few weeks later, the ulcer burst and the victim died. The trial judge had told the jurors that, to find the defendant guilty, they must be convinced that the decision not to operate was reasonable. They also had to believe that the original injuries had made a significant contribution to the death. They found the defendant guilty and the Court of Appeal upheld the conviction.

6 Where the medical treatment given is inadequate

In the cases just discussed, medical treatment was actually refused by the victim or considered to be unwise by the doctors. In the following cases, treatment was given but was either wrong or, at best, given in a very negligent way. The courts had to decide whether this was enough to break the chain of causation. In line with the situations already examined, it will be noted that the courts are very reluctant to allow this to happen and, in most cases, the liability of the person starting the injuries which lead to the death will remain.

The law on this subject is complicated by the case of *Jordan 1956*, which took a contrary approach, but, although this decision has not been overruled, it appears that it will not be followed in the future, unless the new circumstances are very similar to those in that case.

The victim had been stabbed. He was admitted to hospital but died eight days later. The defendant was convicted of murder. Later, evidence came to light that the medical treatment had been 'palpably wrong' and the defendant successfully appealed against his conviction.

The new evidence showed that the victim had been given terramycin, to which he had proved allergic. It had then been withdrawn but inadvertently reintroduced later by another doctor. Large quantities of liquid had also been given intravenously and broncho-pneumonia had set in. On the other hand, at the time of his death, the stab wounds had nearly healed.

The conviction, therefore, was quashed, Hallett J stated:

> Not only one feature but two separate and independent features of treatment were, in the opinion of the doctors, palpably wrong and these produced the symptoms discovered at the post-mortem examination which were the direct and immediate cause of death . . .

The court did, however, take pains to point out that in cases where normal treatment was given, the original injury would be considered to have caused the death.

The decision in *Jordan* caused concern among members of the medical profession who felt that wrongdoers might escape liability if it could be shown that any treatment given to try to save the victim was abnormal in some way.

The doctors need not have worried. The case of Jordan was later distinguished in *Smith 1959*, although, in this case too, the treatment given left a lot to be desired.

The victim had been stabbed twice in a barrack room fight between soldiers of different regiments. While being carried to the medical reception centre, the injured man was dropped twice. When he reached his destination, the doctor on duty failed to realise the seriousness of his injuries and administered treatment which was said at the trial to be 'thoroughly bad and might well have affected his chances of recovery'. An hour later, the victim died.

The defendant was still found guilty of murder and this was upheld by the Courts-Martial Appeal Court. It was stated that provided that the original wound was still an operating and substantial cause at the time of the death, the defendant would still be liable for the death even though some other cause

of death was also operating. Lord Parker went on to say:

> Only if it can be said that the original wound is merely the setting in which another cause operates can it be said that the death did not result from the wound.

In the case of *Malcherek,* mentioned above, the judges of the Court of Appeal believed that the decision in *Smith* was preferable to that in *Jordan*, but decided that there was no need to make such a choice because of the different facts which indicated that *Jordan* had not been wrongly decided.

The matter was raised again in the case of *Cheshire 1991*, where the statements made in *Smith 1959*, appear to have been taken a step further.

The victim had been shot in the stomach and the leg by the accused, during an argument in a fish and chip shop. He was operated upon but later developed breathing difficulties and had to have a tracheotomy tube inserted. He died two months later. It was discovered that his windpipe had narrowed and this had caused the severe breathing difficulties that he was experiencing at the time of his death. It was argued that this was due to the negligence of the hospital when the tracheotomy tube was fitted and that this, therefore, had broken the chain of causation. The trial judge directed the jury that a *novus actus interveniens* would only have occurred if the doctors had acted recklessly and the defendant was found guilty. He appealed against his conviction.

The Court of Appeal criticised the trial judge's reference to recklessness but still upheld the conviction. The court came to this conclusion despite the fact that the immediate cause of the victim's death was due to the possible negligence of the doctors, not from the gunshot wounds inflicted by Cheshire. The court stated that this would not excuse the defendant from liability unless the negligent treatment:

> . . . was so independent of his acts, and in itself so potent in causing death, that they regard the contribution made by his acts as insignificant.

COMMENT

It has been shown from the many cases on this subject, that an offender is going to find it very difficult to prove that the chain of causation has been broken, even in cases where the intervening act appears to be substantial and the negligence of a third party is of a high degree. Some would argue that this view is to be commended because the victim would not have met his death or other fate if the accused had not put in motion the chain of events leading to the death. Others would argue that, in some instances, particularly those involving gross negligence by medical staff, where it is clearly shown that the original wounds are healing well, it is unjust to hold the original attacker liable for the full extent of the injuries.

KEY FACTS

- There is no legislation on this subject, only case law
- When deciding on the factual cause of death, the courts use the 'but for' test, i.e. but for the defendant's act, the death would not have happened (*Dalloway 1847, White 1910*)
- When deciding upon the legal cause of death two further issues are examined, i.e. did the act of the defendant play a significant part in causing the death of the victim? (the term significant means more than a minimal role), and has any other event occurred to break the chain of causation?
- It has been decided that an event breaking the chain of causation must be something completely unforeseeable
- It is not considered unforeseeable that the police might return the fire of a gunman (*Pagett 1983*), or that the victim might try to escape, (*Pitts 1842, Roberts 1971, Mackie 1973, DPP v Daley 1980*, and *Williams 1992*)
- It is also not unforeseeable that others might be involved in the death (*Benge 1849, Towers 1874*), that the victims might already have a pre-existing medical condition (*Hayward 1908*), might refuse treatment (*Holland 1841* and *Blaue 1975*) or that they themselves might aggravate their injuries (*Wall's Case 1802*)
- It is also not unforeseeable that doctors might have to switch off life support machines (*Malcherek and Steel 1981*), or refuse to operate because of the dangers involved (*McKechnie 1992*)
- Lastly, it is not unforeseeable that, on some occasions, the medical treatment might be negligently given or even be thoroughly bad (*Smith 1959, Cheshire 1991*)
- It will only be an accepted as a *novus actus interveniens* if the new act is completely independent and in itself 'so potent in causing death' that the original defendant's acts are insignificant (*Cheshire 1991*). The case of *Jordan 1956* provided an example of this but such cases are rare

FIGURE 3.3 *Key facts chart on causation*

activity

1 In group discussion or in essay form, decide whether the rules of causation are now weighted too far against the interests of the defendant

2 Mike made an unprovoked attack on Henry during the half-time break at a football match and seriously injured him. Henry's friends took him to the first aid centre in the ground to receive attention but, because of the crush, they twice dropped him on the way. The centre was crowded with other people needing attention and Henry was not treated until two hours' later because the paramedic had not believed that his condition was life-threatening. In fact, Henry was a haemophiliac and was bleeding to death and, when this was discovered, it was too late to save him.

Advise Mike, who has been charged with Henry's murder.

summary

By the end of Chapter 3, it should be possible to distinguish between the main fatal offences against the person, namely murder, voluntary manslaughter and involuntary manslaughter.

We should know the definition of murder in detail, plus the rules relating to causation.

We should also have discovered that the accused will be criminally liable if his unlawful act is considered to be more than a minimal cause of the death and the 'but for' test is satisfied.

Once these two matters have been established, it will be very difficult for the defendant to argue that the chain of causation has been broken, even in cases where another party is also blameworthy.

CHAPTER 4

UNLAWFUL KILLING II: VOLUNTARY MANSLAUGHTER

4.1 INTRODUCTION

THERE HAVE ALWAYS been problems associated with this area of law. Lord Atkin made the following comment in the case of *Andrews v DPP 1937*:

> ... of all crimes manslaughter appears to afford most difficulties of definition, for it concerns homicide in so many and so varying conditions.

It will be seen that this statement still reflects the position today as the offence can cover many different situations and widely differing degrees of blame. It includes situations where it is obvious that the defendant intended to cause the death of the victim. It also encompasses other situations where it is clear that nothing could have been further from his mind, but due to a momentary lapse, albeit a very serious one, the accused has brought about the death of another person.

In this chapter, we are concerned with intentional killings but ones where the law has decreed that the person will escape liability for murder because certain conditions exist. These crimes come under the heading of voluntary manslaughter. Non-intentional killings, but ones in which the defendant is still considered to be blameworthy, will be dealt with in Chapter 5.

4.2. THE CRIME OF VOLUNTARY MANSLAUGHTER

This crime is similar to murder in that an unlawful homicide has taken place, with the requisite malice aforethought on the defendant's part, but here special circumstances exist which permit the less serious verdict of manslaughter to be brought in, with more discretion allowed to the judge on sentencing. The maximum sentence he can bestow is life imprisonment, the minimum is an absolute discharge.

The law on voluntary manslaughter is a mixture of common law rules and statutory additions. At common law only one type of voluntary manslaughter existed, that of provocation, but two further defences were added by the Homicide Act 1957. Voluntary manslaughter can now also be pleaded where the defendant is suffering from diminished responsibility or is the survivor of a suicide pact. If one of these three defences is successfully established, the crime will be reduced from murder to voluntary manslaughter. For the defence of provocation to succeed, the defendant must have killed another while suffering from a sudden and temporary loss of self control caused by someone's provoking acts or words. If the defendant wishes to use the defence of diminished responsibility, he has to show that he was suffering from such an abnormality of mind that it has affected his mental responsibility for his actions. The third defence under the Act can be used where two or more people decide to commit suicide and one of them survives and is prosecuted. These three defences are illustrated in the following diagram:

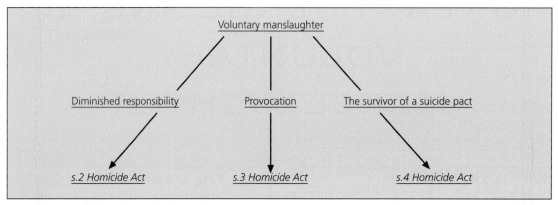

FIGURE 4.1 *The three defences reducing murder to voluntary manslaughter*

It is very important to realise that the defences are only applicable to the crime of murder, and to appreciate that they only reduce the offence from murder to manslaughter. Sections 2, 3, and 4 Homicide Act 1957 cannot be used as defences for lesser crimes.

These special defences now need to be examined in turn, to ascertain precisely what has to be established for the defence to succeed.

4.3 DIMINISHED RESPONSIBILITY

S.2 Homicide Act 1957 states that a person may be found guilty of the lesser offence of voluntary manslaughter, rather than murder, if he was suffering from an abnormality of mind, caused by an inside source, that substantially affected his responsibility for his actions.

The precise wording is to be found in s.2(1). This states:

> Where a person kills or is a party to the killing of another, he shall not be convicted of murder if he was suffering from such abnormality of mind (whether arising from a condition of arrested or retarded development of mind or any inherent causes or induced by disease or injury) as substantially impaired his mental responsibility for his acts and omissions in doing or being a party to the killing.

s.2(2) puts the burden of proof on the defendant; he will have to prove his abnormality of mind on a balance of probabilities and generally he must be the one to raise the defence. If, however, the accused is charged with murder and he pleads not guilty by reason of insanity, the prosecutor might, instead, show evidence of diminished responsibility. If the defendant relies on another defence, such as provocation, and during the trial evidence of diminished responsibility comes to light, the judge is only under an obligation to draw the attention of the jury to the possibility of this other defence. If the defendant pleads not guilty, but his version of events is not believed by the jury and he is convicted, it will only be in rare cases that he will be allowed to introduce the defence of diminished responsibility on appeal. An example where this was successful was *Borthwick 1998*.

The body of a man who had been strangled was discovered in Borthwick's flat, with the latter's dressing gown cord around his throat. There was some evidence to suggest that the death may have been as a result of a homosexual sex act that had gone tragically wrong, although other points indicated an unlawful homicide. There was also evidence that Borthwick had underlying personality problems, but he refused analysis of this or of his history and relationships and made the decision to plead not guilty. He maintained that someone else had been in the flat and had slept with the accused. The jury did not believe his story and convicted him of murder. He later admitted the killing to a psychiatrist, alleging that the death was accidental and had been caused by a bungled bondage session. This same doctor found that he was suffering from a form of mental illness, which could amount to paranoid schizophrenia and affect the sufferer's understanding, judgement and perception. He declined to say whether the abnormalities would have affected the defendant's mental responsibility for his acts as he felt that this was a matter for a jury to decide.

The Crown argued that it was the defendant's own fault that such evidence was not available at the trial. The Court of Appeal rejected this line of reasoning. The court decided that, if there was overwhelming evidence that a plea of diminished responsibility would have succeeded and it was the mental illness itself that caused the defence not to be put forward, then either a retrial or a substitution of a manslaughter verdict should be considered.

It will be seen that the defence of diminished responsibility is wider, in the range of abnormal states of mind it covers, than is allowed under the general defence of insanity under the M'Naghten rules, which are examined in Chapter 10. As mentioned earlier, however, it is vital to remember that the defence under s.2 is limited in that it is only available as a defence to a charge of murder.

It can be seen from a study of s.2, that three elements have to be proved before diminished responsibility can be established:

1 There has to be an abnormality of mind.
2 This abnormality must arise from an inside source, such as mental illness or handicap or other diseases of the mind.
3 The abnormality of mind must have substantially affected the defendant's mental responsibility for his actions.

These three points need looking at in more detail.

4.3.1 AN ABNORMALITY OF MIND

This is a state of mind a reasonable man would find abnormal. It is the task of the jury to decide this, not the medical experts, although the jury will obviously take notice of medical opinion. The jurors will also be strongly influenced by the summing up of the judge. It is therefore vital that this gives the correct statement of the law. This was not held to be the case in *Byrne 1960* and the defendant was successful in his appeal against a murder conviction.

Byrne had strangled a young girl living in a YWCA hostel and then carried out horrific mutilations on her body. He claimed that he was suffering from diminished responsibility and that he had killed the girl while in the grip of an irresistible impulse caused by his perverted sexual desires. Three medical experts had testified that he was, indeed, a sexual psychopath. The judge had told the jury that s.2 was not there to give protection 'where there is nothing else than what is vicious and depraved' and had earlier given the impression that a difficulty or even inability of the defendant to control his acts would not amount to an abnormality of mind. The jury then convicted him of murder.

The Court of Appeal quashed the murder conviction, believing that, if properly directed, the jury would certainly have found that the defence of diminished responsibility had been made out. Lord Parker stated that the term 'abnormality of mind' included a lack of ability to form a rational judgement or exercise the necessary willpower to control one's acts. He said that the term was:

> wide enough to cover the mind's activities in all its aspects, not only the perception of physical acts and matters and the ability to form a rational judgement whether an act is right or wrong, but also the ability to exercise willpower to control physical acts in accordance with that rational judgement.

The appeal against the murder conviction was allowed and a verdict of manslaughter substituted. The sentence of life imprisonment was not, however, disturbed.

COMMENT

One of the problems with this defence is the fact that the defendant is often sent to prison, rather than to a mental institution and, while there, there is no duty imposed on the State to ensure that he has treatment for his abnormality. He could then, at a later time, be released, uncured, back into the community. (I wrote these words before the Michael Stone case. Hopefully, the publicity from that trial will result in more action being taken to treat such offenders).

It has been noted that the defence of s.2 covers 'the mind's activities in all its aspects'. In *Hobson 1997*, the Court of Appeal held that the cumulative effects of 'battered woman's syndrome' could lead to an abnormality of mind, thus affording a defence to a charge of murder if the abused woman turned on her tormentor and killed him.

Evidence of diminished responsibility in respect of such physical abuse was accepted in the retrials of two battered wives, *Ahluwalia* and *Thornton*. These cases will be discussed more fully under provocation.

4.3.2 CAUSED BY AN INSIDE SOURCE

The second element of the defence of diminished responsibility states that the abnormality must be caused by 'arrested or retarded development of mind or any inherent causes or induced by disease or injury'. This means that the abnormality must have been caused by an inside source, i.e. some malfunctioning of the mind. Evidence, therefore, of mere intoxication, caused by drinking or drug taking (i.e. outside sources), cannot be put forward for this defence, unless the drinking or drug taking has actually damaged the mind itself, or where there was such a craving for drink or drugs that it could not be controlled.

In *Tandy 1989* the female defendant was an alcoholic who, on the day in question, had drunk almost a whole bottle of vodka. Her normal drink was said to be Cinzano, which is less potent. She had then strangled her 11-year-old daughter after the latter claimed that she had been sexually interfered with by the defendant's husband and wanted to go to live with her grandmother. The accused made the significant admission that her drinking was not totally involuntary and that she did initially have some control over her choice of drink and the time she started drinking. The judge, therefore, withdrew the defence of diminished responsibility from the jury and she was convicted of murder. The Court of Appeal upheld the conviction stating that, for the defence to succeed, it was necessary for the abnormality of mind to be induced by the alcoholism. This would only have arisen if the defendant's mind had been damaged or there was evidence that she had no control over her drinking at the outset.

Similarly, in *Egan 1992*, the defendant was not allowed the defence of diminished responsiblity when he killed a woman of 79 after drinking an abnormally large quantity of alcohol, (15 pints of beer and several gins and tonics). He was not an alcoholic but there was evidence that he suffered from retarded development and, possibly, a psychopathic disorder. The jury was told to disregard his drinking and to decide whether he would have killed without this. The jury obviously believed that his mental abnormality was not great enough on its own to substantially affect his mental responsibility and convicted him of murder. The Court of Appeal upheld the decision.

While intoxication temporarily affecting the mind will not amount to an abnormality in this context, the defendant does not have to be insane to use the defence. Lord Parker's comment that he thought that the phrase 'diminished responsibility' meant something bordering on insanity was later criticised by the Court of Appeal in *Seers 1984*. The defence has been allowed for someone who killed while in a fit of jealousy (*Miller 1972*) and for women suffering from post-menstrual tension, (*Smith 1982* and *Reynolds 1988*). Chronic depression may also suffice, as was the case in *Seers* and *Gittens 1984*.

In the latter case, the defendant, after a violent quarrel, killed his wife by clubbing her to death and then raped and killed his step-daughter. He claimed that he was suffering from chronic depression although he had also acted under the effects of drink and drugs. The Court of Appeal allowed his appeal against a conviction for murder on the grounds of a misdirection by the trial judge, although as in *Byrne*, mentioned above, the sentence of life imprisonment remained.

4.3.3 WHICH SUBSTANTIALLY AFFECTED HIS MENTAL RESPONSIBILITY

The difficulty which the defendant faces here, is that his abnormality of mind must have been substantially greater than would have been experienced by an ordinary person. The impairment need not be total but must be more than trivial, as stated in *Simcox 1964*. There should be medical evidence to support this contention. Generally, the jury will accept such evidence, but it need not if there is other evidence available to suggest a more calculated killing.

In *Sanders 1991*, the defendant's conviction for the murder of his long-standing mistress was upheld by the Court of Appeal, despite the fact that two psychiatrists had testified that the accused was suffering from reactive depression amounting to an abnormality of mind. The jury had convicted him despite such evidence, because it was shown that he had also written letters to others stating that he was going to commit suicide but had not written to his mistress, nor included her in his will.

In *Campbell 1997*, the defendant did succeed in pleading diminished responsibility at his second appeal. He had picked up a female hitchhiker and had attacked her when she refused his advances. When he discovered that she was not dead, he tried to strangle her and eventually hit her across the throat with his hockey stick. He maintained that he was suffering from diminished responsibility caused by his epilepsy and frontal lobe damage and at his second appeal the court heard the evidence of two eminent psychiatrists in this field. Lord Bingham C J stated:

> Having studied the available evidence of what the appellant did and said at the time, both doctors were of the clear opinion that at the time of the killing the appellant had been suffering an abnormality of mind of such significance as seriously to diminish his responsibility for the act he carried out.

A retrial was therefore ordered, although it was made clear that this could not lead to an acquittal, only a possible reduction of the murder conviction to manslaughter.

- The defence is to be found in s.2 Homicide Act 1957
- It is only a partial defence, reducing the conviction from murder to manslaughter
- In cases of homicide, it has largely replaced the general defence of insanity, which will be discussed in Chapter 10
- Three elements have to be proved before the defence will succeed, an abnormality of mind, caused by an inside source, which substantially impairs the defendant's mental responsibility for his actions
- The term 'abnormality of mind' encompasses a greater variety of situations than the general defence of insanity. It covers a person's inability to distinguish right from wrong but also includes the 'irresistible impulse' situation, where the defendant is unable to exercise the necessary will power to control his physical acts, as in *Byrne 1960*
- The abnormality must derive from the mind itself, although the accused need not be insane, (*Seers 1984*). Those suffering from alcoholism which is shown to have affected the mind, battered womans's syndrome (*Aluwahlia 1992, Thornton (No.2) 1995, Hobson 1997*) depression, (*Seers, Gittens*, both *1984*), epilepsy, (*Campbell 1997*), fits of jealousy, (*Miller 1972*, and post menstrual tension, (*Smith 1982, Reynolds 1988*), have all been able to use the defence. Those suffering from temporary intoxication cannot, (*Tandy 1988, Egan 1992*).
- The abnormality must be great enough to substantially reduce the defendant's mental responsibility for his acts and the jury will be the body to decide this after listening to the evidence of doctors, (*Sanders 1991* and *Campbell 1997*).

FIGURE 4.2 *Key facts chart on diminished responsibility*

There are many criticisms of this defence. The following are examples:

It has been suggested that it is too readily available for defendants who kill but then produce medical evidence of long-term depression caused by emotional problems, such as a partner being unfaithful. In such cases, the sentence is often quite low, in comparison with the severity of the crime, as the following newspaper cutting illustrates.

Conversely, it appears that the defence may, at times, be refused on the grounds of public policy. There was obviously some sort of abnormality in the mind of Peter Sutcliffe, the notorious 'Yorkshire Ripper' and counsel for both sides wished to introduce the defence. The judge refused and Sutcliffe was found guilty of murder, a result that was welcomed by the public and relations of the victims. He has, however, spent most of his sentence in solitary confinement in a mental institution.

Women's groups and sections of the media have argued that the defence of diminished responsibility is less readily available for women. There have, however, been advances in this, as can be seen by the courts' recognition that pre-menstrual tension might result in an abnormality of mind. They have also accepted that mental and physical abuse over a long period, a condition which has become known as 'battered woman syndrome' might reduce a woman's mental responsibility and cause her to turn on the abuser and kill him.

Fury over Army killer's release

A FORMER Ulster Defence Regiment Greenfinch who stabbed her lover's wife to death after luring her to a forest was freed yesterday after four years in jail.

The release of Susan Christie, 27, brought immediate criticism from the parents of her victim, Penny McAllister, who was almost decapitated in the attack in 1991.

Mrs McAllister's father, Desmond Squire, 54, a retired primary school principal, said: "I hope what she did haunts her to the grave and beyond."

Christie, 27, whose story was told in a television drama, *Beyond Reason*, was jailed for five years at Downpatrick Crown Court in June 1992 for the manslaughter of Mrs McAllister, 24, wife of her lover, Capt Duncan McAllister, 30.

The court heard that Christie killed her victim with a butcher's boning knife. The jury accepted a plea of manslaughter through diminished responsibility.

The Court of Appeal ruled that the five-year term was "unduly lenient" and increased the sentence to nine years. With good behaviour, she was entitled to 50 per cent remission under prison rules in Northern Ireland. This took account of more than a year spent on remand in custody before her trial. Christie left Magheraberry Prison , Co Antrim, early yesterday.

Mrs McAllister's parents had been on their way from their home in Arundel, West Sussex, to Northern Ireland to join their daughter for a holiday when she was killed at Drumkeeragh Forest Park, near Ballynahinch, Co Down. Mr Squire and his wife, Norma, arrived at Belfast airport to be told that their daughter was dead.

Mr Squire said yesterday of Christie: "She seems to be realising that during her meagre time in prison, she was cosseted by an environment rather than punished by it.

"Now she has to face the real world of ordinary folk who might consider that acquiring a new knife, sharpening it, luring an innocent person into a forest and cutting their throat is a hideous deed.

"I think she will see mistrust, doubt and fear in the eyes of people she meets, even those people closest to her.

"Even if she never sees a friendly face again, she will have inside her head the knowledge of how she planned and carried out her crime. She is going to have to live with herself and the reality of her memories.

"I hope they haunt her to the grave and beyond it. If they don't, then she should have been locked away for always in order to protect society because there is no doubt she must be mad."

Psychiatrists told Christie's trial that, at the time of the killing, she was suffering from "a major depressive episode" and "acute stress reaction", a mental illness that diminished her responsibility for her actions.

They said this was caused by the affair she was having with Capt McAllister, whom she met when she joined a military diving club that he organised. Capt McAllister was on a tour of duty in Ulster with the Royal Corp of Signals.

After the captain made it clear some months into the affair that he would never leave his wife, Christie, who admitted she was infatuated with her lover, attacked Mrs McAllister while the two women were walking their dogs in a remote part of the forest and cut her throat.

For the previous nine months, Christie had been involved in the secret affair. During her trial, she admitted killing her rival "to get Duncan for myself". Capt McAllister had already received Army papers posting him to Germany.

Hours before her release, Christie spoke of her "deep remorse" for the killing and said she had considered writing to her victim's parents. She said she would carry the burden of her guilt for the rest of her life.

In an interview with PA News, Christie said: "I've wanted to write to them and apologise. But what could I ever say to them? I'm sorry I killed your daughter."

Christie, from Lisburn, Co Antrim, said she had not seen or been in contact with Capt McAllister, who has left the Army.

"I am not going to try and defend myself now," she said. "I accept my responsibilities for the part I played. I don't wish to try and justify what I did. All I can say is that at my trial it was accepted by the court that I was not in my right mind when I killed Penny.

"I don't really have any feelings for Duncan any more. I neither love him or hate him."

She said her future was uncertain. "I was hoping to work for a Third World charity, but I really can't see that happening. It would cause too many problems. Whatever charity or organisation I work for would come under the spotlight for all the wrong reasons.

"I haven't decided where I'll go from here. My only aim is to get outside and pick up the pieces. If I move away from Northern Ireland I will lose the support of my family and friends. I don't think I could exist without their support."

4.3.4 POSSIBLE REFORM OF DIMINISHED RESPONSIBILITY

The Draft Criminal Code wishes to alter the wording of this defence to 'such mental abnormality as would be substantial enough to reduce the charge of murder to manslaughter'. To date, there are no immediate plans to put this change into effect.

activity

Read the following article and imagine that you are conducting Burton's defence. Describe what has to be established before the defence of diminished responsibility will succeed.

Random killer picked on judge's daughter

A LONER murdered a judge's daughter, slashing her throat because she refused to give him money, Liverpool Crown Court was told yesterday. Hours later Nicholas Burton, 27, ambushed a 17-year-old student at knifepoint, threatened to kill her and forced her to drive 100 miles before she managed to escape.

Mr Burton, from New Mills, Derbyshire, who said that he heard voices in his head, had selected his first victim, Rachel McGrath, 27, at random as she waited at closing time on a Friday night last April to pick up her boyfriend outside the Victoria Tavern, in Bramhall, Greater Manchester.

He inflicted "appalling injuries" on Miss McGrath, a building society assistant manager, and left her dying on the pavement to be discovered by her boyfriend.

Anthony Gee, QC, for the prosecution, said that Mr Burton maintained that he was not guilty of any offence because he was insane. His defence counsel will seek to prove that at the time he killed Miss McGrath he was suffering from diminished responsibility, attracting the lesser charge of manslaughter.

However, Mr Gee said Mr Burton had confessed to a fellow inmate at Strangeways prison that he murdered Miss McGrath because she would not give him money and that he planned the attack.

Taken from an article by Russell Jenkins in *The Times*, 25 March 1998

4.4 PROVOCATION

It has been suggested that as many as 45 per cent of all killings are committed by people who have lost their temper. The defence of provocation may exist if this loss of control is caused by the provocative act of the other party.

The defence has existed for many years, at least for men. It was recognised by the common law where the defendant had been provoked after being subjected to a violent physical attack. Provocation was also allowed for a man who discovered his wife committing adultery, as in *Maddy 1671*, and killed her or the lover or both. Blackstone's early Commentaries (iv 192) stated that such a crime was of 'the lowest degree of manslaughter', a view to which not all would subscribe! The defence was at first limited to husbands but, as the cases of *Larkin 1943* and *Gauthier* of the same year illustrate, it was extended to men killing their mistresses in similar circumstances. In *Fisher 1837*, a father who killed a man he discovered in the act of sodomy with his son was also entitled to the defence. It can be seen from these circumstances that, at common law, there had to be a provocative act of some sort; mere words were not enough. In *Lesbini 1914*, the defence was not available for a man who shot and killed a girl in charge of a firing range in an amusement arcade, after she had made derogatory remarks about him. This approach was affirmed by the House of Lords in the case of *Holmes v DPP 1946*. Their Lordships decided that the defence could not be used by a husband who had killed his wife after hearing her verbal confession of adultery.

The restrictive nature of this defence was lifted in 1957. Under s.3 Homicide Act 1957 it states:

> Where, on a charge of murder, there is evidence on which the jury can find that the person charged was provoked (whether by things done or by things said or by both together) to lose his self control, the question whether the provocation was enough to make a reasonable man do as he did shall be left to be determined by the jury.

This section of the Homicide Act clearly recognises and builds upon the common law defence of provocation. There has to be evidence of provocation but it now clearly states that this can arise from 'things said' in addition to 'things done'. It also reaffirms the position that it is the jury who will decide the issue, by measuring the conduct of the accused by the standard of the reasonable man, a concept first introduced in this context at common law in the case of *Welsh 1869*.

Under the Homicide Act 1957, therefore, the revised defence of provocation has three elements to it which have to be satisfied:

1 There has to be evidence that the defendant was provoked.
2 The accused must then have lost his self control.
3 The jury must be satisfied that a reasonable man might have acted in a similar way.

These three elements need to be looked at in turn.

4.4.1 THERE HAS TO BE EVIDENCE OF PROVOCATION

Initially, it is the judge who will decide whether there is enough evidence of provocation to be put before the jury. As mentioned earlier, the provocation can, under s.3 Homicide Act, arise from either things done or things said. In addition, the words or actions do not need to have come from the deceased, as was the case at common law, nor need they be directed at the defendant. In *Davies 1975*, the action of the wife's lover, of walking towards her place of work to meet her, was taken into account when the husband lost control and killed his wife. In *Doughty 1986*, the Court of Appeal held that even the continuous crying of a very young baby should have been considered by the jury as a possible provoking event, even though it was obviously not directed at the accused. Similarly, in *Pearson 1992*, the ill-treatment meted out over a period of eight years by the victim had not been principally directed at the defendant but towards his brother. The Court of Appeal decided that this was still an act of provocation, which the accused could use in his defence when he killed his father by attacking him with a sledgehammer.

Self-induced provocation

To stop the possibility of a later appeal, therefore, the accused should usually be given the benefit of the doubt. This even includes cases where the accused himself has started the trouble, which in law is known as 'self-induced provocation'. A case illustrating this is *Johnson 1989*. The accused had started an argument in a night club, during which he made threats against the victim and his woman friend. A fight developed in the course of which the victim was fatally stabbed. The accused alleged that he had been provoked by the fear of being 'glassed' by the victim but the judge declined to put this matter before the jury.

The Court of Appeal allowed the defendant's appeal, despite the fact that he had been the one who had started the trouble and even though he had been armed with a knife and the other only had a broken glass. Watkins L J, for the Court of Appeal stated:

> In view of the express wording of s.3 ... we find it impossible to accept that the mere fact that a defendant caused a

reaction in others, which in turn led him to lose his self-control, should result in the issue of provocation being kept outside a jury's consideration.

In *Baille 1995*, a similar appeal was successful. The defendant had arrived at the house of a drug dealer armed with a sawn-off shotgun and a cut-throat razor, after serious threats had been made by the dealer to the defendant's three sons, who were addicts who had been among his customers.

The father, who was strongly opposed to the taking of drugs, violently attacked the drug dealer with the razor and seriously injured him. When the victim tried to escape, the defendant fired the shotgun after him. The drug dealer was killed by particles of pellets blasted towards him from a wire mesh fence by the force of the shots.

The defendant tried to plead provocation, arguing that he had suffered from a temporary loss of control after his son told him about the threats and that this had lasted up to the time of the shooting. In the alternative, he also tried to claim that he had lost his self control when the victim tried to wrestle the gun from him, i.e. that this was self-induced provocation. The judge allowed the latter defence to be put before the jury but not the first issue, deciding that the loss of self control must have ceased by the time the killing took place.

The appeal court followed an earlier decision in *Cambridge 1994* and held that the failure to put the issue of possible provocation to the jury was a material misdirection. The murder conviction was therefore quashed and one of manslaughter substituted.

Other provoking events

Similarly, in *Dhillon 1997,* the Court of Appeal held that it was essential, where there was any evidence of possible provocation, that the matter should be put to the jury for this body to decide the issue.

In this case, the prosecution claimed that the accused had deliberately run over the victim in his car during a heated quarrel. The defendant, on the other hand, argued that the death was caused accidentally while he was trying to escape from another man, who had been using a hockey stick as a weapon. There was enough conflicting evidence to support both versions of events. The defence of provocation was obviously inappropriate if the defendant's story was thought to be true and after consultation with both sides, the judge withdrew the issue from the jury. This body went on to find the defendant guilty of murder, obviously preferring the prosecution's account of what had happened. The defendant then appealed.

The Court of Appeal held this was a misdirection and decided that both issues should have been presented to the jury. The court therefore substituted a manslaughter verdict.

From the cases just discussed, it can be seen that almost anything can amount to evidence of provocation. It would be wise of the judge to let the jury decide on the matter after looking at all the circumstances. There are limitations, however. From the wording of s.3, it has been seen that the provocation must have been something done or something said, which would exclude naturally occurring acts. For example, if a landowner lost his self control and killed his gardener after discovering that his gardens had been destroyed by a terrible storm, he would not be able to plead provocation. Similarly in *Acott 1997*, the House of Lords decided that there was no evidence of any provoking words or conduct by another party, even though the savagery of the attack on the victim might have indicated that the perpetrator had lost his self control for some reason. The defendant had claimed that his mother's death was an accident caused by a fall but, on his conviction for murder, he had appealed, arguing that the defence of provocation should have been put to the jury. Neither of the appeal courts found evidence of any provoking act and the man's conviction for murder was upheld by the House of Lords.

4.4.2 THE DEFENDANT MUST HAVE LOST HIS SELF CONTROL

It is not enough for the defendant to show that he has been provoked. He has two further hurdles to overcome before the threat of a murder conviction is lifted. He has to show that the provocation affected him so strongly that he lost his self control. This obviously is a subjective test. Lastly, however, the jury will need to be convinced that a reasonable man might have acted in the same way, a question, therefore, which is decided objectively.

The classic definition of provocation was uttered by Lord Devlin in the case of *Duffy 1949* and, despite the changes made by s.3 Homicide Act, the latter part of his direction still appears to be an authoritative statement of the law. It has been firmly upheld in later cases, as, for example by the House of Lords in *Baille 1995*, mentioned earlier.

The definition in *Duffy* allows the defence of provocation to be used where it has caused:

> a sudden and temporary loss of self-control rendering the accused so subject to passion as to make him or her, for the moment, not master of his mind.

In *Richens 1993*, the Court of Appeal stated that these words should not be extended to mean that there had to be a complete loss of control to the extent that the person did not know what he was doing, simply that the defendant been provoked to lose his self control and had killed.

The definition of provocation was not satisfied in the case of *Cocker 1989*, where the defendant killed his incurably ill wife, after she had repeatedly asked him to end her suffering. At the time of the killing, she had continually attacked him during the night, both mentally and physically, for not honouring his promise to kill her. The defendant then suffocated her with a pillow. Although he tried to argue that the actions that night were 'the last straw', the defendant's appeal on the grounds that he had lost his self control was not accepted.

The words 'sudden and temporary loss of self-control' have also caused problems in cases where the accused has waited some time before acting. The jury (and the Court of Appeal) are less inclined to believe that a person has lost his self-control if he or she has had time for a 'cooling off' period and has then gone on to commit the offence.

This was the position in *Duffy 1949*, *Thornton 1992* and *Ahluwalia 1992*, all cases concerning 'battered wives'.

In *Duffy 1949*, an abused wife, after a quarrel, left the room, changed her clothes and then returned with a hammer and a hatchet when her husband was in bed and killed him. Lord Devlin gave the now famous direction and decided that the woman's actions did not fall within it. Her conviction for murder, therefore, was upheld.

In the case of *Thornton 1992*, the couple had a very stormy relationship. Both of them drank heavily and in this state, the husband sometimes became violent and assaulted his wife.

On the night in question, after a serious quarrel, Mrs Thornton went into the kitchen, allegedly to find a truncheon to protect herself, and when she could not find it, sharpened a kitchen knife instead and returned to where her drunken husband was sleeping on a sofa. She asked him to come to bed but he refused and, after a further acrimonious exchange, she slowly plunged the knife into his stomach and killed him.

The defence relied on the plea of diminished responsibility at the trial but the trial judge also introduced the possible defence of provocation. Both pleas were unsuccessful and the jury convicted her of murder. The issue of provocation was again raised on her first appeal but this, too, was unsuccessful because it was felt that her actions of obtaining a knife and sharpening it did not indicate a loss of self control. After several years in prison, another appeal was allowed and, at this, a retrial was ordered. At

Oxford Crown Court, the defence of provocation was again dismissed but the alternative plea of diminished responsibility was accepted by the jury and a verdict of manslaughter substituted for murder. A sentence of six years imprisonment was given, which in view of the time already served, meant that Thornton could walk free from the court.

In *Ahluwalia 1992*, the defendant, who had been subjected to an arranged marriage, had suffered serious physical abuse by her unfaithful husband over a number of years. At the time of the killing, she had been threatened with a further beating in the morning. She therefore waited until her husband was asleep and then poured petrol over the bed and set fire to it. The victim later died of his injuries. Once again, it was difficult for the defence to show a sudden loss of self control and Ahluwalia was convicted of murder. After a strenuous campaign to free her, the murder conviction was changed to one of manslaughter but only because the defence of diminished responsibility, caused by what has become known as 'battered woman syndrome', and 'learned helplessness', was accepted. The Court of Appeal was prepared to accept that acts of provocation could take place over a period of time, a 'slow burn' effect but Lord Taylor, the Lord Chief Justice at that time still reiterated that the actual loss of self control at the end of the period had to be a sudden one. He said that 'the longer the delay and the stronger the evidence of deliberation on the part of the defendant, the more likely it will be that the prosecution will negative provocation'.

In the case of *Duffy*, mentioned previously, the judge had followed his classic statement with the following comment:

> circumstances which induce a desire for revenge are inconsistent with provocation, since the conscious formulation of a desire for revenge means that a person has had time to think, to reflect, and that would negative a sudden temporary loss of self

> control, which is of the essence of provocation.

Revenge, rather than provocation, was said to be the reason for the crime in the case of *Ibrams and Gregory 1981*. The defendants had been terrorised and bullied by the victim, the last act of provocation arising on 7 October. They and another woman involved in the case had failed to obtain satisfactory police protection so decided to take matters into their own hands. A few days later, therefore, they devised a plan for the woman to lure the man to bed, whereupon the defendants would burst in, attack him and break his arms and legs. Instead, the victim was killed and the defendants were found guilty of murder.

The Court of Appeal upheld the conviction, deciding that the formulation of a plan negatived a loss of self control. This, therefore, was fatal to the plea of provocation.

4.4.3 THE JURY MUST BE SATISFIED THAT A REASONABLE MAN WOULD HAVE ACTED IN A SIMILAR WAY

This involves examining the behaviour of the accused and assessing the extent of his reaction to the provocation. After this, the jury will decide whether a reasonable man might have acted in the same way.

In *Phillips 1968*, Lord Diplock, for the Privy Council, stated:

> The test of provocation is two-fold. The first, which has always been a question of fact for the jury, assuming that there is any evidence upon which they can so find, is 'Was the defendant provoked into losing his self control?' The second, which is one not of fact but of opinion, is 'Would a reasonable man have reacted to the same provocation in the same way as the defendant did?'

He went on to say that the trial judge's summing up, where he made it clear to the jurors that it was their responsibility, not his, to decide upon this matter, was 'an impeccable direction'.

In *Brown 1972*, a married couple had a violent quarrel after the husband suspected that his wife was being unfaithful to him. The wife attacked the defendant with a knife but not seriously, merely scratching his neck. He then attacked her with a poker and cut her throat with a razor. His conviction for murder was upheld because the jury believed that a reasonable man would not have reacted in such an extreme way.

Before the leading case of *Camplin 1978*, the view of a reasonable man was decided by an objective test. This was applied in the case of *Bedder* v *DPP 1954*. The accused had tried, in vain, to have intercourse with the victim, a prostitute. He claimed that she had struck him and taunted him about his impotence and that he had then he lost his temper and killed her.

The House of Lords dismissed his appeal against the conviction for murder, stating that a reasonable man would not have lost control in this way. No allowance was made for the special circumstances of the man's impotency.

This objective test was modified by the House of Lords in *DPP* v *Camplin 1978*. Their Lordships felt that a better test should be: 'would a reasonable man with the same characteristics as the accused have acted in this way'.

In this case, Camplin, a 15-year-old boy had been drinking and went with a middle aged man to the latter's house, where the boy was forcibly subjected to a homosexual assault. When he expressed shame at what had happened, the older man was alleged to have laughed and taunted him. The boy then attacked him with a heavy chipatti pan and killed him. He was convicted of murder after a direction from the judge about the qualities of a reasonable man.

His appeal eventually reached the House of Lords, where it was decided that, while certain of the boy's characteristics should not be taken into account for policy reasons, such as his drunkenness and excitability, other character-istics, such as his young age, could be. The question for the jury, therefore, was whether a reasonable youth of 15, in similar circum-stances, would have acted as he did. Because this was a possibility, the appeal against the murder conviction was allowed.

Unfortunately, the use of the word characteristics, and the question of which of these may or may not be taken into account, has caused confusion among both judges and juries, leading, inevitably to further appeals.

In *Newell 1980*, the accused had killed the victim by hitting him with a heavy ashtray, after the friend had made homosexual advances to him. The defendant was an alcoholic who, at the time of the attack, was recovering from a drug overdose. He was in a bad emotional state because his girlfriend had recently left him.

The Court of Appeal held that, when looking at the characteristics of the accused, the jury should only take into account permanent ones and ones that actually relate to the provocation. Therefore the effects of his drinking and drug taking could not be considered. It was decided that alcoholism could be a permanent factor, which in some situations could be taken into account, but not in this case because it was unre-lated to the actual attack. The appeal against the murder conviction was therefore unsuccessful.

While the appeal was unsuccessful, this case seemed to mark a turning point where a greater range of factors could be classed as character-istics that could be attributed to the reasonable man. The Court of Appeal had relied on a New Zealand authority, that of *McGregor 1962* and it appeared that mental characteristics could also be taken into account, thereby blurring the distinction between provocation and dimin-ished responsibility.

In *Humphreys 1995*, a young girl had been convicted of murder when she stabbed to death the man with whom she was living.

Humphreys had been brought up by an alco-holic mother and stepfather and had developed severe anti-social behaviour, often culminating in suicide attempts. She became a prostitute at the age of 16 and later moved in with the deceased, a much older man. The latter was of a violent disposition and unfaithful to her.

On the night of the stabbing, the deceased, in a pub with the accused and several others, had made remarks about the possibility of a 'gang bang' later that night. Humphreys alleged that, on their return to his house, he had started to undress and she had feared that he was about to rape her. She had earlier made an unsuccessful effort to slash her wrists and he jeered at her about this failed suicide attempt. She stated that she had then lost control and had stabbed him.

At her trial, she tried unsuccessfully to plead provocation, stating that the sneering remarks about her failed suicide attempts, coupled with her past history and the earlier events that evening had caused her 'to snap'.

As in the cases of Thornton and Ahluwalia, a campaign was mounted to secure her release, and her case was eventually referred back to the Court of Appeal. A manslaughter verdict was then substituted in place of the murder conviction because of two misdirections by the trial judge. Firstly, he had told the jury that they should consider the effect of the taunts on a reasonable woman in the same situation as Humphreys, not a woman with a distorted and explosive personality. Secondly, he had failed to give them full details of her history and the events leading up to the stabbing.

The Court of Appeal decided that the girl's characteristics of immaturity and attention seeking could be likened to an illness like anorexia. They could be seen as part of a psychological illness and were sufficiently permanent characteristics to be attributed to the reasonable young woman.

The court also stated that, in a complex case such as this, the jury should have been given a more detailed analysis of the possible areas of provocation and not have been left without guidance simply to make its own decision. The appeal was allowed.

As was stated earlier, both Ahluwalia and Thornton were also the beneficiaries of this more liberal approach to the subject of characteristics which could be held by the reasonable man. While their retrials succeeded on the issue

of diminished responsibility, the Court of Appeal, in an obiter statement in *Ahluwalia 1992* had stated that post traumatic stress disorder and battered woman syndrome could come under the heading of characteristics for the purposes of the defence of provocation. This view was supported in *Thornton (No. 2) 1996*.

In *Dryden 1995*, the defendant's 'eccentric and obsessional personality traits' were considered, on appeal, to be mental characteristics which should have been pointed out to the jury.

The defendant had failed to obtain the required planning permission to build on his land and was ordered to demolish a bungalow he had built there. When he refused to comply with this order, he was told that steps were being taken to enforce the decision. A great deal of publicity attended the subsequent proceedings and the defendant had implied that he would be prepared to use violence to stop the demolition. He became increasingly agitated, moody and eccentric, traits which were exacerbated by the death of his mother. One of the planning officers came to remonstrate with him at the locked gate, prior to the enforcement procedures being carried out. The defendant went back to his house, obtained a gun and, in full view of the TV cameras and police, shot dead the planning officer. He then shot him again as he lay dying on the ground and also tried to shoot another person against whom he held a grudge.

At his trial, he put forward the defences of both diminished responsibility and provocation but was convicted of murder. With regard to diminished responsibility, the doctors had disagreed as to whether his abnormality of mind was sufficient to substantially impair his mental responsibility for his acts. He then appealed.

The Court of Appeal decided, that when the defence of provocation was being explained to the jury, the judge should have discussed the possessiveness and eccentricity of the defendant which distinguished him from others. The court held that these factors amounted to characteristics of sufficient permanence to be

UNLAWFUL KILLING II: VOLUNTARY MANSLAUGHTER

attributed to the reasonable man. Despite the misdirection, however, the appeal failed because it was felt that no jury would have believed that a reasonable man, even one possessing the qualities of the accused, would have acted in a similar way.

In *Morhall 1995*, it had to be decided whether glue-sniffing was a characteristic that the court could take into account or whether it should be treated in the same way as drunkenness and drug abuse.

The defendant had been taunted about his addiction to glue-sniffing several times on the day in question. He had also been involved in a fight with the victim, which had been broken up. The deceased had then followed the defendant up to his room to try to continue the quarrel and later emerged after having been stabbed seven times. Morhall was convicted of murder, a decision that was upheld by the Court of Appeal. The court refused to consider glue-sniffing as a characteristic to be taken into account, likening it to drunkenness or drug-taking, which were felt to be repugnant to the idea of a reasonable man. The House of Lords, however, reversed the decision and substituted a conviction for manslaughter.

Their Lordships decided that a distinction had to be made between cases where the accused is taunted about an addiction he possesses, such as drug addiction, or being an alcoholic or, as in this case, a glue-sniffer, who then loses his self control, and cases where, because of his drugged state or his drunkenness, he loses that self control more readily. In the first type of situation, provocation could be pleaded but, in the latter case, it is felt that a reasonable man, or ordinary man as the House of Lords now chose to call him, would not have been drunk or drugged.

The House of Lords approved of the reasoning in *DPP* v *Camplin* mentioned earlier, but decided that, since that case, too much emphasis had been placed on the word 'characteristic' and attempts to decide which of these could or could not be taken into account.

They decided that, instead of being asked to look at various characteristics of the accused,

the jury should be asked to look at 'the entire factual situation'. This could include other factors that might be relevant to the provocation, in addition to the characteristics of the accused. These could include various addictions if they had been the subject of the provocation, as was the case here.

Lord Goff, while appearing to widen the ambit of provocation in this respect, did, however, add a note of caution. He stated that, in cases such as *Newell* and those following it, too much reliance had been put on dicta in the New Zealand case of *McGregor 1962*, a point he returned to in the case of *Luc Thiet Thuan 1996*.

This concerned an appeal made to the Privy Council from Hong Kong. The defendant claimed that he had killed his ex girlfriend after tying her up and forcing her to reveal her bank code number, because she had taunted him about his inferior sexual prowess compared to that of her new boyfriend. The defendant declared that 'some heat had popped up into my head and I told her not to say any more'. When she continued in the same vein, he stabbed her. There was medical evidence to show that he suffered from organic brain damage that made it difficult for him to control his impulses. The trial judge had directed the jury on this matter when dealing with the defence of diminished responsibility, but had not mentioned it in connection with provocation. The Court of Appeal in Hong Kong dismissed his appeal on the latter ground, stating that such mental abnormality was not a characteristic for the purposes of provocation unless it was this characteristic which had been the subject of the taunts.

The case reached the Privy Council, which again rejected the appeal. The court of five judges decided, four to one, that factors like mental instability which have reduced the defendant's powers of self control cannot be attributed to the reasonable man.

Lord Goff stated that the English Court of Appeal had, in the case of *Newell 1980*, taken a wrong turning regarding provocation and the characteristics to be attributed to the reasonable man, after it had adopted, 'without analysis', statements made in the New Zealand case of *McGregor 1962.* That case had allowed 'purely mental peculiarities' to be included as characteristics in the defence of provocation, which Lord Goff believed was wrong. He pointed out that New Zealand does not have a separate defence of diminished responsibility and therefore needed to take its own steps to rectify this shortcoming, as was discussed later in another New Zealand case, that of *McCarthy 1992.* English law, however, does have two separate defences, so he felt that such an approach should not have been adopted here.

He declared that the possible use of the defence of provocation in the cases of *Ahluwalia,* (post traumatic stress disorder or battered woman syndrome), *Dryden,* (eccentric and obsessional personality traits), and *Humphreys,* (abnormal immaturity and attention seeking) would have been decided differently if the case of *McCarthy* had been brought to the Court of Appeal's attention. If this had been done, he argued, such mental characteristics would not have been considered. He stated that it was necessary to look at the law as stated in *Camplin,* although argued that the case of *Morhall,* (in which Lord Goff himself gave the main judgment!), was 'in no way inconsistent' with it. Factors concerning mental infirmity, however, were not consistent with *Camplin* and should not be permitted.

Be that as it may, it appears that the Court of Appeal, is not yet prepared to admit it has been wrong. Under the doctrine of precedent, earlier decisions of the Court of Appeal are normally binding on the Court of Appeal in later cases, whereas decisions of the Privy Council are only persuasive. In *Campbell 1997,* therefore, mentioned earlier under diminished responsibility, the Court of Appeal stated that it would still abide by its own earlier decisions until such time as it was ordered not to do so by the House of Lords. So where does this conflict leave the law student?

The current state of the law is, at present, that which has been laid down by the Court of Appeal in *Campbell* and cases like *Thornton.* This court accepts that the main statement of the law regarding the third element in provocation is to be found in the cases of *Camplin* and *Morhall.* When looking at characteristics, however, it also allows mental characteristics, such as those discussed in *Ahluwalia, Humphreys* and *Dryden,* to be considered, until such time as the House of Lords decrees otherwise.

It would appear that this time may well be approaching. In *Smith (Morgan James) 1998,* the defendant suffered from a severe depressive illness which, he argued was a characteristic to be shared by the reasonable man. The judge allowed this but declared that it was only relevant when looking at the gravity of the provocation, not with regard to the reasonable man's loss of self control. The jury then convicted him of murder.

The Court of Appeal followed its own line of authority, laid down in cases such as *Ahluwalia, Humphreys* etc, and stated that cases like *Thornton* were a logical extension of *Camplin.* They did, however, certify a point of law on the matter to be put before the House of Lords. This means that the conflict between the Privy Council and the Court of Appeal may soon be resolved.

COMMENT

Not before time, one might add! It is very unsatisfactory to have such disagreement between the Court of Appeal and the Privy Council on such an important issue. It is bound to lead to more appeals, more public expense and greater uncertainty in the law.

When one studies s.3 Homicide Act, it looks deceptively simple. The second half of the section states that:

'. . . the question whether the provocation was enough to make a reasonable man do as he did shall be left to be determined by the jury; and in determining that question the jury shall take into account everything both done and said according to the effect which, in their opinion, it would have on a reasonable man.'

As can be seen, the section states that the jury must take all the things which were said or done into account. In the case of *DPP v Camplin 1978*, Lord Diplock stated that the section was intended to lessen the harshness of the common law approach to provocation, as interpreted in cases like *Bedder*, mentioned earlier. If, therefore, there was any evidence pointing to the loss of self control, this should be put before the jury for that body to decide the issue.

In *Morhall*, the House of Lords itself stated that 'the entire factual situation must be looked at'. It could be argued that this should also include matters like previous abuse, as in *Ahluwalia* or perceived injustice causing a change in character, as in *Dryden* or even a fall causing a personality change as in *Luc Thiet Than*. If all of these matters are put to the jurors, it can then be left to their good sense to decide if the ordinary person in a similar situation to the accused might have lost his self control. The House of Lords, however, may well come to a different conclusion and decide that the lines between diminished responsibilty and provocation have become blurred. It should be remembered that these judges also sit in the Privy Council so may well uphold the previous decisions of that body, rather than those of the Court of Appeal.

KEY FACTS

- The law is to be found in the common law and in s.3 Homicide Act 1957
- The aforementioned Act extended provocation to things said as well as things done
- The provoking words or action need not be directed at the accused, (*Doughty 1983, Pearson 1997*), nor need they come from the victim, (*Davies 1975*), but do need to be something said or done
- The defendant can use the defence of provocation, even if he started the trouble, as in *Johnson 1989*, and *Baille 1995*: this is known as self-induced provocation
- Three elements have to be established before the plea can be used: there has to be evidence of provocation, the accused must have lost his self-control and the jury must be convinced that a reasonable man might act in the same way
- It appears that if there is any possible evidence of provocation, the jury should be advised of this, even if it is felt that the plea would not succeed (*Doughty 1983, Baille 1995* and *Dhillon 1997*)
- When looking at whether the defendant has lost his self control, the direction in *Duffy 1949* is still approved of, although a complete loss of control is not necessary (*Richens 1993*)
- As the law currently stands, this can now come after a 'slow burn' (*Ahluwalia 1992*) or some delay (*Baille 1995*), but there still must be a final loss of self control (*Cocker 1989*)

- Evidence of premeditation is usually fatal to a successful plea (*Ibrams and Gregory 1981*)
- The concept of the reasonable man, first laid down in *Welsh 1869*, has now changed to that of the 'ordinary' man (*Morhall 1995*)
- The question of whether an ordinary man would have acted the same way, is decided by the jury
- In the past, a purely objective approach was used, as in *Bedder* v *DPP 1954*. This was changed in *DPP* v *Camplin* to whether a reasonable person, sharing the same characteristics of the accused would have acted in the same way. In *Morhall 1995*, it was suggested that the whole factual situation needed to be looked at
- Drunkenness or drug taking which might accelerate a person's loss of control will not be taken into account, although, if the defendant is, for example, an alcoholic, drug addict or glue-sniffer, taunts actually relating to such factors can be taken into account (*Morhall 1995*)
- The Court of Appeal is prepared to attribute certain mental characteristics to the reasonable man, such as learned helplessness caused by long-term abuse, as in *Ahluwalia 1992*, eccentric and obsessional personality traits (*Dryden 1995*), abnormal immaturity and attention seeking, as in *Humphreys 1995*, and a severe depressive illness as in *Smith 1998*
- The Privy Council, in the case of *Luc Thiet Thuan 1996*, disapproved of this extension of provocation and stated that the courts should return to the law as laid down in *DPP* v *Camplin 1978* and applied in *Morhall 1995*, so, at present, a dispute between the courts exists
- The Court of Appeal has stated in *Campbell 1995*, that it will continue to follow its own earlier decisions until these have been officially overruled by the House of Lords and in *Smith 1998*, proceeded to do just that! The court did, however, certify a point of law for the House of Lords, so, hopefully the conflict will be resolved
- There is no rule of law that the act of violence has to be proportionate to the provocation as was originally laid down in *Mancini* v *DPP*. The jury will decide the matter as in *Phillips 1968* and *Brown 1972*

FIGURE 4.3 *Key facts chart on provocation*

activity

Decide whether the defence of provocation is available to Jules and Jim.

Jules, an alcoholic, killed his partner by hitting her over the head with a frying pan after she taunted him about his drinking problem.

Jim was often beaten by his domineering wife. He brooded about this for several months, but then crept into her bedroom and smothered her with a pillow.

4.5 THE SURVIVOR OF A SUICIDE PACT

Until the Suicide Act 1961 was passed, suicide was a crime and the person faced prosecution if he survived. In addition, if another was involved in a plan to commit suicide and he survived, he would be charged with murder. Suicide is no longer a crime and the law has decided that aiders and abettors in suicide pacts should be treated more leniently if they do not die.

Under s.4(1) Homicide Act 1957, should two or more people enter into a suicide pact and one of them survive, that survivor would be charged with manslaughter, not murder. The burden of proving such a pact, should the accused have originally been charged with murder, will be on the defendant, s.4(2). Under s.4(3) of the Act, a suicide pact is defined as:

an agreement between two or more persons which has as its objects the death of all parties to it.

The defendant therefore must have had a settled intention of dying.

summary

This chapter has looked at voluntary manslaughter. Most of the law on this subject is to be found in the Homicide Act 1957, ss2, 3, and 4.

There are three situations where, although the defendant has the mens rea of murder, the law has decided to treat him more leniently.

These situations are when the accused is suffering from diminished responsibility, has been provoked or is the survivor of a suicide pact.

Three elements have to be proved to establish the defence of diminished responsibility, an abnormality of mind, caused by an inside source, which has substantially reduced the defendant's mental responsibility.

Three elements also have to be shown before the defence of provocation can be used. There must be enough evidence of provocation causing a loss of self-control by the defendant and the jury must be satisfied that an ordinary man, sharing similar characteristics to the defendant might also have reacted in the same way.

The successful establishment of these two defences will reduce the charge from murder to manslaughter.

A survivor of a suicide pact will also only face a manslaughter charge, not a murder one.

CHAPTER 5

UNLAWFUL KILLING III: INVOLUNTARY MANSLAUGHTER AND OTHER UNLAWFUL DEATHS

5.1 INVOLUNTARY MANSLAUGHTER

With both murder and voluntary manslaughter, an intention to kill or cause grievous bodily harm has to be proved. With involuntary manslaughter, no such intention is necessary. It is enough that the defendant either has committed an unlawful and dangerous act and from that act a death has resulted or that the accused has been so grossly negligent that someone has died. These two types of involuntary manslaughter have been given the names of constructive manslaughter and manslaughter by gross negligence. A third category of involuntary manslaughter has also been recognised over the years, that of reckless manslaughter, but at the present time it appears that this type of manslaughter has been merged with killings as a result of gross negligence. We shall be looking at the two current forms of involuntary manslaughter and examining how changes have been effected over the years regarding reckless manslaughter. We shall also note that major reforms of the law have been suggested in this widely debated area. At the end of the chapter, other unlawful killings will be examined.

5.2 CONSTRUCTIVE MANSLAUGHTER

Constructive manslaughter is also known as unlawful act manslaughter because it is committed where the defendant has caused the death of a person by an unlawful and dangerous act. The distinction between this type of manslaughter and that of gross negligence manslaughter was clearly stated by Humphreys J in the case of *Larkin 1943*.

If a person is engaged in doing a lawful act, and in the course of doing that lawful act behaves so negligently as to cause the death of some other person, then it is for the jury to say, upon a consideration of the whole of the facts of the case, whether the negligence proved against the accused person amounts to manslaughter, and it is the duty of the presiding judge to tell them that it will not amount to manslaughter unless the negligence is of a very high degree [...] That is where the act is lawful. Where the act which a person is engaged in performing is unlawful, then if at the same time it is a dangerous act, that is an act which is likely to injure another person, and quite inadvertently he causes the death of that other person by that act, then he is guilty of manslaughter.

It can be seen therefore that, like the defences of diminished responsibility and provocation, there are three elements which have to be established before a person is liable for constructive manslaughter.

1 There must have been an unlawful act.
2 This act must have caused the death.
3 The unlawful act must also have been a dangerous one, in that it must have been an act that was likely to injure someone.

These three points now need to be examined in more detail.

5.2.1 THERE MUST BE AN UNLAWFUL ACT

It was noted above that if the act causing the death was a lawful one but one that was committed carelessly, it will not come into this category of manslaughter. Gross negligence manslaughter will be the course to pursue in such a case. Lord Atkin had also made this point clear in *Andrews* v *DPP 1937*, when he said:

there is an obvious difference in the law of manslaughter between doing an unlawful act and doing a lawful act with a degree of carelessness which the legislature makes criminal.

With regard to unlawful acts, it was held in earlier times that the unlawful act causing the death could be a civil wrong in addition to a criminal act. In *Fenton 1830*, it was held that a person could be liable for unlawful act manslaughter when he committed the tort of trespass. The accused had thrown stones down a mine-shaft and this act had caused the scaffolding to collapse, which resulted in the death of some of the miners in the shaft. It was decided that the act of the accused was enough to create liability for constructive manslaughter.

In the later case of *Franklin 1883*, however, this view was not sustained. The defendant had thrown a box belonging to a stall holder in Brighton, into the sea, where it had struck a swimmer and caused his death. The judge, Field J stated:

… the mere fact of a civil wrong committed by one person against another ought not to be used as an incident which is a necessary step in a criminal case.

Such a defendant could, of course, be convicted on the grounds of manslaughter by gross negligence if it was felt that the degree of negligence was very high and, in the event, this is what happened.

When a person is charged with constructive manslaughter, the unlawful act often consists of an assault, as was the case in *Larkin 1943*, mentioned earlier. It will be not be a viable defence for the defendant to argue that he did not intend to injure the person who was actually harmed, provided that the assault itself has been established.

In the case of *Larkin*, the accused had discovered his mistress in the company of another man, had brooded about this for a while and had returned with an open razor. He alleged that he had only meant to frighten the man but that his mistress, who had been drinking, staggered into the path of the razor and cut her throat on it. Despite this claim, the conviction for unlawful act manslaughter was upheld because an assault had been committed and this assault had caused the death in question. For liability to be established, however, an unlawful act must be clearly be shown to have taken place. This was not proved in the following two cases.

In *Lamb 1961*, the accused and his friend

had been playing with a revolver. This had two bullets in it, neither of which was opposite the barrel. Believing that this meant that the gun was safe, the defendant pointed it at his friend and pulled the trigger. It was established that he did not intend to harm the friend and the latter was not in fear of his acts. Unfortunately, the gun fired a live bullet and the friend was killed.

The Court of Appeal quashed the manslaughter conviction because it was decided that there had not been an unlawful act. It will be noted later, when looking at non-fatal offences against the person, that the crime of assault requires the victim to be put in fear that a battery will be inflicted upon him. In this case, no such fear existed.

In *Ariobeke 1988*, there was certainly fear on the victim's part but the actions of the defendant did not amount to criminal acts. There had been evidence of bad relations between the two men and the accused had been peering into the carriages of a train apparently looking for the victim. The latter appeared to have panicked and ran across a live railway line to try to escape. He was then electrocuted when he stepped on a live rail. Ariobeke was convicted of manslaughter but the Court of Appeal quashed the conviction on the grounds that an assault had not been established.

A similar approach was taken in *Scarlett 1993*. A publican ejected a drunken customer and the latter fell, hit his head and died. The Court of Appeal quashed the conviction, deciding that an unlawful act had not been clearly established. There was insufficient evidence that the publican had intentionally or recklessly used excessive force to remove the victim.

In two earlier cases, *DPP* v *Newbury and Jones 1977* and *Cato 1976*, the appeal courts had no trouble in upholding the convictions for constructive manslaughter, although they did not specify precisely what constituted the unlawful act. In the first case, two young boys had thrown a slab of paving stone from a bridge into the path of a passing train, which was travelling from Pontypridd to Cardiff. This entered the window of the cab and killed the guard. The *mens rea* of assault requires that the

accused must have foreseen that his act would cause harm and the boys claimed that they had not foreseen the possibility that anyone would have been injured by their actions. Despite this allegation, the House of Lords upheld the conviction for unlawful act manslaughter, a decision that has been questioned by legal writers. Their Lordships merely accepted that an unlawful act had been committed and proceeded to answer the point of law put forward on that basis. While it might have been difficult to establish an assault against the guard, because of a lack of intention or subjective recklessness on the part of the defendants, it has been persuasively argued that an unlawful act could still have been established, either in the form of criminal damage or, alternatively, by endangering passengers contrary to s.34 Offences Against the Person Act 1861. It is, however, unfortunate that the matter was not clarified by their Lordships. As stated, they merely assumed that the unlawful act had been established and then went on to decide that the act was also a dangerous one.

The actual point of law that the House of Lords was asked to consider was whether a defendant, who was not affected by drink or drugs, could still be found guilty of this type of manslaughter if he had not foreseen that his act might have caused harm to another. The answer was given in the affirmative.

Similar problems about establishing an unlawful act occurred in *Cato 1976*. The defendant and the person who died were drug users, who had agreed to give each other their 'fixes'. The defendant injected the victim several times during the night with a mixture of heroin and water, although the victim himself had actually prepared the mixture. The amount taken proved to be fatal and the defendant was charged with both manslaughter and with administering a noxious thing, contrary to the Offences Against the Person Act 1861. The jury found him guilty on both counts. Cato then appealed.

He argued that, while it is an offence to possess or supply heroin under the Misuse of Drugs Act 1971, it is not an offence under that act merely to take a mixture, already prepared by another person and then just give it to him. The Court of Appeal decided that there was no need to refer to the Misuse of Drugs Act, because the unlawful act had been established by the other charge, i.e. the defendant had administered a noxious thing contrary to the Offences Against the Person Act 1861. An unlawful act had therefore been committed. Despite this, Lord Widgery C J decided to deal with the point raised by the defence. He stated:

> But since he, [the defence counsel], went to such trouble with the argument, and in respect for it, we think we ought to say that had it not been possible to rely on the charge under s.23 of the 1861 Act, we think that there would have been an unlawful act here, and we think the unlawful act would be described as injecting the deceased … with a mixture of heroin and water which at the time of the injection Cato had unlawfully taken into his possession.

5.2.2 THE UNLAWFUL ACT MUST HAVE CAUSED THE DEATH

As we have noted in Chapter 3, the unlawful act of the accused must be closely connected to the death that has resulted, and a *novus actus interveniens* (a new intervening act), must not have arisen to break the chain of causation. The unlawful act need not, however, be the sole cause of the death, provided that it made a significant contribution to it.

It was originally decided by the courts that the unlawful act had to be directed at a human being, even if the wrong person actually died, as occurred in *Latimer*, mentioned earlier. The Court of Appeal upheld this view, and in fact went further than this, in the case of *Dalby 1982*, where it stated that the unlawful act must be directed at the victim. The defendant and the victim were drug users but, unlike *Cato*, the defendant in *Dalby* had not injected the other

person with drugs. He had obtained a drug called diconal lawfully on prescription, but had then given some of the tablets to his friend and they had injected themselves intravenously before going to a discotheque. While they were out, the friends had parted company and there was evidence that another person had also injected the victim at least twice more with unspecified drugs. The latter died the following day.

Dalby was charged with supplying drugs and also with the offence of constructive manslaughter and was found guilty on both counts. One of the questions the jurors were asked to consider was whether the supply of the diconal was a substantial cause of the victim's death. They were told that it did not have to be the only cause, but that it had to be a substantial cause, i.e. one which was not merely trivial. The jury found him guilty of manslaughter.

The Court of Appeal quashed the manslaughter conviction, stating that:

> The difficulty in the present case is that the act of supplying a controlled drug was not an act which caused direct harm. It was an act which made it possible, or even likely, that harm would occur subsequently, particularly if the drug was supplied to someone who was on drugs. In all the reported cases, the physical act has been one which inevitably would subject the other person to the risk of some harm from the act itself. In this case, the supply of drugs would itself have caused no harm unless the deceased had subsequently used the drugs in a form or quantity which was dangerous. In the judgment of this court, the unlawful act of supplying drugs was not an act directed against the person as such and the supply did not cause any direct injury to him.

The Court of Appeal then went on to state categorically that:

> In the judgment of this court, where the charge of manslaughter is based on an unlawful and dangerous act, it must be an act directed at the victim and likely to cause immediate injury, however slight.

Later cases have modified the strong statements made in *Dalby*. In the case of *Mitchell 1983*, it was decided that an act intended for another person could, under the doctrine of transferred malice, be classed as being directed at the victim.

In this case, the defendant had tried to 'jump the queue' in a busy post office and a 70-year-old man had remonstrated with him. The accused hit him in the mouth and then either hit him again or pushed him backwards so that he fell against others in the queue, including an even older woman who suffered a broken leg. As a result of this, she had to have an operation to have a hip joint replaced. At first she appeared to be recuperating well but then died suddenly.

The defendant was convicted of manslaughter but appealed. The Court of Appeal had to decide whether the person at whom the act is aimed must also be the person whose death is caused. Staughton J stated:

> We can see no reason of policy for holding that an act calculated to harm A cannot be manslaughter if it in fact kills B. The criminality of the doer of the act is precisely the same whether it is A or B who dies.

After this case, therefore, it was the law that, while the unlawful act must be directed at someone, it need not be at the person who dies. In *Goodfellow 1986*, the Court of Appeal went further and decided that the accused could also be liable when he did not direct his unlawful act at a person at all.

The accused was being harassed by two other men and wanted to move from his council accommodation, but knew that his chances of a transfer were slight. He therefore decided to take matters into his own hands and set fire to his house, making it look as if it had been petrol-bombed, hoping that this would lead to him being re-housed. Unfortunately, the intensity of the fire was greater than was planned and Goodfellow's wife, son and his son's girlfriend all died in the blaze. The Court of Appeal upheld his conviction for manslaughter even though the unlawful act of arson was not directed at the people who died. The court held that the accused could have been liable for both reckless manslaughter, which existed at that time and for unlawful act manslaughter. With regard to the latter charge, the court held that it had to be shown that the act was committed intentionally, that it was an unlawful one, that reasonable people would recognise that it was likely to cause harm and that a death had resulted. The Court of Appeal felt that all these points had been established and the conviction was upheld.

The very clear comments made in *Dalby* stating that the act must be directed at the victim were dealt with in a rather unconvincing way. The lack of clarity caused by these cases has been strongly criticised by academics.

5.2.3 THE UNLAWFUL ACT MUST ALSO BE A DANGEROUS ONE

The third element that needs to be established for constructive manslaughter is that the act must be a dangerous one. The act, therefore, has to be both unlawful and dangerous, which in this context means an unlawful act that is also likely to injure another person. This two-fold approach was clearly stated in *Larkin 1943*, mentioned earlier.

Whether the act is considered a dangerous one is decided objectively, i.e. it must be an act that a sober and reasonable man would regard as dangerous.

This was affirmed in the case of *Church 1966*. The Court of Criminal Appeal, as it was then, stated:

> An unlawful act causing the death of another cannot, simply because it is an

unlawful act, render a manslaughter verdict inevitable. For such a verdict inexorably to follow, the unlawful act must be such as all sober and reasonable people would inevitably recognise must subject the other person to, at least, the risk of some harm resulting therefrom, albeit not serious harm.

The defendant had panicked after having hit a woman who had mocked his inability to satisfy her. Believing her to be dead, he had thrown her into a river, where she had drowned. His conviction for manslaughter was upheld.

In *DPP v Newbury and Jones 1977*, the House of Lords specifically approved of the dicta in *Church* and decided that an act of throwing a paving slab in front of a passing train was one which all reasonable people would look upon as dangerous.

Similarly, in *Ball 1989*, the defendant's argument that he believed that the cartridge in his gun was merely a blank, and so should not be liable, was rejected by the Court of Appeal.

There had been a great deal of ill-feeling between the accused and the victim. The woman had climbed over a wall, accompanied by two men and had been shot by the defendant. The latter alleged that he had been in great fear of them and had therefore grabbed a gun and a handful of cartridges in order to frighten them. He claimed that he kept both live and blank cartridges in the pocket of his overall but believed that a blank was in the gun. He argued that when the question of whether a reasonable man would believe that his actions were dangerous was looked at, this mythical person should consider the fact that the accused believed the gun was harmless.

The appeal court refused to accept this, stating:

> … the question whether the act is a dangerous one is to be judged not by the appellant's appreciation but by that of the sober and reasonable man, and it is

impossible to impute into his appreciation the mistaken belief of the appellant that what he was doing was not dangerous because he thought he had a blank cartridge in the chamber. At that stage the appellant's intention, foresight or knowledge is irrelevant.

Ball's counsel had tried to use the earlier case of *Dawson 1985* to support his argument, where the defendant had been luckier and his appeal allowed. Dawson and masked accomplices had attempted to rob a garage. They had threatened the 60-year-old garage attendant with a pickaxe and an imitation gun. After he had pressed the alarm, however, they had fled empty handed. The attendant, who suffered from a heart disease, had a fatal heart attack shortly after the police arrived on the scene. Dawson was convicted of unlawful act manslaughter.

The Court of Appeal decided that the conviction had to be quashed because the trial judge had told the jurors that they must decide whether the act of the robbers was a dangerous one and that they should approach this from the point of view of a reasonable man 'who knew the facts that you know'. The jury, however, had knowledge of the victim's heart condition, whereas a reasonable man, at the time of the attack, would not have known this fact. He therefore might not have assumed that the acts of the defendant might cause the victim injury: fear, perhaps but not physical harm.

Dawson was distinguished in the case of *Watson 1989*, another case where the victim's heart attack may have been brought about by the unlawful acts of the accused. The latter and an accomplice had thrown a brick through the window of the victim's house and had disturbed the 87-year-old resident. They had then fled without taking anything. The elderly man, however, had died shortly afterwards from a heart attack.

The Court of Appeal held that the defendant should have become aware of the great age and frailty of the victim during the course of the

▼ **COMMENT**

The Court of Appeal obviously felt that it had no choice but to quash the conviction in Dawson because of the misdirection. It is submitted, however, that the ruling is not laying down a more general proposition that a defendant could never be liable in such a situation. It is interesting to speculate on the possible decision of the jury if the correct explanation of the law had been given. It should be remembered that the ruling in *Church* was as follows:

> the unlawful act must be such as all sober and reasonable people would inevitably recognise must subject the other person to, at least, the risk of some harm resulting therefrom, albeit not serious harm.

It is not inconceivable that a sober and reasonable man might well have decided that waving a pickaxe, plus a gun not known at that time to be a replica, at a victim might subject that person to the risk of harm. It can be seen, however, that the direction in *Church* is strongly phrased, using the words 'inevitably' and 'must'.

▼ **KEY FACTS**

- Constructive manslaughter occurs where there is an unlawful and dangerous act and, as a result the victim dies; it is also known as unlawful act manslaughter
- The *actus reus* is the death resulting from the unlawful act
- The *mens rea* will be that which is required by the unlawful act
    In the case of assault and battery, an intention to commit the assault or battery will need to be proved or *Cunningham* style recklessness, i.e. subjective recklessness. There is no requirement to prove an intention to cause the death of the victim, nor to prove recklessness that such a death might occur.
- Three elements have to be established for constructive manslaughter, an unlawful act, which is also dangerous, which has brought about the death of the victim
- The unlawful act must be a criminal wrong, not merely a civil one (*Franklin 1883*), and must be clearly established. In *Lamb 1961, Ariobeke 1988* and *Scarlett 1993*, it was decided, on appeal, that the alleged assaults had not been proved. In *DPP* v *Newbury and Jones* and *Cato*, however, the unlawfulness of the acts was upheld, perhaps for reasons of public policy
- The unlawful act must have been a substantial cause of the victim's death, although it need not be the only cause. Despite the dicta of the Court of Appeal in *Dalby 1982*, it now appears that the unlawful act need not be directed at the victim nor, indeed, at a human being at all (*Mitchell 1983* and *Goodfellow 1986*)
- A dangerous act is one which carries with it the risk of some harm resulting, although not necessarily serious harm (*Church 1966*)
- Whether the act is dangerous is to be assessed objectively, i.e. by the view of a sober and reasonable person (*Larkin 1943* and *Church 1966*)
- When deciding whether the act is dangerous, these sober and reasonable people will look at the situation encountered by the defendant (*Dawson 1985*), but may not accept his claim that his mistaken belief frees him from liability (*Ball 1989*). They may also expect him to become aware of the vulnerability of his victim (*Watson 1989*)

FIGURE 5.1 *Key facts chart on constructive manslaughter* burglary. In the event, the defendant's conviction was quashed because it could not be satisfactorily established that the burglary had caused the heart attack or the entry of the police workmen afterwards. The dicta of the Court of Appeal, however, could ensure that liability can be imposed in future.

activity

While waiting on the edge of the platform for a train to take them to college, Bill and Ben started to argue loudly about the merits of two pop groups currently in the charts. Their heated discussion turned into anger and they began to throw punches at each other. Bill's second punch sent Ben reeling. He was pushed against Daisy, who fell in front of the incoming train and was killed.

Advise Bill, who has been charged with the manslaughter of Daisy.

having regard to the risk of death involved, the conduct of the defendant was so bad in all the circumstances as to amount in their judgment to a criminal act or omission.

- The *actus reus* of the offence is the death which has resulted from the negligent act

- The *mens rea* of the offence is the defendant's grossly negligent behaviour

Manslaughter by gross negligence has had a chequered history and, before the above case, it seemed to have virtually disappeared and to have overtaken by reckless manslaughter. The position now appears to have come full circle and there is serious doubt as to whether reckless manslaughter continues to exist. In *Adomako*, it was firmly decided by the House of Lords that the gross negligence test is the correct one to use in all cases where a duty of care has been broken. It may also be the test to use for all cases of manslaughter where there is no unlawful act.

5.3 MANSLAUGHTER BY GROSS NEGLIGENCE

In the preceding paragraphs, we have been looking at defendants who have committed criminal acts that have resulted in a death. There may also be other situations in which it is felt that the defendant should face a manslaughter charge, even though he may not have been involved in any criminal activity. Under this second form of involuntary manslaughter he may be charged because his behaviour has been so grossly negligent that it has brought about the death of another person.

In *Adomako 1994*, Lord Mackay decided that liability for this type of manslaughter will arise where the jury decides that:

5.3.1 THE DEVELOPMENT OF GROSS NEGLIGENCE MANSLAUGHTER

The leading cases on gross negligence-manslaughter are *Bateman 1925*, *Andrews 1934* and *Adomako 1994*.

In *Bateman 1925*, the accused took away part of a woman's uterus during childbirth and did not remove her to hospital until five days later, where she subsequently died. Bateman's conviction for manslaughter was quashed because it was felt that he had been carrying out normal procedures which were approved of by the medical profession. The procedure itself had been at fault.

The Court of Appeal stated that manslaughter by gross negligence should not be found lightly. It would only arise where:

> in the opinion of the jury, the negligence of the accused went beyond a mere matter of compensation between subjects and showed such disregard for the life and safety of others as to amount to a crime against the State and conduct deserving punishment.

In *Andrews* v *DPP 1937* the defendant was charged with manslaughter after a pedestrian was killed by his dangerous driving. Andrews had been sent by his employers to help when a corporation bus broke down. On his way to the scene, he had driven over the speed limit, had overtaken a car and, while well over on the other side of the road, had struck a pedestrian. The victim was carried along the road on the bonnet of the defendant's van, then thrown from this and run over. The defendant did not stop. He was later convicted of manslaughter but appealed.

The House of Lords stated that manslaughter caused by bad driving was to be treated in the same way as other cases of homicide caused by the defendant's negligence, and went on to state that a person would only be criminally liable if his behaviour was very bad. Their Lordships laid down the following test:

> Simple lack of care which will constitute civil liability is not enough. For the purposes of the criminal law there are degrees of negligence and a very high degree of negligence is required to be proved.

The appeal had been based on a possible misdirection by the trial judge and their Lordships admitted that some parts of his summing up was open to criticism. On balance, however, they felt that there had been a proper direction about the high degree of negligence that needed to be established for this type of manslaughter and the conviction was upheld.

5.3.2 THE RISE OF RECKLESS MANSLAUGHTER

The development of gross negligence manslaughter came to a halt for a while after the case of *Seymour 1983*. In this case, the House of Lords followed the cases of *Caldwell* and *Lawrence*, mentioned in Chapter 2 and decided that this type of involuntary manslaughter should be redefined as reckless manslaughter.

In *Seymour 1983*, the defendant and his woman friend had quarrelled and her car and his lorry had been involved in a collision. The woman got out of her car and went towards the accused. The latter then drove his lorry at the car, claiming that he only intended to push it away but the woman was crushed between the lorry and her own vehicle. She died later of her injuries and the defendant was found guilty of manslaughter. The House of Lords stated that the ingredients for causing death by reckless driving (now replaced by dangerous driving), and the type of involuntary manslaughter which did not come within the definition of constructive manslaughter, were identical. From this case, and later cases modifying the principle to some extent, it appeared that criminal liability would arise if the defendant's conduct caused an obvious and serious risk of some personal injury and, as a result, someone died.

The Privy Council supported this approach in the case of *Kong Cheuk Kwan 1985*, a case concerning the collision of two hydrofoils near Hong Kong, and denied that a separate category of manslaughter by gross negligence was still appropriate.

By 1993, therefore, it appeared that the concept of gross negligence manslaughter had given way to *Caldwell*-style reckless manslaughter. Enough doubts remained, however, to make it inevitable that the matter would be reopened.

5.3.3 THE RE-EMERGENCE OF GROSS NEGLIGENCE MANSLAUGHTER

This occurred in the case of *Prentice & Others 1994*, when the Court of Appeal resurrected manslaughter by gross negligence for cases where there was a breach of duty of care by the defendant.

In *Prentice & Others*, three separate appeals were heard together by the Court of Appeal to decide on the correct test to be used in involuntary manslaughter cases, other than those of constructive manslaughter. These three appeals concerned the cases of *Prentice and Sullman*, *Holloway* and *Adomako*, and only in the last case was the conviction upheld.

The case of *Prentice and Sullman* concerned two junior hospital doctors. Prentice, the most inexperienced, had wrongly injected a drug directly into the spine of a patient suffering from leukaemia. This very serious error was compounded by the wrong action being taken when the mistake was discovered. This resulted in damage to the patient's brain and spinal cord and ultimately caused his death.

Prentice had been supervised by Sullman and had assumed that the latter was overseeing of the whole procedure. Sullman, on the other hand, believed that he was only supervising the actual injection.

The trial judge had felt bound by the case of *Seymour* and had therefore directed the jury on the lines of *Caldwell*-style recklessness. There was an obvious and serious risk of harm and the patient had died, so the defendants were found guilty.

In the second appeal of *Holloway*, a qualified and experienced electrician had installed a new domestic central heating system and afterwards family members began to get electric shocks. The electrician checked his work and found no faults in the wiring but, when the trouble continued, he made arrangements to replace the heating programmer. Before this new part could be obtained, a member of the family received a fatal electric shock.

It was discovered that some of the wires were 'live' and that the circuit breaker, which should have afforded protection, was ineffective. The electrician was charged with manslaughter and found guilty after the judge, as in *Prentice*, directed the jury on the lines of reckless manslaughter.

In both cases, the Court of Appeal quashed the convictions, stating that the correct test to use in these cases, where a duty of care was owed to the victim, was not that of recklessness but that of gross negligence manslaughter.

In *Adomako 1995*, the last of the three cases, the manslaughter conviction was upheld. The defendant was an anaesthetist in a hospital who had been left in sole charge after the senior anaesthetist was called away. Adomako had failed to notice that a tube leading from the patient to the ventilator had become disconnected. When the alarm sounded, his first thought was that the machine itself was faulty and he therefore took the wrong action. By the time the mistake was discovered, the patient had died.

Rather surprisingly in this case, the jury had been directed on the issue of gross negligence, rather than recklessness, despite the fact that gross negligence manslaughter was currently in decline. The defendant was convicted by a majority of ten to one. Adomako based his appeal on the issue that the jury should have been directed with regard to recklessness.

The Court of Appeal was satisfied that the jury had, in fact, been properly directed and upheld the conviction for manslaughter. A duty of care had been owed (in this case by the anaesthetist to the patient), and this duty had been broken by the high degree of negligence of the defendant.

As stated earlier, the Court of Appeal looked at these three appeals together to decide on the correct test to use in such cases. Lord Taylor, the former Lord Chief Justice, decided that manslaughter by gross negligence should be revived and should be classed as the proper test to use in all cases where a breach of duty had arisen. He decided that only cases of motor manslaughter should be treated differently, where the test of reckless manslaughter (*Caldwell*

Canoe disaster chief is freed on appeal

THE managing director of an activities centre, jailed for the manslaughter of the four young victims of the Lyme Bay canoeing disaster, is to be freed. Peter Kite, 46, who has spent 14 months in jail, had his three-year sentence cut by a year by the Court of Appeal yesterday. With remission he is eligible for immediate release.

Kite, of Richmond, south-west London, had his appeal against conviction on four manslaughter charges dismissed by the same judges, Lord Justice Swinton Thomas, sitting with Mr Justice Harrison and Mr Justice Thomas, said that they were "wholly satisfied" that the verdicts returned by the jury at Winchester Crown Court in December 1994 were not in any way unsafe.

But they agreed to cut the sentence after hearing from Edmund Lawson, QC, representing Kite, that the longest sentence passed for similar charges of manslaughter caused by gross negligence was 21 months.

The trial judge had based his sentence on the fact that the charges were serious and demanded a term "of substance". Lord Justice Swinton Thomas said: " We entirely agree with that comment by the judge, but in all the circumstances of the case is three years too long?" He said the judges had agreed that an appropriate sentence would be two years.

Parents of the victims gathered outside the court, comforting each other. Denis Walker, father of Rachel Walker, 16 said: "Kite was sentenced to three years, but will soon be free. My daughter was sentenced to death, Why couldn't Kite behave like a man and serve the rest of his sentence?"

Caroline Langley, mother of Claire Langley, also 16 said: "I am just sad and angry about what has happened. This is a life sentence for the parents of the victims."

Kite was head of the St Albans Centre which was also convicted of four manslaughter charges and fined £60,000 at the Winchester trial. Four sixth-formers from Southway School, Plymouth, died on March 22, 1993, during what was described at the trial as an "ill-conceived and poorly executed" canoe trip.

The teenagers took part in what was meant to be a two-hour paddle to Charmouth, Dorset, but the weather worsened and the canoes became swamped, forcing the teenagers into the water for hours. The other victims were Dean Sayer, 17, and Simon Dunne, 16. Four children and three teachers were rescued.

Dean Sayer's father, Gerry, said at his home in Plymouth that he was disgusted with the decision to free Kite. "I cannot believe it, he should have done three years because that is what he was given," he said.

Taken from an article in *The Times*, 9 February 1996

style), should be retained. (The Court of Appeal felt obliged to make this distinction because in motor manslaughter cases it was bound by the House of Lords' decision in *Seymour*.)

There was a further appeal in the *Adomako* case to the House of Lords. Their Lordships agreed with the revival of the gross negligence test set out by the Court of Appeal with regard to criminal negligence involving a breach of duty and approved of the cases of *Bateman* and *Andrews*, cited in that court. Lord Mackay stressed that it was no longer appropriate to refer to the detailed definition of recklessness stated in *Lawrence* and said that the test in cases such as this should be one which is clear to an ordinary member of the jury with no particular knowledge of the law. He felt that complicated definitions that the jury could not later remember, gave 'no service to the cause of justice'. He did, however, agree that, in some circumstances, it would not be a misdirection for a judge to use the word 'reckless' in its ordinary

sense, if this was felt to be necessary to indicate the seriousness of the behaviour.

In addition to agreeing with the Court of Appeal's new direction in *Prentice & Others*, their Lordships went further and stated that motor manslaughter should not be put into a separate category. It was clearly stated that the gross negligence test was the one to be used in all forms of involuntary manslaughter where no unlawful act was found.

When deciding whether a person is criminally liable, therefore, the House of Lords agreed with the Court of Appeal that ordinary principles of negligence should be adopted to see if the defendant had broken a duty of care to the victim and this breach had caused his death. If the answer was in the affirmative, then the jury should be given the task of deciding whether the negligence was so gross that it should be considered to be a crime. Lord Mackay put it succinctly:

> The essence of the matter, which is supremely a jury question, is whether, having regard to the risk of death involved, the conduct of the defendant was so bad in all the circumstances as to amount in their judgment to a criminal act or omission.

The very vagueness of this test, and the continued use of the word reckless in some cases, is bound to cause further discussion and possible appeals in the future.

The case of *Kite 1996*, shown in the previous article, illustrates the difficulties the judges face when sentencing for gross negligence manslaughter. If the sentence is felt to be too severe, there will invariably be an appeal; if the sentence is too light, the families of the victims are outraged.

Similar difficulties existed concerning the sinking of the Pescado in 1991 as described in the following article. A conviction for manslaughter was obtained against the owner of the vessel at first instance but was quashed on appeal.

Owner and manager blamed for loss of trawler

THE owner and manager of the trawler, Pescado, which sank off the Cornish coast were severely criticised in a report yesterday.

Relatives of the six who died on board repeated their calls for a public inquiry into the incident after the release of the Marine Accident Investigation Branch's report.

But yesterday John Prescott, the Deputy Prime Minister, ruled it out, saying: "I believe that no further safety lessons can be learned through such an inquiry."

The beam trawler sank 13 miles off Dodman Point after sailing from Falmouth in February 1991 for scallops. Relatives and the boat's manager have repeatedly claimed that it was struck by a submarine, claims which the Ministry of Defence denies.

The MAIB inquiry, which was delayed by criminal proceedings against the owner and manager of the vessel, concluded yesterday that the trawler was unsafely operated and foundered after snagging its fishing gear on the sea bed.

It blamed the failings on those who managed and owned the vessel, Mr Alan Ayres, and Joseph O'Connor.

Both men faced charges for manslaughter at Bristol Crown Court in 1996 over the deaths of the five men and one woman on board.

Mr Ayres was acquitted. Mr O'Connor was jailed for three years but his conviction was quashed on appeal.

Hours after the report was published, officials from the Maritime and Coastguard Agency moved to seize a ship which they discovered Mr O'Connor had bought from Customs and Excise last week.

Officials are preventing the Orion Star from leaving Devonport Dockyard, Plymouth, until a full safety inspection is carried out, as its UK Fishing Vessel Certificate has lapsed. Mr O'Connor, 46, of Plymouth, still holds a skipper's certificate.

Taken from an article by Sandra Laville in the *Daily Telegraph*, 23 September 1998. © Telegraph Group Limited, London, 1998.

KEY FACTS

- This form of manslaughter is to be used in all cases where there is no unlawful act but where a death has arisen because of the high degree of negligence of the defendant (*Adomako 1994*)
- The cases of *Bateman 1925* and *Andrews 1937* on gross negligent manslaughter have been specifically approved by the House of Lords
- Reckless manslaughter, in the form of the detailed direction in *Lawrence 1982*, seems to have disappeared and should no longer be used
- The *actus reus* of gross negligence manslaughter is a death arising from the negligent act of the accused
- The *mens rea* is the gross negligence of the accused
- The jury will decide this, after considering whether, having regard to the risk of death involved, the defendant's conduct was so bad that it should be classed as criminal
- At present, the maximum punishment for this type of involuntary manslaughter is life imprisonment

FIGURE 5.2 *Key facts chart on gross negligence manslaughter*

activity

1 In *Adomako*, Lord Mackay made the following comment: 'I entirely agree with the view that the circumstances to which a charge of involuntary manslaughter may apply are so various that it is unwise to attempt to categorise or detail specimen directions.'

In group discussion or in essay form, discuss whether this is the correct approach for the law to take or whether you feel that it puts too much responsibility onto the jury.

2 Bonnie was the director of a company running weekend adventure courses in Snowdonia. She was left short-staffed after two of her experienced guides had taken up positions elsewhere. After criticising the lack of instruction being given on basic safety procedures. Bonnie then engaged two teenagers on a part-time basis, hoping that they would gain experience 'on the job'.

Thelma and Louise were among those attending a course on a very cold weekend in November. They were sent off to climb Mount Snowdon, in the company of one of the new part-timers. Bonnie had been informed about the likelihood of adverse weather conditions but had ignored them, hoping that the reports were an exaggeration. In fact, the temperature dropped sharply and it started to snow. Thelma, who was only wearing ordinary trainers, slipped and fell down a crevasse. She was roped to Louise but the latter managed to cut the rope just before she, too, would have been pulled over.

Discuss the possible liability of Bonnie and Louise.

5.4 REFORM OF THE LAW ON INVOLUNTARY MANSLAUGHTER

The state of the law on involuntary manslaughter has been widely criticised over the years. Some have argued that constructive manslaughter is unfair to the accused and should be reformed or abolished together; Professor Smith, for example, declared in the Criminal Law Review in 1986, when discussing the case of *Goodfellow*, that the law in this area was in 'a discreditable state of uncertainty'. Other commentators have disapproved of the constant changes regarding reckless and gross negligence manslaughter.

The Law Commission considered the matter and published a report on the subject (Law Com. No. 237, Involuntary Manslaughter 1996.) It recommended the complete abolition of constructive manslaughter and suggested modifications to the law on gross negligence manslaughter.

In more detail, the Commission suggested the creation of two new offences, that of reckless killing and killing by gross carelessness.

Reckless killing would be committed where the accused is aware of a risk that his conduct will cause death or serious injury and it is considered unreasonable for him to have taken that risk. When considering the latter, all the circumstances known or believed by him to exist will be taken into account.

The maximum sentence for this would be life imprisonment.

The second new offence would be killing by gross carelessness. Unfortunately for the student, the wording is rather complicated. The offence will be committed where a person's careless conduct has caused a death and it would have been obvious to a reasonable person in the defendant's position that this would happen. The defendant will only be liable if he was capable of appreciating such a risk and it is established either that his conduct had fallen far below the standard expected or that he had intended by his conduct to cause injury or was aware of the risk that this might occur.

This offence is not considered so blameworthy as that of reckless killing and this is reflected in a maximum sentence of ten years.

COMMENT

The proposed abolition of unlawful act manslaughter is no surprise and is a logical step forward. In earlier times, an unlawful act causing death would have resulted in a murder charge. This came to be seen as unjust where there was obviously no intention to kill or cause serious injury to the victim. Taken further, it could be argued that, in similar circumstances, a person should not face a manslaughter charge either. Others would argue that those who are guilty of unlawful or grossly negligent acts should incur criminal liability to deter others. It remains to be seen whether the new offences, if ever enacted, will afford this. If the unlawful act is considered a manifestly reckless way to act, the defendant could be charged with the new offence of reckless manslaughter. It should be remembered, however, that a more subjective approach is taken here when establishing possible liability so there are bound to be people who would not be found guilty under reckless killing who would have been liable for constructive manslaughter.

It is also interesting to note that the Law Commission proposes to revive the concept of recklessness with regard to homicide, after its recent curtailment by the House of Lords, although this is similar in form to *Cunningham* recklessness, and subjective in approach, a move which brings the new offence in line with other offences against the person.

With regard to the second offence, the change from the word 'negligence' to that of 'carelessness' shows an intention to move away from civil law concepts of liability which, some have argued, have no place in criminal law. It will also solve the problem of having to establish whether a duty of care exists. Under the new offence, the defendant will be *prima facie* liable if the conduct causing the death falls far below that which is expected and he knows this.

5.5   OTHER UNLAWFUL HOMICIDES

5.5.1   CAUSING DEATH BY DANGEROUS DRIVING

This was changed from causing death by reckless driving by the Road Traffic Act 1991, which amended s.1 Road Traffic Act 1988 after the North Report, in 1988, favoured such a move. It had been decided that the definition of reckless driving was too narrow and difficult to prove and allowed some offenders to escape with the lesser charge of careless driving or even be acquitted.

S.1 Road Traffic Act 1988, as amended, states that:

> A person who causes the death of another person by driving a mechanically propelled vehicle dangerously on a road or other public place is guilty of an offence.

The amended offence carries a maximum punishment of ten years imprisonment and a possible fine. This doubles the original punishment and helps to reflect public concern about this offence, which causes so much anguish.

A person is held to drive dangerously if his driving falls below the standard expected of a competent and careful driver and it would be obvious that driving in this way would be dangerous. A person would also be criminally liable if his vehicle is in a dangerous state.

The offence is now extended to 'any mechanically propelled vehicle', not just motor vehicles. It can be committed on a road or other public place.

S.3A Road Traffic Act 1988, as amended, also creates a new offence of causing death by careless or inconsiderate driving when under the influence of drink or drugs. This is also triable only on indictment and carries the same maximum punishment as causing death by dangerous driving.

5.5.2   INFANTICIDE

The law is in s.1(1) Infanticide Act 1938. It is available to a woman who 'by any wilful act or omission' causes the death of a child of hers under 12 months but does so because the balance of her mind is disturbed because she has not fully recovered from the effect of giving birth or from breast feeding the baby. In such a case she will be guilty of infanticide instead of murder and will normally be dealt with more leniently.

5.5.3   ABORTION

This is an offence under s.58 Offences Against the Person Act 1861 where it states that it is an offence to procure a miscarriage. The offence can be committed by the woman herself or by another, by use of 'a poison or other noxious thing' or by 'an instrument or any other means'.

There is no requirement to show that there has actually been a miscarriage as a result. To commit the crime, however, the woman herself must actually be pregnant whereas with others who try to procure the miscarriage this is not necessary. Where others are involved the woman could be charged with aiding and abetting the bringing about of a miscarriage, or be charged with conspiracy to procure her miscarriage. In practice such charges are rarely brought.

The word 'poison' refers to a recognised poison and the administrators of it would be guilty however small the amount as laid down in *Cramp 1880*.

The words 'noxious thing' covers things that are harmful in the quantity given, even if harmless in small doses (*Marcus 1981*).

Lawful abortions

By s.1(1) Abortion Act 1967, (as amended in 1990), there is no offence if the pregnancy is terminated by a registered medical practitioner, provided that the correct procedures are laid down.

5.5.4 CHILD DESTRUCTION

It is an offence under s.1(1) Infant Life Preservation Act 1929 for any person, intending to destroy the life of a child capable of being born alive, to wilfully cause the child to die before it has an existence of its own.

There is a defence if the act was done in good faith to save the mother's life and in *Bourne 1939*, this was held to cover a doctor who carried out an abortion on a 14-year-old girl who had been raped.

In *Rance* v *Mid-Downs Health Authority 1991*, it was held that a child is capable of being born alive if it is able to exist as a living child breathing through its own lungs alone.

This offence fills in the gap between abortion and infanticide.

summary

We have discovered that a person can be liable for involuntary manslaughter in two different ways, first, where he commits an unlawful and dangerous act and, as a result, another person dies, and secondly, if he is grossly negligent and this behaviour leads to the death of another.

A party may also incur liability for causing death by dangerous or careless driving or by killing an unborn child. A mother may also be liable for infanticide.

CHAPTER 6

NON-FATAL OFFENCES AGAINST THE PERSON

6.1 INTRODUCTION

In Chapters 3, 4 and 5, we looked at homicide, i.e. fatal offences against the person. This chapter deals with non-fatal offences against the person. Not all such offences will be dealt with; only the ones most commonly found in examination syllabuses. These include common assault, battery, actual bodily harm and grievous bodily harm in its two forms, laid down in s.18 and s.20 Offences Against the Person Act 1861. Knowledge of such offences is now required by all the main boards. In addition, there will be a brief mention of certain offences against the police, indecent assault and rape.

In this chapter, the offences of assault and battery will be examined first, then assault occasioning actual bodily harm. This will be followed by the offence of malicious wounding or inflicting grievous bodily harm, defined in s.20 Offences Against the Person Act 1861. After this, the most serious of these offences short of homicide will be discussed, that of malicious wounding or causing grievous bodily harm, with the intent to cause grievous bodily harm, an offence laid down by s.18 Offences Against the Person Act 1861. Towards the end of this chapter, there is a brief mention of certain offences against the police, and the crimes of indecent assault and rape.

It can be seen by its date that the Offences Against the Person Act (not, as one student delightfully described it, the Offensive Person's Act!), is an ancient one, which contains some very archaic terms. In addition, it will also be discovered that, although in English law, the words 'assault' and 'battery' have very different meanings, the two terms are often confused, not only by laymen but also by the judges and the draftsmen of the statutes relating to this area of law. In many cases, the word assault is used to encompass both an assault and a battery or, indeed, either one of these. This will be made clear as we progress through this chapter. It will come as no surprise, therefore, to learn that there have been strong calls for the urgent reform of this whole area of law.

6.2 ASSAULT

An assault, (or common assault as it is sometimes called), is committed when the accused intentionally or recklessly causes the victim to apprehend immediate and unlawful violence. The House of Lords recently confirmed this definition in the case of *Ireland 1997*. A battery, on the other hand, is a separate offence and concerns the actual infliction of the force.

The two separate crimes were created by the common law but were classified as indictable offences under s.47 Offences Against the Person Act 1861 (noted in future as OAPA 1861), which also laid down the punishment. This part of s.47 has been repealed and now s.39 Criminal Justice Act 1988 decrees that the offences of common assault and battery are to be treated as summary offences. The same section also lays down a maximum sentence of six months imprisonment and a fine not exceeding level 5.

It was generally believed that the two crimes remained as common law offences, despite the fact that certain procedural information, such as the provisions just mentioned, were put into statutory form. In *DPP* v *Taylor, DPP* v *Little 1992*, however, the Divisional Court stated that common assault and battery had been classed as statutory offences since the enactment of s.47 OAPA 1861! A prosecutor, therefore, should now charge the defendant with either assault or battery under the amended law, i.e. under s.39 Criminal Justice Act 1988.

6.2.1 THE *ACTUS REUS* OF ASSAULT

The *actus reus* of assault occurs when the defendant causes the victim to apprehend immediate and unlawful violence.

It can be seen that no force need actually be applied to constitute this offence. The victim need only apprehend personal injury. The word 'apprehend' could mean simply 'to grasp the meaning of' or 'to understand', up to higher degrees of emotion such as 'to expect with anxiety or fear'. Examples of such apprehension include situations where the accused directs some sort of physical movement at the victim, such as raising a fist or pointing a gun at him. The victim must, however, be aware that violence might be enacted. In *Lamb 1967*, mentioned in Chapter 5 under constructive manslaughter, the victim at whom the gun was pointed did not fear the possible infliction of violence because neither he nor his friend believed that the gun with which they were playing would fire. No assault, therefore, had taken place. Conversely, an assault would have been committed if an imitation weapon had been used but the victim believed it to be real.

Can words alone constitute an assault?

It has been clearly decided that conduct causing the victim to believe that harm might be inflicted may amount to an assault but there was, until very recently, far less certainty as to whether words alone could do this. Earlier dicta suggested that they could not. In *Meade and Belt 1823*, the judge stated that 'no words or singing are equivalent to an assault'.

Over the years, however, the judges have changed their opinion that words alone cannot amount to an assault. In the case of *Wilson 1955*, Lord Goddard stated, *obiter*, that the words 'get out the knives' would, on their own, be sufficient to constitute an assault. Similarly, in the civil case of *Ansell* v *Thomas 1974*, a verbal threat to eject the plaintiff was considered to be a civil assault. The most important landmark has occurred very recently, when the Court of Appeal in *Constanza 1997* stated categorically that an assault could arise from words alone and held that older authorities stating otherwise rested on 'a dubious foundation'. It will also be seen, when looking at the case of *Ireland 1997*, under actual bodily harm, that the House of Lords has also upheld that in certain circumstances, even silence can amount to an assault, as where the defendant terrorised women with silent phone calls.

What was established much earlier was that words could prevent an action from being an assault. In the very early case of *Tuberville* v *Savage 1669*, the accused put his hand on his sword and said 'if it were not assize time I would not take such language from you'. The act of putting his hand on his sword was threatening but this had to be weighed against his words, which clearly implied that no physical action would be taken because the judges were in the vicinity!

When looking at the wording of the *actus reus* of assault, it will be seen that the victim must believe that immediate violence will be inflicted upon him. The courts, however, have adopted a liberal interpretation of the word 'immediate', in order to give justice to the victim.

It was stated in *Smith* v *Chief Superintendent of Woking Police Station, 1983* that 'When one is in a state of terror, one is very often unable to analyse precisely what one is frightened of as likely to happen next'.

In this case, the victim, who was in her nightclothes, was badly frightened by the accused, who had trespassed onto private property and was staring in at her through the windows of her ground floor bed sitting room.

The Divisional Court upheld the defendant' conviction for being on enclosed premises for an unlawful purpose (i.e. an assault), The defence tried to argue that the accused could not have committed an immediate assault because the windows and doors were all locked. The appeal court held that it was enough that the woman believed that she was in danger of having immediate violence inflicted on her. Her fear did not have to be rationalised.

It will be seen, when looking at cases on actual bodily harm that a similar approach was taken by the Court of Appeal in the case of *Constanza 1997*.

6.2.2 THE *MENS REA* OF ASSAULT

The *mens rea* of assault is satisfied when the defendant intends to cause the victim to apprehend immediate physical violence or does this recklessly.

The Court of Appeal stated in the case of *Venna 1976* that

> We see no reason in logic or in law why a person who recklessly applies physical force to the person of another should be outside the criminal law of assault.

The defendant was actually convicted of assault occasioning actual bodily harm but the principles laid down relate also to assault and battery.

It will be remembered that there are two types of recklessness in English law, *Cunningham* recklessness and *Caldwell* recklessness. In *Venna*, Cunningham style recklessness, i.e. subjective recklessness, was applied but after the decision in *Caldwell 1981* it was for a short while assumed that it would be sufficient to establish the more objective type of recklessness in all criminal offences where recklessness was

part of the *mens rea. Caldwell* style recklessness was therefore accepted by the Divisional Court in *DPP v K 1990*. As noted in Chapter 2, this change in the accepted position did not last long with regard to offences other than criminal damage. *DPP v K* was overruled by the Court of Appeal in *Spratt 1991* and, although that case was itself overruled on another point, this stricter approach to the *mens rea* of assault and battery was affirmed by the same court in *Parmenter*, also in 1991. When the latter case went to the House of Lords, this point was not directly discussed but *obiter dicta* by Lord Ackner appears to support the Court of Appeal's view. *Cunningham* recklessness, therefore, must be established for the offences of assault and battery.

6.3 BATTERY

This consists of an act by which the defendant intentionally or recklessly applies unlawful physical force to another person, as affirmed by the House of Lords in *Ireland 1997*.

The difference between assault and battery, therefore, is that an assault is committed where the victim believes that he is likely to be subjected to some sort of harm, whereas a battery does not take place until the force is applied. While the latter offence is known by the term 'battery', however, it is not usual to use the verb 'to batter' and state that the defendant has battered the victim. Instead, to the great confusion of all, the word 'assault' is used in its wider layman's form.

With regard to a battery, the law takes the view that an individual has a right to be protected from molestation. Blackstone, the eminent jurist, stated in his early Commentaries that:

> the law cannot draw the line between different degrees of violence and therefore totally prohibits the first and lowest stage of it; every man's person being sacred and

no other having a right to meddle with it,
in any the slightest manner.

In the case of *Collins* v *Wilcock 1984*, described below, Goff L J affirmed this approach. He declared that 'The fundamental principle, plain and incontestable is that every person's body is inviolate'. He went on to quote with approval, the statement in *Cole* v *Turner 1704*, that 'the least touching of another in anger is a battery'.

It can be seen from these quotations that the degree of physical force need not be high. In *Collins* v *Wilcock*, it was considered that a battery had been inflicted when a policewoman took hold of the arm of the defendant in order to detain her but without the intention to effect an arrest.

The police officer came to the conclusion that two women in the street were soliciting; they were loitering and one of them was a known prostitute. The officer therefore wanted to question them but the defendant was abusive and uncooperative. She then made to walk away but the policewoman took hold of her arm to prevent this happening. The defendant reacted by scratching the police officer with her fingernails and was later charged with assaulting a police officer in the execution of her duty.

The Divisional Court of the Queen's Bench Division decided that the action of the policewoman amounted to an unlawful battery and quashed the defendant's conviction for the assault upon her.

This decision followed a succession of cases where the police were held to be acting unlawfully in detaining suspects. They should not, therefore, try to prevent a suspect leaving unless they wish to arrest him and this was not the position in *Kenlin* v *Gardner 1967* and *Ludlow* v *Burgess 1971*, so the detentions were unlawful. In *Donnelly* v *Jackman 1970*, however, the court held that the officer in question did not commit a battery when he merely tapped on the other's shoulder to attract his attention.

The courts have also decided that touching the clothing of a person amounts to touching the person himself, provided, of course that the defendant has the necessary *mens rea* of battery. In the case of *Day 1845* the defendant slashed the victim's clothes, while in *Thomas 1985*, even though the actual offence was not made out, the rubbing of a girl's skirt was held to amount to a battery.

Naturally, not all touching will have this effect. In *Collins* v *Wilcock*, Goff went on to state that:

> most of the physical contacts of ordinary life are not actionable because they are impliedly consented to by all who move in society and so expose themselves to the risk of bodily contact. So nobody can complain of the jostling which is inevitable from his presence in, for example, a supermarket, an underground station or a busy street; nor can a person who attends a party complain if his hand is seized in friendship, or even if his back is (within reason) slapped.

The courts have long since decided that the battery need not be directly inflicted on the victim. In *Scott* v *Shepherd 1773*, a civil case, the court held that the defendant had committed a battery when he threw a live squib into a market place and, after two people had picked it up and thrown it further away, it injured a third party. In *Martin 1881*, an even more serious offence was committed when the defendant placed an iron bar across an exit in a theatre, turned out the lights and shouted 'fire!' In the ensuing panic, several people were injured as they rushed out of the theatre. The defendant's conviction for grievous bodily harm was upheld. More recently, this view was supported in the case of *Fagan* v *Metropolitan Police Commissioner 1969*, mentioned earlier in Chapter 2. It will be remembered that a police officer had ordered the defendant to park his car close to the kerb, and Fagan had reluctantly complied. In doing so, he drove the car onto the policeman's foot. This was done accidentally but, when asked by the policeman to remove the car, he said 'F. . . you, you can wait' and proceeded to turn off the ignition.

He unsuccessfully tried to argue on appeal that no offence had been committed. The Divisional Court disagreed, stating: 'it matters not, in our judgment, whether the battery is inflicted directly by the body of the offender or through the medium of some weapon or instrument controlled by the action of the offender. . .' The judges believed that there was no difference between 'the action of stepping on to a person's toe and maintaining that position and the action of driving a car on to a person's foot and sitting in the car while its position on the foot is maintained.'

6.3.1 THE *ACTUS REUS* OF BATTERY

This consists of the application of unlawful physical force on another, as confirmed by *Ireland 1997*. It will be seen, when discussing actual bodily harm, that the House of Lords decided in the latter case that the causing of psychiatric injury by silent telephone calls will not constitute a battery, although such an action may well be an assault.

6.3.2 THE *MENS REA* OF BATTERY

This is satisfied where the defendant intends to do such an act or is reckless about whether such force will be applied.

As with assault, this is *Cunningham* style recklessness, as laid down in *Venna 1976*. It is necessary, therefore, to prove that the accused himself was aware that he was acting recklessly.

A battery may start off as an innocent, accidental act but may later become a battery during a sequence of events among which the *mens rea* of the offence is formed. This was the position in the case of *Fagan*, mentioned above.

The defendant had also argued that he did not have the necessary *mens rea* for the offence. The Divisional Court held that 'there was an act constituting a battery which at its inception was not criminal because there was no element of intention, but which became criminal from the moment the intention was formed'. The conviction, therefore, was upheld.

6.3.3 THE DEFENCE OF CONSENT IN RELATION TO OFFENCES AGAINST THE PERSON

General defences, which can be put forward in response to many different types of crime including offences against the person, will be examined in Chapters 10 and 11, but the defence of consent, which is of special relevance to offences against the person, will be examined in this chapter. The courts have decided that if the alleged victim has given a valid consent to the assault and/or battery inflicted upon him, no offence will have been committed. This position was clearly affirmed by Lord Lane, a former Lord Chief Justice in *Attorney General's Reference (No. 6 of 1980) 1981*. He stated that as a general starting point:

> it is an essential element of an assault that the act is done contrary to the will and without the consent of the victim. . .

Should the defence of consent be accepted it will be a complete defence and the defendant will be acquitted.

As one would expect, however, strong restrictions have been put upon this general proposition. It was stated in the same case that 'It is not in the public interest that people should try to cause, or should cause, each other bodily harm for no reason'. The court therefore decided that the defence of consent could not be used when a fist fight in the street took place, even though the parties wanted to settle their differences in this way. This followed an early decision in *Coney 1882*, where the courts held that a prize fight conducted with bare fists was unlawful, despite the agreement of the parties. In *Leach 1969*, the defendants were unable to argue that the victim consented to his injuries even though he had asked to be crucified on Hampstead Heath! Fortunately, in this case, the misguided victim lived but it was also noted in Chapters 3 and 4 that it is not possible for a person to give someone else permission to kill him, no matter how strongly the first party wishes to die. Consent may, however, be available in limited circumstances for the less serious offences against the person. These circumstances were described in *AG's Reference (No. 6 of 1980)1981* as 'properly conducted games and sports, lawful chastisement or correction, reasonable surgical interference, dangerous exhibitions, etc.' These exceptions need to be examined more closely.

Properly conducted games and sports

With many games and sports there is always a risk of some bodily harm occurring. The most obvious and perhaps difficult case to justify is boxing, where, by the very nature of the sport, the participants intend to cause harm to the other. Despite this, it was clearly affirmed by the House of Lords in *Brown 1994*, that the sport of boxing is a lawful activity. 'Cudgels, foils and wrestling' were other examples which came under the heading of 'manly diversions' which were said 'to give strength, skill and activity, and may fit people for defence, public as well as personal, in time of need'. This early view was quoted with approval in *Donovan 1934*.

With regard to these 'manly diversions', which include related sports like football, rugby and hockey, the victim is said to consent to harm that occurs within the rules of the game, provided the defendant did not intend to cause serious injury. If he did have such an intention, then it would, of course, be immaterial that he was playing within the rules. Bramwell L J made this point clear in *Bradshaw 1878*, where the victim died during a game of football.

Public school boy locked up for rugby kick that broke jaw

A FATHER lashed out today after his son was put behind bars for smashing an opponent's jaw during a rugby match at his public school.

Civil engineer Chris Calton, 50, said outside court: "It seems to me to be ridiculous that an incident on a rugby pitch should end up in court."

David Calton, 19, now a tourism student at Sheffield Hallam University, was given a 12-month youth custody sentence at Sheffield Crown Court for kicking another boy with such force that one spectator said the impact "sounded like a gunshot".

The court heard how Calton, while a pupil at Mount St Mary's Catholic College, Spinkhill, near Sheffield, was playing "a hard fought and closely contested game" at Pocklington School, east Yorkshire, when he attacked 16-year-old Andrew Wilson late in the game. Mr Mark Bury, prosecuting, said: "The victim was knocked out with a kick to the head which broke his jaw while he was getting up from a ruck.

"There was a crowd at the game and Pocklington headmaster David Grey said the kick was levelled with all his might." The victim was taken to York District Hospital and underwent surgery.

The court heard how, since the incident in January, the boy had been left with throbbing pains in his jaw which makes "cracking sounds" when he eats.

Calton told police that Wilson had been aggressive towards him during the game, which was abandoned with the score at Pocklington 12, Mount St Mary's 17. But he admitted kicking out at him.

Mr Richard Woolfall, defending, said Calton came from a respectable home and was of previous good character. He said he had played rugby since he was seven and had county trials and a chance of playing at national level.

Calton, of Ketton Avenue, Sheffield, pleaded guilty to causing grievous bodily harm.

As his son was sentenced, Mr Calton, visibly shaking, shouted from the public gallery: "This is not justice. It was only a boy's game."

Judge Robert Moore told Calton: "The injured boy was taken out after the ball had gone while he was still trying to get up off the ground. Any sportsman, boy or adult, amateur or professional, who deliberately assaults another will face immediate custody to prevent others from doing the same."

Outside the court, Calton's father said: "This case should never have been brought this far. This was a school rugby match which was supervised by respectable professionals and teachers who should have been responsible."

Visibly shaking and with emotion in his voice, he added: "I am angry with the court's decision. We are going to appeal. I think the sentence is harsh and that sort of incident happens on every rugby pitch.

"I think it is ridiculous. I am staggered by what has happened to my son today. Does this mean that anything that happens on a rugby pitch could now end up in court?"

Taken from an article in the *Evening Standard*, 28 September 1998

Similarly, the defence would not be available to someone who deliberately broke the rules, as the previous article shows.

Lawful chastisement

Parents have always been allowed to use reasonable force to chastise their children, but not where the punishment is inflicted 'for the gratification of passion or rage or if it be immoderate or excessive in its nature or degree'. This view was taken in the case of *Hopley 1860* and currently there is much less tolerance of such physical punishment, as shown by a 1998 decision of the European Court of Human Rights. The stepfather of a boy was held by that court to have used excessive force, even though the English court had acquitted him of occasioning actual bodily harm on his stepson. The UK Government was ordered to pay damages to the boy.

Reasonable surgical interference

A person may consent to the infliction of bodily harm for good medical reasons, even in some cases where the risk is substantial, such as an operation with only a small chance of success. The matter is not so clear cut in situations where the operation or other process has little medical advantage. It is generally believed, however the act is acceptable if it has some therapeutic value to the person requesting it. The defence of consent, therefore, could normally be raised by those performing operations such as cosmetic surgery, ear-piercing or tattooing, (though not tattooing of a minor as this is forbidden by legislation). Legal attitudes are constantly changing in this area to keep abreast of advances in medical science. Circumcision of males, as required in some religions, has long been accepted as lawful although female circumcision is banned by statute. Sterilisation, sex change operations and organ transplants have been added more recently, provided that they are conducted properly and are not for an unlawful purpose. In *Richardson 1998* patients were held by the Court of Appeal to have con-sented to their dental treatment, even though they might have been less willing to undergo this if they had known that the woman had been struck off by the General Dental Council!

Dangerous exhibitions, etc.

Within the field of entertainment, the law allows a person to consent to the possibility of some harm arising, as, for example where a person allows knives to be thrown at him or a cigarette shot from his mouth. It is, however, uncertain how much licence the law will permit, in either civil or criminal law. In the quest for larger audiences, it is possible that stunts involving contestants could become even more flamboyant and potentially more dangerous. If this transpires, the criminal law might well intervene.

Horseplay

In addition to the categories mentioned in *AG's Reference (No. 6 of 1980)1981*, other exceptions where a person may be held to have consented to an assault or battery have, over the years, been recognised. These include what the judges have called horseplay and some forms of sexual activity (see next page).

From time immemorial people have been prone to play jokes upon each other. The law might become involved where the joke had backfired and someone has been harmed. Examples can be seen in the cases of *Jones* and *Aitken*, where that the courts took a tolerant view of such horseplay.

In *Jones 1987*, two young schoolboys were injured after being tossed in the air by the defendants but the Court of Appeal quashed the convictions for grievous bodily harm. The judges decided that the boys' consent to such 'rough and undisciplined play' could provide a defence.

In *Aitken & Others 1992*, the practical jokes engaged in by RAF officers were even more potentially dangerous. The defendants had set fire to the victim's supposedly fire resistant suit but the joke had backfired and the victim had received severe burns. The Court of Appeal held that it was a misdirection to state that such an activity could never be lawful and the convictions were set aside.

Consent to harmful sexual activity

The extent to which a person can consent to be harmed when indulging in sexual activity has also caused problems for the courts, with different approaches being taken by different judges. A controversial early example was the case of *Clarence 1888*, where the defendant escaped liability for both assault and rape because his wife had consented to the actual act of intercourse. She unsuccessfully contended that she would not have given this consent if she had been made aware of the fact that her husband was suffering from venereal disease which was then communicated to her.

The defendant may be held liable, despite the other's consent, if the harm inflicted is more than trivial and is directly inflicted on the victim, as in *Nichol 1807*, where the defendant harmed a 13-year-old pupil. In *Donovan 1934*, a young girl of 17 was beaten on her buttocks with a cane merely to give sexual gratification to the defendant, and in *Boyea 1992*, the victim was held to have consented to the sexual intercourse but not to the harm that this caused. In the latter case, the defendant was aware of his actions. In *Slingsby 1995*, there was no liability after vigorous sexual activity had taken place because the defendant had not committed any direct harm. He had been charged with unlawful act manslaughter because the woman had died from blood poisoning when internal cuts caused by the defendant's signet ring became infected but the case was dismissed.

The position becomes more difficult where the participants actually desire the infliction of pain.

The House of Lords dealt with this issue in *Brown & Others 1993 1994*. The case attracted a great deal of publicity because it involved the sexual activities of a group of homosexual males who took part in sado-masochistic activities, apparently enjoyed by all concerned. They burnt each other with matches and metal wires,

beat each other with whips and indulged in unusual and painful forms of genital torture. Their activities came to light when the police found a video detailing them, which was passed to group members. The instruments were sterilised and the wounds dressed so none of the men suffered permanent injuries. Nevertheless, they were convicted of offences under ss.47 and 20 OAPA 1861 and were sentenced to terms of imprisonment ranging from two to four and a half years. The House of Lords upheld the convictions by a majority of three to two.

For the majority, Lord Templeman stated that in cases where no actual bodily harm is caused, the consent of the person affected precludes him from complaining, thereby recognising the defence of consent in relation to common assault and battery. He also added that Parliament, under the Sexual Offences Act 1967 had permitted homosexual sexual activities in private between consenting adults. He refused, however, to accept the contention of the defendants that their sexual appetites could only be satisfied by the infliction of bodily harm because, as he pointed out:

> sado-masochism is not only concerned with sex. Sado-masochism is also concerned with violence. The evidence discloses that the practices of the appellants were unpredictably dangerous and degrading to body and mind and were developed with increasing barbarity and taught to persons whose consents were dubious or worthless.

He ended with a very clear message, stating that 'I am not prepared to invent a defence of consent for sado-masochistic encounters which breed and glorify cruelty and result in offences under sections 47 and 20 of the Act of 1861.'

Lord Jauncey discounted the argument that there needed to be hostility, as laymen understood the word, on the part of the person inflicting the bodily harm. He decided that if the act was unlawful, it was also a hostile one under the legal meaning of the word. He went on to stress the dangers to health inherent in these activities and the possible corruption of younger participants and decided that if such acts were to be rendered lawful it was up to Parliament to do this.

Lord Lowry also refused to recognise such acts as being in the category of 'manly diversions'. He also stated that 'Sado-masochistic homosexual activity cannot be regarded as conducive to the enhancement or enjoyment of family life or conducive to the welfare of society'.

Lord Mustill, in one of the two dissenting judgments, took a more liberal view. He stated that the state should intervene 'no more than is necessary to ensure a proper balance between the special interests of the individual and the general interests of the individuals who together comprise the populace at large.' He believed that the acts indulged in by the group were not, at present, criminal ones and was not prepared to create a new offence to make them so. He argued that this was Parliament's role, if it was deemed to be necessary.

The Law Commission issued a Consultation Paper (No. 139), entitled 'Consent in the Criminal Law 1995', asking for opinions on the proposition that 'the intentional causing of any injury to another person other than a serious disabling injury should not be criminal if, at the time of the act or omission causing the injury, the other person consented'.

This was only a consultation paper so it is important to keep track of the current position. Despite their differences on other points, all five Law Lords in Brown 1993 appeared to accept that consent could be a complete defence to common assault and battery. The majority, however, went on to decide that consent is not a defence to actual bodily harm or grievous bodily harm unless it comes within one of the recognised exceptions. In Wilson 1997, the Court of Appeal was prepare to include 'bottom branding' in the recognised catagories of tatooing and ear-piercing.

A doctor had discovered that Wilson's wife had scars on her buttocks in the form of the initials A and W and reported the matter to the police. They discovered that her husband, at her request, had burnt his initials onto her buttocks with a hot knife. Wilson was charged with assault occasioning actual bodily harm under s.47 OAPA 1861. Unsurprisingly, the judge decided that he was bound by the cases of *Donovan* and *Brown* and directed the jury to convict.

The Court of Appeal quashed the conviction and expressed its disquiet that the prosecuting authority should have thought it necessary to bring the proceedings, which, it claimed served no useful purpose and yet involved considerable public expense. The court decided that *Brown* did not lay down a proposition that consent was never a defence to actual bodily harm, deliberately inflicted, as all five Law Lords had recognised that there were exceptions to the general rule.

The court also decided that it was preferable for the law to develop on a case by case basis and likened the current case to that of tattooing or ear-piercing, which did come within the recognised exceptions.

The Court of Appeal believed that the current case was vastly different to the cases of *Donovan* and *Brown*. It felt that the first case involved aggression on the part of the defendant and the second physical torture that carried risks of serious physical injury and blood infection. The court felt that in the current case, there was no aggression and the act was more akin to a desire for physical adornment. It was therefore decided that the ublic interest did not demand that the defendant's activities should be treated as criminal.

6.3.4 SUGGESTED REFORM OF ASSAULT AND BATTERY

As mentioned earlier in this book, there have been calls for the codification of the whole of criminal law, which at present is a confusing mixture of common law principles and statutory provisions, and various bodies have been involved in preparing this. The greatest difficulty is finding enough Parliamentary time or

COMMENT

There are many problems concerning the defence of consent. The following are examples:

The current position, involving as it does a possible disagreement between the House of Lords and the Court of Appeal as to the extent to which consent can be a defence for the more serious cases of bodily harm leaves a lot to be desired. The House of Lords appears to have decided that the defence of consent to actual or grievous bodily harm is not available unless it comes within one of the recognised exceptions. It could be argued that the Court of Appeal is taking a different approach and stating that the defence of consent is available unless this is felt to be against public policy.

Some would argue that the defence should not be available for 'horseplay', so that the participants in such activities would know that they cannot rely on the law to help them if the joke goes tragically wrong. This approach has been taken in civil law and has helped to curtail some of the more harmful practical jokes and rituals, particularly in the field of employment.

While it is accepted that attitudes change and the law should, in most cases, keep abreast of prevailing attitudes, the adoption of a 'case by case approach', as suggested by the Court of Appeal in *Wilson*, renders the law uncertain, which is both undesirable and unfair.

There also appears to be a fundamental disagreement among the judiciary about how to treat cases of bodily harm inflicted at the request of the victim. Some argue that the prevention of such activities is an interference with the liberty of the subject and is too paternalistic in approach. Increasingly, it is considered that what consenting adults do in the privacy of their homes is their own concern and the State should not intervene.

Critics of this view would argue that any intentional infliction of pain degrades both the aggressor and the victim and can lead to an escalation of the violence. As stated earlier, Lord Templeman subscribed to this view. The horrific case of Frederick and Rose West illustrates the lengths to which such cruelty can go, although in this case the poor victims were obviously not consenting.

These critics believe that, even in these more permissive days, society has a duty to draw the line somewhere and state the limits of what is acceptable. If the participants then wish to continue and hope that they will not be discovered, then that is their affair. One has some sympathy for those who can only obtain sexual gratification in such a fashion and, in many cases, their activities would never come before the courts. If they did, and the circumstances were not too excessive this could be reflected in the sentence. The state, however, by retaining the general rule that such behaviour comes under the heading of unacceptable violence, is not then being seen to condone such acts.

In *Laskey & Others* v *United Kingdom 1997*, The European Court of Human Rights refused to uphold a complaint by the men in *Brown* that their convictions were an unjustifiable interference with their right to respect for private life. Even that famously liberal court decided that their prosecutions were necessary in a democratic society for the protection of health.

It is also maintained that the young may well be corrupted by such actions. In the case of *Brown*, the 'victims' were young men and the perpetrators of the violence were middle-aged. There was also some evidence that a youth had been initiated into what were known as 'bondage affairs' at the age of 15.

It can be argued that, even in the less extreme situation in *Wilson*, a doctor was obviously concerned enough about the degree of harm to report the matter to the police. Why then should not the law take the matter seriously?

The law makes a distinction between actual consent and mere submission but, in practice, the two states may be confused. It was clear in *Wilson* that the wife desired to be branded but there could be other cases where a partner merely submitted to the infliction of harm, through fear, perhaps or for love of the partner. The decision in *Wilson*, which apparently sets the law's seal of approval on some violent acts, may make it more difficult for the victim to protest. It is submitted that a better approach in cases like *Wilson* would be not to prosecute or to take all the circumstances into account when sentencing.

In conclusion, it appears from the cases that Parliament badly needs to take the initiative in this matter and lay down clear guidelines on the use of consent as a defence.

indeed, the Parliamentary will to tackle the issue. Some offences will not require too much in the way of change, but other parts of the criminal law are considered to be so outdated that reform is urgently needed. As stated earlier, the whole of the area of offences against the person is just such an example and various bodies have been involved in studying this. The Criminal Law Revision Committee was one of the first to do so back in 1980, and most of their proposals were incorporated into later proposals.

In 1993, the Law Commission published a report (Law Com. No. 218), *Legislating the Criminal Code: Offences against the Person and General Defences*, which was carefully scrutinised by many bodies, among them the Home Office. In 1998, the latter produced a Home Office Consultation Document on the subject, together with a Draft Bill.

The Draft Bill incorporates the current offences of assault and battery into one new offence called assault with different components to it. Clause 4(1) of the Bill states that:

A person is guilty of an offence if:

a he intentionally or recklessly applies force to or causes an impact on the body of another or

b he intentionally or recklessly, causes the other to believe that any such force or impact is imminent.

It can be seen that the essence of the two old offences is still present but the wording is much improved. Professor Smith calls this reform 'an admirably clear restatement of the common law offences of assault and battery', although he has some misgivings about the different *actus reus* and *mens rea* required by 4(1)(a) and 4(1)(b), which he feels might leave loopholes in the law. The section is also different from that suggested by the Law Commission in that it makes no specific mention of consent, although a later clause states that the provisions are subject to any existing defences.

It is important to realise that this is only a consultation docment and has not yet been debated in Parliament.

KEY FACTS

- Assault and battery are two distinct offences, although the word 'assault' is often used as a verb to cover both types of offence
- Both offences were created at common law but are now held to be statutory offences under s.39 Criminal Justice Act 1988 (*DPP* v *Taylor*, *DPP* v *Little 1992*)
- The maximum sentence for either offence is six months imprisonment, coupled with a fine
- The definition of an assault is where the accused intentionally of recklessly causes the victim to apprehend immediate and unlawful violence
- The *actus reus* of assault is causing the victim to apprehend immediate and unlawful violence, (*Ireland 1997*), although the word 'apprehend' can cover states of mind which are less acute that than real fear. Anxiety would probably be sufficient

- The *mens rea* of assault is satisfied where such apprehension is caused either intentionally or recklessly (*Venna 1976*). The type of recklessness to be proved is *Cunningham* style recklessness (*Parmenter 1991*)

- The Court of Appeal, in *Constanza 1997*, decided that words alone could, in some circumstances, be enough to constitute an assault. The House of Lords went even further in *Ireland 1997* and held that even silent telephone calls could, if the *mens rea* of the defendant was established, amount to an assault. The court decided, however, that a battery could not be committed in such a fashion

- The victim must apprehend immediate violence but the courts will not inquire too deeply into the rationality of the fear, provided that it is a genuinely held belief (*Smith 1983*, *Ireland 1997*)

- A battery occurs where the defendant intentionally or recklessly applies unlawful physical force to the victim. Psychiatric injury caused by silent telephone calls will not suffice (*Ireland 1997*)

- The force applied need only be minimal, provided that it is unlawful (*Cole v Turner 1704*, *Collins v Wilcock 1984*). The slashing and even touching of someone's clothes could be included (*Day 1845*, *Thomas 1985*), although there is implied consent to a certain amount of touching in everyday life (*Collins v Wilcock 1984*)

- There is no requirement that the force must be directly inflicted (*Scott v Shepherd 1773*, *Martin 1881*, *Fagan v Metrpolitan Police Commissioner 1969*)

- The *actus reus* of a battery is the application of physical force on the victim (*Ireland 1997*)

- The *mens rea* is doing this intentionally or recklessly. Like assault, *Cunningham* or subjective recklessness must be proved (*Venna 1976*). The *mens rea* may be formed at a later time provided that the sequence of events is continuing (*Fagan v Metropolitan Police Commissioner 1969*).

- Consent by the victim may be a defence to assault and battery (*Attorney General's Reference (No. 6 of 1980) 1981*, *Brown & Others 1994*), provided that the activity comes within one of the recognised categories. Included are properly conducted sports like boxing, football, rugby and similar games (*Bradshaw 1878*, *Brown 1994*). Prize fights with bare knuckles and fist fights in the street are not (*Coney 1882*, *Donovan 1934*)

- Consent can also be given expressly or impliedly for lawful chastisement, (which was not the case in *Hopley 1860*), for lawful surgical operations and other procedures if there is some benefit in the activity, for dangerous exhibitions and for horseplay which goes wrong (*Jones 1987*, *Aitken 1992*)

- Consent will not be a defence where actual bodily harm is inflicted during the course of sexual activities (*Nichol 1807*, *Donovan 1934*, *Boyea 1992* and *Brown & Others 1994*), although the Court of Appeal appears to have made an exception to this with regard to 'bottom branding', likening this to a mere tattoo (*Wilson 1997*)

FIGURE 6.1 *Key facts chart on assault and battery*

activity

Using the cases of *Brown* and *Wilson* as a basis for your arguments, decide whether the defence of consent should be extended, curtailed or remain as it is.

6.4 ACTUAL BODILY HARM

This offence is found under s.47 Offences Against the Person Act 1861. It concerns an aggravated assault. It was stated, rather confusingly, by Hobhouse L J in *Chan-Fook 1994* that the offence 'must be an assault which besides being an assault (or assault and battery) causes to the victim some injury.'

There is no definition in the act itself as to what constitutes actual bodily harm, although case law has provided assistance, as seen below. The offence of occasioning actual bodily harm was created at common law and s.47 merely describes the penalty. In the case of *Courtie 1984*, however, the House of Lords decided that the offence of actual bodily harm should be treated as a statutory offence, despite the fact that the section merely states that:

> whosoever shall be convicted on indictment of any assault occasioning actual bodily harm shall be liable to imprisonment for not more than five years.

The offence has since been made a triable either way offence and the section lays down a maximum sentence of five years for when the offence is tried in the Crown Court. If the magistrates agree, however, the offence can be dealt with summarily, with a maximum prison sentence of only six months.

As mentioned earlier, actual bodily harm is a form of aggravated assault so before it is decided that the victim has suffered such harm, it is first necessary to establish that he has been subjected to either an assault or a battery. It is therefore very important to remember the constituents of these offences.

In the case of *Constanza 1997*, the Court of Appeal upheld a conviction under s.47 after deciding that an assault had been established and this assault had caused actual bodily harm.

The defendant, a former work colleague, had subjected the victim to a sustained campaign of harassment. This included numerous telephone calls, over 800 letters, following the victim, daubing offensive words on her door and making other unsolicited visits. As a result, the woman became clinically depressed and, after receiving two further letters, of the belief that the man was going to harm her physically.

The Court of Appeal stated that there was sufficient evidence that the victim was in fear of immediate violence because it might have occurred at any time, particularly as the defendant lived quite close.

The Court of Appeal also decided that there was no actual rule that an assault could not be committed by words alone and said that earlier authorities on this which stated otherwise rested on a dubious foundation.

In *Ireland 1997*, another case concerning harassment, the House of Lords upheld the view that repeated silent telephone calls could constitute an assault.

The court decided, however, that a battery could not be committed in this way, because this offence required proof that unlawful force had been applied.

6.4.1 THE DEFINITION OF ACTUAL BODILY HARM

In *Miller 1954*, the definition was said to include 'any hurt or injury calculated to interfere with the health or comfort of the victim'.

In *Chan-Fook 1994* the Court of Appeal stated that the words 'actual bodily harm':

> are three words of the English language which require no elaboration and in the ordinary course should not receive any. The word 'harm' is a synonym for 'injury'. The word 'actual' indicates that the injury (although there is no need for it to be permanent) should not be so trivial as to be wholly insignificant . . . The body of the victim includes all parts of his body, including his organs, his nervous system and his brain. Bodily injury therefore may include injury to any of those parts of his body responsible for his mental and other faculties.

In this case, the Court of Appeal held that the judge had misdirected the jury when he said that it was enough to amount to actual bodily harm if the victim had been put in 'a nervous, maybe hysterical condition'. She had been questioned roughly by the defendant and locked in a room, after being suspected of stealing an engagement ring.

From this it is apparent that, while actual bodily harm encompasses physical harm, psychiatric injury and other identifiable clinical conditions, it does not cover emotions like fear, distress or panic. There may well have been a common assault and even a battery if the victim was manhandled but the more serious offence under s.47 would not exist.

6.4.2 THE *ACTUS REUS* OF ACTUAL BODILY HARM

This is simply an assault, (with the word used in its wider sense), causing actual bodily harm. As with a battery, it appears that the bodily harm need not be directly applied. In *DPP* v *K (a minor) 1990*, a 15-year-old boy left his chemistry class alleging that he needed to wash acid from his hand. He took a boiling tube of concentrated sulphuric acid with him to the toilet block in order to conduct some tests of his own. While he was experimenting with the acid, he heard footsteps and, in his panic, poured the remaining acid into a hot air hand and face dryer. The footsteps then receded but the boy left the acid in the dryer and returned to class, intending to deal with the problem at a later time. Unfortunately for him and the victim, the latter went into the toilets before this and his face was permanently scarred after he turned on the dryer and the acid was ejected. K's conviction for actual bodily harm was upheld by the Divisional Court.

6.4.3 THE *MENS REA* OF ACTUAL BODILY HARM

Originally, there was a great deal of confusion over the *mens rea* for this offence but in *Savage and Parmenter 1992*, the House of Lords clearly stated that the *mens rea* is the same as that required for common assault and battery. This means that all the prosecution has to show is

that the accused intended or was reckless about putting the victim in the state of apprehending immediate physical violence or intended or was reckless about touching the victim unlawfully. There is no requirement to go further and prove that he intended or was reckless about causing actual bodily harm.

This restated the position laid down in the case of *Roberts 1971*. Following this case there had been confusion over the subject in the Court of Appeal. In *Roberts*, the victim had jumped out of a car travelling between 20 and 40 miles per hour, after the driver, who was giving her a lift to a party, had told her to undress and had grabbed her coat. He had claimed earlier that he had beaten up other girls who had refused his advances.

The Court of Appeal upheld his conviction for actual bodily harm because, although he had not directly inflicted the injuries, he was responsible for them. The defendant had inflicted a battery on the girl and her action of jumping out of the car was one which could reasonably have been foreseen as a consequence of this. The court stated that the matter would have been different if the girl had done something 'so 'daft' ... or so unexpected ... that no reasonable man could be expected to foresee it'.

This view prevailed until the case of *Spratt 1991*. The defendant had fired his air gun out of his window and had injured a child playing below. He claimed that he had been aiming at a sign and was unaware that children were in the vicinity. The Court of Appeal, without referring to *Roberts*, suddenly decided that subjective recklessness about causing, not just a battery, but actual bodily harm itself, was required. The court therefore quashed the defendant's conviction for actual bodily harm because the jury had not been directed in this way. This new view of the law was later followed in the case of *Parmenter 1991*.

By a strange and embarrassing coincidence, however, in the case of *Savage 1991*, decided on the same day as Spratt, the original view of the law had been upheld by another sitting of the Court of Appeal! The defendant had thrown a glass of beer over a former girlfriend of her husband. While attacking her rival, the beer glass had also left her hand (she claimed this was an accident), and had broken and cut the victim's wrist. The conviction for grievous bodily harm was quashed but the defendant was found guilty of the lesser crime of actual bodily harm. With regard to the *mens rea* required for this latter offence, the Court of Appeal restated the position in *Roberts*, although, once again, the name of that case was not mentioned.

There were therefore two conflicting views as to the *mens rea* required for actual bodily harm and, as stated, the House of Lords was called upon to decide the matter in the joint appeals of *Savage and Parmenter 1992*.

The House of Lords decided that the law was correctly decided in *Roberts*. Lord Ackner tactfully suggested that the Court of Appeal had gone astray in the cases of *Spratt* and *Parmenter* because the case of *Roberts* did not appear in Archbold's Criminal Pleading. The latter book did however state that the *mens rea* required for actual bodily harm was the same as for common assault.

The position has now been clarified and there is now no doubt that the *mens rea* for actual bodily harm is the same as for common assault and battery. If actual bodily harm results as a consequence of either putting the person in fear of a battery intentionally or recklessly, or intentionally or recklessly touching the victim unlawfully, then the greater crime under s.47

has been committed. There is no extra requirement to prove that the defendant intended to cause actual bodily harm itself or had been reckless about whether this would happen.

It should be remembered that, when recklessness is alleged, *Cunningham* style recklessness must be proved, as was clearly affirmed by the Court of Appeal in the case of *Venna 1976*.

Before we leave this offence, it should be noted that a person charged with wounding under s.20 may, instead, be convicted of the lesser offence of actual bodily harm.

It is not, however, possible for a person charged under s.47 to be convicted, in the alternative of common assault or battery, if he has not been charged with those offences. Assault and battery are summary offences only.

6.4.4 THE DEFENCE OF A CITIZEN'S ARREST

General defences will be looked at in Chapter 10 but one deserving a special mention here is the common law right to make a citizen's arrest, as affirmed by the Court of Appeal in the case of *Kelbie 1996*.

The court quashed the latter's conviction for actual bodily harm after hearing conflicting versions of events. The victim alleged that the defendant had accused her of begging, had

KEY FACTS

- Actual bodily harm is an aggravated assault, details of which appear under s.47 OAPA
- The offence is a statutory one (*Courtie 1984*), for which the maximum punishment is five years imprisonment
- The prosecution must first establish that the existence of an assault or a battery (*Constanza 1997*)

If fear of immediate harm is present, an assault may arise from harassment caused by words alone or even by silent telephone calls (*Constanza 1997, Ireland 1997*)

- A battery, however, cannot be committed this way; it requires unlawful force (*Ireland 1997*). Such force can, however, be inflicted indirectly, as in *DPP* v *K (a minor) 1990*
- The word 'actual' means more than trivial, the word 'harm' means some injury and the words 'bodily harm' include psychiatric injury. The words do not cover mere emotions like distress, fear and panic (*Chan-Fook 1994*)

- The *actus reus* of s.47 is an assault causing actual bodily harm
- The *mens rea* is the same as for an assault or a battery, i.e. the defendant has intentionally or recklessly caused the victim to apprehend that a battery might be inflicted upon him (assault) or has intentionally or recklessly unlawfully touched the victim (a battery)
- There is no further requirement to show that the defendant intended to cause actual bodily harm (*Roberts 1971, Savage and Parmenter 1992*)
- The recklessness must be subjectively proved, as with all non-fatal offences against the person (*Cunningham 1957, Venna 1976*)

FIGURE 6.2 *Key facts chart on actual bodily harm*

roughly taken hold of her and marched her to a police station.

The accused, on the other hand, claimed that the victim had approached him and had assaulted him when he asked for her authorisation. He argued that he had only taken hold of her when she refused to stop her attack. The judge, however, had refused to direct the jury on the right to make such a citizen's arrest and only described the possible defence of self defence.

The Court of Appeal held that the jury should have been told of the survival of this ancient right, where the degree of force that was permitted might well differ from that in self defence. As stated, the appeal succeeded.

6.5 MALICIOUS WOUNDING OR GRIEVOUS BODILY HARM UNDER SECTION 20 OAPA 1861

S.20 states that:

whosoever shall unlawfully and maliciously wound or inflict any grievous bodily harm upon any person, either with or without any weapon or instrument shall be guilty of an offence.

The maximum punishment for this offence is, surprisingly, the same as for actual bodily harm, i.e. imprisonment for five years.

COMMENT

The Offences Against the Person Act 1861 was merely a consolidating act and made no attempt to rationalise the law which came from several different sources. S.20, however, has always been thought of as the more serious offence and it appears very strange to a layman that it attracts the same maximum penalty as actual bodily harm. It is one more reason why reform in this area of law is long overdue.

It can be seen from the definition of s.20 that the offence has two aspects to it, the malicious wounding of another or the malicious infliction of grievous bodily harm. It is important for the prosecution to make a correct charge, as otherwise the defendant could escape liability. This unfortunate state of affairs occurred in *C (a minor)* v *Eisenhower 1984*, where pellets from the defendant's air gun had caused injury to the victim's eye. There was bruising under his eye and rupturing of the internal blood vessels surrounding it but, crucially, no breaking of the skin. The Divisional Court held that no wounding had taken place. It was decided that there must be 'a break in the continuity of the whole skin'. It was, however, pointed out that the term 'skin' may also include the skin of an internal cavity where it is continuous with the outer skin. It is also important to realise that if there is proof of a wounding, the actual injury need not be severe; any breaking of the skin will suffice.

▼ COMMENT

The latter fact has also been criticised. Many people would be puzzled to learn that the degree of harm needed for malicious wounding need not be as high as that required for the second aspect of the defence, i.e. the infliction of grievous bodily harm. To the non-legal eye, the infliction of a minor wound would equate more easily to the offence of actual bodily harm. On the other hand, the law takes the view that the use of a weapon to cause any sort of wound is a serious matter, however small the actual harm.

With regard to the second part of the offence, it has to be established that the defendant has unlawfully and maliciously inflicted grievous bodily harm upon the victim. In the case of *DPP* v *Smith 1961*, the House of Lords held that the words 'grievous bodily harm' simply mean really serious harm. In *Saunders 1985*, it was also decided that it would not be a misdirection to leave out the word 'really'; the words 'serious harm' would suffice.

6.5.1 THE *ACTUS REUS* OF THE OFFENCE UNDER S.20

This consists of an unlawful wounding or the unlawful infliction of grievous bodily harm.

The word 'inflict' in s.20 has caused problems. It will be seen that, in s.18 OAPA, where the offence of grievous bodily harm with intent is laid down, the word 'caused' is used, rather than 'inflict'. The courts have therefore been faced with the problem of whether the words cause and inflict are synonymous or should be interpreted differently. If the latter approach is taken, it has to be decided whether the word 'inflict' in s.20 means that any harm done to the victim has to be directly inflicted upon him. Until the House of Lords' decision in *Burstow 1997*, there seemed to be conflicting authorities on this. One strain of cases suggested that the

word 'inflict' should be interpreted narrowly and only apply if the defendant had caused direct harm. An example of this approach was the early case of *Clarence 1888*, noted earlier in the chapter relating to the issue of consent. The defendant was not held to have inflicted grievous bodily harm on his wife by infecting her with venereal disease because he had not made a direct assault upon her. She had consented to the sexual intercourse, even though she would not have done so if she had known the full facts.

The other line of cases treated the word 'inflict' in the same way as the word 'cause'. The judges took the view that the defendant could be convicted if the harm was caused in a more indirect way. The case of *Martin 1881*, mentioned above, is an example, where the defendant was convicted under s.20 when he placed a wire across the gangway in a theatre, because he had indirectly caused the injuries. Similarly, in *Halliday 1889*, a man was convicted of grievous bodily harm when he so frightened the victim that the latter jumped through a window and sustained serious injuries. In *Lewis 1970*, a husband was equally liable when his wife broke her legs in her efforts to escape him.

In *Wilson 1984*, the House of Lords looked at this conflict and preferred the latter approach. The law, therefore, is that there may be liability under s.20, even though there was no direct assault. Their Lordships relied on an Australian case, that of *Salisbury 1976*, to support their contention, although certain exceptions were detailed in that case.

In *Burstow 1997*, a similar view was taken. The defendant had refused to acknowledge that a relationship was over and had subjected the victim to a campaign of harassment. He sent letters and photographs, made telephone calls, followed the woman, stole her washing and planted offensive items in her garden. He refused to stop his campaign even though he had been warned about his behaviour, had been prosecuted and even imprisoned. As a result of this obsessive attention, the woman had suffered a severe depressive illness amounting to grievous harm of a psychological nature.

The Court of Appeal, and subsequently the

COMMENT

The decisions in *Constanza*, *Ireland* and *Burstow*, show a willingness on the part of the judges to take a liberal approach to the wording in the ancient OAPA, and are, therefore, to be welcomed. It has been officially recognised that cases on stalking are on the increase and, at a time when there was no specific legislation to deal with this problem, the courts needed to be flexible to avoid the injustice of a person walking free from the court after engaging in conduct which devastated the victim.

The position has been partially rectified by the Protection from Harassment Act 1997, which creates two new offences. The less serious summary offence is committed where the defendant pursues a course of conduct that amounts to harassment of the victim. It requires harassment on at least two occasions. It is specifically laid down in s.7 that the word 'conduct' can include words alone. The maximum punishment is six months imprisonment and a fine on level 5 of the scale.

Despite its short time in existence, the courts have made it clear that the act is to be confined to clear cases of actual harassment and cannot be used to take away civil liberties such as the rights to meet, march and demonstrate, even by extremists.

The more serious offence, of putting a person in fear of violence appears in s.4. Once again, there must be conduct causing such fear on at least two occasions and the defendant must have known or should have been aware that his conduct would cause such fear.

This offence is a triable either way offence and, if tried on indictment, the maximum punishment is five years imprisonment.

The creation of these new offences means that the judges will no longer have to strain the meaning of existing words in the OAPA. It also gives out a clear statement that the State is not prepared to tolerate stalking and other obsessive behaviour. Burstow, for example, has not given up his campaign of harassment and, in January 1999, was given a fourth term of imprisonment by Bracknell magistrates.

House of Lords, ignored the limitations on which type of harm could result in liability, imposed in the case of *Salisbury*, and stated that there could be liability for grievous bodily harm without any direct or indirect application of physical violence.

6.5.2 THE *MENS REA* OF THE OFFENCE UNDER S.20

It can be seen from the definition of the offence, that the wounding or infliction of grievous bodily harm must be done 'maliciously'. This word requires explanation. It was decided in the case of *Cunningham 1957*, discussed earlier in Chapter 3 in relation to the subject of murder, that the word has a very precise meaning in law and should not be equated with wickedness. Use of the word in law means that the defendant must be shown to

have intended to inflict harm or have been reckless as to whether such harm would occur.

In *Cunningham*, (not the same *Cunningham* as in recklessness), it was decided that the defendant would only be liable if he had actually foreseen that his actions would cause grievous bodily harm, i.e. really serious harm. Currently, the defendant can be convicted more easily. It was decided by the Court of Appeal in *Mowatt 1968*, that foresight of such a high degree of harm need not be proved. It is enough for the prosecution to show that the accused must have foreseen that some harm would result. The House of Lords, in *Savage and Parmenter 1992*, approved of this diluting of the *mens rea* for grievous bodily harm under s.20.

In the same case, it was also affirmed that it is possible for a defendant charged under s.20 to be convicted, instead, of actual bodily harm, provided that the jury has been properly directed about this.

6.6 MALICIOUS WOUNDING OR GRIEVOUS BODILY HARM UNDER SECTION 18 OAPA 1861

This is the most serious form of assault other than homicide.

S.18 OAPA 1861, as amended by the Criminal Law Act 1967, states:

> Whosoever shall unlawfully and maliciously by any means whatsoever wound or cause any grievous bodily harm to any person . . . with intent to do some grievous bodily harm . . . or with the intent to resist or prevent the lawful apprehension or detainer of any person, shall be guilty of an offence.

At first glance, this seems to be very similar to the offence under s.20 and the words 'wounding' and 'grievous bodily harm' have similar meanings. There are, however, important distinctions to be made between the offences.

As was noted earlier, the s.18 offence is committed when the accused has 'caused' grievous bodily harm to another. Taken literally, therefore, the offence is wider than s.20 and there is no requirement that the wounding or bodily harm must be directly inflicted. The section also uses the words 'by any means whatsoever' which reinforces this.

In *Mandair 1994*, the House of Lords decided that a charge of grievous bodily harm under s.18 is wide enough to cover an allegation of 'inflicting' grievous bodily harm under s.20 in a case where the full requirements of the s.18 offence cannot be made out. This approach allows the defendant to be convicted on the lesser charge, even though he has not been charged with it.

The House of Lords also used this opportunity to overrule the Court of Appeal decision in *Field 1993*, in which it had been held that a wrong drafting of an offence under s.20, which stated that the defendant had 'caused' grievous bodily harm, instead of having 'inflicted' it, was not known in law! Their Lordships stated that the wrong word could be interpreted to mean causing grievous bodily harm by inflicting it.

6.6.1 THE ACTUS REUS OF THE OFFENCE UNDER S.18

The *actus reus* of s.18 is committed when the accused unlawfully and maliciously wounds another or causes him grievous bodily harm by any means whatsoever.

6.6.2 THE MENS REA OF THE OFFENCE UNDER S.18

It is very important to realise that recklessness will not suffice for liability under s.18. The wounding or grievous bodily harm must be

---

KEY FACTS

- There are two offences describing these crimes laid down in s.18 and s.20 OAPA 1861
- Both offences have two aspects to the *actus reus*, malicious wounding and grievous bodily harm
- To constitute a wounding, there must be a breaking of the whole skin (*C (a minor) v Eisenhower 1984*), but the injury itself need not be a severe one
- The word 'inflict' in s.20 is to be interpreted in the same way as the word 'cause' in s.18 (*Wilson 1984, Burstow 1997*)

- This approach enables a conviction to be obtained in cases of psychiatric harm caused by stalking and other obsessive behaviour (*Constanza 1997, Ireland 1997, Burstow 1997*), although the creation of the two new offences under the Protection From Harassment Act 1997 will lessen the need for this
- To decide on the *mens rea* of s.20, the word 'malicious' needs to be examined. It now means intending to wound or inflict some harm on the victim or being reckless about this. The earlier requirement that the defendant must have intended to inflict serious harm has been changed, (*Mowatt 1968, Savage and Parmenter 1992*). *Cunningham* style recklessness is required
- It is possible for the defendant to be convicted of the lesser offence under s.47, if a s.20 offence cannot be proved (*Savage and Parmenter 1992*)
- The offence under s.18 OAPA is, apart from rape, the most serious of the non-fatal offences against the person
- The maximum sentence is life imprisonment
- The *actus reus* occurs where the defendant wounds or causes grievous bodily harm by any means whatsoever. *Prima facie*, it is therefore wider than s.20
- The *mens rea* will only be established if it can be proved that the defendant intended to cause grievous bodily harm or intended to resist or prevent an arrest or detention
- The word 'intention' has the same meaning as for murder, The prosecution must, as a minimum, show that the defendant foresaw as a virtually certain consequence that his actions would cause serious harm. The jury will then be the body to decide the matter
- If this cannot be proved, the word 'cause' has been held to be wide enough to allow, in the alternative, a conviction under s.20

FIGURE 6.3 *Key facts chart on grievous bodily harm*

done maliciously but also with a further intention to either cause grievous bodily harm or with intention to resist or prevent a lawful arrest or detention.

The word 'intention' has the same meaning as required for the crime of murder. The prosecution must therefore prove that it was the defendant's purpose to cause grievous bodily harm or to resist arrest or that he foresaw this as a virtually certain consequence of his actions. If the latter is shown, then the jury may infer that he had the necessary intention, just as in the murder cases looked at earlier in this book.

activities

1 Evaluate the following statement:

❝ *The state of the law concerning non-fatal offences against the person is uncertain, unjust and badly in need of reform.* ❞

2 Describe the offences which might, (or might not), have been committed in the following scenario.

Al Corleone and Michael Capone were the leaders of two notorious London gangs, the Jets and the Comets. They agreed to merge the two gangs and to have a fist fight to decide who should be in overall charge. During the fight, Al's eye was badly bruised by the knuckle-duster used by Michael and there were signs of internal bleeding. Al then landed a heavy punch on Michael, which broke the latter's collarbone. While trying to deflect further blows from Al, Michael was outraged to hear the abuse being heaped upon him by Sonny, a member of the opposing gang. Michael shouted, menacingly, 'If I were not so busy right now, I would not take such language from you!'

Mrs Malone, a bystander, was jeered at as she tried to pass by and, although she wasn't hurt, she was jostled and pushed by a member of the gang and her skirt was grabbed.

Meanwhile, Moll, Al's ex girlfriend has complained to the police about his obsessive behaviour. She said that he is refusing to accept that their relationship is over, is following her everywhere and has made so many silent telephone calls to her that she is in a state of mental collapse.

6.7 POSSIBLE REFORM OF NON-FATAL OFFENCES AGAINST THE PERSON

The latest Draft Bill from the Law Commission, attached to the Report (Law Com. No. 218), *Legislating the Criminal Code: Offences Against the Person and General Principles*, would sweep away the old fashioned wording of these offences and provide more modern and sensible definitions.

A person would be guilty of assault if he intentionally or recklessly applied force to or caused an impact on the body of another:

● Without the latter's consent or

● Where the act was intended to cause injury, with or without the consent of the other, or

● Where he intentionally or recklessly, without the consent of the other, caused the other to believe that any such force or impact was imminent

● Ordinary touching in everyday life would be excluded

● Actual bodily harm would be replaced by the offence of intentional or reckless injury

● The offence of reckless serious injury would be implemented in place of s.20 OAPA, and the crime of intentional serious injury would replace s.18 OAPA. The word 'injury' would include physical and mental injury. The words 'serious harm' are not defined and would be left to the jury.

COMMENT

It can be seen that the Commission favours abolishing the offence of battery and including this within the new definition of assault. The wording of the other offences would be much improved. It is obviously an unsatisfactory state of affairs that the judges are still having to deal with old-fashioned wording laid down in 1861.

It remains to be seen, however, whether either this Bill or the one produced by the Home Office in 1998 will ever become law. One would hope that, at last, we are seeing some signs of action, but the will of Parliament to effect such much-needed reforms still needs to be demonstrated.

6.8 OTHER OFFENCES

6.8.1 OBSTRUCTING A POLICE OFFICER IN THE EXECUTION OF HIS DUTY

A person who resists or wilfully obstructs a police officer in the execution of his duty or someone helping the police officer in his duty, will be guilty of an offence under the Police Act 1996. This offence carries a maximum penalty of one month's imprisonment and a fine not exceeding level 3 on the standard scale.

6.8.2 ASSAULTING A POLICE OFFICER IN THE EXECUTION OF HIS DUTY

This offence is also found in the Police Act 1996 and is obviously more serious. To reflect this, it has a maximum punishment of six months imprisonment and a fine not exceeding level 5.

One of the most difficult aspects of these offences is to decide exactly when the officer is acting in the execution of his duty. If the courts are not convinced of this, the conviction will be quashed.

6.8.3 INDECENT ASSAULT

Under ss.14 and 15 Sexual Offences Act 1956, as amended, it is an offence for a person to make an indecent assault on either a woman or a man. The maximum penalty is ten years imprisonment.

In *Court 1988*, the House of Lords stated that there were three requirements for this offence:

1 An intentional assault on the victim.
2 An assault which was considered by 'right-minded persons' to be indecent.
3 A further intention to commit an indecent act.

This offence covers a wide range of cases, including those where the crime of rape cannot be established, as where the victim is forced to engage in oral sex or other acts as in *Court*, where the defendant admitted putting a girl of 12 across his knee and spanking her.

6.8.4 RAPE

Reports about this offence have been escalating since the Second World War. One reason for this could be the increasing willingness on the part of women to complain about such conduct, although, sadly, it is estimated that only one in four rapes actually gets reported at all.

The offence of rape is defined in s.1(1) Sexual Offences Act 1956, as amended by the Criminal Justice & Public Order Act 1994. The amended section states that it is an offence for a man to rape a woman or another man. Under s.1(2), a rape is committed if the man has sexual intercourse, either vaginal or anal, with someone who does not consent, and at the time, the man knows that the other does not consent or is reckless as to whether the person has consented.

Under s.44 of the Act, the act of sexual intercourse need not be completed, proof of penetration will be enough. The man need not ejaculate, nor need the woman's hymen be ruptured. The offence is also committed if the man refuses to withdraw after being asked to do so, as in *Kaitamaki 1985*.

One of the essential elements of the offence is that the woman (or man) does not consent to sexual intercourse. The word is not defined but, over the years, the cases have established that a woman is not consenting when she is asleep, unconscious, mentally backward, too young to give a proper consent, as in the case of *Howard 1966*, or senseless through drink or drugs, as in *Malone 1998*. The burden of proof is on the prosecution to show a lack of consent. This was established in *Harling 1938*, where a girl of 13 was shown to have a weak intellect and was therefore not held to be capable of giving a valid consent.

The victim in *Flattery 1877*, was not held to have consented when she thought the intercourse was part of a medical examination, nor was the woman in *Williams 1923*, when she was told that the act was being performed in order to improve her singing! In *Olugboja 1982*, the Court of Appeal stressed the difference between an active assent and a mere submission through fear. The court decided that the young girl in question had not consented because, although actual violence had not been used against her, the man had threatened to keep her all night in a bungalow if she did not submit.

As mentioned earlier in this chapter, the wife in *Clarence 1888* was held to have consented to the act of sexual intercourse even though she would not have done so if she had known the man had a venereal disease. Presumably, the same principle would apply to a man with the HIV virus, although the decisions in *Burstow* and *Ireland* would suggest that he could now be convicted of grievous bodily harm. Perhaps less seriously, it was held in *Linekar 1994*, that a prostitute had given a valid consent even though she would not done so if she had known that she was not going to be paid.

Under s.1(2) Sexual Offences (Amendment) Act 1976, it is stated that an honest belief in the woman's consent will mean that the offence has not been committed. This put into statutory form the decision, in *DPP v Morgan 1976*, where the House of Lords also decided that an honest but unreasonable belief in the other's consent could afford a defence.

This view has been criticised so the amended section goes on to say that the fact as to whether the man has reasonable grounds for his belief is a matter to be taken into account with all the other evidence to see whether the belief is honest.

Rape within marriage – the changing law

Until 1994, when further amendments were made to the Sexual Offences Act 1976, the definition of rape included the word 'unlawful'. The view prevailed, therefore, that sexual intercourse within marriage, even without the woman's consent, could not be termed unlawful. In 1736, a quote by Hale, an eminent jurist, illustrated a view of marriage that has persisted until very recent times. He stated that a man 'could not be guilty of a rape committed by himself upon his lawful wife for by their mutual matrimonial consent and contract, the wife hath given herself as in this kind unto her husband which she cannot retract'.

Fortunately for women, the position gradually changed. In *Miller 1954*, it was decided that whereas a husband could not be convicted of rape within marriage, he could be found guilty of actual bodily harm. In *O'Brien 1974*, a husband was found guilty of raping his wife when the parties had already obtained a decree nisi for divorce. In *Steele 1976*, a husband was convicted when he disobeyed a undertaking he had given not to molest his wife and in *Roberts 1986*, a husband was found guilty when he raped his wife when a formal separation agreement was in existence.

The Law Commission was busily preparing a report on this subject when, in 1992, in the case of *R*, the House of Lords finally decided that a husband could commit the offence of rape within marriage even when these situations did not exist.

summary

We have discovered that the main offences to be considered for examination purposes are assault and battery, actual bodily harm and grievous bodily harm under ss.18 and 20 OAPA 1861.

All these offences are now classed as statutory offences, although the first three were developed at common law.

The *mens rea* for all the offences, except the most serious one under s.18, includes recklessness. This is subjective recklessness as laid down in *Cunningham 1957*.

We have noted that it is possible for those charged under s.18 and s.20 to be convicted of a lesser offence, even if this not included in the charge. On the other hand, it is not possible for a person charged under s.47 to be convicted in the alternative with common assault or battery.

We have seen that there is an urgent need for reform of the law relating to assault and battery and the more serious offences. We have seen that a start has been made with the Home Office Consultation Paper on non-fatal offences and by the creation of the new offences to deal with stalking.

We have also looked at certain offences against the police and the crime of rape, which is sexual intercourse, committed intentionally or recklessly, without the other's consent. The offence may be against a woman or a man and can now be committed while a marriage is still subsisting.

....

CHAPTER 7

PROPERTY OFFENCES I: THEFT AND RELATED OFFENCES

7.1 INTRODUCTION

IN THIS CHAPTER, we shall be looking in depth at the law of theft, the definition of which is found in s.1 Theft Act 1968. We shall also be discussing, albeit more briefly, the related offences of robbery, found under s.8 of the same act, burglary and aggravated burglary described under ss.9 and 10 and blackmail under s.21. In Chapter 8, offences concerning deception will be explored and in Chapter 9 criminal damage will be examined.

The law of theft encompasses many different forms of stealing, from the shoplifting of a single low priced article to the stealing millions of pounds from a large company. Robbery can be loosely defined as theft plus violence, whereas burglary could be described as trespass, plus theft or other serious crimes, such as grievous bodily harm or rape. The defendant will be charged with aggravated burglary if he commits the crime armed with a firearm or other weapon. Lastly, blackmail occurs where money or other property is demanded with menaces.

7.2 THEFT

Stealing from others has always been considered a reprehensible crime. Number Eight of the Ten Commandments states firmly that 'Thou shalt not steal', and nearly every jurisdiction has some sort of sanction against stealing from others. In this country, the law is to be found in the Theft Act 1968. This Act was passed after the Criminal Law Revision Committee looked at this topic and suggested important changes. It was decided that the time was right for 'a new law of theft and related offences ... embodied in a modern statute'. The idea was to replace old-fashioned terms like larceny and, instead, to try to make the law more understandable and more easily accessible. Whether this aim has been achieved is debatable but, even with its shortcomings, it is a definite improvement on the old law. Arguably, much of the current confusion in this area has been caused by the prosecutors, rather than by the drafters of the Act. The Crown Prosecution Service and other bodies have caused problems on occasion by charging offenders with the crime of theft rather than the offence of obtaining property by deception. The judges, particularly those in the House of Lords, have then felt obliged to strain the meanings of the words in the Theft Act in order that the obviously guilty should not be allowed to escape liability, thereby causing difficulties in later cases.

Theft is a triable either way offence. Originally, the maximum penalty was ten years imprisonment if tried on indictment. Now, under s.7, as amended by the Criminal Justice Act 1991, the maximum sentence has been reduced to seven years.

The first point to note is that the whole of the

law of theft is to be found in just seven sections of the Theft Act 1968. S.1 contains the complete definition of theft, and ss.2–6 give further information on this. It will be seen that s.2 and s.6 contain further detail on the *mens rea* of theft and that ss.3,4 and 5 elaborate on the *actus reus*. As noted above, s.7 lays down the punishment.

The definition, under s.1 Theft Act 1968, states that a person is guilty of theft if he 'dishonestly appropriates property belonging to another with the intention of permanently depriving the other of it'.

The *actus reus* is appropriating property belonging to another. The offender will have the necessary *mens rea* if he does this in a dishonest way, intending to permanently deprive the true owner of it. This can be seen more easily in Figure 7.1.

The following newspaper article gives detail of a carefully planned crime in which all the elements of theft appear to be present.

Thieves target power bikes

POLICE believe a team of thieves are stealing high-powered motorcycles to order and driving them away in a refrigerated van to mask the noise of the alarm.

Well over £50,000 worth of top class machines have disappeared in mid-Essex in the last month.

One was in a locked shed and apparently securely chained when it was stolen.

The last victim was the owner of a silver Kawasaki 1100, worth £7,000, stolen from Sycamore Way, Chelmsford in the early hours of Monday. And a BMW K100 was taken from High Chelmer, Chelmsford recently.

Police believe the thieves could be targeting owners and their machines for some time before they strike – usually late at night or in the early morning.

They also think the machines could eventually be loaded into a container and shipped abroad. Detectives know one particular gang are using refrigerated vans.

Taken from an article in the *Essex Chronicle*, 11 September 1998

The *actus reus* and *mens rea* of theft now need to be examined in more detail.

7.2.1 THE *ACTUS REUS* OF THEFT

It has been noted that the *actus reus* of theft is committed when a person 'appropriates property belonging to another'.

The words 'appropriates', under s.3, 'property', under s.4, and the phrase 'belonging to another', under s.5, need to be looked at more fully.

Appropriates (s.3)

This part of the definition of theft is the one that has caused the greatest problems for the courts. The word is described in s.3 of the Act and the current major authority on its interpretation is found in the case of *Gomez 1993*, a House of Lords' decision.

S.3 Theft Act states that:

Theft		
Section	Word or phrase	*Actus reus* or *mens rea*
2	dishonestly	*mens rea*
3	appropriates	*actus reus*
4	property	*actus reus*
5	belonging to another	*actus reus*
6	with the intention of depriving the other of it	*mens rea*

FIGURE 7.1 *The elements of theft*

> any assumption by a person of the rights of an owner amounts to be an appropriation, and this includes, where he has come by the property (innocently or not) without stealing it, any later assumption of a right to it by keeping or dealing with it as owner.

A person appropriates property, therefore, when he assumes the rights of the true owner. It is easy to see that he would be classed as doing this if he unlawfully took away the property of another, sold it or destroyed it without permission, retained goods after they should have been returned or treated the property of another as his own. In the case of *Pitham and Hehl 1977*, the Court of Appeal decided that a man who invited the two defendants into his friend's house while the latter was in prison and then sold them some of his furniture, had been assuming the rights of the owner. He was therefore held to have appropriated the property and this decision meant that the defendants' conviction for handling stolen goods could be upheld.

At first sight, the explanation of appropriation in s.3 appears to be straightforward but, unfortunately for the student, over the years since the passing of the Act, various problems have arisen with it. One point which needed to be addressed by the judges was whether the thief has to assume all the rights of the real owner to be classed as appropriating his property or whether it is enough for him to assume some, or even just one of the real owner's rights. A second difficulty was to establish at what time the appropriation of property takes place and, following on from this, whether there can be more than one appropriation of the property. The third area of contention has given rise to a great deal of comment from both judges and academics. The courts have had to decide whether an appropriation of property can be said to have taken place in cases where the real owner appears to have given his consent. It should be noted that this point is often the subject of essay or problem questions set by examination boards. Other problems faced by the courts included the position of whether there has to be an actual taking to amount to an appropriation and what course of action should be taken in cases where the principles of criminal law and civil law appeared to be in conflict. These problems are all dealt with below and most of them were covered in the case of *Gomez 1993*.

Does the thief have to assume all the rights of the real owner?

This question was addressed by the House of Lords, in *Morris; Anderton v Burnside 1984*. Lord Roskill stated clearly that it is enough for the prosecution to prove that any of the rights of the owner have been assumed. The House of Lords later affirmed this view of the law in the case of *Gomez 1993*.

In *Morris*, mentioned above, the defendant had taken some goods from a supermarket shelf and substituted lower price labels for the ones currently on the goods. He then went to the checkout desk and paid the lower price and was subsequently arrested.

In *Anderton v Burnside*, a shopper had removed the price label from a joint of pork and replaced it with a much lower price from another item. He reached the checkout but was arrested before he had attempted to pay for the goods.

Both offenders were appealing against their convictions for theft. Their contention was that they had not appropriated property belonging to another, because they had not assumed all the rights of the real owner. Both appeals were dismissed. The House of Lords decided that they had assumed at least one of the rights of the real owners of the store by switching the labels on the goods and this action was sufficient to amount to an appropriation.

At what time does the appropriation take place?

In *Gomez 1993*, Lord Keith refused to follow another statement by Lord Roskill that the appropriation only occurred when the labels were switched and the goods were placed into a supermarket basket. Lord Keith decided that the appropriation took place earlier than this. He stated that:

the switching of the price labels on the article is in itself an assumption of one of the rights of the owner, whether or not it is accompanied by some other act such as removing the article from the shelf and placing it in a basket or trolley. No one but the owner has the right to remove the price label from an article or to place a price label on it.

He dealt with the possible problem of a practical joker being convicted of theft by arguing that such a person would not have the *mens rea* for the offence because he would not be dishonest and would not have intended to permanently deprive the owner of the goods. He would, however, have committed the *actus reus* of theft because he had appropriated property belonging to another.

It can be seen, therefore, that *Gomez* has decided that an appropriation takes place the moment that the offender assumes any of the rights of the real owner. Cases such as *Skipp 1975* and *Fritschy 1985*, where the courts had decided that an appropriation did not take place until the defendant had done something that he had not been authorised to do, were overruled.

This new view of the law meant that the convictions of the defendants in *Atakpu and Abrahams 1994* could not be sustained. The offenders had devised a plan to hire expensive cars abroad and then to bring them to England to sell them. Suspicions were aroused, however, when the men reached Dover and they were arrested. The case came to trial before the decision in *Gomez* and it was decided at first instance that the men were guilty of conspiracy to steal. The state of the law at that time decreed that the theft would have taken place in England, i.e. when the cars had been retained after the hire period had expired. By the time the case reached the Court of Appeal, however, *Gomez* had been heard by the House of Lords and it was reluctantly decided that the offenders had, instead, appropriated the property when they had, with dishonest intent, hired the cars

in Brussels and Frankfurt. The men, therefore, could not be said to have been conspiring to steal in England and the convictions had to be quashed. The Court of Appeal was prepared to recognise that an appropriation could be a continuing act while the act of stealing was taking place, but would not stretch this to include actions taken days after the cars had been obtained. The following propositions were put forward by Ward J, after he had reviewed the authorities. He stated that:

1 Theft can occur in an instant by a single appropriation but it can also involve a course of dealing with property lasting longer and involving several appropriations before the transaction is complete.
2 Theft is a finite act – it has a beginning and it has an end.
3 At what point the transaction is complete is a matter for the jury to decide upon the facts of each case.
4 Though there may be several appropriations in the course of a single theft or several appropriations of different goods each constituting a separate theft [...] no case suggests that there can be successive thefts of the same property (assuming of course that possession is constant and not lost or abandoned, later to be assumed again).

Can an appropriation still take place in cases where the true owner appears to be giving his consent to the taking?
Lord Roskill, in *Morris*, believed that, for an appropriation to arise, there had to be an adverse interference or a usurpation of the rights of the real owner. This statement, however, seemed to be in direct contradiction with an earlier House of Lords' decision, made in *Lawrence* v *Metropolitan Police Commissioner 1972*. In that case it had been decided that an appropriation had taken place, and a theft committed, when the real owner had apparently agreed to the taking of the money.

An Italian student had arrived at Victoria Station in London on his first visit to England. Mr Occhi spoke little English but showed a taxi driver a piece of paper on which was written an address in Ladbroke Grove. The taxi driver falsely indicated that the journey was a long and expensive one and, when offered a £1 note, took a further £6 from the student's open wallet.

The driver was convicted of the theft of the £6 but appealed on the grounds that the owner had consented to the taking. The case eventually reached the House of Lords, where their Lordships decided that there could be an appropriation 'even though the owner has permitted or consented to the property being taken'. The actual point of law which was certified for the House of Lords to consider was 'whether s.1(1) of the Theft Act 1968, is to be construed as though it contained the words "without having the consent of the owner"'. Their Lordships decided unanimously that the answer was no.

Until the case of *Gomez 1993*, therefore, there were two conflicting House of Lords' decisions on this subject, despite the averred intention of the House of Lords, in the Practice Statement of 1966, that the criminal law should be kept as certain as possible! In the civil case of *Dobson* v *General Accident Fire and Life Assurance Corp 1990*, the Court of Appeal made it clear that it preferred the decision in *Lawrence*. The court stated that 'whatever *R* v *Morris* did decide it cannot be regarded as having overruled the very plain decision in Lawrence's case that appropriation can occur even if the owner consents. . .'.

The House of Lords upheld this view of the law in the case of *Gomez 1993*. The defendant was employed as assistant manager at a store selling electrical goods and agreed with an acquaintance to supply goods to him in return for two stolen, unsigned building society cheques, amounting to £17,200.

The manager of the shop was presented with a list of goods to the value of the first of the stolen cheques, told that it was a genuine order and asked for his authorisation for the payment to be made by cheque. He requested that the bank be contacted to confirm that the cheque was a valid one. The defendant pretended that he had taken this step and declared that he had

been informed that the cheque was 'as good as cash'.

The goods were duly delivered to the accomplice, with the defendant helping to load up his van.

A similar procedure was taken with regard to the second cheque, (although one of the items ordered was not delivered), and this time the manager merely accepted the position. Some time later, the cheques were returned bearing the words 'Orders not to pay. Stolen cheque'.

Gomez, together with another employee and the man posing as the genuine buyer, was arrested and subsequently sentenced to two years imprisonment. He claimed that he could not be said to have appropriated the property in question because the manager had authorised the sale. The Court of Appeal accepted this defence and quashed the conviction.

A point of law of general public importance was, however, certified for the attention of the House of Lords. The question asked took the following form:

> when theft is alleged and that which is alleged to be stolen passes to the defendant with the consent of the owner, but that consent has been obtained by a false representation, has (a) an appropriation within the meaning of s.1(1) of the Theft Act 1968 taken place, or (b) must such a passing of property necessarily involve an element of adverse interference with or usurpation of some right of the owner?

Lord Keith gave the main judgment. He decided that *Lawrence* was right and *Morris* was wrong and was, in addition, only *obiter dicta*. He stated that:

> The decision in *Lawrence* was a clear decision of this House upon the construction of the word 'appropriates' in s.1(1) of the 1968 Act, which has stood for 12 years when doubt was thrown

upon it by the *obiter dicta* in *Morris*. *Lawrence* must be regarded as authoritative and correct, and there is no question of it now being right to depart from it.

The conviction for theft was reinstated.

It is now clearly the law, therefore, that there may still be an appropriation of property even if the owner appears to have consented to the taking. Earlier company cases, such as *McHugh 1993*, in which the Court of Appeal had stated that 'An act done with the authority of the company cannot in general amount to an appropriation', are no longer good law. After *Gomez*, directors or others holding a majority share holding in a company who appropriate company property for their own use, can be found guilty of theft.

Lords Jauncey, Browne-Wilkinson and Slynn agreed with Lord Keith's judgment in *Gomez*. Lord Lowry, however, made a powerful dissenting speech and stated firmly that cases such as *Gomez* should be dealt with under s.15 of the Theft Act, i.e. by charging the offender with obtaining property by deception, not with theft. He was the only judge to refer back to the Eighth Report of the Criminal Law Revision Committee that preceded the Theft Act. (Lord Keith had decided that this would serve no useful purpose!) This Report had clearly stated that, while it was possible for some cases of deception to also come within the definition of theft, it would not be theft where the owner obtained ownership of the goods.

COMMENT

The actual point of law in *Gomez* was quite a narrow one, concerning as it did a case where the consent was only given after a false representation had been made. The judges of the House of Lords, however, did not confine their reasoning solely to this type of situation, so therefore the implications of the decision are far wider. Smith and Hogan state that 'the effect is to create an extraordinarily wide offence, embracing many acts which would more naturally be regarded as merely preparatory acts'. It also means that every case of obtaining property by deception under s.15 (to be discussed in the next chapter) will also be theft.

Professor Smith obviously disapproves of the decision in *Gomez*. In his commentary in the *Criminal Law Review* on the case of *Mazo*, which is discussed below, he roundly condemns it as 'one of a long roll of disastrous decisions by the House of Lords'. Strong words! He does, however, accept that *Gomez* is now the authority on the subject of appropriation and believes that it would take a very brave Court of Appeal to defy it. It will be seen that the latter court is, at least, prepared to try to limit its effect in some instances, as noted in the cases of *Gallasso 1993* and *Mazo 1996*, discussed below.

Does there have to be an actual taking of property to constitute an appropriation?

We have seen that the House of Lords, in *Gomez*, implied that the answer to this question was 'no' because the court decided that an appropriation occurs the moment that the defendant assumes any of the rights of the owner, whether or not he goes on to take the property. (It would, of course, be more difficult to establish the *mens rea* of theft at such a point because it would have to be shown that the defendant was acting dishonestly and had an intention to permanently deprive the owner of the goods.)

The Court of Appeal, however, appeared to come to a different decision in *Gallasso 1993*, decided on the same day as *Gomez*. The accused was a nurse in charge of a house for people with severe learning difficulties and was authorised to deposit and withdraw money from the patients' accounts to meet their daily needs.

One of the residents received three cheques, one for £4250, another for £4000 and the third for £1800.32p but, instead of depositing the money in the existing account, Gallasso opened other accounts in the patient's name and withdrew some of this money for her own use. She was charged with various counts of theft but disputed that a theft had occurred by the opening of the separate accounts in the resident's name.

The Court of Appeal quashed the conviction for theft on this count and decided that, although *Gomez* had laid down that an appropriation could take place even though the real owner appears to have given his consent, it was still necessary to have a taking. In this situation, while the nurse had obviously intended to commit criminal acts, it was felt that, at this stage, there had not been any appropriation of the resident's property.

This decision does not sit easily with the case of *Gomez* and is felt by many to be wrongly decided. The defendant was certainly assuming some of the rights of the owner by the opening of other accounts and *Gomez* has decided that this is enough to amount to appropriation.

What position should be adopted in cases where the principles of criminal law and civil law conflict?

This matter came to the attention of the Court of Appeal in the case of *Mazo 1996*. A maid was appealing against a conviction for the theft of large sums of money from her employer, an elderly woman whose mental faculties were weakening. The maid alleged that the money was a gift from a grateful employer and this point seemed to be made out because the employer had authorised the cashing of the cheques after the bank had made inquiries about them. The Court of Appeal decided, therefore, that a valid gift of the money might well have been made and held that, in such a situation, there could not be a conviction for theft. The Court of Appeal did pay lip service to the decision in *Gomez*, by stating that the act would have been theft, even though the owner had apparently consented to the taking, if that

consent had been secured by deception. The court, therefore, was recognising the narrowest ratio of the House of Lords in *Gomez*. In the present case, however, the judges felt that no such deception existed, the jury had been misdirected on the issues and therefore the defendant should be given the benefit of the doubt.

Once again, this decision has been questioned as not standing with *Gomez* but has been rationalised by saying that, in this case, the defendant had acquired 'an absolute, indefeasible right to the property'. In such a case, a conviction for theft would conflict with civil law principles, under which, if the money were to be taken from the defendant, she could use a civil court in which to sue for its return!

It would appear, therefore, that wide as the decision in *Gomez* is, it does have limits and one of these is where a finding would conflict with civil law.

There was no such conflict in *Kendrick and Hopkins 1997*, because, in this case, a valid gift had not been made. The facts contained some similarities to both *Gallasso* and *Mazo*. The defendants were in charge of a residential home and had taken over management of the affairs of a 99-year-old resident. They had obtained a power of attorney, cashed her investments and had also persuaded her to make a new will naming them as beneficiaries. They were convicted of conspiring to steal and the Court of Appeal upheld the decision. The judges distinguished *Mazo*, arguing that in the current case, the elderly resident did not have the mental capacity to make a valid gift and therefore the ownership of the property had not passed to the defendants. The jury was therefore entitled to conclude that dishonesty had been present.

Before leaving the subject of appropriation, it should be noted that a person who obtains property in good faith, which later turns out to have been stolen, would not be guilty of theft for assuming the rights of the true owner. This is stated in s.3(2.)

activity

Read the preceding information on appropriation and discuss whether the decision in *Gomez* has widened the law on theft in an unacceptable way.

Property (s.4)

The word 'property' is widely defined in s.4(1) to include:

> money and all other property, real and personal, including things in action and other intangible property.

It can be seen, therefore, that nearly every type of property may be stolen. The definition includes both real and personal property, although, under s.4(2), this is qualified to some extent. This section states that a person cannot steal land, or things forming part of the land, except in the circumstances specified. These include situations where a trustee or personal representative disposes of the land under his control in an unauthorised way, where a person not in possession of the land severs something from it or where a tenant misappropriates fixtures which should have remained attached to the land.

It has been decided that blood and urine samples can be classed as property, allowing the defendant in *Welsh 1974* to be convicted when he removed the urine sample he had provided for the analysis by the police! Similarly, body parts preserved for scientific examination can also be stolen, as confirmed in *Kelly 1998*.

'Things in action', mentioned in the definition, are known in civil law as choses in action, and consist of intangible property like patents, copyrights, shares, debts and insurance policies. The courts have had to decide how far the term 'things in action and other intangible property' will extend.

In *Oxford* v *Moss 1978*, an engineering student at Liverpool University acquired the proof of an examination paper, intending to read its contents and then return it. The student was obviously intending to cheat and the advantages he would have gained by his unlawful behaviour would have been grossly unfair on other students who had not seen the contents of the paper. What had to be decided, however, was whether his actions satisfied the definition of theft.

It was clear that the student had no intention to steal the actual paper, which was obviously the property of the university. The point of law sent by the prosecutors to the Divisional Court to decide upon, therefore, was whether the information contained in the examination paper could amount to property within the meaning of the Theft Act 1968. The Court decided that the right to confidential information was not in the category of intangible property laid down in s.4(1) of the Act. The student, therefore, could not be convicted of theft.

The term 'other intangible property' widens the definition of property to encompass things like quotas allowed for the export of textiles. This enabled the director of a company in *AG of Hong Kong* v *Chang Nai-Keung 1987* to be convicted of stealing his company's property when, without authorisation, he sold his company's excess quota for a grossly reduced price to another company in which he had an interest.

'Other intangible property' has also been held to include things like gas stored in a container, but, owing to difficulties under the previous law, the dishonest abstraction of electricity has been made a separate offence under s.13 Theft Act 1968, punishable by a maximum term of imprisonment of five years.

Sections 4(3) and 4(4)

S.4(3) and s.4(4) are easy to understand. They deal with wild flowers, plants and animals. Under s.4(3) no offence is committed if a person picks mushrooms which are growing wild, or wild flowers, fruit or foliage, provided that this is not done for a commercial purpose. S.4(4) lays down that a person will not commit theft if he captures a wild animal which has not been tamed or reduced to captivity.

activity

Decide whether the following people have stolen property. Give clear authority for your answers:

> Anthony arranged for the Barchester Bank Ltd to debit the account of Joanna and credit his own.

> Jane picked a quantity of bluebells from Austen Wood and sold the blooms in her local market.

> Charlotte, a student at Bronte University, discovered the whereabouts of the English examination paper, memorised the questions and returned it to the filing cabinet.

> Anna captured a wild pony on Sewell Moor, tamed it and kept it for her own use.

> William was given notice to quit Hathaway Cottage and, in a fit of temper dismantled and took with him all the fitted bookcases.

Belonging to another (s.5)

These words are given a wide meaning under s.5(1), which states that:

> property shall be regarded as belonging to any person having possession or control of it, or having in it any proprietary right or interest. . .

It can be seen, therefore, that the property can belong, not only to the actual owners of it, but also to those who are currently in possession of it or have some sort of right over it.

This can mean that it is possible, in certain circumstances, for a person to be convicted of stealing his own property, if others have rights over it.

This point is illustrated in the case of *Turner (No. 2) 1971*. The defendant put in his car for repairs but then returned after the repairs had been carried out and took away the car from the road in which it had been put without informing the garage owner and without paying for the repairs. His conviction for theft was upheld. Lord Parker stated that:

> This court is quite satisfied that there is no ground whatever for qualifying the words 'possession or control' in any way. It is sufficient if it is found that the person from whom the property is taken, or to use the words of the Act, appropriated, was at the time in fact in possession or control.

In *Meredith 1973*, however, it was decided that the police did not have rights over the defendant's car which had been impounded for causing an obstruction while the owner was at a football match, only the right to enforce the statutory charge. It was held by the trial judge, therefore, that the accused had no case to answer in theft when, as in Turner, he removed the car, plus a police Krooklok immobilising it, without authority.

▼ COMMENT

> The decisions in these two cases are very difficult to reconcile. It should be borne in mind, however, that *Turner (No. 2) 1971* was decided by the Court of Appeal, so is obviously of higher authority. Nowadays, the two offenders would probably be charged, not with theft but with the crime of making off without payment, an offence created in 1978, and dealt with in Chapter 8.

When looking at the term 'proprietary interest', it should be noted that the Crown has such an interest in 'treasure', discovered on land. Until the Treasure Act 1996, this was known as 'treasure trove'. 'Treasure' now consists of items of predominantly gold or silver, at least 200 years old, where the true owner is unknown. In *Hancock 1990*, the defendant had been charged with stealing from the Crown some Celtic silver coins, which he had discovered with the aid of a metal detector and had not disclosed to the authorities.

The Court of Appeal decided that the mere fact that an item may later be classed as treasure would not, at that point in time, be an established proprietary interest. It was therefore necessary for the jury to decide on this point before a conviction for theft could be sustained. The passing of the Treasure Act 1996 will make it easier to establish this as, unlike the previous law, it is no longer necessary to prove that the find has been deliberately hidden. It has also been made a criminal offence not to report such a find within 14 days.

Waverley Borough Council v *Fletcher 1995*, a civil case, established that, if an item is not classed as 'treasure', the owner of the land will have a better claim to the article than the finder, provided that the article is attached to the land or found within it. If the find is not attached to the land, the owner will only have a better right if he has exercised some clear form of control over the land and what is on it. In the early civil case of *Bridges* v *Hawksworth 1851*, the finder of some bank notes on the floor of a shop was held to have a better title than the shopkeeper.

Sections 5(2) and 5(3)

Ss.5(2) and (3) deal with situations where the defendant has acquired ownership or control of property, so that, in law, it would normally be taken as belonging to him, but special circumstances exist to prevent him doing as he likes with the property.

With the vast majority of trusts, there are identifiable beneficiaries and if their interests are adversely affected they can take action

under s.5(1) as being the holders of a proprietary interest. S.5(2) plugs a possible loophole where there are no ascertainable beneficiaries. It states that where the property in question is the subject of a trust, the property shall be taken as belonging to any of the people who have rights under the trust. Accordingly, if the person is in charge of a charitable trust which, as yet, has no ascertainable beneficiaries, and absconds with the proceeds, action can be taken against him. The property over which he has control would be deemed to belong to another and, provided that the other elements of theft are established, he could be charged with theft.

S.5(3) covers situations where a person receives property under the obligation to deal with it or the proceeds of the property in a special way. Once again, the property will be held to 'belong to another' if he does anything unauthorised with it.

An illustration of this is the case of *Davidge* v *Bennett 1984*, where the defendant was given money by her fellow flat sharers to pay the communal gas bill. When she spent the money on Christmas presents instead, she was held to be guilty of theft.

The difficulty with this subsection has been to establish exactly when there is such an obligation to deal with the property in a particular way. It was stated in the case of *Hall 1973*, that 'each case turns on its own facts'. One example, where the holder of money appears to be obliged to deal with it in a particular way, is where the public puts money into special collecting tins. In these circumstances, the collector cannot use the money for his own purposes. Another such example is where a builder is given money specifically to purchase supplies; he, too, cannot use the money advanced for other purposes. Other cases, where most laymen would assume that the subsection would apply, do not appear to be covered. In *Hall 1972*, a travel agent took deposits from customers, among them teachers paying a lump sum on behalf of their pupils for air trips to America, and placed the money in the firm's general trading account. The firm subsequently foundered and the flights never materialised.

Nor were any of the deposits returned. At first instance, Hall was convicted of theft but the Court of Appeal reluctantly decided that the partner was not, in these circumstances, under an obligation to deal with the customers' money in a particular way. While the defendant was undoubtedly dishonest in his dealings and his conduct held to be 'scandalous', he was not appropriating property belonging to another. A similar problem was found in *DPP* v *Huskinson 1988*, when a person spent his housing benefit on other things. He, too, did not fall foul of this subsection because there was nothing in the Social Security and Housing Benefits Act 1982 laying down an obligation that the actual funds received had to be put to a particular use.

The question appears to turn on whether there is a clearly agreed obligation to deal with the money or proceeds in a particular way. Usually, this will arise where there is a stipulation that the money or proceeds should be kept in a separate fund but, in special circumstances, liability might continue even when permission has been given for the money to be transferred to another fund, as in *Wain 1995*.

The defendant in *Wain* had raised over £2000 for charity in a 'telethon' organised by Yorkshire Television and paid it into a separate bank account. He made several excuses for not sending it to the television company and was eventually allowed to pay the money into his own account and to send a cheque drawn on that account. The cheque was subsequently dishonoured and Wain was convicted of theft. His appeal against this was rejected. McCowan L J stated:

> It seems to us that by virtue of s.5(3), the appellant was plainly under an obligation to retain, if not the actual notes and coins, at least their proceeds, that is to say the money credited in the bank account which he opened for the trust with the actual property. When he took the money credited to that account and moved it over to his own bank account, it was still the proceeds of the notes and coins

> donated which he proceeded to use for his own purposes, thereby appropriating them. . .

People generously sponsoring the deeds of others for charity will be heartened to note that the Court of Appeal took the opportunity to disapprove of the earlier case of *Lewis* v *Lethbridge 1987*. In that case the Divisional Court had decided that a competitor in the London Marathon was not under a specific obligation to account to the charity for the actual sponsorship money or its proceeds; he was merely a debtor who had to account for the amount he had collected.

Similarly, in *Klineberg 1998*, although the appeal succeeded in part, the Court of Appeal affirmed that where a party, (in this case buying a time-sharing property) is induced to contract on the understanding that his money would be protected by a trusteeship, there was a legal obligation under S.5(3) to deal with the money in a particular way.

Section 5(4)

S.5(4) deals with circumstances where a person receives property by mistake. In such a case, he is under an obligation to restore the property to its rightful owner. If he fails to do this, he will be classed as intending to deprive the other of it.

The actual section is rather a lengthy one. S.5(4) states that:

> Where a person gets property by another's mistake, and is under an obligation to make restoration (in whole or in part) of the property or its proceeds or of the value thereof, then to the extent of that obligation the property or proceeds shall be regarded (as against him) as belonging to the person entitled to restoration, and an intention not to make restoration shall be regarded accordingly as an intention to deprive that person of the property or proceeds.

As under s.5(3), the obligation imposed on the current owner of the property, in this case to restore the property to another, is felt to be a legal, rather than merely a moral obligation. It might well be argued, therefore, that an overpayment of a gambling win would not be recoverable, as any agreements relating to wagering or gaming are generally unenforceable in law.

In the case of *Gilks 1972*, however, the Court of Appeal did not seek to rely on s.5(4), preferring, instead, to confirm the view of the trial judge, who had cited the ancient case of *Middleton 1873*. In *Gilks*, the defendant had visited one of Ladbrokes' betting shops and bet on a horse called Fighting Scot. This horse was not placed but, by a strange coincidence, another horse called Fighting Taffy won! By mistake, the defendant was paid out a sum of over £100 as if he had won on this latter horse. He was convicted of theft when he failed to disclose the mistake and, as stated, his appeal against this conviction was dismissed.

The Court of Appeal stated:

> that where a person was paid by mistake . . . a sum in excess of that properly payable, the person who accepted the overpayment with knowledge of the excess was guilty of theft. . .

The court decided that s.5(4) was merely designed to change the law in relation to cases like *Moynes* v *Cooper 1956*, where an employee who later realised he had been overpaid wages could not, at that time, be convicted of theft.

S.5(4) is often invoked where employees have been overpaid and have failed to return the money. The following point of law came to the attention of the Court of Appeal in *AG's Reference (No. 1 of 1983) 1985*:

COMMENT

With respect, there are problems with this decision. It is true that, following civil law principles, there are recognised categories where it can be shown that ownership of the property has not passed to another party but these do not appear to apply to this case. With regard to s.5(4), it clearly states that a person will be treated as depriving the other of property when he comes by the property by mistake and is under an obligation to restore it. The word 'legal' is not actually included in the section but it has always been assumed that a legal obligation is required and that a moral obligation will not suffice. In fact, the Court of Appeal in *Gilks* clearly affirmed this view of the law, when Cairns L J stated:

> An alternative ground on which the trial judge held that the money should be regarded as belonging to Ladbrokes was that "obligation" in s.5(4) meant an obligation whether a legal one or not. In the opinion of this court that was an incorrect ruling. In a criminal statute, where a person's criminal liability is made dependant on his having an obligation, it would be quite wrong to construe that word so as to cover a moral or social obligation as distinct from a legal one. . .

It could be argued, therefore, that as ownership of the money had passed to Gilks and s.5(4) did not place him under a legal obligation to pay it back, he could not be said to have committed theft, however much he might have been morally at fault.

> whether a person who receives an
> overpayment of a debt due to him . . . by
> way of a credit to his bank account
> through the 'direct debit' system . . . and
> who knowing of that overpayment
> intentionally fails to repay the amount . . .
> may be guilty of theft. [The answer was
> said to be 'yes'].

In this case, a policewoman had been paid an additional sum of £74.74, had discovered this fact but had failed to inform her employer. The trial judge had ordered an acquittal. The Court of Appeal decided in the *Reference* that, on the wording of s.5(4), a person should be found guilty of theft even though he had not touched the money and had merely left it in an account. It would, of course, be a different matter if the employee really believed that he was entitled to the money or was genuinely unaware of the overpayment.

The position in equity regarding mistake

S.5(4) applies in law where the ownership of goods has passed to the alleged thief but where he is held, in special circumstances, to be under an obligation to restore the property or risk being convicted of theft. It has been argued that the subsection may be superfluous because the wrongdoer may also be under a fiduciary duty to restore such property to the original owner because that person still retains an equitable interest in it. This is known as the Chase Manhattan principle, after the case of *Chase Manhattan Bank NA* v *Israel-British Bank (London) Ltd 1981*. In this case, it was decided that the bank in question, which by mistake had paid over £2 million to a third party, was entitled under equitable principles to have the whole amount restored to it, after the third party had gone into liquidation.

This principle was used in *Shadrokh-Cigari 1988*, another banking case. A mistake had been made whereby a child's account had been credited with the amount of £286,000, instead of a mere £286! The child's guardian had arranged for the child to authorise bank drafts using this money and, when the guardian was arrested, only £21,000 remained.

The Court of Appeal upheld the guardian's conviction for theft, deciding that the bank had retained an equitable interest in the property and that, therefore, the defendant had appropriated property belonging to another under s.5(1).

▼ **COMMENT**

It has to be said that the use of such a principle makes an already complicated area of law even more difficult. It should be remembered that equitable remedies are discretionary so there is no guarantee that such help would be forthcoming. It appears, therefore, that s.5(4) will still be helpful when property is gained by mistake.

activity

Decide whether the defendants in the following circumstances have appropriated property 'belonging to another'. Give full legal reasons for your answers:

Del booked a holiday in the Carribean with Peckham Travel and forwarded a large deposit. The travel agent, Rodney, used Del's money on other ventures and did not arrange the holiday, as promised. The firm then went into liquidation and Rodney was arrested.

Dorothy obtained sponsorship money of £5000 for abseiling down the White Cliffs of Dover. The money was given to help a children's charity but Dorothy has spent it on clothes.

> Sharon put her grandfather clock into the local antique shop for repair and, after the work had been effected, she entered the shop while the owner was unloading his van and removed the clock without his knowledge.

> Tracey, a traffic warden, discovered that she had been credited twice with her monthly salary. She decided to keep silent about this.

> Gary was paid an amount of £50,000 by mistake by his local bookmaker. The correct amount should have been £50 but he decided to keep the money in the belief that the bookmaker could afford the loss!

....

7.2.2   THE *MENS REA* OF THEFT

As stated earlier, the *mens rea* of theft requires that the accused should 'dishonestly' appropriate property 'with the intention of permanently depriving the other of it'. These two terms need to be examined.

Dishonestly (S.2)

The drafters of the Theft Act preferred to use the word 'dishonestly' to the word 'fraudulently' which was used in the old law on larceny, because it was believed that a jury would find it easier to understand this new word. There is no actual definition of dishonesty under s.2 of the Act and it is the jury that has to decide the matter. What the Act does, instead, is to describe three situations in s.2(1) where a person is not to be classed as dishonest and two situations in s.1(2) and s.2(2) where he would be.

Section 2(1)(a)

In the first instance, s.2(1)(a) states that a person will not be regarded as dishonest if he appropriates property, for himself or a third party, believing that he has a right in law to deprive the other of it. It appears from the case of *Holden 1991*, that it is not necessary for the accused to prove that his belief is a reasonable one, providing that it is genuinely held. The defendant must, believe, however erroneously, that he has a legal, as opposed to a moral right to the property.

In *Holden 1991*, the defendant had been accused of stealing scrap tyres from Kwik-Fit, a previous employer. His defence was that he knew that others had taken the tyres with the permission of a supervisor. On the other hand, the depot manager gave evidence that the taking of the tyres was disciplinary offence, meriting dismissal. The jury was directed that the question to be asked was whether the defendant had a reasonable belief that he had a right to take the tyres.

This was held, on appeal, to be a misdirection. The Court of Appeal held that a person was not dishonest if he had an honest belief that he had a right to take the property. Obviously, however, if the belief is a very unreasonably held one, the jury is less likely to believe that it is an honest one.

Section 2(1)(b)

Secondly, under s.2(1)(b), a person will not be considered dishonest if he takes property believing that the other would consent to this course of action if he knew about it. An example would be if you were to borrow a fellow student's law books while that person was away, in the belief that your friend would approve of this course of action.

Section 2(1)(c)

The last exception is more controversial. Under s.2(1)(c) a person will not be held to be dishonest if he appropriates property belonging to another believing that the person to whom it belongs cannot be discovered by taking reasonable steps. This section helps to protect a finder of property from a conviction for theft, who would otherwise satisfy the *actus reus* of theft; this sub-section prevents him having the *mens ea,* provided that he fits the criteria laid down.

In *Small 1988,* the defendant tried to claim that the car he had appropriated had been abandoned by its owner. It had been left in one place for over a week with the keys in the ignition. The jury obviously did not believe his story but the Court of Appeal decided that his conviction ought to be quashed if he had honestly believed that this was the case.

The sub-section specifically excludes trustees and personal representatives, so they may well be dishonest in the circumstances laid down. It is believed that such people should not become entitled to the property of others in such circumstances because, if the beneficiaries cannot be found, the property would revert to the Crown.

Sections 1(2) and 2(2)

The sections mentioned above provide defences to a charge of theft. Conversely, s.1(2) decides that a person may still be convicted of theft despite the fact that his appropriation of property is not made with a view to gain, or for his own benefit and s.2(2) states that he may still be classed as dishonest even if he is willing to pay for the property.

It will still be theft, therefore, for a Robin Hood type figure to steal from the rich and give to the poor. It is also theft if property is merely removed for spite and is just destroyed or thrown away.

The basic test for dishonesty

This has changed over the years. There were differing opinions as to whether the test for dishonesty ought to decided in an objective way or according to the defendant's own belief, i.e. subjectively. In *McIvor 1982,* the Court of Appeal sought to reconcile these differences, deciding, rather strangely, that a subjective approach should be taken where the charge was conspiracy to defraud, but that the question of

dishonesty in theft should be decided objectively. A little later, in the case of *Ghosh 1982,* the Court of Appeal re-thought the matter and rejected this distinction. Currently, therefore, the same test is to be used for both these offences and for the crime of obtaining property by deception, contrary to s.15 Theft Act 1968. The test, however, has been altered and is now a mixture of an objective and subjective approach. The rather complicated twofold test asks the jury to decide upon the following matters:

1 Whether, according to the ordinary standards of reasonable and honest people what was done was dishonest. If the jury decides that it was not, that is the end of the matter.
2 If, however, the jurors decide that it was dishonest, they should then consider whether the defendant himself must have realised that what he was doing was by those standards dishonest.

The accused can only be convicted if the answer to both questions is 'yes', but in *Price 1989* Lord Lane stated that there was no requirement for the judge to give the *Ghosh* direction in the vast majority of cases. It was only necessary in cases where the defendant appeared to believe that his actions were not dishonest but there was some doubt about whether he really thought that others would share this view.

For example, the test would be applicable where the defendant was accused of stealing from the rich to give to the poor and argued that he honestly believed that ordinary reasonable people would not think he was doing wrong. In such a case, using the *Ghosh* test, he could not be said to be acting dishonestly.

If, however, the accused merely liked to think of himself as a latter day Robin Hood but knew that others would think that he was acting wrongly, he would be considered dishonest.

COMMENT

The *Ghosh* test is not an easy one for juries, and indeed students, to understand. It has been subjected to a great deal of criticism, with some opponents of it calling, instead, for a statutory definition of dishonesty. In the earlier Australian case of *Salvo 1980*, the judge felt that it was not always the case that a citizen 'knows dishonesty if he sees it', and that further help was needed in some cases. At present, however, it is important to realise that *Ghosh* does represent the law on the subject until there is an intervention by either the House of Lords or Parliament.

With the intention of permanently depriving the other of it (S.6)

Edmund Davies L J in *Warner 1970* made it clear that, as with the word 'dishonestly', there is no definition of the phrase 'intention of permanently depriving the other of it' in the Theft Act 1968. The Criminal Law Revision Committee had believed that the term required no further explanation but made it clear that mere borrowing, even dishonest borrowing, was not normally meant to be included. S.6, however, was added later and, while said by J R Spencer in the Criminal Law Review in 1977 to sprout 'obscurities at every phrase', gives extra illustrations of where such an intention to permanently deprive can be assumed even when it is argued that there is no such intention. Summarising these instances, s.6(1) provides that a person will be taken as permanently depriving the other of property if he intends to treat the property as his own to dispose of regardless of the real owner's rights and states that this may sometimes occur even in cases where the offender is claiming that he has only borrowed the goods.

The full, rather obscure wording of s.6(1) is as follows:

A person appropriating property belonging to another without meaning the other permanently to lose the thing itself is nevertheless to be regarded as having the intention of permanently depriving the other of it if his intention is to treat the thing as his own to dispose of regardless of the other's rights; and a borrowing or lending of it may amount to so treating it if, but only if, the borrowing or lending is for a period and in circumstances making it equivalent to an outright taking or disposal.

This would cover situations where a person borrows property without intending to return it or takes the property of another intending to sell or otherwise dispose of it. In *Downes 1983*, the Court of Appeal upheld a conviction for theft when the defendant sold some tax vouchers, made out to him but belonging to the Inland Revenue, to others so that they could obtain tax advantages. The same court also refused to quash the conviction in *Velumyl 1989*. The defendant took over £1000 from his employer's safe in breach of company rules and was convicted of theft. He was unsuccessful in his allegation that he had not committed the crime of theft because he had intended to repay the money after the weekend break and, therefore, had no intention permanently to deprive the employer of his property. The Court of Appeal showed scant sympathy for this argument and upheld the conviction on the grounds that he could not have intended to pay back the exact notes and coins he had taken.

In the earlier case of *Lloyd, Bhuee and Ali 1985*, the defendants had been luckier. Lloyd was chief projectionist at the Odeon Cinema in Barking and over a period of months had temporarily removed films from the cinema in order that his accomplices could take illegal copies of them and sell the pirate videos at a substantial profit. The films were only taken for a few hours and then returned but the defendants had been caught red-handed while making a copy. It had to be decided whether the defendants had committed the offence of theft. The Court of Appeal decided that there were circumstances where there could be an intention to permanently deprive even though the goods were actually returned, but stated that this would be in cases where the value of the item stolen was affected. Here, it was decided that 'the goodness, the virtue, the practical value of the films to the owners has not gone out of the article... The borrowing, it seems to us, was not for a period, or in such circumstances, as to make it equivalent to an outright taking or disposal'.

In *Bagshaw 1988*, the defendant's conviction had to be quashed because these matters had not been properly explained to the jury. Bagshaw had been charged with the theft of some glass cylinders but alleged that he had only borrowed them. The trial judge had failed to explain to the jury that he could only be convicted in such a case if he had intended to keep the cylinders until all the 'goodness' in them had been utilised. His appeal against his conviction on the grounds of this misdirection was therefore upheld.

From these decisions it can be seen that a person would be permanently depriving the other of property if he took an article like a season ticket, used it until it had expired and then returned it. The value, (or goodness or virtue) in the article would have been removed. A person would also be held to be permanently depriving the other if he took the property and then put conditions on its return. Here, it may be safely assumed that if the conditions were not met, the property would not go back to the rightful owner. Lord Lane has quoted the example of an offender taking a valuable painting and refusing to return it until a large sum of money had been paid.

An examination of the cases shows that people steal the oddest things! In *DPP v Lavender 1994*, the alleged theft concerned two doors. The defendant had removed these from property being renovated by the local council

and used them to replace two damaged doors in his girlfriend's residence. Despite the difficulties caused by the fact that this property, too, was owned by the local authority, the defendant was classed by the Divisional Court as treating the doors as his own to dispose of and this, it was felt, was enough. This appears to widen the law and sits uneasily with the view of the Court of Appeal in *Cahill 1993*, that there had to be more than a mere intention to use the thing as one's own because of the inclusion of the words 'to dispose of'. Hopefully, there will be a further discussion of this issue in the future.

A last point regarding s.6(1) which needs examination is whether an offender can be classed as permanently depriving the other of goods, and so be guilty of attempted theft, when he is trying to assess whether there is anything worth stealing. An example would be where he breaks into a car in order to see if it contains a radio or, as in *Easom 1971*, rifles through a handbag to see if the contents are worth stealing and then returns it when nothing of value is found. In this case, the handbag had been attached, by a string, to the wrist of a policewoman and, despite the fact that the bag had been returned to her, the defendant was convicted of the theft of the bag and its contents. The Court of Appeal quashed the conviction stating that 'a conditional appropriation will not do' and this view of the law was upheld in *Husseyn 1977*, where the article in question was a holdall containing valuable sub-aqua equipment. In *AG's References (Nos 1 and 2 of 1979) 1980*, however, the Court of Appeal decided that this would only be a problem in cases where the indictment specifically mentioned a particular article. In other cases, there could be a conviction for theft.

S.6(2) states that person may be regarded as treating the property of another as his own in cases where he parts with possession of it 'under a condition as to its return which he may not be able to perform'. An example would be where he pawned the goods in question, knowing that it might not be possible to redeem them.

In conclusion, it can be seen that the law of theft has grown quite complex, mainly because of the uncertainty generated by changing decisions on the interpretation of various words and phrases making up the definition of theft in s.1 and the explanations provided in ss.2–6. It is very important, therefore, to know these sections well and to be fully conversant with the latest case law on the subject.

activity

Decide whether Dennis has the *mens rea* for theft in the following situations:

He removed several mattresses from a large furniture store without paying for them, in order to distribute them to the people 'sleeping rough' in London doorways.

He borrowed a book from the library and gave it to his cousin for a Christmas present.

He saw a bicycle resting against the railings in the town centre, which was identical to the one he had lost in that same place the previous week, and took it home. In fact, the bicycle belonged to the local postman.

He found a gold watch in the railway station. He took it to the lost property office but, finding this closed, decided to keep it.

He was suddenly invited to a 'black tie' event at a local hotel, so decided to wear a dinner jacket belonging to his absent flatmate. The friends often 'swapped' clothes. Would your answer be different if Dennis had taken £30 from the till of his employer in order to pay for the hire of such a jacket, with the intention of returning the money after the weekend?

On the dance floor at the hotel, he found two expensive tickets for the musical 'Miss Peking' and pocketed them. He took his girlfriend to see the show a few days later and later returned the ticket stubs to the hotel.

KEY FACTS

- The law on this subject changed in 1968 with the passing of the Theft Act 1968
- S.1 lays down the definition of theft. A person is guilty of theft if 'he dishonestly appropriates property belonging to another with the intention of permanently depriving the other of it'
- Ss.2–6 give further explanations and/or examples of key words in the definition
- S.7 Theft Act, as amended, states that the maximum punishment for theft is seven years imprisonment
- The *mens rea* of theft occurs when the defendant is 'dishonest' in his appropriation of property and has 'the intention of permanently depriving the other of it'
- Further explanation of the *mens rea* of theft is to be found in ss.2 and 6 Theft Act
- There is no definition in the Act of what is meant by dishonesty and it is up to the jury to decide this. Normally no direction on this will be needed (*Price 1989*). In cases where the defendant is disputing his lack of honesty, however, *Ghosh 1982* states that the jury should look at two points; first, whether according to the ordinary standards of reasonable and honest people what was done was dishonest. Secondly, if they decide that it was dishonest by those standards, did the defendant himself realise this?

- S.2(1) states that a person will not be classed as dishonest if he believes that he has a right in law to the article. The belief need not be a reasonable one, provided it is honestly held (*Holden 1991*). Neither will he be dishonest if he believes that he would have the other's consent if he knew of the matter, or if he believes that the real owner cannot be traced by taking reasonable steps (*Small 1988*)

- Conversely, s.1(2) decides that a person may still be convicted of theft despite the fact that his appropriation of property is not made with a view to gain or for his own benefit, and s.2(2) states that he may still be classed as dishonest even if he is willing to pay for the property.

- There is also no definition of the phrase 'intention of permanently depriving the other of it' (*Warner 1970*). S.6, however, describes certain situations where this will be assumed, as where the offender has an intention to treat the property as his own to dispose of regardless of the other's rights. This includes situations where he borrows or lends property in circumstances which amount to an outright taking of it (*Downes 1983*, *Velumyl 1989* and *Lavender 1994*), or where he pawns or otherwise disposes of property belonging to another in circumstances where he may be unable to get it back. If he uses the property of another but then later returns it, he will only be classed as permanently depriving the other of the goods if the value in them has been used up (*Lloyd 1985*, *Bagshaw 1988*).

- Provided that the indictment is correctly worded, it appears that the defendant can be convicted of attempted theft in cases where he searches property in order to discover whether there is anything worth stealing and then discards it (*AG's References Nos 1 and 2 of 1979*)

- The *actus reus* of theft is satisfied where the defendant 'appropriates property belonging to another' and explanations and illustrations of these terms are found in ss.3, 4, and 5 of the Theft Act 1968

- The word 'appropriates' described under s.3 has caused problems for the courts but is now settled as meaning to assume any of the rights of the owner (*Morris 1984*, *Gomez 1993*)

- The appropriation takes place the first time that the defendant assumes any of these rights (*Gomez 1993*)

- *Gomez 1993* also firmly supported *Lawrence* v *Metropolitan Police Commissioner 1972* and affirmed that there may still be an appropriation in cases where the true owner consents to the taking. *Morris 1984*, which decided that there had to be an adverse interference with the true owner's rights, was overruled on this point

- *Gomez* also decided that there was no necessity for there to be an actual taking of property to amount to an appropriation, although, in some cases, it might well be difficult to prove the *mens rea* at this point. It would appear that the Court of Appeal decision in *Gallasso 1993*, suggesting that there had to be a taking, was wrongly decided

- *Atakpu 1994* established that there cannot be successive thefts of the same property and the men's convictions for attempted theft were quashed

- It appears that there will not be an appropriation in cases where the civil law has decided that a valid gift has been made, as in *Mazo 1996*

- Property is widely defined in s.4 to include most types of tangible and intangible property (*Welsh 1974*, *AG of Hong Kong* v *Cchang Nai-Keung 1987*) but not, it appears, confidential information like examination secrets (*Oxford* v *Moss 1978*). It also does not include land unless something is severed from it, a trust is involved or a fixture is removed, nor wild animals, fungi, fruit, flowers and foliage unless taken for profit. With regard to trusts without any beneficiaries, s.5(2) states that the trust property shall be taken as belonging to any people who have rights under the trust.

- Under s.5(1), property can belong to another if that person has temporary possession or control of it (*Turner No. 2 1971*)

- Treasure belongs to the Crown and other finds belong to the owner if attached or found within the land (*Waverley BC* v *Fletcher 1995*). Only in other cases will they belong to the finder
- Where property is given to the defendant to deal with in a particular way, s.5(3) states that he will be guilty of theft if he uses it for his own purposes (*Davidge* v *Bennett 1984*). It appears, however that this will only apply where the property should be kept apart to be forwarded to a third party, as in *Wain 1995*. The defendants in *Hall 1973* and *Huskinson 1988* were under no such obligation
- S.5(4) imposes a duty on the defendant to return property to the rightful owner if the defendant has come by it by mistake and is under a legal obligation to restore it (*AG's Reference (No. 1 of 1983) 1985*)
- In addition, there may also be such a duty under s.5(1), where a proprietary interest is involved and the Chase Manhattan principle is invoked, as in *Shadrokh-Cigari 1988*.
- It is arguable whether there is such a duty at common law, once ownership of the goods has passed to the defendant but in *Gilks 1972* the Court of Appeal upheld his conviction on this ground, while making it clear that a moral obligation would not suffice for s.5(4)
- It is vital to remember that all the elements of the definition of theft in s.1 Theft Act 1968 have to be established. If not, the defendant is entitled to an acquittal

FIGURE 7.2 *Key facts chart on the law of theft*

Now that the elements making up the offence of theft are known, it is appropriate to look at certain other offences, not involving deception, for which most examination boards require knowledge and which are also to be found in the Theft Act 1968. These are robbery, burglary, aggravated burglary and blackmail.

7.3 ROBBERY

S.8 Theft Act 1968 defines this. It states:

> A person is guilty of robbery if he steals and immediately before or at the time of doing so and in order to do so, he uses force on any person or seeks to put them in fear of being then and there subjected to force.

In the following article it can be seen that Russell Grant-McVicar put fear into the hearts of several young women by his violent acts.

John McVicar's robber son jailed for 15 years

THE ARMED robber and fugitive son of John McVicar was jailed for 15 years by the Old Bailey today "to protect the public".

Russell Grant-McVicar, 33, whose father was once Britain's most wanted man, was sent to prison "for what you did but not for who you are".

Grant-McVicar carried out a series of armed robberies "with skill and considerable panache" but deliberately and ruthlessly put innocent people, mostly young women, in fear of their lives, said judge Geoffrey Grigson.

Like his father, who was sentenced to 26 years in 1968 before escaping from Durham prison, Grant-McVicar went on the run after twice evading police and prison warders.

John McVicar, now 58 and a respected writer, believes his son's crimewave was a deliberate attempt to punish him for being in prison during his childhood. Grant-McVicar changed his name to distance himself from the notoriety of his father who he claims neglected him and his mother.

Before being sentenced today he sent a letter to the judge which was not read in court.

However, Judge Grigson told him: "I have read what you have said about your family but you must understand that the effect on them is your responsibility. My responsibility is to the public and you must understand that I sentence you for what you did but not for who you are. You appreciate that only a substantial sentence is appropriate and it is necessary to protect the public from your activities."

The judge added that Grant-McVicar claimed in his letter he regretted the trauma caused to his victims, but said "that was the effect of what you did".

Grant McVicar was convicted yesterday of eight robberies, including ripping a £650,000 Picasso from the walls of a leading West End art gallery. He was also found guilty of two charges of escaping custody, one attempted robbery and five firearms offences. Further counts of abducting a 14-year-old girl and unlawful sex were allowed to lie on the file.

Grant-McVicar told the judge he had had "a fair trial", and, as he was led from the dock, he nodded his thanks to police and the jury.

Taken from an article by Paul Cheston in the *Evening Standard*, 22 May 1998

It should be noted that the defendant might have been fortunate to be jailed for only 15 years. S.8(2) Theft Act 1968 provides that the maximum sentence is life imprisonment.

It can be seen by the definition that robbery is aggravated theft so it is very important to realise that, firstly, theft, with all the elements discussed earlier in this chapter, must be established. There must, therefore, be a dishonest appropriation of property belonging to another with the intention to permanently deprive the other of it. In addition, the theft must be accompanied by the use of force or the threat that immediate force may be used.

The elements of theft were not established in the case of *Robinson 1977*. The defendant ran a clothing club and was owed money by the victim's wife. A fight took place and in the course of this a £5 note fell from the victim's pocket which the defendant appropriated. He further claimed that he was still owed £2.

The Court of Appeal quashed the conviction for robbery. The defendant had an honest belief that he was entitled to the money so could not be held to have stolen it. He could, of course, have been charged with other crimes, such as actual bodily harm but should not have been convicted of burglary.

The additional elements required before a robbery is committed would also not be made out in cases where the force is used first and then the wrongdoer then goes on to steal. This could occur, for example, where the offender attacked another who made derogatory comments about him and when his victim was lying unconscious, stole his wallet. It would also not be robbery where a theft took place and violence was used when the getaway was prevented. In these situations, the force is not being used or threatened 'in order to' steal and is not taking place 'before or at the time of' the theft. The courts, however, take a pragmatic approach to these words and have decided that a theft can be a continuing affair, as in *Hale 1978*.

The defendant and an accomplice, wearing stocking masks, forced their way into the victim's house, put a hand over her mouth to stop her screaming and later tied her up. Meanwhile, the accomplice had stolen a jewellery box from the rooms upstairs. They were later convicted of robbery but appealed, arguing that the theft was over when the force took place. The court refused to accept this claiming that 'the act of appropriation does not suddenly cease. It is a continuous act and it is a matter for the jury to decide whether or not the act of appropriation has finished'.

The court was also prepared, in the alternative, to accept that the act of putting a hand over the victim's mouth was also using force and this, too was done to facilitate the theft.

The Criminal Law Revision Committee,

when devising this section, made it clear that there had to be more than a mere snatching of property from an unresisting owner before it could be held to be a robbery. The courts, however, have decided that it is enough that there is some resistance to the taking. In *Clouden 1987*, for example, the defendant's conviction for robbery was upheld when he used both hands to wrench a shopping bag from the victim and ran off with it. In the earlier case of *Dawson 1976*, jostling the victim was also held to be enough force. Lawton L J stated that 'Force is a word in ordinary use. It is a word which juries understand'. He decided, therefore, that the jurors 'were entitled to the view that force was used'. In *Corcoran* v *Anderton 1980*, it was held to be immaterial that the robbery had not been effected. This case concerned another bag-snatching attempt, of the type that has become so commonplace in recent times. The attack had been planned and the victim was pushed from behind and her handbag snatched from her. She then screamed and fell and the two youths ran away without taking the bag. The Divisional Court was asked to decide whether 'the tugging at the handbag, accompanied by force, amounted to robbery, notwithstanding the fact that the co-accused did not have sole control of the bag at any time'.

The Divisional Court decided that 'there cannot possibly be, save for the instance where a handbag is carried away from the scene ... a clearer instance of robbery than that which these justices found was committed.' They held that the forcible tugging of the handbag was a sufficient exercise of control by the accused.

activity

Mickey has borne a grudge against members of the acting profession ever since he was rejected for a part in a popular soap opera. Decide whether he has committed robbery in the following instances:

> He visited a film premiere and, as Liz was going into the cinema, pulled one of her diamond earrings from her ear.

> He had a fight with Sylvester and knocked him out. While Sylvester was on the floor, Gordon decided to steal his Rolex watch.

> He forced his way into Demi's house and stole the contents of her safe. He then tied her to a chair and made his escape.

> He wrestled with Arnold as the latter was leaving a film set and snatched his camera. Arnold then started to fight back so Mickey dropped the camera and ran away.

7.4 BURGLARY

S.9 Theft Act 1968 lays down a rather complicated definition of burglary. To summarise this, s.9(1)(a) states that:

> Burglary is committed where the defendant enters a building or part of one as a trespasser, with the intent to steal, to inflict grievous bodily harm or to rape therein or to do unlawful damage to the building or anything inside it.

S.9(1)(b) provides that burglary will also be committed when a person steals or inflicts grievous bodily harm on another, after he has entered as a trespasser, or attempts to do either of these things.

The maximum sentence for this offence is laid down in s.9(3) and is 14 years imprisonment.

It can be seen that one difference between these two sections is that, in subsection (a), the offender must intend to steal or commit the other offences laid down at the time he trespasses, but in subsection (b) the intent to steal can be formed after the trespass. Another difference is that the offence under s.9(1)(b) only applies to theft and grievous bodily harm, but, unlike s.9(1)(a), also includes attempts to do either of these things.

The words 'entry', 'trespasser' and 'building' have caused problems and need looking at further.

Entry

The first point to note is that the entry must have been effective. In earlier cases it was decided that the entry had to be both substantial and effective, as held in *Collins 1973* but this is no longer necessary, as the cases of *Brown 1985* and *Ryan 1996* illustrate.

Collins is a case known to nearly every law student because of its peculiar facts. Edmund Davies stated that if the facts of this case were to be put in a novel or a play they 'would be regarded as being so improbable as to be unworthy of serious consideration and as verging at times on farce'.

The defendant, who was 19, had seen the girl in question when he worked near her house and after drinking a considerable amount he had decided to visit the premises. He had seen a light in her bedroom and had fetched a ladder to reach the room. He then saw the girl naked and asleep in a bed very near the window. He descended the ladder, took off all his clothes except his socks, and then re-climbed the ladder and reached the window sill. He alleged that he was pulling himself into the room when the girl awoke. He claimed that she had then got up, knelt by the bed, embraced him and appeared to pull him towards it. They then had sexual intercourse.

The girl argued that she had awoken at about 3.30am and seen a vague form with blond hair in the open window. She was unable to say categorically whether the person was on the outside part of the window sill or actually inside the room. She firmly believed at that point that her boyfriend had come to make a nocturnal visit but later, during the intercourse, started to have doubts about this! She then

turned on the light, discovered that her fears were justified and slapped the defendant's face. When she visited the bathroom, the defendant made his escape.

Collins was later convicted of burglary. The girl, not unnaturally, argued that she would not have agreed to the intercourse if she had known that the man in question was not her boyfriend. The defendant, on the other hand, claimed that he would not have entered the room if the girl had not beckoned him in. Despite this contention, he was convicted. He later appealed on the basis that he had not entered as a trespasser.

The Court of Appeal decided that, in a case such as this, three ingredients to the offence of burglary had to be proved. Firstly, there had to be an entry into the building. This point was soon proved. Secondly, the defendant needed to have entered as a trespasser, which was far more difficult to decide upon. Lastly, he had to have intended, at the time of entry, to commit rape.

The Court of Appeal decided that the judge had misdirected the jury on both of these points, particularly the second one. The court stated that 'Unless the jury were entirely satisfied that the appellant made an effective and substantial entry into the bedroom without the complainant doing or saying anything to cause him to believe that that she was consenting to his entering it, he ought not to be convicted of the offence charged. The point is a narrow one, as narrow maybe as the window sill which is crucial to this case. But this is a criminal charge of gravity and, even though one may suspect that his intention was to commit the offence charged, unless the facts show with clarity that he in fact committed it he ought not to remain convicted'. The conviction, therefore, was quashed.

The fact that there must be a substantial and effective entry followed the earlier common law position but has since been disputed. In *Brown 1985*, the Court of Appeal upheld a conviction for burglary even though the defendant argued that his entry was ineffective because a major part of his body was still on the highway. He had been caught while leaning through a broken shop window and sorting through the goods. In *Ryan 1996*, the Court of Appeal went even further and refused to entertain the idea that there could not be an effective entry because the wrongdoer had got stuck trying to effect one! The defendant had got himself into this unfortunate position by trying to climb through a small window of a residential property in the dead of night. Eventually, the fire brigade had rescued him. At his trial, Ryan tried to argue that he was only attempting to recover his baseball hat, which his friend had thrown through the window. The jury refused to believe such a story and the Court of Appeal upheld his conviction for burglary, despite the fact that he was unable to go any further in his efforts to gain entry.

Trespasser

It is now necessary to examine the word 'trespasser'. Usually, it will be easy to show that the wrongdoer is trespassing but occasionally there are problems, as, for example, when the defendant claims that he has a right to be there. This was the case in *Jones and Smith 1976*. The defendants removed two television sets from the home of Smith's father during the night and were convicted of burglary. At the trial, however, the father had tried to protect his son by arguing that he was not a trespasser because he had unreserved permission to enter the house. The Court of Appeal was not prepared to accept this and decided that the word 'trespasser' also covered cases where a person acts in excess of the permission given. The court quoted with approval the civil case of *Hillen and Pettigrew* v *ICI 1936*, and particularly the comment that 'When you invite a person into your house to use the staircase you do not invite him to slide down the banisters'. The appeals, therefore, were dismissed. The court made it clear that a person is a trespasser if he enters premises of another knowing that he is entering in excess of the permission that has been given to him, or being reckless as to this fact.

Building

Lastly, the word 'building' needs investigation. There is no definition of this word in the Act but s.9(4) states that the word includes an inhabited vehicle and a vessel, even if they are not inhabited at the time of the offence. In the early civil case of *Stevens* v *Gourley 1859* it was suggested that a building was 'a structure of considerable size and intended to be permanent, or at least endure for a considerable time'. In *B and S* v *Leathley 1979*, there appeared to be an extension of this definition because a locked freezer container, resting on sleepers and connected to the main electricity supply, was held to be a building. In *Norfolk Constabulary* v *Seekings and Gould 1986*, however, the courts were not prepared to widen the definition to include two lorry trailers; these remained as mere vehicles.

Burglary will also be committed where the trespasser enters 'any building or part of a building'. This point was at issue in the case of *Walkington 1979*. The defendant went up to the first floor in Debenham's department store, went behind one of the moveable counters and looked into the open drawer of the till. He discovered that it was empty, slammed it shut and tried to leave the store. He was arrested and later convicted of burglary. The Court of Appeal quoted from Professor Smith's book, *The Law of Theft*, in which it is stated:

> A licence to enter a building may extend to part of a building only. If so, the licensee will trespass if he enters some other part.

If the offender then intends to commit a crime in that other part, he will be guilty of burglary. The Court of Appeal also decided that such a person still commits the offence even if he only intends to steal on the condition he finds something worth stealing.

7.4.1 THE *MENS REA* OF BURGLARY

The offender must know that he is a trespasser or be reckless as regards this fact and then must have the intention to commit the ulterior offence.

7.5 AGGRAVATED BURGLARY

S.10 Theft Act 1968 is easy to understand. S.10(1) states that:

> A person will be guilty of aggravated burglary if he commits any burglary and at the time has with him any firearm or imitation firearm, any weapon of offence, or any explosive.

S.10(2) states that the term 'firearm' also includes airguns and air pistols and 'imitation firearm' means 'anything which has the appearance of being a firearm, whether capable of being discharged or not'. This obviously brings a wide range of real and imitation guns within the definition. The term 'weapon of offence' has caused some problems. It is defined as 'any article made or adapted for use for causing injury to or incapacitating a person or intended by the person having it with him for such use'.

It can be seen from these sections that the aggravated offence is established if the defendant possesses any of these articles at the time of the offence; he does not have to use them or even intend to do so. In *Stones 1989*, the defendant had a household knife in his possession but claimed that this was merely for self-defence because 'some lads from Blyth' were after him. The prosecution admitted that this was not an article 'made or adapted for use', etc. but decided that the person intended to use it for the causing of injury or to incapacitate someone. The Court of Appeal upheld the conviction on the grounds that it was not necessary to prove that the defendant intended to use the article in the burglary; it was enough that he had the article with him and intended to use it in any way.

In the earlier case of *O'Leary 1986*, the defendant had not been armed when he entered the house but took a knife from the kitchen upstairs with him. His conviction under s.10 was upheld as he had the weapon with him when he made the decision to steal.

7.6 BLACKMAIL

In days gone by, the word 'blackmail' described 'gifts' given by border landowners to chieftains in Scotland to prevent raids on their property, i.e. the word described an early form of protection racket. Gradually, the word was extended to cover other forms of extortion and made a serious criminal offence. The cry of the highwayman 'Your money or your life' is an example of blackmail, and the offender would have been subjected to the full rigours of the law if he were caught.

Britvic blackmail case man is jailed

THE man who tried blackmailing Chelmsford's soft drink giant, Britvic, by threatening to poison their apple juice, was a top security officer in Bass Charrington, part of the company's group, a court heard.

Paul Bovingdon, 49, of Copmanthorpe, Yorks, was jailed for six years on Monday. He admitted blackmail.

Judge Benjamin Pearson, sitting at Chelmsford Crown Court, told Bovingdon: "Your position as regional security manager for Bass Charrington gave you specialist knowledge which you employed in your criminal design.

"You knew your threat to poison your victim's product was a threat to ruin that company. Blackmail is a serious and disgusting offence. Companies involved in the retail trade with products for human consumption are entitled to the court's protection."

Robert Neill, prosecuting, said part of Bovingdon's job was to arrange company lectures on "crisis management" of terrorist threats, bomb hoaxes and menacing demands.

On March 31 he sent a carton of Britvic apple juice to the Chelmsford office of Stephen Davis, managing director of Britvic.

The carton had been injected with a harmless dye. A letter demanded £5,000 or a poison would be injected into cartons for sale.

Other communications with Bovingdon's code title "Panic" followed with directions to toss the money over a five-barred gate into a Yorkshire field near Bovingdon's home.

HELICOPTER

Essex police mounted one of their largest-ever investigations and Britvic appeared to go along with the demand.

A police officer acting as courier delivered the money as directed. A police helicopter with heat-seeking device then homed in on Bovingdon.

He was curled up in the undergrowth wearing a home-

made camouflage outfit. With him was night sight equipment supplied by Bass Charrington. He said he was looking for badgers.

Later he said he needed £5,000 to clear domestic debts and did not demand more because he thought there was a more realistic possibility of success.

Peter Morris, mitigating, said: "Bovingdon acted out of character when he was at the end of his tether. He is destroyed."

Taken from an article in the *Essex Chronicle*, 11 September 1998

The crime of blackmail is now under found under s.21 Theft Act, which states that a person will be guilty of blackmail if:

> with a view to gain for himself or another or with intent to cause loss to another, he makes an any unwarranted demand with menaces.

The above article in the local press shows that this unpleasant crime is alive and well in the latter half of the twentieth century.

Gain and loss

The first thing to note is that, under s.34 Theft Act, the words 'gain' and 'loss' only apply to gains or losses in money or other property, although this is normally what will be demanded. The words 'with a view to gain for himself' mean, however, that it would also be blackmail if the defendant demanded a superior job or better housing, if such a demand was unwarranted and was made with menaces, because extra money would be involved or better property.

In *Bevans 1987*, a man crippled with osteo-arthritis produced a gun and demanded a mor-

phine injection from a doctor he had summoned. He threatened to shoot the doctor if he did not comply. The court decided that the morphine came under the heading of 'property' and his conviction for blackmail was upheld.

It would not, however, be blackmail if services were demanded with menaces. An example would be where sexual favours were demanded, accompanied by a threat to expose some unsavoury conduct of the victim should the service not be performed. In a case like this, there would be no gain or loss of money or other property.

Unwarranted

Next, to satisfy the definition, the demand must be 'unwarranted'. The Criminal Law Revision Committee held that two of the essential features of blackmail are that the defendant is demanding something to which he knows he has no right and, secondly, that he knows that the use of menaces is wrong. The approach, therefore, is subjective; it is not what the reasonable man believes but, instead, the defendant himself must know that he is not entitled to the property demanded or at least have knowledge that it is wrong to demand it in this way.

In *Harvey 1980*, the defendants tried to argue that they had a right to act as they did but the jury obviously did not agree and they were convicted. They had arranged to pay £20,000 to a person called Scott, in return for a large supply of cannabis. Scott supplied worthless goods and the enraged defendants then kidnapped his wife and child and demanded the repayment of their money. They were convicted of blackmail along with other offences but appealed.

The Court of Appeal acknowledged that the trial judge had failed to make it clear to the jurors that it was up to them to decide whether the defendants genuinely believed that they had reasonable grounds for making the demand. It was decided, however, that this misdirection would not have prejudiced the defendants. The appeal, therefore, was dismissed.

Demand

It is now necessary to look at the word 'demand'. This is the essence of the offence. The crime of blackmail will still exist even in cases where the defendant fails to receive what has been asked for, provided that a clear demand has been made. The courts have also decided that the demand can be implied from the circumstances, as well as being made in a more express way. In *Collister and Warhurst 1955*, the defendant was intended to overhear the comments of two police officers, suggesting that the charges might be dropped if a payment was made by the accused. This was held to constitute a demand. It also appears from the case of *Treacy* v *DPP 1971*, that, if the demand is made by post, it takes effect as soon as the letter is posted and it is immaterial whether the letter actually reaches the proposed victim.

Menaces

The word 'menaces' used only to cover threats of violence but has since been widened. In *Thorne* v *Motor Trade Association 1937*, it was said to be 'an ordinary English word which any

jury can be expected to understand'. In the same case it was held to include 'threats of action detrimental to or unpleasant to the person addressed'. The threat 'Unless you pay me within seven days . . . you will have to look over your shoulder before you step out of doors', had been made by roof repairer who had not been paid because the work was thought by the householder to be sub-standard. Later, other threatening words had been uttered and the defendant's conviction for blackmail was upheld.

In *Clear 1968*, the word was narrowed slightly when it was held that the menaces should be:

> of such a nature and extent that the mind of an ordinary person of normal stability and courage might be influenced or made apprehensive.

There will be some cases, therefore, where the demand is not considered to be in this category. This view was taken in the case of *Harry 1974*, where a treasurer of a college rag committee sent letters to over 100 shopkeepers asking them to buy posters for charity. The poster was stated to protect the shopkeeper 'from any Rag Activity which could in any way cause you inconvenience'. A few of the people to whom the letter was addressed felt unhappy with the tone of the latter and, later, the prosecution agreed that it contained 'the clearest threat or menace however nicely it was couched'. Judge Petre of Chelmsford Crown Court (perhaps remembering his own student days!), did not agree. He stated 'Menaces is a strong word' and directed the jury to acquit.

- The crime of robbery is defined in s.8 Theft Act 1968; the maximum sentence is life imprisonment, (s.8(2))
- The elements of the crime of theft must first be established (*Robinson 1977*). It then has to be proved that the defendant used force, or threatened to use it, immediately before or at the time of the crime, although the courts have been prepared to find that a robbery can be a protracted affair (*Hale 1978*)
- A simple snatching of property would be theft rather than robbery but the latter may be established if the victim resists the attack (*Clouden 1987*) and maybe even where the victim has merely been jostled (*Dawson 1976*). There is no requirement that the goods have to be taken (*Corcoran v Anderton 1980*)
- Burglary is defined in s.9 Theft Act 1968 and can be committed in one of two ways. Both require a trespass by the defendant. Most trespasses will be obvious but a person will also be a trespasser if he acts in excess of any permission given to him (*Jones and Smith 1971*)
- Under s.9(1)(a) burglary committed where the defendant enters a building or part of one intending to steal, to inflict gbh, to rape or to cause criminal damage. It will also be burglary where the defendant steals or inflicts gbh after having entered as a trespasser (s.9(1)(b))
- The entry must be considered to be an effective one but the courts now take a broader view of this. There is no longer a requirement that the entry should be substantial (*Collins 1973, Brown 1985* and *Ryan 1996*)
- A building is not defined in the Act but will include a vehicle or vessel which is inhabited. The courts have also included a freezer container with mains electricity attached in this category (*B and S v Leathley 1979*) but were not prepared to recognise two stationary lorry containers as such (*Norfolk Constabulary v Seekings and Gould 1986*)
- A person will become a trespasser if he enters a prohibited part of a building and commits one of the prescribed crimes there (*Walkington1973*)
- Aggravated burglary is defined in s.10 and takes place where the burglar has a real or imitation firearm, other weapon or explosive with him at the time he commits the offence. He does not have to bring the weapon with him so long as he has it at the time of the crime (*O'Leary 1986*)
- The term 'other weapon' includes things made or adapted to cause injury or incapacitation (s.10(2)) and it is immaterial that the burglar does not intend to use the article during the commission of the crime (*Stones 1989*)
- Blackmail is defined in s.21 Theft Act 1968 and takes place where the defendant makes an unwarranted demand with menaces with a view to obtaining a gain for himself or another of money or other property or a loss of the same to some other person. The unlawful obtaining of drugs, even those which have to be injected, will come under the definition of property (*Bevans 1987*)
- The demand can be made expressly or be implied from the circumstances (*Collister and Warhurst 1955*), and if posted, takes effect at the time of posting (*Treacy v DPP 1971*). It will be unwarranted when the defendant knows that he is demanding something to which he has no entitlement or when he knows that the use of menaces is wrong (*Harvey 1980*)
- The word 'menaces' is to be given its ordinary meaning, and there is now some doubt as to whether a threat to do something which is merely unpleasant would suffice (*Thorne v Motor Trade Association 1937, Clear 1968*, and *Harry 1974*). In *Clear 1968*, it was decided that the threat must be such that it would influence an ordinary person of normal stability and courage

FIGURE 7.3 *Key facts chart on robbery, burglary and blackmail*

activity

Decide whether the following people have committed any offences under ss.9, 10 and 21 of the Theft Act 1968:

Jack fell asleep at the end of a working day. He awoke to find the building empty so decided to steal one of the computers from the office of his boss.

Jill was desperate for money and planned to steal the silver candlesticks in her local church. She had just put her head through the window when the parish priest discovered her. He then invited her to take the candlesticks as a gift.

Simon, a junior clerk, was having an affair with the Managing Director and threatened to tell her husband unless he was made company secretary.

Mary broke into a department store and then stole a knife from the kitchen department. She used this to force the security officer to give her the contents of the safe.

Tom was a member of a fanatical group of activists. He sent a demand to the management of Tessbury, that all their cosmetic range, allegedly tested on animals, should be withdrawn from the shelves in all their stores. The letter stated that if this action were not taken, a bomb would be planted in one of their busiest branches.

summary

We have discovered that most examination boards require knowledge of the offences of theft, robbery, burglary and blackmail, all of which are to be found in the Theft Act 1968.

We have noted that the offence of theft needs to be known in depth, partly for its own sake and also because it forms the basis of liability for robbery and burglary. Details of both the *actus reus* and the *mens rea* of theft, therefore, laid down in ss.1–6 of the Act, have been examined in detail and then the additional requirements for robbery and burglary have been studied.

Lastly, the offence of blackmail was looked at which normally involves the making of an unwarranted demand for money or other property, accompanied by menaces.

CHAPTER 8

PROPERTY OFFENCES II: DECEPTION OFFENCES

8.1 INTRODUCTION

THIS CHAPTER LOOKS mainly at crimes where some sort of deception is involved. Knowledge of these offences is required for all the examination boards except AEB so it would be very unwise not to learn them. The information acquired could also be useful in everyday life to help maintain your guard against possible confidence tricksters!

It will be seen that five offences involving deception need to be learned, three of which are found in the Theft Act 1968 and two others in the far shorter Theft Act 1978. For convenience, another offence has also been included in this chapter, because this also appears in the Theft Act 1978. This is the offence of making off without payment found under s.3 of that Act.

It is intended to deal with each of these offences in turn, in as simple a way as possible without losing the essential elements of each crime and then to conclude the chapter by examining the offence of making off without payment, found in s.3 Theft Act 1978.

8.2 OBTAINING PROPERTY BY DECEPTION

As stated above, this offence is found in s.15 Theft Act 1968. S.15(1) lays down both the definition and the maximum sentence. It states:

> A person who by any deception dishonestly obtains property belonging to another, with the intention of permanently depriving the other of it shall on conviction on indictment be liable to imprisonment for a term not exceeding ten years.

It can be seen that the definition of this offence is very similar to that of theft, under s.1. It should also be remembered that, since the case of *Gomez*, every time an offender satisfies the definition of obtaining property by deception, he also satisfies the definition of theft under s.1 and could be charged with this offence. In certain situations, this could make it easier for the prosecution to prove its case. There are, however, some important differences between the two crimes. The first is that, under s.15, there is a need for a deception to have been practised so while anyone alleged to have obtained property by deception can also be found guilty of theft, the reverse is not true. Secondly, under s.15, the word 'obtains' is used, rather than the word 'appropriates' in theft. The third difference is in the sentence; the maximum sentence for theft has been shortened to seven years, whereas it is ten years for the s.15 offence.

The *actus reus* of s.15 is satisfied where the defendant by any deception obtains property belonging to another.

The *mens rea* exists when the accused does this dishonestly and with the intention of permanently depriving the other of it. This can be seen more easily in Figure 8.1.

Word or Phrase	Actus Reus	Mens Rea
By any deception	yes	
Whether deliberate or reckless		yes
Dishonestly		yes
Obtains	yes	
Property	yes	
Belonging to another	yes	
With the intention of permanently depriving the other of it		yes

FIGURE 8.1 *The* actus reus *and* mens rea *of deception*

8.2.1 THE *ACTUS REUS* OF OBTAINING PROPERTY BY DECEPTION

The various components of the *actus reus* now need to be studied.

By any deception

This phrase is the key element of this offence. Obviously, there can be no liability under s.15 if the victim has not been deceived. It was stated in *Re London and Globe Finance Corporation 1903* that to deceive is 'to induce a man to believe that a thing is true which is false and which the person practising the deceit knows or believes to be false'. It can be seen from this that a person must be involved, it is not possible to deceive a machine. There would be no liability under s.15, therefore, if an offender put worthless tokens in a machine to obtain something of value from it. Likewise, a deception would not operate where the buyer makes it clear that he was not influenced by the words or conduct of the other party. In *Laverty 1970*, the defendant had changed the registration and chassis number plates on a car and then sold it. His conviction under s.15 was quashed on appeal, as the court was not convinced that the buyer had bought the car solely as a result of this action.

S.15(4) helps to clarify the word 'deception' by stating that it includes deliberate and reckless deception by either words or conduct. In addition, the courts have decided that the deception can be either express or implied. There could, therefore, be liability where goods were paid for by cheque in circumstances where the drawer of the cheque knows that the bank would not honour it, provided that it can be shown that someone had been deceived. This could cause problems where a guarantee card accompanies the cheque because, in such circumstances, the retailer is relying upon the card and knows that the cheque will be honoured. It could be argued that he is not therefore concerned about the fact that there are no funds to meet it. The House of Lords, however, has taken a robust attitude towards the word 'deception' to ensure that cases like this are covered and the offender does not escape liability. This approach can be seen in the case of *Metropolitan Police Commissioner v Charles 1976*, a case which will be discussed more fully on page 148 under obtaining a pecuniary advantage by deception. The House of Lords decided that the defendant's cheques had only been accepted because of the belief that he was acting properly. It followed, therefore, said Lord Edmund-Davies, that the victim was being deceived, even though he may not have been concerned about the deception and may not have incurred any loss.

A similar approach was also taken in *Lambie 1982*, regarding the misuse of a credit card. The defendant used her Barclaycard over 60 times after her credit limit had been exceeded, including a transaction at Mothercare. Lambie had been convicted of obtaining a pecuniary advantage by deception but, on appeal, the conviction had been quashed. The House of Lords then restored the conviction. Their Lordships decided that she had made a representation that she had actual authority to make a contract with Mothercare on the bank's behalf that the bank would honour the voucher on presentation. Lord Roskill also queried why the charge of obtaining property by deception had been rejected and decided that it would have been made out. He rejected the contention that it was necessary in every case to call the person on whom the fraud was first perpetrated, arguing that if this were so, the guilty would often go free.

These cases also illustrate that it is possible to practise a deception by conduct as well as by words.

Another example of this was the case of *DPP v Stonehouse 1978*, where the extraordinary conduct of the MP John Stonehouse hit the headlines all over the world. His financial affairs were in chaos so he decided to fake his death while on a business trip to Miami. He gave the impression that he had drowned by leaving his clothes on the beach and fled to Australia to start a new life with his mistress. He had earlier transferred his money to Australia so that his estate would be insolvent but, to provide for his wife after his 'death', had taken out insurance policies in her favour. Suspicions, however, were aroused and he was later discovered live and well in Australia. The press, of course, had a field day and the MP later returned to this country to face charges of attempting to obtain property by deception. The Court of Appeal upheld his conviction, deciding that 'the accused ... had done all the physical acts lying within his power that were needed to enable Mrs Stonehouse to obtain the policy moneys if all had gone as he intended'.

Another cruel attempt to obtain property by deception was practised on an elderly widow in the case *King and Stockwell 1987*. The defendants pretended that they were from a reputable firm of tree surgeons and falsely told the victim that many of the trees in her garden were dangerous and needed to be removed. They then offered to do the work immediately for the sum of £470, if paid in cash. Their deception came to light when a sympathetic building society cashier noted the woman's distress as she attempted to withdraw the money for the work and called the police. The Court of Appeal upheld the convictions of the two men.

Neill L J stated 'there was ample evidence on which the jury could come to the conclusion that had the attempt succeeded the money would have been paid over by the victim as a result of the lies told to her by the appellants'.

Obtains

The word 'obtains' is explained under s.15(2), which states that a person is treated as obtaining property 'if he obtains ownership, possession or control of it'. He is also classed as doing this if the obtaining is for another person.

A gap in the law was disclosed in cases like *Collis-Smith 1971*, where the defendant obtained the property first and then practised a deception on the other party. Collis-Smith had filled up his car with petrol; therefore, at that moment, ownership in the property had passed to him. He then falsely indicated that his company would pay for it. The conviction under s.15 was quashed because the property had not been obtained by the deception. Ownership had come earlier. It will be seen later in this chapter that this gap has now been closed by the passing of the Theft Act 1978 and that the defendant could now be charged with evading a liability by deception under s.2.

Property

The word 'property' is not defined in s.15 but s.34 states that the definition of property in s.4(1) will apply to all sections of the Act. The word therefore includes 'money and all other property, real or personal, including things in action and other intangible property'. The limitations under s.4(2), however, imposed with regard to the offence of theft, do not apply to s.15. It would appear, therefore, that almost anything might be obtained by deception, including land. An example of this would be where an impostor claimed the estate of a deceased person.

Belonging to another

Under s.34, this phrase, too, will be taken to have the same meaning as in theft. It is possible, therefore, to obtain by deception property that belongs to the offender but is in the temporary control of another.

8.2.2 THE *MENS REA* OF OBTAINING PROPERTY BY DECEPTION

It will be remembered that the *mens rea* of this offence will be present when the defendant obtains the property 'dishonestly' and 'with the intention of permanently depriving the other of it'. In addition, he must have made the deception, discussed above, deliberately or recklessly. These points require further examination.

Dishonestly

It is very important to realise that, in addition to any deception, it is also necessary to prove a dishonest intent. This was clearly stated by the Criminal Law Revision Committee when the bill was being drafted and is also obvious from the definition. To clinch matters, the Court of Appeal affirmed this position in *Feeny 1991*, when it was said that the offence could not be committed 'unless dishonesty is established as a separate and essential ingredient'.

When deciding whether the defendant is dishonest, the *Ghosh* test, mentioned under theft, will be used. The jury needs to be convinced of two things, first, that the defendant's behaviour was dishonest when judged against the standards of reasonable and honest people and secondly, that the defendant himself realised that he was doing wrong by those standards. As stated in *Price 1990*, however, on many occasions this will be obvious and, if so, it is not necessary for the trial judge to give the *Ghosh* direction.

In *Lightfoot 1993*, the defendant had obtained a Barclaycard issued in the name of Plummer, a fellow firefighter. Lightfoot had used the card to purchase goods to the value of £3000. There was some doubt as to whether he had done this with the consent of the named person and Plummer strongly denied this. The direction of the trial judge did not follow exactly the words laid down in the *Ghosh* test but they were similar. The Court of Appeal

held that this was good enough and upheld the conviction on the grounds that the defendant must have appreciated that he was doing wrong by the standards of reasonable and honest people.

With regard to dishonesty in theft, s.2(1) lays down situations where a person is not classed as being dishonest; it is important to realise that there is no corresponding section with regard to obtaining property by deception.

With the intention of permanently depriving the other of it

S.15(3) states that the extended definition of this phrase, laid down in s.6 concerning theft, also applies to s.15. A person will commit the offence, therefore, if he treats the property as his own to dispose of, provided, of course, that the other elements of obtaining property by deception are present.

Whether deliberate or reckless

In addition to the two phrases within the definition of s.15(1), s.15(4) also states, indirectly, that the deception must be practised deliberately or recklessly. In *Staines 1974*, the Court of Appeal held that the term 'recklessness' meant more than mere carelessness or negligence on the part of the defendant. It is also made clear by the cases that in all the deception offences, *Cunningham*-type recklessness must be proved.

Greenstein 1976 can be cited as a rare example of a reckless deception. The case concerned the very questionable activity of 'stagging', whereby large blocks of shares were applied for by the defendant, 'paid for' with a cheque for which funds were not available. This was done in the knowledge that the shares would be over-subscribed and only a proportion of the shares applied for would be issued. When this reduced allocation was assessed, a cheque would then be sent to cover the difference between the amount of the shares applied for and the ones received. This amount would then be banked so that when the original cheque was presented at the applicant's bank, there would then be enough money to honour it, if not on the first presentation, then on a subsequent one. In this way, the applicants would receive a higher allocation of shares than if they had only applied for shares to the amount that they could afford and had then been given a proportional allocation of this quantity. The practice of stagging was considered to be highly irregular and to try to combat it, the issuers of the shares would sometimes ask applicants to give an assurance that the cheque would be met on its first presentation. This was the position in this case and the defendants were charged with obtaining the shares by deception, when such a declaration was held to be a false one. The defendants tried to argue that they had not been dishonest because in the vast majority of cases where such a practice had been employed in the past, the cheques had almost always been honoured. The Court of Appeal decided that the cheques could only be met if the applicants were successful in their deception on the issuers of the shares. This deception was that their application was a genuine one. It could also be argued that the defendants were reckless because, while they hoped that their cheques would be met, there was always a chance that they would not be. They were aware that in 14 out of 136 transactions the return cheque had not been cleared in time to cover the amount needed for the first cheque.

8.3 OBTAINING A MONEY TRANSFER BY DECEPTION

The law on this is to be found in a new s.15A, inserted into the Theft Act 1968 by the Theft (Amendment) Act 1996. The very swift change in the law followed the controversial finding of the House of Lords in *Preddy 1996*, that no existing deception offence had been committed when the defendants had obtained mortgages by giving false information. Their Lordships had come to this conclusion because no property had passed from the payer to the payee; there had merely been a transfer of money between the two accounts.

S.15A states:

> A person is guilty of an offence if by any deception he dishonestly obtains a money transfer for himself or another.

Such an offence occurs where money is debited from one account and credited to another and 'the credit results from the debit or the debit results from the credit' (s.15A(2)). The maximum punishment is laid down in s.15A(5) and is ten years imprisonment.

8.3.1 THE *ACTUS REUS* OF OBTAINING A MONEY TRANSFER BY DECEPTION

The *actus reus* of this offence is satisfied when a person by any deception obtains a money transfer for himself or another.

8.3.2 THE *MENS REA* OF OBTAINING A MONEY TRANSFER BY DECEPTION

The *mens rea* occurs when the deception is deliberate or reckless (s.15B states that the word is to have the same meaning as in s.15), and the obtaining is done dishonestly.

8.4 OBTAINING A PECUNIARY ADVANTAGE BY DECEPTION

The offence and the punishment for it are laid down in s.16(1) Theft Act 1968, which states that:

> a person who by any deception dishonestly obtains for himself or another any pecuniary advantage shall on conviction on indictment be liable to imprisonment for a term not exceeding five years.

S.16(2) states the circumstances when such an offence will occur.

Under s.16(2)(b), a person unlawfully acquires a monetary advantage for himself if, by deception, he is permitted to become overdrawn, take out an annuity or insurance policy or to secure an improvement on the terms of any such transaction. An example would be where the wrongdoer falsely tells his bank that he needs an overdraft for repairs to his house but, in reality, intends to spend the money on a trip to the Bahamas.

Similarly, the defendant in *MPC v Charles 1977*, mentioned earlier in this chapter, also committed this offence. He visited a gaming club called the Golden Nugget and, in just one evening, used all the cheques in his book to purchase chips for gaming. Each of them was made out for the sum of £30 and covered by a cheque guarantee card so each cheque subsequently had to be honoured by the bank. The defendant tried to argue that the casino owner was not deceived, because he was unconcerned as to whether the defendant had the bank's authority to issue these cheques; he would be paid in any event. As noted previously, however, the House of Lords took a liberal approach to the question of deception and his conviction was upheld.

S.16(2)(c) states that a person also commits this offence if, by his deception:

> he is given the opportunity to earn remuneration or greater remuneration in an office or employment.

Such an offence would be committed if the defendant lied about his qualifications and thereby obtained a higher paid job, as shown in the following article.

Teacher lied over degree to get a better-paid job

A TEACHER who lied about his qualifications to get a job and boost his pay was yesterday ordered to do 180 hours community service.

Timothy Steel, 31, was found out after four years when he applied for another post and was discovered to have been overpaid by almost £14,000.

York Crown Court was told that he claimed to hold a second class BA Honours degree from Liverpool Poiytechnic where he had, in fact, obtained a third class business studies degree.

James Robinson, prosecuting, said the lie enabled him to get an interview and secure the job at Filey School, North Yorks, in 1994 for which he was paid a rate above his qualifications.

He said it was only when Steel resigned as the school's information technology co-ordinator last May for another job that his false application became apparent.

Adrian Robinson, defending, said Steel had repaid the local authority in full the amount he was overpaid, which was put at nearly £14,000.

He told the court that Steel had enhanced GCSE pass rates at every school he taught at including Filey and schools in Crystal Palace and Elephant and Castle, south London.

Mr Robinson said: "He was and still is a capable and confident teacher. He is hard working and enthusiastic and has found a new job at a London school. There has never been a complaint about his aptitude."

His current school, where he is an information technology teacher, was aware of the proceedings and Steel's job was still open to him.

"He is a valued member of the new school and of the teaching profession," added Mr Robinson.

Steel, of Catford, south London, was appearing for sentence after admitting obtaining a pecuniary advantage by deception from North Yorkshire county council.

Judge Trevor Kent-Jones said it would be in the interests of everyone to allow him to carry on in the classroom by making him do unpaid work for the community.

He said: "I am sure this will be a lesson to you and clearly you must act honestly in the future. It is unfortunate that a check was not made if a salary depends on it. They took what you said at face value."

Taken from an article by Paul Stokes in the *Daily Telegraph*, 26 September 1998. © Telegraph Group Limited, London, 1998.

In *Callender 1992*, the wording of s.16(2)(c) was held to cover self-employed people as well as employees. The defendant had been engaged to prepare the accounts for several small businesses, had received payment for the work but had not performed his side of the bargain. It was discovered that he had lied about his professional qualifications and was not, as claimed, a qualified accountant. He was therefore charged under s.16. In his defence, Callender tried to argue that he did not come under the definition of 'an office or employment'. The Court of Appeal decided that this term should be interpreted liberally and upheld his conviction.

The observant student might have noted that there has been no explanation of s.16(2)(a). This section was repealed after criticism of its ambiguous wording and the difficulty of obtaining convictions under it. In its place, s.2 Theft Act 1978 created a new offence of evading a liability by deception. A case illustrating the now defunct section is that of *DPP* v *Ray 1974*.

The defendant, together with his three friends, ordered a meal in a restaurant. The defendant did not have enough money to pay his share but an arrangement was made that the others would lend him the money. After the meal, however, they all decided not to pay, and, later, when the waiter was out of the room, they ran out of the restaurant.

The defendant was convicted of obtaining a pecuniary advantage by deception under s.16(2)(a) but this was quashed, on appeal, by the Divisional Court. There was a further appeal to the House of Lords where the conviction was restored. Their Lordships decided that the defendant had evaded his debt by deceiving the waiter. This deception had been practised by the defendant remaining in the restaurant after finishing the main meal thereby giving the impression that he and his friends were 'ordinary honest customers'. In this way, they had encouraged the waiter to lower his guard and disappear into the kitchen.

8.4.1 THE *ACTUS REUS* OF OBTAINING A PECUNIARY ADVANTAGE BY DECEPTION

This takes place when a person by any deception obtains for himself or another a pecuniary advantage.

8.4.2 THE *MENS REA* OF OBTAINING A PECUNIARY ADVANTAGE BY DECEPTION

The mental element of this offence is satisfied when the deception is practised deliberately or recklessly, (s.16(3)), and the obtaining is done dishonestly.

Ten years after the passing of the Theft Act 1968, the Theft Act 1978 came into force to help remedy some of the shortcomings found in the earlier Act. Three new offences were created, two of them dealing with deception. The third offence was formulated to address the problem of offenders knowingly decamping without paying for the goods or services they had obtained. These offences will be looked at in the order that they appear in the Act.

8.5 OBTAINING SERVICES BY DECEPTION

This offence is found in s.1 Theft Act 1978, which states:

> A person by any deception dishonestly obtains services from another is guilty of an offence.

S.4 states that the maximum punishment for this offence is five years imprisonment and s.5 states that deception is to have the same meaning as in s.15 Theft Act 1968.

S.1(2) gives further detail on the obtaining of services. This occurs when the other party is induced to confer a benefit on the understanding that it will be paid for. Examples quoted by academics include car repairs, taxi rides and house painting, provided that these acts are done for gain. The benefit given by the other party includes doing an act or causing or permitting one to be done, so would also cover the provision of hotel accommodation or a seat at a theatre. This section, could, on occasion, overlap with the offence under s.15 of the 1968 Act.

It is important to realise that, on the wording of s.1 Theft Act 1978, the deception must occur before the services are obtained. Forms of deception are various; they could include paying for services with a worthless cheque, pretending to be a pensioner to obtain a discount for a service or posing as a wealthy client so that payment is deferred.

There was great consternation when it was decided by the Court of Appeal, in *Halai 1983*, that a mortgage advance was not a service under this section and that the correct charge should have been one under s.15. *Halai* was distinguished in *Widdowson 1985*, where the Court of Appeal decided that a hire-purchase agreement was not to be treated in the same way as a mortgage advance. The court announced that it was rejecting the suggestion 'that the obtaining of a hire-purchase agreement cannot amount to the obtaining of services'. The same court suggested in *Teong Sun Chuah 1991* that *Halai* was wrongly decided and overruled it in *Graham 1997*. At roughly the same time, Parliament also decided to deal with the problem. The Theft (Amendment) Act 1996 inserted a new subsection into s.1 Theft Act 1978. S.1(3) now decides that a mortgage advance is to be treated as a service.

8.5.1 THE *ACTUS REUS* OF OBTAINING SERVICES BY DECEPTION

This occurs where a person by any deception obtains services from another.

8.5.2 THE *MENS REA* OF OBTAINING SERVICES BY DECEPTION

The required *mens rea* exists when the offender deceives the other party deliberately or recklessly and obtains the service dishonestly. S.5 of the Act states that the word 'deception' is to have the same meaning as in s.15 Theft Act 1968.

8.6 EVASION OF LIABILITY BY DECEPTION

This offence is to be found in s.2 Theft Act 1978. It was designed to cover many different situations where the accused, by deception, has tried to avoid the payment of a debt so has three parts to it.

Section 2(1)(a)
Under s.2(1)(a) a person commits an offence if, by any deception, he:

> dishonestly secures the remission of the whole or part of any existing liability to make a payment, whether his own liability or another's.

This means that by deceiving the other party and by acting in a dishonest way, the defendant has managed to get all or part of his debt extinguished, or the debt of someone else extinguished.

For example, if a person dishonestly convinced his creditor that he, (the debtor), was dying and thereby persuaded him not to enforce the debt, he would be liable under this subsection. The offence was also committed in *Jackson 1983*, when the defendant paid for petrol with a stolen credit card. The court decided that he had an existing liability to pay for the petrol already poured into the tank of his motorbike and he had deceived the garage owner about the validity of the credit card.

The *actus reus* of this part of the offence is

where the defendant secures the remission of his own or another's liability.

The *mens rea* of the offence is doing this dishonestly and by practising a deliberate or reckless deception. S.5(1) states that the word 'deception' in all parts of s.2 is to have the same meaning as in s.15 Theft Act 1968.

Section 2(1)(b)

Under s.2(1)(b) a person evades liability if:

> with intent to make permanent default in whole or in part on any existing liability to make a payment, or with intent to let another do so, [he] dishonestly induces the creditor or any person claiming payment on behalf of the creditor to wait for payment . . . or to forgo payment.

A person who writes a cheque or uses a credit card knowing that he is exceeding his authorisation to do this would be liable under this subsection, because s.2(3) specifically provides for this.

A person who convinces the creditor that payment has already been made would also be liable.

In *Holt and Lee 1981*, the Court of Appeal decided that the defendants were rightly convicted of attempting to commit this offence. They were sitting in a pizza restaurant after having consumed a meal and devised a scheme that they would tell their waitress that payment had already been made to another member of staff. They then planned to leave when the coast was clear. Unknown to them, however, their conversation had been overheard by another diner. He was an off-duty policeman who promptly proceeded to arrest them!

The *actus reus* of s.2(1)(b) is satisfied if the defendant by deception, somehow induces a creditor to wait for his money or to forgo payment altogether.

The *mens rea* is present if this is done in a dishonest way, with a deliberate or reckless deception and is meant to be permanent. Temporary stalling devices by the debtor in order to obtain more time to pay would not be enough to incur liability.

Section 2(1)(c)

Under s.2(1)(c) a person will also commit this offence if, by any deception, he:

> dishonestly obtains any exemption from or abatement of liability to make a payment.

An example would be where a person deceives the Inland Revenue into giving him a lower tax assessment or wrongfully gains a rate rebate by making a false statement. It was also decided in *Sibartie 1983* that liability could also arise where the defendant by deception tries to prevent a debt from arising at all.

The defendant passed a ticket inspector and waved an invalid season ticket in his direction. The Court of Appeal decided that he had been correctly convicted of an attempt to commit this offence. He had tried to give the impression that he was the holder of a valid season ticket and was therefore under no liability to pay and, by these means, was trying to gain an exemption. It could be argued that he was also attempting to induce the other to forgo payment under s.2(1)(b).

It is possible to practise such a deception under s.2(1)(c) by failing to reveal certain information in the knowledge that the other is being deceived by this omission. In *Firth 1990*, the defendant was a consultant gynaecologist/obstetrician who performed both National Health and private work. He failed to inform the hospital that two of his patients were private patients so was not billed for the services provided for them. The Court of Appeal upheld the conviction under this section because he had thereby gained an exemption from liability.

The *actus reus* of s.2(1)(c) occurs if the defendant by any deception obtains any exemption from or abatement of liability to make a payment.

The *mens rea* occurs if the deception is effected deliberately or recklessly and the exemption is obtained dishonestly.

- Obtaining property by deception is an offence found under s.15 Theft Act 1968 and carries a maximum punishment of ten years
- Since the case of *DPP* v *Gomez*, all those liable under s.15, would also be guilty of theft under s.1
- The *actus reus* of s.15 is established when, by any deception the defendant obtains property belonging to another (*DPP* v *Stonehouse 1978*, *Lambie 1982*, *King and Stockwell 1987*)
- The *mens rea* is said to exist when the defendant does the obtaining in a dishonest way, intending to permanently deprive the other of the property and his deception is practised deliberately or recklessly (s.15(4), *Greenstein 1976*, *Lightfoot 1993*)
- S.15A Theft Act 1968 creates a new offence of obtaining a money transfer by deception (Theft (Amendment) Act 1996)
- The punishment for this is ten years imprisonment (s.15A(5))
- The *actus reus* exists when a person by any deception obtains a money transfer for himself or another (s.15A(1))
- The *mens rea* is established when the obtaining is dishonest and the deception is deliberately or recklessly practised (s.15A(1), s.15B(2))
- S.16(1) lays down the offence of obtaining a pecuniary advantage by deception and states that the maximum punishment is five years imprisonment
- S.16(2)(a) has been repealed
- S.16(2)(b) states that the offence will occur when a person, by his deception is allowed to become overdrawn, to take out an annuity or insurance policy or to obtain an improvement on existing terms (*MPC* v *Charles 1976*)
- Under s.16(2)(c) the offence is also committed when the offender deceives another in order to gain remuneration or a higher salary or other payment 'in an office or employment'
- The case of *Callender 1992* decides that the term 'in an office or employment' is to be construed widely, so it will cover self-employment
- The *mens rea* of the offence of obtaining a pecuniary advantage by deception is acting dishonestly (s.16(1)) and deliberately or recklessly deceiving the other party (s.16(1), s.16(3))
- The Theft Act 1978 created two additional offences, obtaining services by deception under s.1 and evading a liability by deception in s.2
- S.4 decrees that the maximum punishment for both these offences is five years imprisonment
- S.1(2) states that a service is obtained under s.1 when the other party 'is induced to confer a benefit by doing some act, or causing or permitting some act to be done on the understanding that the benefit has been or will be paid for'
- Services provided free, therefore, will not be covered, even though a deception may have been practised
- Under s.1(3), the provision of mortgage advances now comes within the meaning of services, overruling *Halai 1983*, (Theft (Amendment) Act 1996)
- The *actus reus* of s.1 occurs when a person by any deception obtains services from another
- The *mens rea* is present when this is done dishonestly, and the deception is deliberately or recklessly practised (s.1(1), s.5)
- The offence of evading a liability by deception under s.2 Theft Act 1978 is in three parts
- S.2(1)(a) states that it will occur when the defendant, by any deception, dishonestly secures the remission of the whole or part of a debt. Payment by a stolen credit card would be an example (*Jackson 1983*)

- Under s.2(1)(b), the offence is also committed when the defendant, by any deception, dishonestly persuades the creditor to wait for payment or to forgo payment entirely with the intention never to pay. Pretending that the debt has already been paid would be covered here (*Holt and Lee 1981*)
- S.2(1)(c) states that the offence will also arise where the defendant, by any deception, dishonestly gains exemption from liability (*Sibartie 1983, Firth 1991*)
- S.5 states that the deception must be made deliberately or recklessly. The courts have decided that it should be *Cunningham*-style recklessness

FIGURE 8.2 *Key facts chart on the deception offences*

8.7 MAKING OFF WITHOUT PAYMENT

As stated earlier, this is not a deception offence, although there was some discussion on this during the formulation of the Theft Act 1978. S.3 was created to plug a loophole in the Theft Act 1968 where people obtained goods without at that time deceiving the other party but later refused to pay for them. An example of this type of behaviour was shown in the case of *DPP v Ray 1974*, mentioned earlier, where a diner in a restaurant made off without paying for his meal. It was also intended to cover the passenger in a taxi who fails to pay the fare and the motorist who drives off after filling his tank with petrol.

S.3 Theft Act 1978 states that:

> . . . a person who, knowing that payment on the spot for any goods supplied or service done is required or expected from him, dishonestly makes off without having paid as required or expected and with intent to avoid payment of the amount shall be guilty of an offence.

J R Spencer in an article in the Criminal Law Review in 1983 put forward the view that the term 'making off' means 'disappearing: leaving in a way that makes it difficult for the debtor to be traced', and the Oxford English Dictionary states that it means 'to depart suddenly'. Others would argue that the term merely means 'to leave'. Whatever interpretation is put on the phrase, the offender must be aware that payment on the spot for either goods or a service is expected from him before liability is incurred.

8.7.1 THE *ACTUS REUS* OF MAKING OFF WITHOUT PAYMENT

This arises in cases where the accused makes off without paying for the goods purchased or a service supplied. In *Aziz 1993*, two men asked a taxi driver to take them to a night-club, refused to pay the £15 requested when they arrived there and offered £4 instead. The taxi driver decided to drive them to a police station but on the journey, the men started to damage the taxi. The driver then went into a garage and asked for the police to be called. The two men ran off but one of them was caught and charged under s.3.

The appellant argued that he had not made off from the spot where payment was due. The Court of Appeal held that in journeys by taxi, payment on the spot could either be in the taxi or outside it and in this case the men were still inside it when payment was requested. The court went further and stated that it was enough that the requirement to pay the money had arisen; a particular location was not necessary.

For liability to arise, the payment must be 'required or expected'. In the case of *Troughton v Metropolitan Police Commissioner 1987*, the taxi driver had not completed the journey so was not held to have the right to demand payment. His passenger had asked to be taken to Highbury but had not specified the exact address. He was under the influence of drink and on the journey had quarrelled with the driver, accusing him of making an unnecessary deviation. The taxi driver was unable to get an address from the passenger so made a detour to take him to a police station to try to clarify matters. The defendant was later charged and convicted under s.3.

The Court of Appeal quashed the conviction, deciding that, as the driver had not completed the contract, the defendant could not be required or expected to pay for the journey.

In a similar vein, payment cannot be demanded if the goods supplied or the service provided is contrary to law. This is made clear in s.3(3) of the Act. A defendant who refused to pay a prostitute, therefore, would not incur liability under this section. He could, however, be charged under s.1 for obtaining services by deception because, under this section, no such limitation is imposed.

The term 'making off' suggests that the defendant must have left the premises. Should he be prevented from doing this, it was stated in *McDavitt 1981* that the correct charge should be an attempt.

8.7.2 THE *MENS REA* OF MAKING OFF WITHOUT PAYMENT

There are three elements to the *mens rea*.

1 The defendant must know that payment on the spot is required or expected.
2 He must then dishonestly make off without making such a payment.
3 He must have the intention to avoid making it.

With regard to the first two elements, the defendant would not be liable in the restaurant type of situation if he genuinely but mistakenly believed that someone else was going to pay the bill.

In *Brooks and Brooks 1982*, the Court of Appeal held that this point had not been made

clear to the jury and the daughter's conviction for obtaining a meal without paying for it was quashed, even though she had left the restaurant early in some haste.

In the same case, the court held that 'the words "dishonestly makes off" are words easily understandable by any jury which, in the majority of cases, require no elaboration in a summing up'. In the case of *Allen 1985*, however, the House of Lords was eventually called upon to decide whether the defendant had been dishonest and had also intended to avoid payment.

KEY FACTS

- This offence is found in s.3 Theft Act 1978 and the maximum sentence is two years imprisonment (s.4)
- The term 'making off' is not defined; it could mean merely 'to leave', or 'to depart suddenly' or 'to leave in a way that makes it difficult for the debtor to be found'
- The *actus reus* exists when the defendant makes off without having paid as required or expected (*Aziz 1993*; contrast with *Troughton 1987*, where no liability was incurred)
- Should the offender be apprehended before he leaves the place where payment is due, the correct charge would be attempting to make off without payment (*McDavitt 1981*)
- The *mens rea* of s.3 consists of having knowledge that payment on the spot is required, being dishonest within the ordinary meaning of the word or under the *Ghosh* test, and having an intention to evade payment altogether (*Allen 1983*)

FIGURE 8.3 *Key facts chart on making off without payment*

He had stayed for nearly a month at a hotel but then left without paying his bill. He contacted the hotel a few days later explained that he was in financial difficulties but stated that he would leave his passport as security for the debt when he came to collect his belongings. Instead, the police were called and he was later convicted under s.3.

The House of Lords quashed his conviction. Lord Hailsham agreed with the Court of Appeal that the words 'with intent to avoid payment' meant an intention to evade payment altogether, not just an intention to defer or delay payment. In this case, it was felt that the accused should be given the benefit of the doubt.

He joins a health club and starts his weight training programme in the knowledge that he cannot afford the yearly subscription.

He tells the bookseller from whom he had purchased his law books on credit, that his father will be paying the debt in the near future. In fact, his father is in prison, having embezzled company funds. The bookseller believes Sly's tale and stops his demands for payment.

activity

Discuss the possible liability of Sly in the following unrelated situations:

He visits an upmarket tailor and purchases two designer suits, using a stolen credit card to make payment.

He then goes for a job interview with a leading firm of solicitors, pretends that he has passed his Legal Practice Course with Distinction and secures a training contract with a leading firm of solicitors.

To celebrate the obtaining of this position, he later dines at Le Gourmet and leaves without paying when the waiter is serving another customer.

He falsifies information on a mortgage application form and acquires a substantial mortgage advance in order to purchase a riverside apartment.

summary

In this chapter we have discovered that five important deception offences need to be studied:

Obtaining property by deception, s.15 Theft Act 1968
Obtaining a money transfer by deception, s.15A Theft Act 1968
Obtaining a pecuniary advantage by deception, s.16 Theft Act 1968
Obtaining services by deception, s.1 Theft Act 1978
Evading a liability by deception, s.2 Theft Act 1978

We have noted that all five offences require proof of dishonesty and a deception that is deliberate or reckless and that the type of recklessness to be proved is *Cunningham* recklessness. In addition, we have noted that the offence of making off without payment was passed to impose liability on those who depart without paying the sums owed, with the intention of avoiding payment altogether.

CHAPTER 9

PROPERTY OFFENCES III: CRIMINAL DAMAGE

9.1 INTRODUCTION

You will be relieved to know that this is a comparatively easy area to learn, compared with the complications concerning theft and deception. The law on criminal damage is in the Criminal Damage Act 1971. This act was largely the work of the Law Commission and was designed to replace the archaic Malicious Damage Act 1861. The Criminal Damage Act now contains, in a more simplified form, most offences concerning damage to property.

S.1 Criminal Damage Act creates three offences

1 The basic offence of criminal damage is laid down in s.1(1).
2 Aggravated criminal damage is to be found in s.1(2).
3 Criminal damage by the use of fire is in s.1(3).

S.2 of the Act creates two offences:

1 Threatening to destroy or damage property.
2 Threatening to do so in a way that is likely to endanger life.

S.3 makes it an offence to have possession or control of something intending to use it or to allow it to be used for either simple criminal damage or for criminal damage likely to endanger life.

9.2 THE BASIC OFFENCE UNDER SECTION 1(1)

A person will be guilty of the basic offence of criminal damage if he destroys or damages property belonging to another, either intentionally or recklessly.

A more precise definition is to be found in s.1(1) of the Act, which states:

> A person who without lawful excuse destroys or damages any property belonging to another intending to destroy or damage any such property or being reckless as to whether any such property would be destroyed or damaged shall be guilty of an offence.

The elements of this offence are discussed in detail below.

9.2.1 THE *ACTUS REUS* AND *MENS REA* OF CRIMINAL DAMAGE

It can be seen from the above definition that the *actus reus* of the basic offence is destroying or damaging property belonging to another and the *mens rea* is doing this intentionally or recklessly.

9.2.2 THE PUNISHMENT

If the damage or destruction is above £5000 in value, the offence comes into the category of a triable either way offence for which the maximum punishment is ten years imprisonment.

For damage of £5000 or less, the offence will be tried summarily, as laid down in s.22 Magistrates' Courts Act 1980, as amended by s.4 Criminal Justice and Public Order Act 1994. Before the amendment was made, the value of the damage had to be £2000 or less to be tried summarily.

This offence now needs to be examined in more detail.

9.2.3 ELEMENTS OF THE BASIC OFFENCE

The words 'destroying' and 'damaging' need to be analysed, as do the terms 'property' and 'belonging to another'. Finally, under this section, the words constituting the *mens rea* of the offence will be examined.

Destroys or damages

Neither of these words is defined in the Act and the courts appear to have taken a common sense approach to their meaning. In most cases, damage to the property will be obvious, as in the following case.

The courts have decided that the word 'destroys' will cover rendering the property useless, in addition to total destruction.

The word 'damage' can be used where property is made imperfect or inoperative or if the harm affects its usefulness or value. A car would

Party mob wrecks girl's home while parents are away

KEITH and Sarah Young have no idea what lies in store when they return from their holiday in Spain.

They know nothing of the ruined carpets, the smashed windows, the graffiti, the thefts and the broken furniture that await them when they come home to White Horse Cottages in Sutton Poyntz, Dorset.

The Youngs have yet to learn that twice on Saturday night police were summoned to this normally quiet village to evict an unruly mob of more than 100 drunken teenagers from their home.

The couple had agreed to let their daughter Caroline, 15, who was being cared for by an aunt, host a sleep-over party for 10 girl friends in the cottage.

They could not have imagined that the party would be gate-crashed by scores of alcohol fuelled teenagers, few of them older than 15, intent on causing mayhem.

At one point 10 police officers and a dog unit chased the youths through the village and surrounding fields.

Amid the chaos, an ambulance crew was attending to a girl who had collapsed beside the mill pond. She was taken to hospital to be treated for alcohol poisoning.

Peter Smith, the landlord of the Springhead public house, said yesterday: "I spent most of the night on the door stopping them from coming in — there must have been 150 or more roaming around the village.

"They brought lots of drink with them and they systematically wrecked the house. They must have done several thousand pounds worth of damage. Some of the neighbours tried to clear the house but this lot were going nowhere, so we called the police."

Officers from Weymouth, two miles away, were on the scene within minutes. Mr Smith said: "One minute there were 150 youngsters here and the next thing the place was deserted. They all ran off into the gardens and fields. The police cleared the house and locked it and took the girl back to her aunt's house."

But the youths returned shortly

before midnight, breaking into the cottage to continue their party. "You could hear them smashing things up so I called the police," Mr Smith said. PC Rick O'Shea, one of the officers who attended the scene, said widespread and deliberate damage had been done to the Young's home.

He said that Caroline had issued a number of invitations for the sleep-over to close friends but one appeared to have fallen into the wrong hands, was copied and widely distributed.

"Some of the people who turned up were from three or four miles away and were not connected with her at all. The damage is malicious and quite deliberate. The electrical fittings have been pulled out, lights, windows and crockery smashed, alcohol poured over the carpets and CDs and tapes destroyed. Most of the youngsters were very drunk and just set about the place."

Taken from an article by Sean O'Neill in *The Daily Telegraph*, 7 October 1998. © Telegraph Group Limited, London, 1998.

be damaged if an important part of it were to be uncoupled as, for example, a brake cable. In *Roper* v *Knott 1898*, beer was held to have been damaged after water had been added to it.

In *Samuel* v *Stubbs 1972*, it was stated that the word damage 'is sufficiently wide in its meaning to embrace injury, mischief or harm done to property'. It was also agreed that property would be damaged where it could no longer serve its normal purpose. It appears that a temporary cessation of its function will sometimes be sufficient. In this case, a policeman's cap had been trampled upon and the court held that the item had, in fact, been damaged, even though the headgear may well have been returned easily to its original state.

In *Hardman* v *Chief Constable of Avon and Somerset Constabulary 1986*, members of CND had been convicted of criminal damage and mounted an appeal against this. In order to mark the fortieth anniversary of the dropping of the atomic bomb on Hiroshima, they had used watersoluble paint to draw silhouettes on a pavement illustrating vaporised human remains.

The defendants tried to argue that their actions did not amount to criminal damage because the harm done was only temporary. They claimed that the paintings would have been erased naturally, if left alone, by the footsteps of pedestrians and by the elements. Despite these submissions, the convictions were upheld because the local authority had been put to the expense of employing people to wash off the paintings with pressurised water jets.

Similarly, in *Roe* v *Kingerlee 1986*, the defendant had smeared mud over the walls of a police cell, which cost £7 to clean off. This was held to amount to criminal damage, even though no lasting damage had been done.

There is, however, a limit to liability. In *A (a juvenile)* v *R 1978*, spitting on a police officer's raincoat was not held to amount to criminal damage because the spittle could easily be removed with a damp cloth and no lasting damage had been done. A different decision may well have been made if the article had been stained and had needed dry cleaning.

In a similar vein, merely running over the land of another would not amount to damaging that land, as decided in *Eley* v *Lytle 1885*, a civil case, whereas the actual trampling down of grass could constitute liability (*Gayford* v *Chouler 1898*).

In *Lloyd* v *DPP 1992*, a person tried to turn the tables on those arguing that he was at fault by accusing the other party of effecting criminal damage to his car by wheel-clamping it.

He had parked in a prohibited place, despite notices warning that illegally parked cars would be clamped and had returned to discover that such action had been taken. He then refused to pay the amount of £25 demanded for the release of the clamp and, instead, had used a disc cutter to prise it off. He was later charged with effecting criminal damage to the clamp. In his defence, he tried to argue that the other party had been trespassing on his property by applying the wheel clamp in the first place and had used some very old authority to support his findings. Despite his novel attempt to evade liability, such arguments were not accepted by the court and his conviction was upheld.

In some cases, the article itself may not be damaged but, instead, an item which helps it to operate. In *Cox* v *Riley 1986*, the defendant was found guilty of criminal damage after he had erased a programme from a plastic circuit card operating a saw to cut wood to specially programmed designs. The court decided that, while no damage had been caused to the saw itself, there had been damage to the card.

A similar approach was taken in *Whiteley 1991*. In this case, a computer hacker had infiltrated JANET, the Joint Academic Network, had altered and deleted files and changed some of the passwords. The computer had not been damaged by this misuse, but it had been rendered inoperable because of the damage to the magnetic particles on the disks.

The problem of computer misuse has now been recognised as a subject worthy of treatment in its own right and the passing of the Computer Misuse Act 1990 has made it easier to obtain convictions for such offences. The Act is not only concerned about harm caused to the actual computer but also the harm caused by the unauthorised use of the material contained within. S.3 deals with this and creates an offence if a person intentionally does any act that causes any unauthorised modification of the contents of any computer. This has lessened the need to stretch the meaning of the word 'damage' under the Criminal Damage Act. If the matter had been left like this, however, it would have caused an overlap between the two Acts, which might have caused future problems. For example, the new offence only carries a maximum penalty of five years imprisonment, whereas criminal damage attracts ten years. In addition, the new offence can only be committed intentionally, whereas offences under the Criminal Damage Act can also be committed recklessly.

S.3(6) Computer Misuse Act, therefore, makes it clear that:

> a modification of the contents of a computer shall not be regarded as damaging any computer or computer storage medium unless its effect on that computer or computer storage medium impairs its physical condition.

Property

Under the Criminal Damage Act 1971, property encompasses all items of a tangible nature, including money and animals belonging to another person. Wild animals that have been tamed and/or kept in captivity will come into this category but wild mushrooms, flowers, fruit or foliage will not.

It can be seen, therefore, that the tearing up of a £50 pound note belonging to another would amount to criminal damage, as would the unlawful shooting of a neighbour's dog. It would also be an offence under this act to poison the trout in a farmer's lake or to injure an animal in a local zoo. It would not amount to criminal damage to stamp on wild flowers, to uproot wild trees or to use a crossbow to shoot a wild bird, although offences under other acts may well arise.

The actual wording of the section is rather lengthy and is to be found in s.10 (1). It states:

> In this Act 'property' means property of a tangible nature, whether real or personal, including money and
>
> (a) including wild creatures which have been tamed or are ordinarily kept in captivity, and any other wild creatures or their carcasses if, but only if, they have been reduced into possession which has not been lost or abandoned or are in the course of being reduced into possession; but
>
> (b) not including mushrooms growing wild on any land or flowers, fruit or foliage of a plant growing wild on any land.
>
> For the purposes of this subsection, 'mushroom' includes any fungus and 'plant' includes any shrub or tree.

This definition of property appears very similar to the one in the Theft Act 1968 but there are some important distinctions. While land, under the law of theft, cannot be stolen, it can, under the Criminal Damage Act, be damaged. Conversely, intangible property rights, such as patents and copyrights can be stolen but do not come within the definition of property under the Criminal Damage Act.

Belonging to another

Under the basic offence the property that is damaged or destroyed has to belong to someone else. It will be noted, later, that this is not the case for the more serious offences which may arise under ss.1(2), 1(3), nor for the offences under s.2 and s.3.

Following on from this, it is obviously not an offence under s.1(1) to damage or destroy one's own property and the person may also be protected if he honestly but mistakenly believes that the property was his, provided, of course, that the jury believes his version of the events.

In *Smith 1974*, a tenant of a ground floor flat gave notice to quit but asked that his brother might be allowed to stay on. The landlord refused to entertain the idea. The tenant then damaged floor boarding, roofing and wall panels in a conservatory, in order, he claimed, to remove some electric wiring which he and his brother had installed, with the permission of the landlord, so that they could use their stereo equipment more effectively. Damage totalling £130 was caused and the appellant was charged under s.1(1). He argued that he had believed that the property belonged to him and that therefore he had a lawful excuse. In fact, the items had become fixtures that should not have been removed.

The trial judge declared in no uncertain terms that such an argument was unacceptable but the Court of Appeal held that this was a fundamental misdirection and the conviction was quashed. The appeal court was influenced by the law preceding that in the Criminal Damage Act. This made it clear that an offence would not be committed by a person who destroyed or damaged property belonging to another, if he had done this in the honest but mistaken belief that the property was his own, or had believed that he had a legal right to do the damage. This was illustrated in the early case of *Twose 1879*.

The Court of Appeal felt that the creators of the revised law on criminal damage did not intend to increase the liability when the Act was passed so decided that:

> no offence is committed under this section (i.e. s.1(1)), if a person destroys or causes damage to property belonging to another if he does so in the honest though mistaken belief that the property is his own, and, provided that the belief is honestly held, it is irrelevant to consider whether or not it is a justifiable belief.

The term 'belonging to another' is given a wide meaning under s.10(2). Property is treated as belonging to another if that other has custody or control of it, a proprietary right in it, a charge over it, or a right under a trust.

It would be an offence, therefore, if the defendant caused damage to his own goods, if

they had been lent to someone else. It is, however essential to prove that that the other had a proprietary right or interest in the goods. An insurer would not come into this category, so if a person destroyed or damaged his own property in order to claim from an insurance company, he would not be committing an offence under this section, as he would not be harming the goods of another.

Before leaving this subject, it should be noted that, if the damaged property belongs to a spouse, the consent of the Director of Public Prosecutions is needed before a charge can be brought. The restriction would not apply where the parties are no longer under a duty to cohabit.

9.2.4 THE *MENS REA* OF THE BASIC OFFENCE

As stated earlier, this is satisfied if the person unlawfully destroys or damages property belonging to another, either intentionally or recklessly. With regard to the word 'intention', it is quite clear that the defendant cannot be found guilty on this part of the count unless he possesses a clear intent to cause the damage. In addition, he must intend to act unlawfully and damage property belonging to another. If, therefore, he is under the mistaken impression that the property is his own, as in the case of *Smith 1974*, described above, he would lack the *mens rea* for the basic offence.

With regard to the word 'reckless', it should be remembered that this is *Caldwell*-style recklessness. As already discussed in Chapter 2, this is the more objective form of recklessness. Lord Diplock stated in *Metropolitan Police Commissioner* v *Caldwell 1982*, that a person is reckless if 'he does an act which in fact creates an obvious risk that property will be damaged or destroyed and, when he does the act he either has not given any thought to the possibility of there being any such risk or has recognised that there was some risk involved, and has nonetheless gone on to take it'.

This definition meant that, in the case of *Caldwell*, the defendant was guilty of an offence under s.1(2), because he had damaged property, reckless as to whether the life of another would be endangered. The risk of harm to others was an obvious one and he had not given any thought to this.

In *Chief Constable of Avon and Somerset Constabulary* v *Shimmen 1986*, a case mentioned in Chapter 2, the defendant had aimed a kick at the window of a store and caused damage of £495 to the plate glass window. He tried to argue that he had given some thought to the possibility of there being a risk of damage to property but had decided that his skills in martial arts were so great that no damage would result. He therefore claimed that he fell outside the *Caldwell* definition of recklessness.

On an appeal by the prosecution to the Divisional Court, the judges decided that there was an obvious risk that property would be damaged, the defendant had recognised that there was such a risk, but had believed, wrongly, that he had taken sufficient steps to minimise it. He had then gone on to take the risk. The appeal court decided that this was not the same as the 'lacuna' situation put forward by academics, i.e. that the party had considered whether there was a risk and had decided, erroneously, that one did not exist. The appeal of the prosecution was, therefore, successful and a direction to convict the accused was given.

Until Parliament steps in to change the law, therefore, it is very important to remember that offences of criminal damage only require proof of *Caldwell* recklessness, not the more subjective recklessness, laid down in the case of *Cunningham*, which is needed for most other offences.

COMMENT

Caldwell was a House of Lords' decision and was followed by that House in *Lawrence 1982*, a case involving causing death by reckless driving (an offence that has now been changed to causing death by dangerous driving). *Caldwell* is, therefore, an authoritative statement of the law regarding recklessness in criminal damage, despite the fact that this type of recklessness was not originally envisaged by the Law Commission, when that body discussed the Criminal Damage Act. It is obvious, when looking at the report on the deliberations of the Commission, that a more subjective test as to the nature of the recklessness was planned. By 1982, however, the House of Lords had come to believe that this was no longer appropriate.

The facts of *Shimmen* would, at first sight, appear to come into the types of situation not covered by Lord Diplock's definition of recklessness in criminal damage but the judges of the Divisional Court were obviously not prepared to open the floodgates in this way. The judges adroitly managed to bring the situation in that case within the definition, while not denying that a lacuna did still exist in very limited circumstances. In *Reid 1992*, in a now outdated reckless driving case, the House of Lords accepted the existence of a possible loophole in the *Caldwell* definition, but did not discuss this in relation to criminal damage. Their Lordships did, however, state that the term recklessness might have different meanings in different contexts.

9.2.5 DEFENCES TO A CHARGE OF CRIMINAL DAMAGE

All the normal general defences, which are described more fully in Chapter 10, are *prima facie* available to a charge of criminal damage and the related offences in the Act. In addition to this, however, there is a special defence provided in the Act itself, the defence of lawful excuse. It is important to note that this special defence is not available for the aggravated offences, where the defendant commits criminal damage or threatens to do so, intending by the destruction or damage to endanger the life of another or being reckless about this. Nor is it available for the aggravated offence in s.3 of possessing something for the purpose of committing criminal damage in a way that he knows is likely to endanger life.

Section 5(2) and section 5(3)

According to s.5(2) Criminal Damage Act 1971, there are two situations where the defendant will be acting with lawful excuse in relation to the property which is alleged to have been damaged or destroyed. The first is where he believes that the other party would have consented to the damage. The second situation is where he destroys or damages the property of another in order to protect other property belonging to himself or another. In the latter type of situation, the defendant must have believed that the property in question was in immediate need of protection and the methods he adopted to do this must be considered reasonable in the circumstances. Should this be the case, s.5(3) goes on to state that it does not matter if his belief is unjustified, provided that it is an honestly held one.

In *Chamberlain* v *Lindon 1998*, the defendant demolished a wall built by a neighbour because he believed that it threatened his own right of access. His defence of lawful excuse was accepted by both the trial judge and the Divisional Court. The latter decided that the defendant had an honest belief that his property was in need of immediate protection and, provided such a belief was honestly held, he was entitled to use the defence.

The actual wording of the section is rather lengthy. It states that a person will be regarded as having a lawful excuse if:

(a) at the time of the act or acts alleged to constitute the offence he believed that the person or persons whom he believed to be entitled to consent to the destruction of or damage to the property in question had so consented, or would have so consented to it if he or they had known of the destruction or damage and its circumstances; or
(b) if he destroyed or damaged or threatened to destroy or damage the property in question or, in the case of a charge of an offence under section 3 above, intended to use or cause or permit the use of something to destroy or damage it, in order to protect property belonging to himself or another or a right or interest in property which was or he believed to be vested in himself or another, and at the time of the act or acts alleged to constitute the offence he believed:
(i) that the property, right or interest was in need of immediate protection; and
(ii) that the means of protection adopted or proposed to be adopted were or would be reasonable having regard to all the circumstances.

For the purposes of this section it is immaterial whether a belief is justified or not if it is honestly held.

The following case illustrates the width of this defence, which allows a defendant to escape liability where he would not be so successful when using the general defence of mistake.

In *Jaggard* v *Dickinson 1981*, the defendant was charged with basic criminal damage, after breaking into a house belonging to a stranger. She acted in the mistaken belief that the house belonged to her friend and that this friend would, if she had been aware of the situation, have consented to the damage! The magistrates stated that she could not rely on s.5(2) because she was intoxicated and her drunkenness was self-induced. It will be noted in Chapter 10, that self-induced intoxication will not normally negative *mens rea* in basic intent crimes, such as criminal damage, so the general defence would not be available.

The Divisional Court refused to deny her the use of s.5. Mustill J stated:

> ... Parliament has specifically isolated one subjective element, in the shape of honest belief, and has given it separate treatment and its own special gloss in s.5(3). This being so, there is nothing objectionable in giving it special treatment as regards drunkenness, in accordance with the natural meaning of the words.

Another case illustrating s.5(2)(a) and s.5(3) is *Denton 1982*. The defendant started a fire at his employer's mill. He claimed that his employer had encouraged him to take this action so that the employer could make a fraudulent claim against his insurance company. His honest belief that the employer had authority to order such an action was sufficient to afford him the defence of s.5.

In *Appleyard 1985*, however, a managing director's claim that he could give himself such authority, by virtue of his position, was rejected by the Court of Appeal.

The case of *Blake* v *DPP 1993* was an unusual one in that the defendant tried to argue that God himself had consented to the vicar's acts of criminal damage! The vicar had used a marker in order to write passages from the Bible on a stone pillar near to the Houses of Parliament. He was protesting against the possible use of force in the 'run up' to the Gulf War.

He also invoked s.5(2)(b) by arguing that he was taking this action to protect the property of people in the Gulf States who would be affected by such military action.

Unfortunately for him, the Divisional Court of Queen's Bench Division was not prepared to accept either of these arguments. The court stated that there was no authority concerning consent given by God and also felt that, when viewed objectively, there was nothing in his action that could effectively protect the property of people so far away from the scene.

A similar approach to s.5(2)(b) was taken in the case of *Hunt 1978*. The defendant had claimed that he was concerned about the defective fire alarms in the block of old people's flats of which his wife was a deputy warden.

He claimed that he had set light to some bedding to draw attention to this deficiency, and that by his action, he was, in reality, seeking to protect the property. The court failed to be convinced of this.

The courts were similarly unmoved in the case of *Hill and Hall 1988*, where demonstrators were protesting against the presence of American military bases in this country. The defendants had gone to the site with equipment to cut the perimeter fences and had tried to use s.5(2)(b) in their defence. They argued that they were taking this action in order to protect their own and other's property in the neighbourhood, which might otherwise be destroyed by a retaliatory attack if military action was undertaken from the base.

The Court of Appeal rejected this, despite the subjective nature of s.5(3). The judges decided that, while the first point needing examination is what the defendant honestly believed, when deciding whether the property was actually in need of protection, a more objective approach should be taken. The jury should decide on this after appropriate direction from the trial judge. Despite the genuine beliefs of the defendants, therefore, the convictions were upheld.

▼ COMMENT

It is apparent that Parliament wanted to retain a subjective element in the special defence given under s.5(2), by the very precise nature of the wording in s.5(3), but it is equally clear that the courts are worried about the possible width of this and are seeking to curtail it. Some would argue that, if the courts did not take this approach, defendants would be able to escape the consequences of their actions by putting forward all sorts of odd beliefs and might then have to be given the benefit of the doubt.

On the other hand, it could be argued that the subjective element in this defence should be retained to help redress the balance against the objective test, used earlier in the proceedings to establish whether recklessness exists in the first place.

▼ KEY FACTS

- The basic offence is under s.1 Criminal Damage Act 1971. The maximum punishment is ten years imprisment if tried on indictment
- It is committed when a person destroys or damages property belonging to another, intending to do this or being reckless about it
- Property is destroyed or damaged if it is totally destroyed, made imperfect or inoperative or where it no longer serves a useful purpose. The damage may well be far slighter than this (*Roper* v *Knott 1898, Samuel* v *Stubbs 1972, Hardman* v *C C of Avon 1986, Roe* v *Kingerlee 1986*), and can cover plastic circuit cards and computer disks (*Cox* v *Riley 1986, Whitley 1991*), but will not normally include spittle or simple trespassing (*A 1978, Eley* v *Lytle 1885*)
- The Computer Misuse Act 1990 now helps with some forms of damage
- Property will include most tangible things but not wild flowers, fruit, fungi and foliage
- A person will have a defence if he mistakenly believes that the property is his or that the owner would have consented to the damage; the belief does not have to be reasonable (*Smith 1974, Jaggard* v *Dickinson 1981*)

FIGURE 9.1 *Key facts chart on basic criminal damage*

9.3 THE AGGRAVATED OFFENCE UNDER SECTION 1(2)

This offence is committed where a person destroys or damages property intending by the destruction or damage to endanger the life of another or being reckless about this.

It is not a requirement that someone's life must actually be put at risk; it is enough that a reasonable man would have believed that there was such a risk (*Sangha 1988*).

The maximum punishment for this offence is life imprisonment.

The actual section is worded as follows:

> A person who without lawful excuse destroys or damages any property, whether belonging to himself or another:
>
> (a) intending to destroy or damage any property or being reckless as to whether any property should be destroyed or damaged; and
> (b) intending by the destruction or damage to endanger the life of another or being reckless as to whether the life of another would thereby be endangered;
>
> shall be guilty of an offence.

It can be seen, therefore, that the same *actus reus* and *mens rea* of the basic offence must be present, with the additional *mens rea* of intending to endanger life or being reckless about this.

9.3.1 DIFFERENCES BETWEEN S.1(1) AND S.1(2)

With the aggravated offence, the property destroyed or damaged does not have to belong to another.

In addition, as noted earlier, the special defence of lawful excuse permitted in s.5 does not apply to this more serious offence, although the more general defence of lawful excuse negativing *mens rea* in the first place could still be argued in appropriate circumstances. The *mens rea* for the part of the aggravated offence relating to recklessness is the same as for the basic offence.

It should be remembered that, in the case of *Metropolitan Police Commissioner v Caldwell 1982*, which has caused so much comment, the defendant was charged with offences under both s.1(1) and s.1(2) and that, while he was prepared to admit to the first count, he strongly argued that he should not be held liable under the second, because, in his drunken state, it had not crossed his mind that someone's life might be endangered. Unfortunately for him, as noted earlier, Lord Diplock in the House of Lords, decided that the test for recklessness in this context had a more objective element in it and his conviction was upheld.

It is also important to realise that, with the aggravated offence, the danger to life must come directly from the damage to property and not from some other source. This is graphically illustrated in the case of *Steer 1988*. In this case, the danger was coming from the rifle that Steer was firing, not from the slight damage to the window.

The defendant had quarrelled with his former business partner and, in the early hours of the morning had gone to his bungalow, armed with an automatic rifle. He rang the bell and woke up the occupants and, when they looked out of the window, he fired one shot in that direction, plus two further shots, one at another window and the other at the front door. Mr and Mrs Gregory were not injured and it was not suggested that Steer had deliberately fired at them.

The defendant was charged under s.1(1) and s.1(2) Criminal Damage Act and also with an offence under another act of possessing a firearm with intent to endanger life. He appealed against the conviction under s.1(2), stating that the judge had misdirected the jury about this. He argued that the danger to life in this case had been caused by the rifle shots, not by the damaged property. The case eventually reached the House of Lords. This body was asked to consider the following point of law:

Whether, on a true construction of s.1(2)(b) of the Criminal Damage Act 1971, the prosecution are required to prove that the danger to life resulted from the destruction of or damage to the property, or whether it is sufficient for the prosecution to prove that it resulted from the act of the defendant . . .

Their Lordships stated that the prosecution had to prove that the danger to life came from the destruction or damage of the property.

Steer's conviction for this offence, therefore, was not upheld.

COMMENT

It can be seen that the wording of the offence of aggravated criminal damage leaves a loophole through which a reckless defendant might escape liability if the damage to the property was too slight to endanger life. In Steer's case, he was carrying a firearm, so he could be convicted of this alternative offence, which carried a maximum penalty of 14 years imprisonment. If, however, he had merely carried a brick, and had thrown this with force at the window but not at the actual people standing there, it might have been difficult to charge him with more than basic criminal damage, despite the seriousness of the act.

Smith and Hogan wonder whether a new offence should be formulated to cover this, such as recklessly endangering life whether by damaging property or otherwise.

9.4 ARSON

The common law offence of arson was abolished by the Act and added to the offences of criminal damage. S.1(3) states that if a person destroys or damages property by fire this will be charged as arson. The maximum penalty for arson is life imprisonment.

In *Miller 1983*, the House of Lords upheld the charge of arson when the defendant accidentally started a fire and failed to take the necessary steps to put it out. Once again, if the risk would have been obvious to most people, the defendant will be liable, despite the fact that he might not have foreseen this.

This can sometimes have harsh results, as was shown in the case of *Elliot* v *C (a minor) 1983*, mentioned earlier in Chapter 2. It will be recalled that an educationally sub-normal girl of 14 was convicted of arson, despite the fact that she could not explain why she had poured white spirit over a carpet in a neighbouring shed and had set it alight. The Divisional Court reluctantly upheld the conviction. Goff L J stated: 'I would be lacking in candour if I were to conceal my unhappiness about the conclusion which I feel compelled to reach'.

COMMENT

When the Law Commission was debating the law on criminal damage, it recommended that arson should not be treated as a separate offence. Parliament, however, was not prepared to accept this and s.1(3) was formulated. A person can be charged under this section, in addition to s.1(1) or s.1(2) if there is any damage caused by fire. It need not be great. The potential punishment, however, is very severe, i.e. life imprisonment and the judges do not flinch from imposing it. It gives cause for concern that a conviction can be sustained if the risk is merely obvious to a reasonable man. Many offenders committing crimes by fire are not reasonable people but, instead, mentally disturbed in some way. While the public obviously needs to be protected from their harmful acts, a very long term of imprisonment is not going to tackle the problem if no further help is given.

9.5 OTHER OFFENCES

S.2 makes it an offence where a person, without lawful excuse, makes a threat to another that he will destroy or damage his property, or that of a third party, intending that other to fear that he will carry out the threat, or threatens to destroy or damage his own property in a way which he knows is likely to endanger life.

S.3 of the act states that a person will be guilty of an offence where he has something in his possession which he intends, without lawful excuse, to use to destroy or damage property belonging to another or to permit or cause someone else to do this, or has something in his possession which he intends to use for destroying or damaging his own property in a way which is likely to endanger the life of others.

KEY FACTS

- Aggravated criminal damage can be committed where the party destroys or damages property intending by that destruction or damage to endanger life or being reckless as to whether life is endangered, s.1(2)
- The maximum punishment is life imprisonment
- The danger to life must be caused by the destruction or damage (*Steer 1988*)
- S.1(3) states that if a person destroys or damages property by fire, this will be arson, for which the punishment is life imprisonment

- The *mens rea* for these offences is intention or *Caldwell* recklessness (*MPC* v *Caldwell 1982*, *Miller 1983*, *Elliot* v *C (a minor) 1983*)
- S.2 makes it an offence, punishable by ten years imprisonment, to make a threat to another, knowing that the other would fear that this will be carried out, to destroy or damage that other's property or to damage or destroy his own property in a way which he knows is likely to endanger life
- S.3 imposes liability on a party who has something in his possession or control which he intends to use, or allow someone else to use, to damage or destroy property the property of another. The second part of the offence is committed where he has something in his possession or control which he intends to use to damage or destroy his own or another's property in a way which he knows is likely to endanger life. Once again, the maximum sentence is ten years

FIGURE 9.2 *Key facts chart on other offences of criminal damage*

activity

Marie, aged 14, ran away from home after an argument with her parents. She broke the lock on the garage of No. 15 Fleming Avenue, believing that she was at No. 13, where her school friend Edison lived. Marie believed that his parents would not mind her staying there. In fact, the garage belonged to Alexander.

As the night progressed, Marie became cold and decided to light a fire. The wood was damp, so she poured petrol over it and then set light to this. The resulting blaze spread to the garden furniture stored in the garage, and the smoke from the burning wood and the fumes from the foam-filled cushions travelled to the flat above the garage, which was occupied by Isaac, Alexander's gardener.

Though partially affected by the fumes,

Isaac still had the presence of mind to phone for the fire brigade. After putting out the blaze, James, one of the fire fighters, turned to Marie and called her 'a stupid girl' for causing so much trouble. This made Marie angry and she snatched off his helmet and threw it into the smouldering remains of the fire. The helmet was not damaged but was blackened by the ash.

Discuss the possible offences and defences that might have arisen under the Criminal Damage Act 1971.

summary

After studying Chapter 9, we should be aware that there are two main offences under s.1, that of destroying or damaging property belonging to another, either intentionally or recklessly, (s.1(1)), and that of destroying or damaging any property either intentionally or recklessly, intending by that damage or destruction to endanger the life of another or being reckless about this, (s.1(2)). We should be able to describe the elements of these offences. We should have noted that, if either of these offences are by the use of fire, the offence of arson might also be charged under s.1(3).

We should realise that the offences can be committed either intentionally or recklessly and know that the test for recklessness is that laid down by the House of Lords in *Metropolitan Police Commissioner* v *Caldwell 1982*. The defendant will be considered reckless even if he did not give thought to the risk involved, provided that a reasonable man would have perceived that a risk existed. It should be noted that the punishment for the basic offence is ten years imprisonment, and is life imprisonment for the aggravated offence or where fire has been used.

A special defence, that of lawful excuse, has been given under s.5(2) of the Act, provided that there is no charge of endangering life. This is in addition to any general defences that may be available. Finally, there are other offences under ss.2 and 3 of the Act, although it is less likely that they will appear in examination questions.

CHAPTER 10

GENERAL DEFENCES I

10.1 INTRODUCTION

WE NOTED WHEN discussing substantive offences, that, in some instances, special defences may be used by the accused in relation to the particular crime in question, such as the limited defences of provocation and diminished responsibility in murder and the full defence of consent in assault and battery. This chapter and Chapter 11 look at the more general defences, which may also be of great help to the defendant in specific instances. There are ten of these to examine and knowledge of them is required for all the major examination boards. They are listed below.

- Infancy (or lack of capacity)

- Insanity (or insane automatism)

- Non-insane automatism

- Intoxication

- Mistake

- Necessity (in very limited circumstances)

- Duress

- Duress of circumstances

- Martial coercion (rare)

- Public and private defence

Infancy, insanity, automatism and intoxication are looked at in Chapter 10 and the remaining defences are examined in Chapter 11.

10.2 INFANCY OR LACK OF CAPACITY

Those of you who have studied contract law will already know that, in civil law, anyone under the age of 18 is classed as an infant, a rather insulting suggestion to young people attaining the age of 17 years and 11 months! The term 'minor' is a more acceptable one that has gradually replaced the word 'infant'. The criminal law, however, treats the matter of age rather differently and, until very recently, put the liability of children and young persons into three categories, those under the age of ten, those between the ages of 10 and 14 and those of 14 and over. With regard to the first category, it is still comparatively rare for children of this age to be involved in serious criminal activity. It is not, however, unknown and some very young children have been involved in horrific acts of violence. One example that resurfaced recently, when the question of payment for her life story hit the headlines, was the case of Mary Bell who, at the age of nine, murdered two very young children. There is also a disturbing increase of some types of criminal activity among the 10 to 14 year-old-age group, mainly in relation to joy riding, criminal damage and minor theft. Fortunately, cases like the James Bulger affair still remain rare. This case, involving the abduction and killing of a two-year-old child by two 11-year-old boys attracted a great deal of publicity because of the brutality and lack of compassion displayed by the young offenders, Jon Venables and Robert Thompson. It was established that they knew that they had done something seriously wrong and they were found guilty of murder. We now need to look at these three divisions in more detail.

10.2.1 CHILDREN BELOW THE AGE OF TEN

It has been decided that, however awful the circumstances, criminal liability should not be imposed upon children under the age of ten. The Latin phrase *doli incapax* is used, which means 'incapable of crime'. The law is to be found in s.50 Children and Young Persons Act 1933, as amended, which states:

> It shall be conclusively presumed that no child under the age of ten years can be guilty of any offence.

It should be noted that, while such a young offender would not face a trial, the child could well be subject to care proceedings if the crime is a serious one. Where the most serious offences are concerned, the child will not be released back into the community until it is decided that he no longer poses a threat to society.

10.2.2 CHILDREN BETWEEN THE AGES OF TEN AND FOURTEEN

The question of liability for children between the ages of 10 and 14 has been the subject of much debate in recent times. The current position is stated in the Crime and Disorder Act 1998. This states that children of this age are now held to be criminally liable for their actions; the presumption that they are incapable of committing a crime, which had been recently affirmed by the House of Lords in *C (a minor) 1996*, has been removed.

Before this change in the law was effected, a presumption existed that a child between the ages of 10 and 14 was not criminally liable for his actions. It was possible to rebut this presumption if the prosecution could establish that the child knew that he was doing something seriously wrong. The law called such knowledge 'a mischievous discretion'. The prosecution had to prove that the child knew that the act he was performing was wrong in law, mere 'naughtiness', as the law put it, was not enough. It was stated in *Gorrie 1919*, that there had to be 'very clear and complete evidence' of knowledge of wrongdoing before the presumption could be rebutted. Such evidence could have been deduced from the child's background, his behaviour after the act, his mental capacity, the replies he made to police questioning or his attitude in court. The mere fact of running away was not in itself conclusive, because the child could have run away after non-criminal acts, if he thought he was likely to get into trouble. The age of the child was always an important factor because the courts rather naturally took the view that the older the child and the more serious the act, the more likely it was that he knew that he was doing something wrong.

In the early case of *Kershaw 1902*, the jury found enough evidence of knowledge of wrongdoing and a boy of 13 was sentenced to ten years penal servitude for manslaughter. Similarly, in *JM (a minor)* v *Runeckles 1984*, the conviction of a 13-year-old girl for actual bodily harm was upheld after she had stabbed another young girl with a broken milk bottle.

Until the mid-1990s, therefore, the law on this subject was clear; a presumption of lack of capacity for children between the ages of 10 and 14 existed and the prosecution had to rebut this. In the case of *C (a minor)* v *DPP 1996*, however, the Divisional Court threw the matter wide open by roundly declaring, in these days of universal education, the presumption was outdated and should no longer form part of English law.

The case concerned a boy of 12, observed by the police on private property holding the handlebars of a Honda motor cycle while his friend tampered with the chain and padlock securing it. The boy ran away when challenged but was caught. He later appealed against his conviction on the grounds that the prosecution had not rebutted the presumption that he lacked criminal liability. The Divisional Court refused to entertain the appeal and made the provocative statements discussed above.

There was a further appeal to the House of Lords and this time it was successful. Their Lordships firmly upheld the existence of the presumption, deciding that it came from 'a long and uncontradicted line of authority'. Lord Lowry decided that the question of punishment for child offenders was a social and political matter as well as a legal one and believed, therefore, that if change were to be effected, this was a matter for Parliament.

COMMENT

It might be argued that the House of Lords was more concerned about the attack on its authority by the Divisional Court, than in regarding the appeal as an opportunity to look further at the question of liability of young offenders. The presumption that children between the ages of 10 and 14 lack the capacity to commit a crime was one which had been developed by the common law so the decision that only Parliament should deal with the matter was questionable to say the least. The presumption had been the subject of much criticism and the Ingleby Committee had already suggested that it should be abolished. In allowing this appeal, it could be argued that the House of Lords was sending a clear message to young offenders that they might be able to escape liability if only they

had the sense to stay silent. Arguably, the most hardened of the young offenders have been the ones to learn this lesson most quickly, and the police may have been hampered in their efforts to try to stop the escalation of crime among certain sections of the young community. It can be seen from the cases following this decision that, although the Divisional Court recognised that the attempts of that court to change the law had failed, it was prepared to take a robust approach to the question of liability, while awaiting action from Parliament.

In *A v DPP 1997*, a 12-year-old boy was charged with indecently assaulting a girl of the same age. Two other boys were also involved and had threatened the girl with violence. The boy refused to answer any questions on arrest, during interviews and at the trial but, nevertheless, was convicted. On appeal, the Divisional Court was asked to decide whether there was sufficient evidence to justify the finding that the boy knew that he was doing something seriously wrong.

The court acknowledged that the presumption, so recently upheld by the House of Lords, meant that such a point had to be proved. The court felt, however, that it was entitled to consider all of the conduct closely associated with the case, in order to see if the required guilty knowledge had been present. The court believed that the following points indicated that the boy clearly knew he was doing wrong.

First, he had seen the two other boys threatening the girl and had adopted a similar stance. Secondly, he had forced the girl to have both oral and ordinary sex with him when her distress was obvious. Thirdly, he had then run away. The appeal against conviction was dismissed.

In *DPP v K and C 1997*, two girls of 14 and 11 had threatened, falsely imprisoned and robbed another 14-year-old girl. A boy, who had not been traced, had also raped her. The girls were charged, among other things, with aiding and abetting this rape. The magistrates were of the opinion that they could not convict on this count so the Crown appealed on a point of law to the Divisional Court.

The boy allegedly committing the rape was said to be between 10 and 14 years of age but, because he had not been traced, the prosecution had not had a chance to rebut the presumption about his lack of criminal liability. The Divisional Court decided that this was not fatal to the possible liability of the two girls. A rape had been established, the girls were present when it took place, had desired that it should happen and had helped to procure the result. The court was therefore of the opinion that a conviction on this count was possible.

In the interim period, provisions removing the presumption that children of this age do not have liability for their criminal acts were being put into statutory form. They finally appeared in the Crime and Disorder Act 1998, which came into force in October 1998.

10.2.3 CHILDREN AND YOUNG PERSONS OVER THE AGE OF FOURTEEN

A child aged 14 or over has always been considered to be 'as responsible for his actions entirely as if he were 40'. This comment was made in *Smith 1845*, and the position is the still same today with regard to his actual liability for his criminal acts. The courts may however, recognise the youth of the offender when it comes to the choice of the court to be used for his trial and, when the case is over, in the matter of sentencing him if he has been found guilty.

10.3 INSANITY

Most people would agree that someone suffering from insanity, who is completely unaware

KEY FACTS

- There is a conclusive presumption that children under the age of 10 are not criminally liable for their actions (s.50 Children and Young Persons Act 1933, as amended)
- With children between the ages of 10 and 14, there used to be a rebuttable presumption that they were not criminally liable (*C (a minor)* v *DPP 1996*)
- The prosecution was obliged to produce evidence that the child committed the act and also knew that the act was seriously wrong. Enough evidence of these two matters was shown in the cases of *Kershaw 1902, Gorrie 1919, JM (a minor)* v *Runeckles 1984, A* v *DPP 1997* and *DPP* v *K and B 1997*, but not in *C (a minor)* v *DPP 1996*
- The presumption has now been abolished and children between the ages of 10 and 14 are now criminally responsible for their actions (Crime and Disorder Act 1998), along with children of 14 or over (*Smith 1845*)

FIGURE 10.1 *Key facts chart on infancy*

of his actions, should not be branded as a criminal. On the other hand, members of the public need reassurance that they will be protected from his violent acts. The criminal law, therefore, has to strike a balance between these two principles and this section will examine how this is done.

The first point to note is that, if possible, such an offender should face trial. If it is then proved that he committed an unlawful act, he will not be found guilty; instead a special verdict will be recorded of 'not guilty by reason of insanity'. The public will normally be protected because the court then has the power to deal with the defendant. It possesses a range of special orders to impose upon him. Before 1991, there was only one such order at the court's disposal; on a finding of insanity, the court was obliged to order that the defendant be admitted to a secure hospital without limitation of time. He could then only be released on the authority of the Home Secretary. In 1991, however, the Criminal Procedure (Insanity and Unfitness to Plead) Act 1991 was passed, to amend s.5 of the Criminal Procedure (Insanity) Act 1964. Despite the complicated name, the purpose of this former Private Member's Bill is laudable. It permits a wider range of disposals to be made when the defendant is found to have committed the crime but is also found to be insane. If the crime is murder, there is still no choice about treatment and a hospital order without limitation of time must still be imposed. In other cases, however, the court is permitted to impose a hospital order, accompanied by a time limit, a guardianship order, a supervision and treatment order or even an absolute discharge.

It is now necessary to look at the question of insanity in more detail and, before this, the three periods of time when this state of mind might be relevant.

10.3.1 INSANITY BEFORE THE TRIAL

If a person is in custody but is obviously insane, it may be considered unwise to bring him to trial, both because of the effect on his mental state and because the public needs to be protected. The Home Secretary, therefore, has the power to detain him immediately in a mental hospital provided that he has confirmation of the offender's state of mind from two doctors.

10.3.2 UNFITNESS TO PLEAD AT THE TIME OF THE TRIAL

If, because of his mental or physical state, the defendant is unable to appreciate the significance of the criminal trial, he may be found unfit to plead. Such a decision is not taken lightly. The Royal Committee on Capital Punishment recommended that, where possible, the defendant should have the benefit of a full trial. In *Podola 1960*, therefore, even though the defendant could not remember anything at all about the crime with which he was charged because he was suffering from amnesia at the crucial time, the trial proceeded because, in all other respects, he was completely sane. The question of unfitness to plead may be raised by the defence, the prosecution or by the judge himself. It may be claimed that the defendant is unable to understand the charges made against him, or is unable appreciate the difference between the pleas of guilty or not guilty. Alternatively, he may be unable to instruct his defence. If the claims are felt to have merit, a special jury will be empanelled to decide upon the matter. This body is only permitted to find the defendant unfit to plead if reports from two doctors support this view and one of the doctors has been approved by the Home Secretary as having special expertise in the field of mental illness.

If matters were left like this, it could result in unfairness to the defendant because the case has not been proved against him. Amendments made to the Criminal Procedure (Insanity) Act 1964 now provide that the jury must also decide whether, on the evidence available, the defendant actually committed the offence. If the jury agrees that he has done the act, then the judge will decide what should happen to the accused. We noted earlier, that under the Criminal Procedure (Insanity) Act, as amended, the judge, in all but murder cases, has a variety of orders from which to choose when deciding how best to deal with the offender. If the jury is not convinced that the defendant did the act, he must be acquitted and no further action will be taken against him. It is also possible for the defence to make the prosecution put its case forward before the issue of unfitness to plead is brought up. If the case is weak and the judge rules that there is no case to answer, the matter of the defendant's unfitness to plead will not be examined at all.

10.3.3 INSANITY AT THE TIME THE CRIME WAS COMMITTED

This is a completely different issue. In this situation the defendant is considered fit to plead, but either the defence, the prosecution or, on rare occasions, the judge, is claiming that he was insane at the time he committed the act in question. In such a case, the question of whether or not he is insane is determined by reference to the rules laid down by the House of Lords after the case of *M'Naghten* in 1843.

If the defence of insanity is successful, an amended s.2 of the offensively named Trial of Lunatics Act 1883, provides that a special verdict has to be recorded, stating that the defendant 'is not guilty by reason of insanity'. Once this finding has been given, one of the orders mentioned above will then be put into force. If the crime is murder, then the judge is required to commit the defendant to a mental hospital at the discretion of the Home Secretary.

In practice, the defence of insanity is rarely used, although the changes made concerning treatment may alter this position. At present, only two or three cases are brought each year. When the crime is homicide, most defendants prefer to use the limited defence of diminished responsibility, which, as noted in Chapter 4, reduces the offence from murder to manslaughter. When this defence is unsuccessful and the accused is sentenced to life imprisonment for murder, he will often be released on licence after serving a period of years in prison. If the defence of diminished responsibility is made out, the period of imprisonment is often considerably shorter. In both cases, prison is often felt to be a more acceptable alternative than incarceration in a mental hospital, and being labelled insane. The rules relating to insanity do, however, need to be learned for the cases where the defence is put forward and to ensure that they can be distinguished from the rules relating to automatism. It is also a popular subject in examinations!

10.3.4 THE DEFENCE OF INSANITY UNDER THE M'NAGHTEN RULES

As mentioned earlier, the rules relating to insanity were laid down after the case of *M'Naghten 1843*.

The accused, Daniel M'Naghten, had tried to kill the Prime Minister at that time, Sir Robert Peel, but, had, instead, shot and killed the Prime Minister's Secretary, Edward Drummond. M'Naghten was found not guilty of murder on the grounds that he was insane. This caused such an outcry that, after the case, the House of Lords consulted with all the judges and, from the responses to a series of questions, the M'Naghten Rules were formulated.

The M'Naghten Rules state that the jury should be informed that a person is presumed to be sane and responsible for his crimes unless it can be proved that, at the time of the offence:

> he was labouring under such a defect of reason, from disease of the mind, as not to know the nature and quality of the act he was doing, or if he did know it, that he did not know he was doing what was wrong.

The burden of proof is on the defendant, who must prove his own insanity on the balance of probabilities. (This is the only general defence where the burden is not on the prosecution to disprove it, once it has been raised.)

It can be seen that there are three stages in proving the defence of insanity.

1 The defendant must prove that he was suffering from a defect of reason.
2 The defect must have been caused by a disease of the mind.
3 The defect has meant that the defendant did not know what he was doing or, if he did, he did not know that his act was wrong.

These three elements to the defence now need to be looked at in turn.

A defect of reason

The courts have decided that this means a complete loss of the power of reasoning, not mere confusion or absentmindedness.

In *Clarke 1972*, the accused was charged with the theft of three items of small value from a supermarket, a jar of coffee, a packet of butter and a jar of mincemeat, which she had transferred from the wire basket to her bag. Her defence rested on the fact of her forgetfulness, which, she claimed, had been caused by depression. The trial judge decided that this raised the issue of insanity. The woman quickly changed her plea to one of guilty but then appealed against the judge's finding. The Court of Appeal held that her behaviour 'fell very far short of showing that she suffered from a defect of reason'. The court decided that the rules are not meant to apply 'to those who retain the power of reasoning but who in moments of confusion or absent-mindedness fail to use their powers to the full'. Her conviction, therefore, was quashed because of the misdirection.

Caused by disease of the mind

It is important to realise that it is the judges who have made the decision as to what constitutes a disease of the mind. It is not a medical decision, although conditions such as schizophrenia are obviously covered. Over the years, it has been decided that the term 'disease of the mind' is not merely confined to diseases of the brain alone; any malfunctioning of the mind caused by an inside source will be included.

This position was made clear in *Kemp 1957*, where the Court of Appeal clearly stated that the law:

> is not concerned with the brain but with the mind, in the sense that 'mind' is ordinarily used, the mental faculties of reason, memory and understanding.

In this case, the accused inflicted grievous bodily harm on his wife with a hammer for no apparent reason. Evidence had been brought to show that he was normally a mild-tempered man and a devoted husband. He claimed that he had lost consciousness because he was suffering from arteriosclerosis, which had caused a congestion of blood in his brain. The prosecution argued that the defect of reason had been caused by a physical illness, not a mental one and was not, therefore, within the definition of the M'Naghten Rules. Devlin did not agree with this view and upheld the trial judge's finding of insanity.

In addition, it might cause surprise and concern to learn that epilepsy, diabetes and the effects of a brain tumour can also lead to a finding of legal insanity. This will occur if it is shown that these diseases have caused a defect of reason resulting in the commission of a crime. Such a condition can be a temporary illness as well as a permanent one, a curable one in addition to an incurable one.

In *Bratty* v *Attorney General for Northern Ireland 1963*, Lord Denning affirmed that the question of insanity could be raised by the prosecution or the judge, in addition to the defence. He also agreed that conditions such as epilepsy and cerebral tumours could come under the definition of diseases of the mind, thus disapproving of the earlier case of *Charlson 1955*, where a contrary statement was made. Lord Denning went on to state firmly that:

> any mental disorder which has manifested itself in violence and is prone to recur is a disease of the mind.

In *Sullivan 1984*, the House of Lords addressed the issue when it looked at the position with regard to epilepsy.

In this case, the accused had kicked and injured an 80-year-old man during an attack of psychomotor epilepsy and was charged with grievous bodily harm. The medical evidence showed that the defendant had committed the offence during the third stage of his epileptic fit when he unaware of what was happening. The judge decided that he would have to direct the jury on the issue of insanity. The accused, therefore, changed his plea to guilty of actual bodily harm and was sentenced to three years probation. He then appealed against the judge's direction.

The House of Lords, although expressing sympathy for the defendant, nevertheless dismissed his appeal. The statements made in *Kemp* were approved of. Their Lordships decided that it was not important whether the impairment of the defendant was organic, as in epilepsy, or functional, or permanent or transient and intermittent, provided that the disease existed at the time of the act.

In *Hennessy 1989*, the accused was charged with taking away a conveyance and driving while disqualified. He had diabetes and argued that he had failed to take his dose of insulin because he was suffering from anxiety, stress and depression and that this had affected his blood sugar level. He contended that this had led to the condition of hyperglycaemia and a state of automatism, thereby allowing him this defence. The judge decided, instead, that this state raised the question of insanity because the hyperglycaemia had arisen from the diabetes itself, not from any outside source. Like Clarke and Sullivan before him, Hennessy did not wish to be tainted with the stigma of insanity. He therefore changed his plea to guilty but then appealed against the judge's finding.

The Court of Appeal upheld the finding of the trial judge. Lord Lane stated that stress, anxiety and depression 'constitute a state of mind which is prone to recur' and could not be classed as outside factors. This meant the defence of automatism was not available to the defendant, only the defence of insanity because of his disease of the mind.

This case can be contrasted with *Quick 1973*, an earlier Court of Appeal decision, where the defence of automatism, which is discussed more fully later in this chapter, was allowed and entitled the possibly unworthy defendant in question to a full acquittal.

The accused was a nurse in a mental hospital and had been convicted of occasioning actual bodily harm to a severely disabled patient. The defendant claimed that the attack had occurred while he was suffering from hypoglycaemia,

caused by low blood sugar in his blood, (as distinct from hyperglycaemia which results from too much sugar), and was unaware of his acts. He therefore argued that the defence of automatism should be available for him. The trial judge decided that this defence could not be used, only the defence of insanity, so, once again, the defendant changed his plea to guilty and appealed.

The Court of Appeal decided that Quick's mental condition was not caused by his diabetes but by his use of insulin and alcohol, which were outside sources. It followed, therefore, that the defence of automatism should have been put before the jury and because it had not been, the appeal had to be allowed, albeit reluctantly.

The courts make a distinction between conditions caused by an outside source, such as a blow to the head causing concussion, or the wrongful use of medication, and diseases of the mind. It is felt that, in the former case, the condition can easily be treated or avoided and, in addition, is unlikely to recur. Where diseases of the mind are involved, however, which might well recur at a later time, the protection of the public is of paramount importance and the court needs to be able to make orders for suitable treatment and/or detention.

Such reasoning is apparent in the case of *Burgess 1991*, where the accused attacked his friend and neighbour while watching television in her flat. She had fallen asleep and, while in this state, the defendant had hit her over the head with a bottle and the video recorder and attempted to strangle her. When she cried out, he appeared to come to his senses and he voluntarily called an ambulance for her. At his trial for malicious wounding, he argued that he remembered nothing of the events and must have been sleepwalking during the attack. He therefore put forward the defence of automatism but this was rejected by the trial judge, who argued, instead, that the evidence suggested insanity under the M'Naghten Rules. After being found not guilty by reason of insanity, the judge ordered that Burgess should be detained in a secure hospital.

The Court of Appeal upheld this verdict. Lord Lane approved of the cases of *Bratty* and

Sullivan. He also noted the views expressed in the Canadian case of *Rabey 1977.* The Supreme Court of Canada had stated that 'the ordinary stresses and disappointments of life which are the common lot of mankind, do not constitute an external cause constituting an explanation for a malfunctioning of the mind which takes it out of the category of a "disease of the mind" '. His opinion of the law was not affected by the later Canadian case of *Parks 1990,* where a man was acquitted when he allegedly drove over 20 kilometres while asleep and killed his mother-in-law! Lord Lane decided that while sleep is a normal condition, sleepwalking, and particularly violence in sleep, is not normal. He noted that the doctors for the defence and prosecution had given conflicting evidence. The prosecution had not believed that this was a case of sleep-walking at all but rather one of a 'hysterical dissociative state'. Lord Lane, therefore, upheld the judge's finding that this was 'an abnormality or disorder, albeit transitory, due to an internal factor, whether functional or organic, which had manifested itself in violence' and decided that it need to be treated, even if recurrence of serious violence was unlikely. He did, however, agree that it was 'incongruous' to label such conditions as insanity and supported Lord Diplock's view, expressed in *Sullivan,* that Parliament could change the wording.

As not to know the nature and quality of the act he was doing. . .

It can be seen from the Rules, that the effect of the disease of the mind must be such that the defendant is 'unaware of what he is doing, or if he does understand this, he fails to appreciate that he is doing something wrong'.

The first part of this statement covers situations where the accused, because of his defect of reason, does not understand the physical nature and quality of his act. In *Kemp 1957,* the defendant's attack occurred when he had lost consciousness and, in *Burgess 1991,* the man claimed that he was asleep. Neither, therefore, knew the nature and quality of their acts. This part of the Rules would also act as a defence if a

man threw his girlfriend from the roof of a building, in the belief that he was flying a kite, or, conversely, his girlfriend chopped off his head, thinking that she was chopping down a tree!

The second part of this statement covers a person who is aware of what he is doing but does not realise that he is doing something wrong. This may be harder to prove. In *Codere 1916,* the appeal court made it clear that the defendant will not be able to rely on such a contention just because he feels that he is not doing anything morally wrong, if he does know that his acts are legally wrong. The man who feels he is morally justified in killing prostitutes would not come under the Rules if he were able to appreciate that he was breaking the law. The case of *Windle 1952* also makes this position clear.

The defendant, a 40-year-old man said to be of weak character, was married to a much older woman who was believed to be insane. She often spoke of suicide and a workmate of the defendant, irritated by Windle's constant complaints about his unhappy home-life, suggested giving her 'a dozen aspirins'. The defendant, instead, gave her 100. A defence doctor believed that the accused was suffering from '*folie a deux*', a form of communicated insanity, but both sets of doctors agreed that Windle knew that he was performing a wrongful act. He had also mentioned to the police that 'I suppose they will hang me for this?' He was found guilty of murder and the Court of Appeal confirmed that the word 'wrong' in this context meant that the defendant knew 'that what he was doing was contrary to law, and that he had realised what punishment the law provided for murder'.

10.3.5 SUGGESTED REFORM OF THE DEFENCE OF INSANITY

We have noted that many doctors, lawyers and laymen have strong reservations about the current law on insanity. The Draft Criminal Code provides for reform of this area. It adopts, with limited amendments, the recommenda-tions made by the Butler Committee. It approves of that body's suggestion that the verdict should be changed to one of 'not guilty by reason of mental disorder'. Clause 35 states that this would be established if it is proved that the defendant, at the time he committed the offence, was suffering from severe mental illness or severe mental handicap. Two medical practitioners, who are experienced in this field, must give evidence to this effect. Clause 36 states that a mental disorder verdict should be brought where the defendant acts in a state of automatism due to mental disorder, or, surprisingly, a combination of mental disorder and intoxication. It should also be brought where the fault for the offence cannot be established for this reason or where, because of his mental disorder, the defendant believes that an exempting circumstance existed.

COMMENT

The law on insanity, particularly in relation to the M'Naghten Rules and the judges' interpretation of them, has been subjected to a barrage of criticism from a variety of sources. The following adverse criticisms have been made:

The Rules were formulated in 1843 and have never been updated.

The Rules are too restricted; they do not cover the defendant who is subject to an irresistible impulse that he knows is wrong but cannot control. The partial defence of diminished responsibility, reducing the liability from murder to manslaughter, does recognise this type of situation.

The Rules lay down a purely legal formula for establishing insanity; they have been criticised by the medical profession as not conforming to medical views of insanity.

They are also disliked by the people they were designed to protect, i.e. the defendants. The latter prefer to use the partial defence of diminished responsibility if the crime is murder. People suffering from epilepsy, diabetes and those who have committed crimes while sleepwalking are outraged to discover that the law labels them insane and, as shown in cases like *Clarke 1972*, *Sullivan 1984* and *Hennessy 1989*, often prefer to plead guilty rather than be tainted with such a stigma.

The judges themselves are uneasy about this development, as shown by the comments of Lawton L J in *Quick 1973*. He stated that 'Common sense is affronted by the prospect of a diabetic being sent to such a hospital when in most cases the disordered mental condition can be rectified quickly by pushing a lump of sugar . . . into the patient's mouth'. It is felt that the condition of too much sugar in the blood could be put right just as quickly. Lord Diplock in *Sullivan 1984* and both the trial judge and Lord Lane, in *Burgess 1991* urged Parliament to look into this matter.

The very different results from a finding of an illness caused by an inside source, such as hyperglycaemia, and an effect on the mind caused by an outside source, such as the wrong dose of medication causing hypoglycaemia, appear to most people to be irrational and unfair. In the first instance, the defendant may be locked away without a time limit being set, whereas in the second case, if automatism is accepted, the defendant will have a complete defence and will walk free from the court. It is a valid argument that the public needs to be safeguarded against violence from offenders who have mental disorders but it might also need to be protected from those who have attacks because they have not followed their correct course of treatment.

This is the only general defence where the onus is on the defendant to prove his insanity, instead of the prosecution having to prove that he is not insane. This again acts unfairly when the alternative defences of insanity and automatism are put forward. In the first case, the defendant must show, on a balance of probabilities, that he is not insane. In the second case, the prosecution will have the task of proving that the defendant was not acting as an automaton.

The state of the law on insanity has been criticised by the Royal Commission on Capital Punishment, the Butler Commission and the Law Commission.

The old-fashioned terminology surrounding the law on insanity also sounds offensive to modern ears. Those who cause harm while suffering from illnesses like epilepsy or diabetes are obviously upset and outraged when the courts label them insane; it must add further pain when they are then found 'not guilty by reason of insanity' under the Trial of Lunatics Act 1883, as amended! Surely it would not have been too difficult a task for Parliament to have repealed the act and modernised the law, rather than merely amending it.

10.4 NON-INSANE AUTOMATISM

We have just discussed the position where the defendant commits a crime but is completely unaware of this because he is suffering from a disease of the mind. This is an example of insane automatism. If, however, an outside factor causes him to act like an automaton, he may be able to use the defence of automatism.

We have already observed that the consequences of the two states of mind are very different. With insane automatism, the verdict will be 'not guilty by reason of insanity' and the judge is obliged to make an order regarding treatment for the defendant. If non-insane automatism is proved, this results in a complete acquittal. The case of *Quick 1973*, noted under insanity, illustrates this. Another very similar example occurred in *Bingham 1991*.

The defendant, who had diabetes, was found guilty of the theft of a can of Coca Cola and a packet of sandwiches, worth just £1.16p. The trial judge would not permit him to put to the jury the defence that he was suffering from hypoglycaemia and had not been aware of any criminal activity.

The Court of Appeal affirmed that the courts had made a clear distinction between hyperglycaemia (an excess of sugar in the blood), which is classed as a disease of the mind and gives rise to the defence of insanity, and hypoglycaemia (a deficiency of sugar in the blood), which is caused by an outside source. If the latter is satisfactorily established, it shows that the accused is in a state of non-insane automatism, which is a complete defence. The court therefore decided that the judge should have directed the jury on this matter and allowed the appeal.

10.4.1 THE LIMITS OF AUTOMATISM

It is now necessary to establish when the defence of automatism will be allowed. After a hectic, high-living weekend, our behaviour might resemble that of an automaton on a grey Monday morning following this. The courts, however, require rather more than wandering around in a dream-like fashion, wishing that lunchtime would arrive! The essence of the defence in law is that the defendant's actions are completely involuntary. Involuntary acts done after a blow to the head, or reflex actions after being attacked by a swarm of bees were cited as examples in *Hill v Baxter 1958*. In *Bratty 1963*, Lord Denning stated that the defence was limited to reflex actions, acts done as a result of a spasm, or acts committed while unconscious or while having convulsions. It was made clear in that case that an act is not involuntary simply because the offender could not resist the impulse to act or did not intend the consequences to take place. Some of the examples given in earlier cases will now come under the heading of insane automatism, after decisions such as *Sullivan 1984* and *Burgess 1991*. In the latter case, the Court of Appeal firmly decided that sleepwalking came under the heading of a disease of the mind, and therefore the defence of insanity applied, not automatism. In the light of these decisions, which have limited the scope of automatism, it is rather surprising to note the decision in *T 1990*. The court accepted that post-traumatic stress, which is surely a disease of the mind, could satisfy the criteria laid down for the defence of automatism, because this condition had been caused by the outside factor of a rape. A woman of 23 had allegedly been acting in a dream-like state during and after her involvement in a robbery. A psychiatrist diagnosed that, at the time of the crime, she was in a dissociative state and not acting with any conscious will. The judge therefore allowed the defence of automatism to be put before the jury and the girl was acquitted of the crime. It is arguable whether this decision is in line with other authorities although it may well have been a just one in the circumstances.

In *Whoolley 1997*, sneezing was accepted as an involuntary act and the defence of automatism allowed.

The defendant admitted that he was driving very close to the car in front in a queue of slow-moving traffic on the M62 near Manchester. He alleged that he suddenly had a sneezing attack and lost control of his HGV wagon. He crashed into the car ahead and this caused a 'domino effect' involving seven other vehicles. The court decided that an attack of sneezing could be the type of involuntary act that came under the defence of automatism and affirmed that a verdict of not guilty by magistrates was allowable.

In *Broome* v *Perkins 1987*, the defence of automatism was not allowed to a person suffering from diabetes who still had some control over his vehicle and this position was affirmed in *AG's Reference (No. 2 of 1992) 1993*. In the case that had given rise to this reference, the jury had found a lorry driver not guilty of the offence of causing death by reckless driving. He had driven 700 yards along the hard shoulder of a motorway before crashing into a parked car and killing two people standing in front of it. He alleged that he had been 'driving without awareness' after a long journey on a straight flat motorway.

The acquittal caused concern and, when the case was referred to the Court of Appeal, it was decided that the defence of automatism is not available where there was merely reduced or imperfect awareness and some degree of control still existed. The court stated that there had to be a 'total destruction of voluntary control' before the defence could apply.

Self-induced automatism

In addition to the limitations noted above, the defence of automatism may not be available even where the defendant is suffering from hypoglycaemia, if it is the defendant's own fault that he is in such a condition. The Court of Appeal addressed this matter in the case of *Bailey 1983*.

The defendant had suffered from diabetes for over 30 years and needed insulin to control his condition. He had become very upset when his girlfriend had ended their relationship and befriended another man.

Bailey had visited this man to discuss the position and after ten minutes or so had complained of feeling unwell and had requested a drink of water and sugar. Before leaving, he asserted that he had lost his glove and, as the other man bent to look for it, Bailey hit him over the head with an iron bar, which had been brought with him. The jury found him guilty of malicious wounding. Bailey appealed.

The Court of Appeal made it clear that automatism arising from the voluntary consumption of drink or drugs is not covered by the defence because the party concerned has been reckless at putting himself in this position, a decision which will be discussed further in the next part of the chapter. The same approach, however, is not normally taken towards someone who fails to take food after an insulin injection, unless he is aware that this might lead to 'aggressive, unpredictable and uncontrollable conduct', and it was felt that this fact was not generally known.

It was decided, therefore, that the jury had been misdirected on this point. Despite this finding, however, the Court of Appeal held that there had been no miscarriage of justice. It was believed that the jury would still have convicted Bailey on the facts; there was ample evidence that he had deliberately gone to the victim's home, armed with an iron bar, in order to teach him a lesson.

activities

1 Do you agree with the contention that the law on insanity is outdated, unfair and in urgent need of reform?

2 Romulus and Remus are twins. They both suffer from diabetes. Romulus was studying so hard for his examinations that he forgot to take his insulin. He became very ill tempered and attacked his law lecturer after the latter had criticised his revision plan.

Remus is more of a 'party animal'. He did not have time to eat, but took a dose of insulin and went off to a club. He was later informed that he had overpowered two of the club 'bouncers' after they had objected to his unruly behaviour at the bar.

Advise the twins, who both face charges of grievous bodily harm. Neither has any recollection of the incidents in question.

10.5 INTOXICATION

In law, the phrase 'intoxication' covers both excessive drinking and various forms of drug taking.

There are rare occasions where the drunkenness or the drugged state is not the fault of the accused at all and, if this is shown to the satisfaction of the court, he may well have a defence. As a starting point, therefore, the law makes a distinction between voluntary and involuntary intoxication.

10.5.1 VOLUNTARY INTOXICATION

As a general rule, the defendant will not be able to rely on the defence of intoxication if he has voluntarily put himself into that state and then committed a crime. In *DPP* v *Beard 1920*, the Lord Chancellor of that time made the following statement:

> Under the law of England as it prevailed until early in the nineteenth century voluntary drunkenness was never an excuse for criminal misconduct; and indeed the classic authorities broadly assert that voluntary drunkenness must be considered rather an aggravation than a defence.

During the nineteenth century, however, the judges began to allow intoxication to be a limited defence in some circumstances where the most serious crimes were involved and the person would otherwise be put to death or, at the least, transported to the colonies. It was also allowed for crimes for which *mens rea* was required for an additional element of the offence. It was gradually recognised that, while voluntary intoxication would never be a defence in crimes of basic intent, like assault, ordinary criminal damage, rape and manslaughter, it might be allowed as either a full or partial defence where crimes of specific intent are involved. Specific intent crimes are normally offences for which some extra element has to be proved before liability is established, although the crime of murder has also been included in this group. The following offences are examples of specific intent crimes:

- Aggravated criminal damage can only be established if a person destroys or damages property, with the intention of endangering life or being reckless whether life is endangered

- Ordinary criminal damage would not normally be in such a category but if the charge specifically mentioned 'intention' only and not recklessness, it would be included

- Theft is definitely a specific intent crime; it can only be committed when the offender

KEY FACTS

- There are three possible times when the question of insanity arises, before the trial, at the time of the trial and at the time the offence was committed
- Two doctors must agree on this and, if the case has reached the trial stage, a special jury must decide the issue taking the doctors' opinion into account. If the jurors hold that the defendant is insane, they must then examine the case against him and decide whether he did the act of which he is accused. If not, he will be released. If so, the judge will choose how to treat him from a range of orders although, in the case of murder, the defendant must be sent to a secure mental hospital, (Criminal Procedure (Insanity) Act 1964, as amended by the Criminal Procedure (Insanity and Unfitness to plead) Act 1991
- If the accused is thought to be insane at the time he committed the act (an issue that can be brought up by the defence, prosecution or the judge), the M'Naghten Rules are used to decide whether legal insanity exists. These state that there must be a defect of reason, caused by a disease of the mind, so that the defendant did not know the nature and quality of his act or, if he did know what he was doing, he did not realise that his act was wrong
- The defendant must prove his insanity on a balance of probabilities. If proved, a special verdict 'not guilty by reason of insanity' is recorded
- The term 'defect of reason' means a complete loss of reasoning powers; forgetfulness is not enough (*Clarke 1972*)
- The term 'disease of the mind' is wider than a disease of the brain; it includes any malfunctioning of the mind that affects reason, memory and understanding (*Kemp 1957*). It includes criminal acts committed while suffering from arteriosclerosis (*Kemp 1957*), in the midst of an epileptic fit (*Sullivan 1983*), while suffering from hyperglycaemia caused by diabetes (*Hennessy 1989*), and even where the defendant is sleepwalking or suffering from a blackout (*Burgess 1991*). It does not include illnesses like hypoglycaemia which are caused by an outside source (*Quick 1973*). In such cases, the complete defence of automatism is available
- Denning's statement that 'any mental disorder which has manifested itself in violence and is prone to recur is a disease of the mind' now seems to have been widened to admit diseases of the mind where the violence is unlikely to recur (*Burgess 1991*)
- The defendant must either be unaware of the nature and quality of his act or not realise that he is doing something wrong (*Codere 1916, Windle 1952*)
- There has been strong criticism of the M'Naghten Rules and many calls for their reform although, in practice, cases where insanity is pleaded are rare
- Automatism is divided into insane automatism, to which the M'Naghten Rules are applied, and non-insane automatism, which is a complete defence, resulting in an acquittal. Non-insane automatism is sub-divided into involuntary automatism and self-induced automatism
- The following acts have been accepted by the courts as involuntary: blows to the head, reflex actions after being attacked by a swarm of bees (*Hill v Baxter 1958*), other involuntary spasms, (*Bratty 1963*), a dissociative state caused by a rape (*T 1990*) and an attack of sneezing (*Whoolley 1997*)
- Automatism cannot now be pleaded for sleepwalking (*Burgess 1991*) or for acts where the defendant still has the power to exercise some control over his actions (*Broome v Perkins 1987, AG's Reference (No. 2 of 1992) 1994*)
- The defence will not be available if the accused has caused the situation by his own reckless conduct (*Bailey 1983*). The Court of Appeal felt that failing to take food after an insulin injection might not come into the category of reckless behaviour because it was not commonly known that such inaction could cause a diabetic person to act aggressively

FIGURE 10.2 *Key facts chart on insanity and automatism* dishonestly appropriates property belonging to another with the intention of permanently depriving the other of that property

- Under s.18 Offences Against the Person Act 1861, the defendant must have unlawfully and maliciously wounded or caused grievous bodily harm to another with the intention to do some grievous bodily harm to be found guilty of this most serious offence in the category of non-fatal offences against the person

All these crimes, therefore, require some further intention to be established and, if this is not the case because extreme drunkenness or a deeply drugged state negatives this, it is felt that the offender cannot be found guilty; he cannot be shown to possess the appropriate *mens rea*. It will be seen from the cases, however, that, in many instances, he can be found guilty of a lesser offence, i.e. manslaughter instead of murder, basic criminal damage rather than the aggravated form and malicious wounding or grievous bodily harm under s.20, instead of s.18. The offence of theft causes difficulty, because no lesser offence exists to put in its place.

It is now necessary to look at some of the important cases concerning the two issues of basic and specific intent.

Basic intent crimes

As stated in *DPP* v *Beard 1920*, intoxication cannot be used as a defence for these crimes. A basic intent crime is a crime where the *mens rea* does not exceed the *actus reus* of the offence. This was stated in *DPP* v *Morgan 1976*. Examples among the crimes we have studied in this book are manslaughter, rape, malicious wounding or grievous bodily harm under s.20 Offences Against the Person Act 1861, actual bodily harm and common assault and battery. The reasoning behind the refusal to allow intoxication as a defence is that the act of getting drunk or putting oneself into a drugged state is a reckless course of conduct which, combined with a criminal act, will amount to

recklessness in law and thus satisfy the *mens rea*. It is probably best to think of this as a policy decision on the part of the courts, rather than trying to reason it through, because there are difficulties with this in cases where *Cunningham*-style recklessness has to be shown. Despite these problems, and despite what is stated in s.8 Criminal Justice Act 1967, the rule that drunkenness is no defence in crimes of basic intent was categorically affirmed by the House of Lords in the case of *DPP* v *Majewski 1977*.

The defendant was convicted at Chelmsford Crown Court of three counts of actual bodily harm and three counts of assault on a police constable in the execution of his duty. Majewski was a drug addict and claimed that on the day in question he had consumed such large quantities of drugs and alcohol that he 'completely blanked out' and had no recollection of committing assaults in the pub in Basildon or later at the police station. The judge told the jury to disregard the fact that there could be a defence on this ground and the defendant appealed.

The House of Lords unanimously upheld the conviction. Their Lordships were obviously concerned about the social as well as the legal implications of allowing such a defence. Lord Salmon stated 'If there were to be no penal sanction for any injury inflicted under the complete mastery of drink or drugs, voluntarily taken, the social consequence could be appalling'. Lord Elwyn-Jones stated that self-induced drunkenness had long been a problem. He went on to say that 'voluntary drug-taking with the potential and actual dangers to others it may cause has added a new dimension to the old problem'.

Majewski's convictions, therefore, were upheld and the defence denied him. Lord Elwyn-Jones approved of the case of Beard, and stated clearly that it was only in crimes of specific intent that drunkenness could ever provide a defence. Lord Salmon admitted that it could seem illogical to allow the defence in one class of case and not in another but felt that treating specific intent crimes differently was justified in order to alleviate the harshness that might otherwise be caused. He did not agree that basic intent crimes should be allowed the defence as the law had been clear on this subject for about 150 years and had not been seen to cause injustice. He believed that the rules were more necessary today, because of the increase in drug taking.

Another basic intent crime is rape and, as in *Majewski*, the defendant could not rely on his drunkenness to avoid liability. In *Fotheringham 1988*, the defendant was appealing against his conviction for the rape of a 14-year-old girl. She had acted as a babysitter for Fotheringham and his wife and had gone to sleep in the matrimonial bed. The defendant claimed that he was very drunk and had got into bed and had sexual intercourse in the mistaken belief that the girl in the bed was his wife. He was appealing because the judge had directed the jury to disregard this fact.

The Court of Appeal upheld the rule that self-induced intoxication cannot be used as a defence to a crime of basic intent and stated that neither could the defence of mistake be raised, if this mistake were caused by self-induced intoxication. The case of *O'Grady 1987* (see Chapter 11), was held to be authority for this.

Specific intent crimes

It has been noted that, with regard to specific intent crimes, if the drunkenness is so advanced that the defendant has not been able to form the *mens rea* for the offence, he may be able to put forward the defence of intoxication. He will not often escape liability completely, because it is usually possible to convict him, instead, of a lesser basic intent crime. An example of this occurred in *Lipman 1970*.

The defendant and the victim were both addicted to drugs and, on the night in question, took LSD. The dead body of the girl was found a day later. She had suffered two blows to the head but had actually died of asphyxia from having part of a sheet crammed into her mouth. The man, an American citizen, had returned to his home country but was sent back to face trial for murder. He claimed that he had experienced a bad LSD 'trip', during which he had believed that he was descending to the centre of the earth and was being attacked by snakes, which he had tried to fight off. He argued that he had no knowledge of the real events and had not intended to harm the girl. The jury found him guilty of manslaughter.

The Court of Appeal upheld this verdict. The court decided that he could not be found guilty of murder, a specific intent crime, if the intention to kill or cause grievous bodily harm could not be established. He could, however, be found guilty of manslaughter; there had been an unlawful act and a death had resulted. Manslaughter was a basic intent crime for which self-induced intoxication was no defence.

In *AG for Northern Ireland* v *Gallagher 1963*, the defendant was not able to show that he lacked the intention to kill. The prosecution claimed that the defendant harboured a grudge against his wife because she had been instrumental in arranging for him to be detained in a mental hospital. He therefore decided to kill her and bought a knife for this purpose. He also bought a bottle of whisky, either to give himself Dutch courage or to drown his conscience after the event.

The jury convicted him of murder but this was quashed by the Northern Ireland Appeal Court. The House of Lords restored the conviction.

Lord Denning gave the main speech. He decided that there were only two possible defences; the first was insanity, the second, intoxication. Denning decided that insanity was not applicable here because, although the man was a psychopath, this state of mind was not active at the time he conceived of the plan to kill his wife. He also affirmed that the defence of intoxication was not available in a crime of basic intent and added that, even in a specific intent crime, it had to be shown that the degree of drunkenness was such that the defendant 'was rendered so stupid by drink that he does not know what he is doing'. Denning agreed that this had been established in the early case where a nurse at a christening had been so drunk that she had put the baby onto the fire, instead of a log of wood. He also quoted with approval a later case where a man had stabbed his friend several times, in the mistaken belief that it was a theatrical dummy in his bed, not a real person.

In *Gallagher*, however, the House of Lords decided that the defendant obviously knew what he was doing and had formed the clear intent to kill. Lord Denning made the following pronouncement:

> My Lords, I think the law on this point should take a clear stand. If a man, whilst sane and sober, forms an intention to kill, and makes preparation for it, knowing it is a wrong thing to do, and then gets himself drunk so as to give himself Dutch courage to do the killing, and whilst drunk carries out his intention, he cannot rely on this self-induced drunkenness as a defence to a charge of murder, nor even as reducing it to manslaughter.

The case of *Gallagher* did, however, affirm that the defence of insanity was available for both specific intent and basic intent crimes if the drunkenness had been so acute that it had led to a 'disease of the mind', as where the defendant was suffering from delirium tremens.

10.5.2 INVOLUNTARY INTOXICATION

In the aforementioned cases, the offenders have deliberately taken alcohol or drugs. We now need to look at the position where the intoxication is involuntary. An example of involuntary intoxication would occur where the drink or drugs were given to the offender without his knowledge, as, for example where his drink has been 'spiked'. In such a case, the defendant might well have a defence, both in cases where the crime is a specific intent one and also where it is a basic intent one, provided that in the latter situation the defendant is not found to have been careless. In the early case of *Pearson 1835*, it was stated that 'If a party be made drunk by stratagem, or the fraud of another, he

is not responsible'. In some circumstances, the courts have gone further than this and have decided that the intoxication may also be involuntary even if taken deliberately, if it can be shown that the defendant believed that he was taking a drug to calm himself when, in reality, it had the opposite effect. In the case of *Hardie 1985*, noted below, it could be argued that the defendant was, at the least, misguided in taking drugs prescribed for his ex-girlfriend. Nonetheless, the Court of Appeal held that the defence of intoxication should have been put to the jury for that body to consider the matter.

The facts were as follows. Hardie's long-term relationship had broken down and he had been asked to leave the flat he had shared with his girlfriend. He had become very upset and during the day had taken several Valium tablets, after being reassured that they were 'old stock' and would not do him any harm.

He later fell asleep and claimed that he could remember very little after this time but, while in this state, he started a fire in a wardrobe at the flat he was vacating. The jury found him guilty of arson but the Court of Appeal quashed the conviction. Parker L J stated 'It is true that Valium is a drug and it is true that it was taken deliberately and not taken on medical prescription, but the drug is, in our view wholly different in kind from drugs which are liable to cause unpredictability or aggressiveness. It may well be that the taking of a sedative or soporific drug will, in certain circumstances, be no answer, for example in a case of reckless driving, but if the effect of a drug is merely soporific or sedative the taking of it, even in some excessive quantity, cannot in the ordinary way raise a conclusive presumption against the admission of proof of intoxication for the purpose of disproving *mens rea* in ordinary crimes, such as would be the case with alcoholic intoxication or incapacity or automatism resulting from the self-administration of dangerous drugs'.

The court distinguished the case of *Bailey 1983*, where the conviction had been upheld despite the judge's misdirection, on the grounds that the error in the law would not have made a difference to the outcome, and quashed Hardie's conviction.

The courts are not, however, prepared to extend this licence too far. In *Allen 1988*, it was affirmed that it was not available to a defendant who had been drinking wine in a voluntary way but had failed to realise the strength of it and had acted out of character as a result.

On the other side of the coin, the defendant who has, in truth, been involuntarily intoxicated will not be able to use this as a defence if he had still retained the ability to form the intent to commit the crime in question. The House of Lords, in *Kingston 1994*, overturned the controversial quashing of the decision by the Court of Appeal and upheld the view of the trial judge that 'a drugged intent is still an intent'.

The defendant had been involved in a business dispute with another couple and the latter had decided to blackmail him. They knew that he had paedophiliac tendencies and arranged for him and their accomplice to visit a flat to which a 15-year-old boy had been lured. The latter had been given drugs and was asleep on the bed. The defendant was then invited to abuse the boy and was photographed and taped as he did so. Kingston claimed that he, too, had been drugged and had performed the unlawful acts while in this state. He asserted that, if he had not been so intoxicated, he would have been able to control his actions.

The Court of Appeal decided that, if this were indeed the case, the defence of involuntary intoxication should be open to him. The House of Lords was clearly worried about the implications of such a move, and refused to allow this. The current state of the law, therefore, is that once the intent to commit the crime in question is proved, intoxication is no defence, whether the offence is one of basic intent or specific intent and whether the intoxication is voluntary or involuntary.

10.5.3 POSSIBLE REFORM OF THE LAW ON INTOXICATION

Over the years, various suggestions have been put forward to reform this area of law. Some reformers are concerned about the fact that intoxication often causes severe social problems and therefore recommend making it a separate offence. The Butler Committee suggested a new offence called dangerous intoxication, which would come into play when the defendant was acquitted of the main charge and which would carry a penalty of one year's imprisonment for a first offence or three years for subsequent ones. This proposal did not find favour with the Criminal Law Revision Committee. This body did not like the idea of the same penalty being applied, whatever the offence against the person and suggested, instead, clarifying the present rule laid down in *Majewski*.

Other reformers believe that it is unfair to treat an intoxicated person in the same way as if he were not drunk or drugged, and disapprove of the current restrictions put upon the defence of intoxication. The defence is more widely available in other jurisdictions, including Australia, Canada, New Zealand and South Africa. The Law Commission, therefore, in a consultation paper in 1993, suggested that our law should follow similar lines and abolish the basic intent/specific intent distinction and allow the defence to be put forward in all instances. The responses to this were not favourable so the Commission now proposes to codify and clarify the present law, with only minor amendments.

KEY
FACTS

- The defence of intoxication is available for specific intent crimes provided that it is established that the defendant is so drunk or drugged that he is not able to form the *mens rea* for the offence in question (*DPP* v *Majewski 1977*). In most cases, the defendant will be found liable for a lesser crime instead, such as manslaughter instead of murder (*Lipman 1970*), basic criminal damage instead of aggravated criminal damage or gbh under s.20 instead of s.18. If intoxication is established where the crime is theft, the defendant is entitled to an acquittal
- If the defendant has been shown to have formed an intent, the defence will not be available. An intent formed by a psychopath while he is not insane (*AG for Northern Ireland* v *Gallagher 1963*), or an intent formed by a person who has been drugged (*Kingston 1994*), will still amount to an intent.
- Specific intent crimes are normally those for which an extra intention has to be established beyond that required for the *actus reus*, although murder has been included in this category
- The offences include grievous bodily harm under s.18 Offences Against the Person Act 1861, aggravated criminal damage, theft and burglary
- The defence of intoxication is not available for basic intent crimes (*DPP* v *Beard 1920*, *DPP* v *Majewski 1976*, *Fotheringham 1988*)
- If the intoxication is involuntary, then, *prima facie*, the defence will be available for both basic intent crimes and specific intent crimes (*Pearson 1835*). It might also be permitted even in cases where the drugs are deliberately taken, if they are believed to be calming drugs rather than stimulants (*Hardie 1985*)

FIGURE 10.3 *Key facts chart on intoxication*

activity

Distinguish between: (a) voluntary intoxication and involuntary intoxication; (b) basic intent crimes and specific intent crimes, giving two examples of each type of crime.

summary

We have learned that the rules on incapacity have recently changed and that, while a child under the age of ten cannot be charged with a criminal offence, those of ten and over are treated in this respect in the same way as adults.

We have learned that the defence of insanity is seldom favoured by defendants because of its archaic form, the interpretation of the M'Naghten Rules by the judges and the alternative verdict that is brought in, and that strong calls for reform of this area of law have been made. We have noted that the defence of non-insane automatism may be available for completely involuntary acts caused by an outside source but is less likely to succeed if this is self-induced.

Towards the end of this chapter, we examined the defence of intoxication and discovered that this defence is rigorously contained because of the social implications of allowing any extension. Generally, therefore, it is not available as a defence. We noted, however, that it can be put forward in cases where the intoxication is purely involuntary, provided that no *mens rea* has been formed. It should be remembered that the case of *Kingston* decided that a drunken intent is still an intent. If the crime is one of specific intent, and no *mens rea* has been formed because of the acuteness of the drink or drugs, the defendant will have this defence although, in most instances, he will still be found guilty of a lesser crime.

CHAPTER 11

GENERAL DEFENCES II

11.1 INTRODUCTION

OUR STUDY OF general defences continues with the defence of mistake. This will be followed by a discussion of three important and interrelated defences, i.e. those of necessity, duress and duress of circumstances. Lastly, the defences of self-defence and prevention of crime will be examined. These two defences are known collectively under the term private and public defence.

11.2 MISTAKE

Generally, making a mistake about the law will not provide a defence. In 1982, Lord Bridge stated that a fundamental principle existed that ignorance of the law is no defence in criminal law. If, for example, the defendant had led a very sheltered life and then killed someone who disagreed with his views, he would not have a defence to the crime of murder even though he may have been unaware that such an offence existed.

With mistakes of fact, however, there could be a defence if the mistake is such that it prevents the accused forming the *mens rea* necessary for the crime in question.

We have noted that special provisions allowing for certain mistakes may be found in the statute laying down the offence, as in the Theft Act 1968 and Criminal Damage Act 1971.

The defence of mistake is also available in a more general way but, until the 1970s, its scope was fairly limited. Before this, the defence was only possible if the defendant could establish that his mistake of fact was a reasonable one and this was not always easy to prove. Fortunately, the accused in *Tolson 1889*, was able to satisfy the court that her mistake was both an honest mistake and a reasonable one to make in the circumstances.

The defendant's husband had deserted her and she later heard from others that he had been aboard a ship bound for America that had sunk with no survivors. Six years later, therefore, she went through a ceremony of marriage with another man. The husband then turned up again 11 months later.

Mrs Tolson was convicted of bigamy but this was quashed on appeal. Stephen J stated:

> The conduct of the woman convicted was not in the smallest degree immoral, it was perfectly natural and legitimate. Assuming the facts to be as she supposed, the infliction of more than a nominal punishment on her would have been a scandal. Why, then, should the legislature be held to have wished to subject her to punishment at all?

This position still exists where the *mens rea* of the offence can be established by mere negligence; any mistake must be both honestly and reasonably held. Where, however, the offence requires the prosecution to establish that the defendant intended to commit the crime in question or was reckless about this, then the decision in *DPP* v *Morgan 1976* comes into operation. This case widened the use of the defence of mistake and allows it to be used in cases where the mistake is an honest one but is not necessarily reasonable.

The defendants were all in the RAF and spent the evening drinking together. Morgan then invited the others to have intercourse with his wife and stated that, if she protested, she did not really mean this and was doing so to increase her pleasure, which was shown to be completely untrue. The men were all convicted of rape but tried to argue on appeal that they believed that the woman was consenting and that the judge had misdirected the jury that their belief had to be a reasonable one.

Their Lordships admitted that there had been a misdirection and clearly stated that, in cases where intention or recklessness has to be proved, an honest mistake, even one that is not reasonably held, could provide a defence. This, then, is the current state of the law. In this particular case, however, the convictions were not quashed because the judges held that the jury would not have believed such a story and would still have convicted even if the point of law had been correctly put to it.

In *W (a minor)* v *Dolbey 1983*, a 15-year-old defendant was able to take advantage of this rule when he was convicted of malicious wounding. He successfully argued that he honestly believed that the air rifle he carried no longer had any pellets in it.

This widening of the defence of mistake was also upheld in two cases of alleged self defence. The first was *Williams (Gladstone) 1987*, where the defendant mistakenly believed that he was watching a mugging. In fact his victim had been the one to see such a crime and had grabbed hold of a youth who had just robbed a woman. The defendant then attacked the man holding the mugger and inflicted actual bodily harm on him! His appeal against his conviction was successful on the grounds that he had made an honest mistake.

Similarly, in *Beckford 1988*, a policeman who shot a man who had been terrorising his family was able to use the defence of mistake because he had believed, wrongly as it transpired, that the victim was armed.

While the decision in *Morgan* has opened up the defence of mistake, it is still not available for mistakes that are made while in the state of voluntary intoxication, as illustrated by the case of *Fotheringham 1988*, mentioned earlier in Chapter 10.

11.3 NECESSITY

The defences of necessity, duress and duress of circumstances are all connected and, for this reason, the key facts chart and the activities will encompass all three defences. In particular, duress of circumstances, only recognised by that name since the 1980s, is felt to be an extension of the defence of necessity. In these three offences, the defendant is claiming that he did not want to commit the crime in question but either the circumstances or other people are forcing him to do this.

KEY FACTS

- There is normally no defence for mistakes about the law
- When a mistake of fact has been made, a defence will exist if the mistake means that the *mens rea* of the crime cannot be established
- Some statutory offences allow the defence of mistake, e.g. Theft Act 1968, Criminal Damage Act 1971
- More generally, an honest mistake about the facts may provide a defence (*Tolson 1889*)
- The House of Lords' decision in *Morgan 1976* now makes it clear that, for crimes where intention or recklessness has to be proved, the mistake need not be a reasonable

> one provided that the belief is honestly held (*W (a minor)* v *Dolbey 1989*)
> - The defence of mistake may be available in cases where another defence is being claimed like self-defence or prevention of crime (*Williams (Gladstone) 1987*, *Beckford 1988*), but it cannot be used if the accused made the mistake as a result of voluntary intoxication (*Fotheringham 1988*)

FIGURE 11.1 *Key facts chart on mistake*

11.3.1 THE SCOPE OF THE DEFENCE OF NECESSITY

There has always been some doubt as to the actual extent of the defence of necessity in English law and this uncertainty was reflected in the comments of members of the Commission drafting the Criminal Code. They stated 'We are not prepared to suggest that necessity should in every case be a justification; we are equally unprepared to suggest that necessity should in no case be a defence'. The cases that have come before the courts also show this ambivalence towards the defence.

In early times, the defence was available in specific instances. For example, it was felt to be justifiable to pull down a house to prevent a fire spreading to others, to jettison the cargo of a ship to save lives or for a prisoner to escape if the jail in which he was kept imprisoned was on fire. Before the passing of the Abortion Act 1967, there was a defence to a charge of carrying out an illegal abortion if this was necessary to safeguard the life of the mother or, as in the case of *Bourne 1939*, a 14-year-old girl who had been raped.

In *Johnson* v *Phillips 1976*, it was held that a police officer, acting in the course of his duty, was permitted to order a motorist to disobey traffic regulations, if this action was felt to be necessary for the protection of people and property. More recently, the courts appear to have extended the defence. In *F (Mental Patient: Sterilisation) Re 1990*, West Berkshire Health Authority, acting with the permission of the girl's mother, sought a declaration that it was not unlawful to sterilise a patient suffering from a very serious mental disability, after the girl had formed a sexual relationship with another patient. It was believed that a pregnancy would be disastrous to her precarious mental health. The Official Solicitor, acting on behalf of the girl who was not able to give her own consent to this operation, challenged the action, doubting its legality. The House of Lords came out strongly in favour of the Health Authority. Lord Brandon stated:

> In many cases ... it will not only be lawful for doctors, on the ground of necessity, to operate on or give other medical treatment to adult patients disabled from giving their consent; it will also be their common duty to do so.

Even more controversially, in 1992, a doctor was allowed to perform a caesarean operation on a pregnant woman who, because of her beliefs, had specifically refused to give her consent to it. The doctor claimed that the operation was necessary to save the life of the unborn baby. Professor Ian Kennedy argued strongly that this decision lowered the status of women, treating them as mere 'chattels and ambulatory wombs'!

11.3.2 LIMITATIONS ON THE DEFENCE OF NECESSITY

While allowing the defence in specific situations, the courts have been wary of expanding the defence in a more general way. Lord Hale, an early writer, made it clear that the defence was not available just because a person was hungry or unclothed. In the latter half of this century, Lord Denning, normally a champion of the underdog, was equally forthright when he stated: '... if hunger were once allowed to be an excuse for stealing, it would open a door through which all kinds of lawlessness and disorder would pass'. He was even less inclined to allow the defence to homeless people, arguing that, if it were allowed 'no one's house could be safe. Necessity would open a door which no man could shut'.

The courts have always been influenced by the notorious case of *Dudley and Stephens 1884*, where the Divisional Court decided that the defence of necessity was not allowed as a defence to murder. Lord Coleridge claimed that if necessity was once allowed in such circumstances, it might 'be made the legal cloak for unbridled passion and atrocious crime'.

The two defendants, another man and a 17-year-old cabin boy had been adrift in the ocean in an open boat, 1600 miles from land. They had been without food for eight days and without water for six. They therefore decided to kill and eat the cabin boy, who had become very weak. Four days later, a passing ship discovered them. The men were charged with murder. The jurors obviously had some sympathy for the plight of the shipwrecked crew because, although they found that the defendants had indeed killed the boy, they wished to record a special verdict. This recognised the fact that the men had little hope of an early rescue and would probably have died if they had not committed the act. It was also acknowledged that the boy was likely to have died anyway although it was stressed that there was no greater necessity to kill him rather than one of the men.

The Divisional Court was not prepared to allow a defence in these circumstances. Lord Coleridge had sympathy with the suffering of the defendants and appreciated the difficulties of resisting temptation in such a dreadful situation but stated that the judges were:

> often compelled to set up standards we cannot reach ourselves and to lay down rules which we could not ourselves satisfy. But a man has no right to declare temptation to be an excuse, though he might himself have yielded to it, nor allow compassion for the criminal to change

> and weaken in any manner the legal definition of the crime. It is therefore our duty to declare that the prisoners' act in this case was wilful murder, that the facts as stated in the verdict are no legal justification of the homicide; and to say that in our unanimous opinion the prisoners are upon this special verdict guilty of murder.

The men were sentenced to be hanged but the sentence was later commuted to just six months imprisonment without hard labour.

Rather surprisingly, in *Buckoke* v *Greater London Council 1971*, Lord Denning decided that the defence of necessity was not even available for firefighters and other rescuers, if they contravened the traffic regulations in their race to the scene of danger. He did go on to say that they should be congratulated rather than condemned for their action and expressed the hope that they would not be prosecuted in the first place. One example noted by Smith and Hogan concerned the behaviour of an army corporal at the time of the sinking of the Herald of Free Enterprise at Zeebrugge. He told the inquest that he had ordered people near a young man on a rope ladder to push him off, as he was preventing the rescue of others because he had become petrified through cold and fear, and would not move despite all attempts to persuade him. The corporal and others involved were never prosecuted. It should be noted that firefighters have now been given a special defence under the Road Traffic Act 1988 in certain situations and other statutes also lay down specific defences akin to necessity as, for example, the Criminal Damage Act 1971, which allows a defence under s.5(2) if the accused acted as he did in order to protect property he thought in immediate need of protection.

Conversely, the courts have decided that the common law defence is not available if the statutory provision expressly or impliedly precludes this, as shown in *DPP* v *Harris 1995*, a careless driving case.

Similarly, in *Cichon* v *DPP 1994*, the defendant was unsuccessful in his attempt to use the defence of necessity because the notorious Dangerous Dogs Act 1991 (now amended), laid down an offence of absolute liability. The defendant, a nephew of the dog's owner, claimed that he had taken off the muzzle of the pit bull terrier in the park to allow it to be sick because it had kennel cough. Despite this, he was still found guilty, fined £50 and the dog ordered to be destroyed. Dog lovers will be pleased to note that the animal later won a temporary reprieve from its death sentence from the Divisional Court, after the owner challenged the fact that the hearing had taken place without her. Mr Justice Rougier (obviously a dog lover!) was scathing about the merits of the Dangerous Dogs Act 1991, believing it to be 'an ill-thought piece of legislation, no doubt drafted in hasty response to another strident pressure group. Add to that a foolish nephew and an over-zealous policeman and a perfectly inoffensive animal has to be sent to the gas chamber'. There were suggestions after this appeal that the dog would be sent to France to be under the protection of Brigitte Bardot, the film actress, in order to ensure its safety in case the CPS instigated further proceedings.

In conclusion, it can be seen that the scope of the defence of necessity is still uncertain. The recognition of the defence of duress of circumstances, which is examined below, is unlikely to make the position clearer, even though it shows a welcome willingness on the part of the courts to accept new situations where a defence to a criminal charge should be made available.

11.3.3 POSSIBLE REFORM OF THE DEFENCE OF NECESSITY

At present, there are no plans to change the common law rules on this defence, uncertain though they are. In 1977, the Law Commission had been in favour of abolishing the defence altogether. It was felt that it only covered rare cases and, where such a defence was felt to be necessary, it could be included in the relevant statute. In other cases, it was argued that the matter could be dealt with when deciding whether or not to charge the offender or when the defendant was sentenced. This view was strongly criticised at the time, causing the Commission to re-think the matter.

Their altered view has now strengthened in the light of the development of the defence of duress of circumstances, for which they have given the seal of approval and which is discussed below. In the Law Commission's Report No. 218, *Legislating the Criminal Code – Offences Against the Person and General Principles, 1993* and the Draft Bill accompanying it, special provisions are included relating to duress of circumstances. None are made concerning the wider defence of necessity but the Commission does recommend that it should remain as a common law defence, to be developed by the judges, as required.

11.4 DURESS (OF THREATS)

The defence of duress has existed for centuries. In *Oldcastle's case 1419*, the defendants were able to put it forward as a defence to a charge of treason. They were able to convince the court that they had only supplied food to rebels because they feared death if they refused. It was again acknowledged as a possible defence to some acts of treason in *McGrowther 1746* and, more recently in *Purdy 1946*. In these cases and the ones described below, the act amounting to duress was caused by another person. This has come to be known in some quarters as duress by threats. It will be seen that, while this defence has been clearly established, it is not available for everyone or for all situations.

Since the 1980s, another form of duress has developed which is actually closer to the defence of necessity, although many of the rules laid down for duress of threats have also been held to apply to this 'new' defence. This is known as duress of circumstances. It can be used when the defendant commits a crime as a result of threatening circumstances. The difference is that no

11.4.1 THE SCOPE OF THE DEFENCE OF DURESS OF THREATS

Prima facie, the defence of duress by threats is available if the defendant is forced to commit a criminal act because another person is using force against him or another or threatening to do so. In *AG v Whelan 1934*, it was stated that the defence of duress should be available when the accused is subjected to:

> threats of immediate death or serious personal violence so great as to overbear the ordinary powers of human resistance.

Parts of this definition need further examination.

At whom must the threat be directed?

The force or threat of it may be made against the defendant himself or against others, although how widely this extends is, at present, uncertain. It certainly covers threats to the defendant's family and appears to cover threats to cohabitees and other loved ones, as suggested in *Hurley and Murray 1967*, an Australian case. There is uncertainty over whether the defence could be used if strangers were threatened with violence unless the defendant committed a criminal act. The Law Commission favours the view that there should no restrictions on who is actually threatened, but it cannot be said with certainty that this is the current position.

What constitutes a serious threat?

It is obvious from the definition in *AG v Whelan* that the threat must be a really serious one; in *Valderrama-Vega 1985*, a threat to disclose details of the defendant's homosexual tendencies was not, on its own, enough to constitute duress. The defendant had been involved in a drug smuggling 'racket' concerned with importing cocaine from Columbia. He claimed that he had committed the crimes because he and his family had been threatened with death or injury if he did not comply. He also argued that the defence of duress should be available to him because he was under severe financial pressure and was therefore forced to turn to crime and also because threats to divulge his homosexual leanings had been made. The judge told the jury to discount the last two fears; he decided that they were not serious enough threats to amount to duress and the Court of Appeal agreed. The judge then went on to tell the jurors that they should only allow the defence if they were convinced that he committed the crimes solely because of the threats of violence and this part of his judgment was held to be a misdirection. Despite this, the conviction was upheld, as it was in the case of *Ortiz 1986*, where, once again the word 'solely' had been used by the judge. In this case, however, only one alleged threat had been made, a threat to harm the defendant's wife and child. Apart from this there had been substantial inducements to commit the crime in question; the defendant had received business advantages, nearly £90,000 in cash, a holiday for himself and his family and a flat in Chelsea, before the threats had been made. The jury refused to accept the defence of duress and convicted him of dealing in drugs and the Court of Appeal upheld this. That court did suggest, however, that it would be better not to direct the jury that the serious threat had to be the sole reason that the defendant committed the crime.

How immediate must the threat be?

The threat must be a reasonably immediate one. Normally, if there is plenty of time to obtain help and protection from other sources, the defendant will not be able to use the defence of duress. In some circumstances, however, the courts are prepared to look at all the circumstances of the case and may take a sympathetic view of the fears of the accused, as in *Hudson and Taylor 1971*. Hudson, a young girl of 17 and Taylor, aged 19, were the principal prosecution witnesses in a malicious wounding case but, through fear of retaliatory action from associates of the accused, changed their stories in court and ensured the acquittal of the defendant. The girls were later charged with perjury and put forward the defence of duress as they had been threatened with serious physical violence if they testified. They had then seen one of the men who had threatened them sitting in the public gallery at the trial, which reinforced their decisions to change their evidence. The jury convicted the girls after the judge made it clear that the defence was not open to them because the threats 'were not sufficiently present and immediate'.

The Court of Appeal disagreed. The court said that the prosecution needed to prove that the girls could have obtained protection and it was then up to the jury to decide the matter after considering the age of the offenders, the circumstances in which they found themselves and any risks which may have been involved.

▼ COMMENT

The courts are in a difficult position where the issue of perjury is concerned. In an increasingly secular age, there needs to be a strong legal deterrent to stop people lying in court or refusing to testify at all. In many cases nowadays, witnesses (and defendants) place less significance on swearing on the Bible, or in other ways, so other methods must be in force to encourage people to tell the truth. If they do not, the guilty will be able to defeat attempts to bring them to justice and cases will be lost or not brought to court at all, after all the expense to the taxpayer of initiating an unsuccessful prosecution. In addition, if the practice of intimidating witnesses is seen to be successful, it might be become more commonplace.

On the other hand, it leaves a nasty taste in the mouth when innocent people are imprisoned when, because of genuine fears, they refuse to testify or change their version of events. Their belief that the police will not be able to protect them effectively may be well founded in these days of diminishing resources. A recent case very similar in its circumstances to *Hudson and Taylor* attracted a great deal of media attention and, again, the girls' release was effected but, as yet, no satisfactory answer to this difficulty has yet been found (*Hurst 1994*).

So great as to overbear the ordinary powers of human resistance

What is meant by the expression in *AG* v *Whelan* that the threats of death or personal injury must be 'so great as to overbear the ordinary powers of human resistance'? This question was looked at in the case of *Graham 1982*. He was a homosexual who lived with his wife and his homosexual lover, King. Graham claimed that he was frightened of King, because he had been violent towards Graham and his wife and had been instrumental in the latter leaving the matrimonial home, shortly before the murder. Graham claimed that the Valium he was taking had increased his fear and had made him more susceptible to the bullying. This had made him agree to help in the murder his wife. Mrs Graham was then lured to the house after her husband falsely claimed that he had attempted suicide, and was then strangled by King with a flex from the coffee percolator. The prosecution claimed that Graham had helped with this and with the disposal of the body.

Graham's conviction for murder was upheld and the defences of intoxication and duress were rejected.

The Court of Appeal held that, if anything, the judge had been too favourable to the accused in his summing up and dismissed the appeal. The proper direction in such cases was said to be a two-fold one and can be summarised as follows:

1 Was the defendant impelled to act as he did because, as a result of what he reasonably believed the other had said and done, he had good cause to fear that, if he did not act as he did, death or serious injury would result?
2 Would a sober person of reasonable firmness, sharing the characteristics of the defendant have acted in a similar way?

It can be seen that three different points have to be proved. The defendant's belief must have been a reasonable one, he must have good cause to fear that death or personal injury will result, and lastly, it must be shown that a sober person of reasonable firmness, sharing the characteristics of the defendant, would have made a similar response.

The question as to which characteristics of the accused can be attributed to the sober person of reasonable firmness has occupied the attention of the court in the last few years.

In *Bowen 1996*, the prosecution claimed that the defendant had visited over 40 electrical outlets and had falsely obtained goods on credit in order to sell them to others and pocket the proceeds. The defendant, on the other hand, argued that he had only committed the offences because two men had threatened to use petrol bombs against him and his family if he refused and had not gone to the police because of his fear of retaliation. Evidence was put forward by the defence that Bowen only had an IQ of 68 and was especially vulnerable to threats.

The Court of Appeal held that these factors were not in the category of characteristics that could be taken into account. His low intelligence fell short of mental impairment and characteristics such as excessive vulnerability, pliability and timidity were not factors shared by a person of reasonable firmness. His appeal against his conviction for obtaining services by deception was therefore dismissed, as it had been earlier on the grounds of a personality

disorder in *Hegarty 1994* and vulnerability falling short of a psychiatric illness in *Horne 1994*.

11.4.2 LIMITATIONS ON THE USE OF DURESS

Voluntary participation in a criminal enterprise

Even if the test in *Graham* is satisfied, the defence will not be allowed to a person who has voluntarily joined a gang or voluntarily taken part in a criminal exercise and is then forced to take part in activities of which he does not approve. This point was established in *Fitzpatrick 1977*, where the defendant had voluntarily joined the IRA but had later tried to leave the organisation. Threats were then made against both him and his mother so he was 'persuaded' to take part in an armed robbery in which he shot and killed an innocent person.

The Court of Appeal for Northern Ireland said that:

> if a person voluntarily exposes and submits himself . . . to illegal compulsion, he cannot rely on the duress to which he has voluntarily exposed himself as an excuse either in respect of the crimes he commits against his will or in respect of his continued but unwilling association with those capable of exercising upon him the duress which he calls in aid . . .

It was also made clear in *Fitzpatrick*, that the ruling was not confined to proscribed organisations like the IRA and this was affirmed in the case of *Sharp 1987*. The latter had been involved in a series of armed robberies on sub-post offices and in the latest attack the shop owner had been killed by another member of the gang. Sharp tried to argue that he had only remained involved because the ringleader had threatened to kill him. The Court of Appeal reiterated that where the defendant:

> voluntarily, and with knowledge of its nature joined a criminal organisation or gang which he knew might bring pressure on him to commit an offence and was an active member when he was put under such pressure, he cannot avail himself of the defence of duress . . .

This view of the law has been extended to those who consort with drug dealers and then cannot pay their suppliers, as in the cases of *Ali 1995* and *Flatt 1996*. In both cases the defence of duress failed, even though both men alleged that they were in fear of being killed by the drug dealers.

The crimes of murder and attempted murder

In addition to the above limitation, the courts have also had to decide whether the defence of duress should be made available for all crimes even the most serious one of murder. Judicial opinion on this has changed over the years. In *DPP for Northern Ireland* v *Lynch 1975*, it was allowed for a secondary offender involved in a murder.

The defendant had been ordered to drive a group of terrorists to the scene of the crime where they had murdered a policeman. The defendant had taken no part in this but had later driven the men away. He claimed that he would have been shot if he refused to help but, despite this, was convicted of murder.

The case reached the House of Lords where it was decided that the defence of duress was available for a secondary offender; a retrial was therefore ordered. Lord Wilberforce stated:

> Heinousness is a word of degree, and that there are lesser degrees of heinousness, even of involvement in homicide, seems beyond doubt. An accessory before the fact, or an aider or abettor, may (not necessarily must) bear a less degree than the actual killer: and

> even if the rule of exclusion is absolute, or nearly so in relation to the latter, it need not be so in lesser cases.

In *Abbott 1977*, the Privy Council had to decide whether the defence of duress was ever available to a principal offender. It was stated that this position had never been argued in an English court, although in Hale's Pleas of the Crown 1736 and Blackstone's Commentaries on the Laws of England 1857, it was accepted that duress was not a defence to murder.

In the case before the Privy Council, the defendant had taken part in a particularly horrible murder where the woman in question had been stabbed with a cutlass and then buried alive. The defendant alleged that he was forced to help because of threats made against him and his mother.

The Privy Council found it 'incredible . . . that in any civilised society, acts such as the appellant's, whatever threats may have been made to him, could be regarded as excusable or within the law'. The judge went on to state that the courts did not have 'the power to invent a new defence to murder which is entirely contrary to fundamental legal doctrine, accepted for hundreds of years without question'.

This precedent was not actually binding on the English courts but was clearly affirmed by the House of Lords in the case of *Howe and Bannister 1987*, a case in which their Lordships then went further and overruled the decision in *Lynch* regarding secondary offenders.

Howe and Bannister had been involved in the vicious murders of two young men, who were alleged to have 'grassed' on other gang members. The defendants had kicked and punched the first victim until he was near death but had not been involved in the final act of strangulation. In the second case, however, they had been the actual killers. After their conviction for murder, they argued that the defence of duress should have been allowed.

The House of Lords unanimously disagreed. Lord Griffiths stated 'We are facing a rising tide of violence and terrorism against which the law must stand firm recognising that its highest duty is to protect the freedom and lives of those who live under it'. He was strongly of the opinion that the defence should not be available to the actual killer. He then went on to decide that it should not be allowed for a secondary offender either, saying that it was neither rational or fair to make such a distinction. This was because, in many cases, the latter was just as blameworthy as the actual killer or often, as in the case of a contract killer, more so. He said that those who were obviously innocent of wrongdoing, as where a woman was forced to drive criminals to the scene of the crime, would not be prosecuted in the first place. He concluded his argument in the following way:

> As I can find no fair and certain basis upon which to differentiate between participants to a murder and as I am firmly convinced that the law should not be extended to the killer, I would depart from the decision of this House in *DPP for Northern Ireland* v *Lynch 1975* and declare the law to be that duress is not available as a defence to a charge of murder or to attempted murder.

Lord Mackay was of the same opinion and questioned whether the law on duress was sufficiently precise to make it right for the House of Lords 'to introduce it for an actual killer for the first time in the law of England'. The judges also rejected the idea that duress should be a partial defence which, if successful, would reduce the offence from murder to manslaughter.

In *Gotts 1992*, the House of Lords confirmed that the defence of duress was not available on a charge of attempted murder either but only on a majority of three to two. As in the case of *Howe*, calls were made for Parliament to intervene and put the law on duress on a statutory footing.

In this case, a boy of 16 alleged that he had been ordered by his father to kill his mother otherwise he, instead, would be shot. He therefore stabbed his mother and seriously injured

her but, fortunately, she survived. The defence of duress was not allowed at his trial so the boy pleaded guilty and was put on probation for three years. The House of Lords was eventually called upon to decide the matter. Lord Jauncey, for the majority, after reviewing the case of *Howe*, stated 'I can therefore see no justification in logic, morality or law in affording to an attempted murderer the defence which is withheld from a murderer'. He added that it was pure chance that the boy had not succeeded in his murder attempt so the fact that it had failed should not make a difference.

11.4.3 POSSIBLE REFORM OF THE LAW ON DURESS BY THREATS

There has been little consensus on this and, as has been seen above, the judges in the cases of *Howe* and *Gotts* felt strongly that it was time for Parliament to intervene in relation to the defence of duress and clarify when the defence should, or should not be available. Some judges favour the complete abolition of the defence and believe that any circumstances excusing the defendant could be looked at when the defendant was sentenced. The minority in the case of *Gotts* felt that the defence should be available for all cases of duress, including murder. Similar confusion is apparent in the views of the Law Commission. This body has been looking at possible reforms on the law relating to duress since 1974 and, currently, takes a similar view of the defence to that of the minority in the cases mentioned above. In its latest proposals, found in the Law Commission Report No. 218, *Legislating the Criminal Code: Offences Against the Person and General Principles 1993*, it suggests that the defence should be available for all crimes, including murder and attempted murder. It does, however, recommend that the burden of proof for this defence should be shifted to the defence, as it is with insanity.

Under these proposed reforms, a person will have a complete defence if the crime was com-

▼ COMMENT

The proposals are a mixture of the current law and new additions. A very important change is that the defence would be available for murder and attempted murder, thus conflicting with the views of the majority in the House of Lords in *Howe* and *Gott*. The report suggests that if Parliament does not favour such a change, the defence could be used to reduce the crime from murder to manslaughter. Neither is a completely satisfactory approach. If the defence is allowed as a complete defence in cases of murder, a person who has taken the life of an innocent party would be entitled to a full acquittal, which could cause great distress to the victim's family. In such situations, the jury might be more inclined to reject the defence and find the accused guilty of murder. He would then be sentenced to life imprisonment, despite the threats made to him. The changes could also encourage people who might have taken a heroic stand to take the easier option. The defence would also become more subjective and could, with the help of clever lawyers, be utilised by less deserving defendants, who will not have to show the reasonableness of their belief in as strict a way as is currently the case in *Graham*. In *Lynch*, Lord Morris made the point the following point: 'Duress must never be allowed to be the easy answer of those who can devise no other explanation for their conduct'. Even where there is an obvious threat of harm to the defendants and more sympathy for their plight, many would argue against a full acquittal. Arguably, the vicious behaviour of defendants like *Abbott, Howe, Bannister* and even *Gott* should not be allowed to go completely unpunished, however horrible the circumstances in which the defendants found themselves.

On the other hand, if the defence can only be used to reduce the crime to manslaughter, a person subjected to the most awful threats, which few could be expected to resist, would still be convicted of a serious crime and, in some circumstances, this would be unjust. It is true that the judge would have the discretion over the sentence and, in appropriate cases, the defendant could be given the minimum sentence to reflect the special circumstances, but he would still be stigmatised as a convicted killer. In addition, many have argued that Lord Hailsham's belief that the ordinary man should be expected to lay down his life rather than kill another is unrealistic. Even those who might be prepared to give up their own lives to save a stranger could yield if their children or other loved ones were the people threatened with torture or death. Even in less extreme cases, it could be argued that the law should not expect such heroism.

The proposed changes allow the threat to be made to 'another', which would deal with the current problem of how far it should be widened from threats to the person or his family.

The belief in the seriousness of the threat and its immediacy, would be viewed subjectively, but the threat itself would have to be one that the defendant 'cannot reasonably be expected to resist', thus retaining an objective element in the defence. An important change is that, under the reforms, more of the defendant's characteristics could be taken into account. The 'sober person of reasonable firmness' would disappear, which, it could be argued, might widen the defence in an unacceptable way.

Another important alteration suggested by the Law Commission concerns the burden of proof. It proposes that, in future, the onus should be on the defendant to prove the duress rather than placing the burden on the prosecution to disprove it, as is currently the law. This is a major reversal but is thought to have been included to make the other changes, such as allowing the defence for murder and attempted murder, more palatable to Parliament.

It remains to be seen whether any of these changes will be effected in the foreseeable future. The current attitude in Parliament appears to favour the increase of criminal liability rather than its reduction. It should also be remembered that other alternatives are available. One would be to abolish the defence completely and make allowance for the duress in the sentencing process, although such a move would be out of line with most other common law jurisdictions and, arguably, would be a step backwards rather than a reform. Another solution would be to retain the rule that duress is not a defence for murder but to change the mandatory aspect of the sentence, so that life imprisonment is not the only option. People against such a move would argue that the deterrent aspect would then be lessened.

mitted because of duress of threats. The defendant must have committed the crime because he knew or believed that he or another was being threatened with immediate death or serious injury or before he or another could obtain 'effective official protection'. A threat to damage property would not suffice. He must also have believed that there was no other way of preventing the threat being carried out. When assessing the seriousness of the threat, the courts would be asked to take both a subjective and objective approach. The threat to the defendant must be 'one which in all the circumstances (including any of his personal characteristics that affect its gravity) he cannot reasonably be expected to resist'. The Commission felt that the more restrictive test in *Graham* was not in line with other defences, especially self defence, and also felt that the present separation of characteristics that could be taken into account, and those that could not, was unsatisfactory. The amended law would therefore change this and would allow any of the characteristics that affect the gravity of the threat. There would be no requirement to show 'good cause' for the fear and all the defendant's characteristics could be taken into account.

The amended defence would not, however, be available to someone 'who knowingly and without reasonable excuse exposed himself to the risk of a threat', so presumably the existing rules on the voluntary joining of a criminal enterprise would remain.

11.5 DURESS OF CIRCUMSTANCES – AN EXTENSION OF NECESSITY

The defence of duress was, until recently, confined to threats from another person against the person or someone close to him. Any other kind of pressure on him was felt to come under the possible defence of necessity and, as has been noted, was not often allowed.

Since the late 1980s, however, a special defence has sometimes been permitted which has become known as duress of circumstances. The following cases show where it can or cannot be used.

11.5.1 THE DEVELOPMENT OF DURESS OF CIRCUMSTANCES

The origins of the new defence began with the case of *Willer 1986*. The defendant was convicted of the old offence of reckless driving. He had been persuaded by a broadcast on a Citizen's Band radio to drive to a shopping precinct in Hemel Hempstead to meet another enthusiast. The directions he had been given led him down a very narrow alley, where he was confronted by a gang of youths shouting that they were going to kill him. The gang surrounded the car, banged on it and tried to drag out the occupants. One of the men got into the car and started fighting. Willer decided that his only way of escape was to mount the pavement and drive through a small gap in the road. He made good his escape, driving very slowly but then discovered that one of his friends was missing. He returned the same way to try to find him but was unsuccessful and therefore went to the police instead. He was then charged with reckless driving which as the appeal court judge said was 'a very surprising turn of events indeed!' The defendant's bad luck continued; he chose trial by jury but the assistant recorder refused to allow him to put the defence of necessity before that body.

The Court of Appeal decided that necessity was not the appropriate defence; this, they argued should have been duress. Watkins L J concluded 'the assistant recorder upon those facts should have directed that he would leave to the jury the question as to whether or not upon the outward or return journey, or both, the appellant was wholly driven by force of circumstance into doing what he did and did not drive the car otherwise than under that form of compulsion, ie under duress'.

It can be seen therefore how the defence

started. It was developed further in the case of *Conway 1988*, another reckless driving case, although arguably one with a lot less merit. In this case the accused drove off erratically after two plain clothed policemen in an unmarked car approached him. His version of events (which was substantially different to that of the prosecution, who strongly maintained that the occupants knew they were policemen) was that one of his passengers had been in a car a few weeks earlier when one of the occupants had been shot and badly injured. This youth, called Tonna, was said to have been the intended target and had only narrowly escaped.

In the present instance, the defendant claimed that Tonna had shouted hysterically at him to drive off, when the two men, who, he alleged, had not identified themselves, approached the car. Believing them to be potential assassins, the defendant had driven erratically, and at high speed, in order to shake them off when they had followed him. The defendant was convicted of reckless driving but argued that he should have been allowed a defence. The Court of Appeal confirmed that:

> necessity can only be a defence to a charge of reckless driving where the facts establish 'duress of circumstances' as in *R* v *Willer* . . . i.e. where the defendant was constrained by circumstances to drive as he did to avoid death or serious bodily harm to himself or some other person.

The court agreed with Smith and Hogan that 'a defence of "duress of circumstances" is a logical consequence of the existence of duress as that term is ordinarily understood, i.e. "do this or else".' The court continued 'This approach does no more than recognise that duress is an example of necessity. Whether "duress of circumstances" is called "duress" or "necessity" does not matter. What is important is that, whatever it is called, it is subject to the same limitations as "do this or else" species of duress'. In this case, the court decided that the matter

should have been put to the jury, even though they doubted that it would have made a difference to the verdict.

After Conway, therefore, it was clear that the new defence had been recognised but also that it was subject to the same limitations as duress, i.e. it was only possible to use it where there was a fear of death or personal injury.

This point was confirmed in the odd case of *Martin 1989*, yet another driving case. The defendant claimed that, even though he had been disqualified from driving, he had been forced to drive his stepson to work because his wife had threatened to commit suicide if he did not comply! Doctors had supported the view that she had suicidal tendencies and was capable of carrying out the threat. She had been shouting and screaming and making such threats because her son had overslept and she had feared that he would be sacked if he were late for work.

Once again, although the Court of Appeal was sceptical as to the success of the defence, it decided that it should have been put before the jury. The court stated that the authorities were now clear and that:

> English law does recognise a defence of necessity. Most commonly this defence arises as duress, that is pressure on the accused's will from the wrongful threats or violence of another. Equally however it can arise from other objective dangers threatening the accused or others. Arising thus it is conveniently called 'duress of circumstances'.

The Court of Appeal again made it clear that there are important limits to this new defence. The defendant must have good cause to fear that unless he acted in the way he had, death or serious injury would follow. It also had to be shown that a sober person of reasonable firmness, sharing the same characteristics as the accused, would have responded in the same way, i.e. the court affirmed that the test laid down in *Graham* is to be applied.

The defendant in *DPP* v *Bell 1992* was able to establish this when he drove off while under the influence of alcohol, because of his fear that those pursuing him intended to harm him. The appeal by the prosecution failed because it was successfully shown that he had good cause for this fear. In addition, the fact that the defendant had only driven a short way before stopping, rather than all the way home, showed that he was acting reasonably. It was on this latter point that the appeals of the prosecution succeeded in the cases of *DPP* v *Davis* and *DPP* v *Pittaway* in 1994 and the magistrates were ordered to convict.

In the first case, the defendant claimed that he had only driven while under the influence of alcohol because of fear engendered by the homosexual advances of a friend. The Divisional Court decided that the fear had not still existed after the defendant had left the friend's flat and, in such circumstances, he had no need to drive for two miles, which was the distance he had covered before he was stopped.

In *Pittaway*, the woman divorcee in question had been involved in a violent marriage and claimed that her fears had returned during a row with her new partner at a party. She had run to her home 200 yards away but had then taken her car out. The appeal court decided that the objective test, that she had good cause to fear death or serious personal injury, had not been satisfied. She had also driven away at a time when she was not being pursued.

In the case of *Cole 1994*, the Court of Appeal decided that neither of the two types of duress was available to the defendant. He claimed that he had robbed two building societies because he needed the money to repay moneylenders. He alleged that they had attacked him with a baseball bat and had threatened him, his girlfriend and their child with further violence if he did not find the money.

The Court of Appeal decided that the defendant could not rely on duress by threats because the moneylenders had not ordered him to rob the banks, i.e. the person making the threats had not nominated the crime to be committed. Neither could he put forward the defence of duress of circumstances, because the court found that the connection between the threat and the criminal act was not as close or immediate as in *Willer*, *Conway* and *Martin*, 'where the offence was virtually a spontaneous reaction to the physical risk arising'. The appeal court may have been alarmed at the escalation in the use of the defence because they echoed an earlier call for Parliament to legislate on the matter and decided that, in the meantime, the defence of duress should be rigidly confined to its present established limits.

It therefore comes as somewhat of a surprise to note the decision in *Pommell 1995*, in which the Court of Appeal held that the defence of duress of circumstances was not just available for driving offences, but is, instead, permitted for all offences except murder and manslaughter. In this case a man was convicted of being in possession of a firearm without a licence. He was discovered in bed with the loaded gun in his hand. He claimed that he had taken possession of the gun because a friend was threatening to shoot someone with it. The defendant added that he had only pleaded guilty because the judge had ruled that his failure to go to the police immediately deprived him of a defence and appealed against this finding. The Court of Appeal confirmed that, *prima facie*, the defence of duress of circumstances was available for all crimes except murder, attempted murder and some forms of treason, and also decided that a delay was not always fatal to the defence. The court held that as the defendant had put forward possible explanations for the delay, these should have been put before a jury. The appeal, therefore, was allowed, but a new trial was ordered. This would enable the jury to decide whether the defendant's act in reloading the gun and concealing it in his bed showed that he was not desisting from the criminal act as soon as he reasonably could.

If the defence of duress of circumstances succeeds, it is a complete defence, entitling the defendant to an acquittal. The Court of Appeal decided that it is not correct, in a dangerous driving case, merely to reduce the offence to careless driving (*Symonds 1997*).

To summarise, it is apparent from the cases that the defence of duress of circumstances has taken firm root in English law. The defence is an extension of the defence of necessity, rather than of duress of threats but is limited in the same way as the latter.

11.5.2 POSSIBLE REFORM OF DURESS OF CIRCUMSTANCES

The Law Commission has recognised the value of the defence of duress of circumstances and has included the defence in its Draft Criminal Law Bill 1993. These current proposals differ from what is in the Draft Criminal Code. The newer version would permit the defence to be used in crimes of murder and attempted murder, but would change the burden of proof, which would now be on the accused. This would bring this defence in line with what it proposed for duress of threats. Under Clause 26, the defence would be available for a defendant who only commits a crime because 'he knows or believes that it is immediately necessary to avoid death or serious injury to himself or another. The danger that he knows or

▼ COMMENT

It will be seen from the reforms that the defence of duress of circumstances has been firmly recognised by the Law Commission and would be extended to cover all offences including murder and attempted murder. The merits and possible problems with this are the same as those discussed under duress by threats. It can also be seen that the test in *Martin* has been watered down, although there is still an objective element when assessing the actions that he has taken in response to the threat. This might result in many more appeals, especially in relation to driving offences, and could overload an already overstretched Court of Appeal.

believes to exist must be such that in all the circumstances (including any of his personal characteristics that affect its gravity) he cannot reasonably be expected to act otherwise'.

activity

1 In small groups, or individually in written form, discuss the following question: 'At the present time, English law recognises the three separate, but related defences of necessity, duress and duress of circumstances. Is this a satisfactory state of the law?'

2 Decide whether a defence of necessity, duress or duress of circumstances is available in the following scenarios:

Alan took part in the killing of Graham after Victoria threatened to commit suicide if he refused to help.

Gary found himself surrounded by a hostile crowd in the middle of town. He saw Mandy's Mercedes parked nearby, with the keys still in the ignition, so jumped in and sped away at 60 miles per hour.

Eric and Kevin were the only survivors of a plane crash. After 15 days without food, Eric killed and ate Kevin.

3 Do you agree with the argument that the relaxation of the rule on duress, allowing the defence for murder or attempted murder, would open the floodgates to a rush of unworthy claims?

11.6 MARITAL COERCION

This very limited defence only applies to a wife who can prove that she committed an offence

▼ KEY
FACTS ▼

- The defence of necessity, if allowed, is said to justify the commission of a crime; for this reason it is a very limited defence, confined to specific situations (*Bourne 1939*, *Johnson* v *Phillips 1976*, Road Traffic Act 1988, (as amended), *F (Mental Patient: Sterilisation): Re 1990*
- It is not available for the crime of murder (*Dudley and Stephens 1884*), or where statutes do not intend the defence to be available (*Cichon* v *DPP 1994*, *DPP* v *Harris 1995*)
- Duress of threats provides an excuse for the commission of a crime. It is definitely available if the person or his family is threatened (*Hurley and Murray 1967*), and may well apply if others are at risk
- It can only be used where the threat is to cause death or serious injury (*AG* v *Whelan 1934*) and a sober person of reasonable firmness, sharing the characteristics of the accused, would have acted in the same way (*Graham 1982*). The word 'characteristics' would include age, sex and mental impairment but not a personality disorder (*Hegarty 1994*), excessive vulnerability, timidity or pliability (*Horne 1994*, *Bowen 1996*) or a low IQ (*Bowen 1996*). Threats to reveal someone's poor financial position or his homosexual tendencies are not enough (*Valderama-Vega 1985*), but the threat of death or serious injury need not be the sole reason for the defendant's act (*Valerama-Vega 1985*, *Ortiz 1986*)
- The threat must be an immediate one, without the prospect of getting official protection, although the courts may look at extenuating circumstances, such as the age of the defendant and the belief that official protection is inadequate (*Hudson and Taylor 1971*)
- Even if the requirements for the defence are satisfied, it is not available for those who voluntarily join gangs or other illegal enterprises (*Fitzpatrick 1977*, *Sharp 1987*, *Ali 1995*, *Flatt 1996*)
- It is also not available for murder, whether for a principal offender (*Abbott 1977*), or a secondary offender (*Howe 1987*). Neither is it a defence for attempted murder (*Gotts 1992*)
- Duress of circumstances is an extension of the defence of necessity but has the same limitations as duress of threats. There is no actual threat from a person; instead it comes from the circumstances. If successful, the defendant is entitled to a full acquittal (*Symonds 1997*), it cannot be used to reduce a charge
- The defence is available where the defendant fears that death or personal injury will result if he does not commit a crime in order to relieve the situation. He must, however, have good cause for his fear and the court must be satisfied that a sober person of reasonable firmness would have acted in a similar way (*Martin 1989*)
- Such a defence was first suggested in *Willer 1986*, although it was not specifically named as such until *Conway 1988*. These cases and *Bell 1992*, *DPP* v *Davis 1994* and *DPP* v *Pittaway 1994* all concerned driving offences but, in *Pommell 1995*, the Court of Appeal made it clear that the defence can be used for all offences, except some forms of treason, murder and attempted murder
- Despite this extension, it was stated in *Cole 1994* that Parliament should legislate on the defence of duress and meanwhile it should be 'rigidly confined'
- As in duress by threats, normally the defence of duress of circumstances can only be used if the threat is immediate (*Bell 1992*). It was felt that the danger had passed in *DPP* v *Davis* and *DPP* v *Pittaway* so the defence failed
- In *Pommell 1995*, however, the Court of Appeal stated that if there were possible explanations for the delay, the matter should be put before the jury

FIGURE 11.2 *Key facts chart on necessity, duress and duress of circumstances* other than treason and murder in the presence of, and under the coercion of, her husband. The defence was originally formulated by the common law, under which it was presumed that a wife was acting under the coercion of her husband unless the prosecution could prove that she had taken the initiative. In 1925, however, the presumption was abolished by s.47 Criminal Justice Act 1927. Currently, marital coercion only exists as a defence in such a situation. It is limited to wives who need to show that they are validly married. In *Ditta 1988*, Lord Lane seemed to have had doubts as to whether the defence could be extended to polygamous marriages.

Many feel that such a defence has little part to play in a more equal society. The Law Commission recommended its abolition back in 1977 but, as yet, no reform has been effected.

11.7 PUBLIC AND PRIVATE DEFENCE

The defences described below come under this blanket heading because a party may lawfully use force, provided that this is not excessive, in the defence of both public and private interests. He is therefore allowed to use such force in defence of the following:

- To prevent crime or assist in the lawful arrest of an offender or a suspected one

- To prevent a breach of the peace

- To protect his property or to prevent a trespass

- To prevent a breach of the peace

- To protect himself from unlawful violence

- To protect himself from unlawful detention

11.7.1 THE STATUTORY OFFENCE

The law on the first two of the situations listed above was developed at common law but is now found under s.3 Criminal Law Act 1967. This states that:

> a person may use such force as is reasonable in the circumstances in the prevention of crime or in assisting in the lawful arrest of offenders or suspected offenders, or of persons unlawfully at large.

In the case of *Renouf 1986*, the defendant had been working on the forecourt of his garage when the occupants of a Volvo car drew up and threw things at him. He suffered an injury to his arm and his car windscreen was damaged. After calling to his wife to call the police, he followed the men in his car and eventually forced them onto a grass verge. He was convicted of reckless driving (still in existence at that time) but appealed. The Court of Appeal held that the possible defence under s.3, that he was trying to assist in the lawful arrest of offenders, should have been put before the jury and quashed the conviction.

In many cases of assault, this statutory defence is also open to a person who is personally threatened, in addition to the common law defence of self defence, discussed below. While he is defending himself against the attack on his person or the person of another, he will, in most cases, also be preventing a crime being committed. The Criminal Law Act makes it clear that the common law defence remains in areas where the act does not provide a defence and in *Cousins 1982* it was stated that both defences exist and can be used in conjunction with each other. It is also possible to make a 'citizen's arrest' without falling foul of the law. Permission to do this is given under s.24 Police and Criminal Evidence Act 1984, if someone is committing an arrestable offence or is reasonably suspected of having committed one.

It has already been noted in Chapter 9 that

S.5 Criminal Damage Act 1971 provides a person with a defence if:

> he destroys or damages the property of another in order to protect his own property or that of someone else, provided that it is in immediate need of protection and the force used is reasonable.

If, however, the person injures another in the process of this protection, or to stop himself being evicted, the same common law rules will be used as apply in the other three examples. This was not always the position; the older rules appeared to give greater protection to someone who was defending himself from unlawful eviction, i.e. defending his property, than when he was protecting his person. A person was allowed to stand firm and fight against the loss of his property whereas, if the attack were against him personally, he was, in earlier times supposed to retreat from the danger where possible. In *Hussey 1924*, the Lord Chief Justice at that time stated that the more favourable common law rule, concerning the defence of property, should have been explained to the jury. He therefore quashed the conviction of a man who had barricaded himself in when threatened with alleged unlawful eviction. He had fired a gun through the door at the three people armed with household tools, who were seeking to remove him, wounding two of them. It is extremely unlikely that a similar decision would be arrived at today but it is still clear that a person can seek the help of the law in protecting his property. In *AG's Reference (No 2. of 1983) 1984*, it was rather surprisingly decided that it was not unlawful for a person to make up petrol bombs to try to prevent crime and defend his property in an area where there had been extensive rioting and further threats were imminent.

11.7.2 SELF DEFENCE AT COMMON LAW

The subjective element

The judges have decided that person may use reasonable force to protect himself or another person if he fears an attack or one actually occurs. The first part of this test is a subjective one, as was noted under the defence of mistake. This means that the defendant's belief that he was forced to act in the way he did might, on occasion, be thought to be an unreasonable one to an outsider. Despite this, the matter should be put before a jury for that body to decide the matter. The cases of *Williams (Gladstone) 1987* and *Beckford 1988*, discussed earlier, are authority for this. In the latter case, the Privy Council stated that:

> the reasonableness or unreasonableness of the defendant's belief is material to the question of whether the belief was held by the defendant at all. If the belief was in fact held, its unreasonableness, so far as guilt or innocence is concerned is neither here nor there.

The belief in whether there is a need to act in self defence is therefore a subjective one, and an honest, albeit unreasonable belief will suffice unless, however, the defendant is making the mistake because he is intoxicated. In such a case, his mistaken belief will not avail him of the defence. This point was made clear in *O'Grady 1987*. The defendant was addicted to drink and, on the night in question had consumed eight flagons of cider. He then retired to his flat with two friends. In the morning, one of these friends found him covered with blood and the other friend dead. O'Grady claimed that he and the victim had been involved in a fight in the night and when he had felt the victim he was cold. The defendant reported the matter to the police and argued that he had only acted in self defence. When he was examined, a number of cuts and bruises were noted which might have supported his version of events, but he was still convicted of manslaughter. The Court of Appeal confirmed that the defence of self defence would be available to a 'sober man who mistakenly believes he is in danger of immediate death at the hands of an attacker' but not to a person whose mistake was caused by voluntary intoxication.

The question of retreating from the danger

In the older cases of common law self defence, it was suggested that the defence would fail unless the defendant could show that he had tried to retreat from the danger. In *Julien 1969*, however, the Court of Appeal decided that this was not essential but did go on to state what action he did need to take:

> It is not, as we understand it, the law that a person threatened must take to his heels and run in the dramatic way suggested by counsel for the appellant; but what is necessary is that he should demonstrate by his actions that he does not want to fight. He must demonstrate that he is prepared to temporise and disengage and perhaps to make some physical withdrawal.

In the following case, the Court of Appeal went further. In *Bird 1985*, the defence of self defence was still held to be open to a 17-year-old girl celebrating her birthday, who had been very upset when an ex boyfriend appeared at her party with a new girlfriend in tow. He had left after a heated argument but later returned alone and the argument continued. The defendant threw a glass of Pernod over him and a physical fight developed. Bird alleged that she had been held up against a wall and had lunged at the victim. The glass was still in her hand when she hit him in the face, causing him to lose an eye. The Court of Appeal decided that the case of *Julien* had placed too great an obligation on the defendant to demonstrate that he did not wish to fight, which was not reflected in the later Privy Council decision in *Palmer 1971*. This case decided that 'there are no prescribed words which must be employed in or adopted in a summing up'. The court also quoted with approval Smith and Hogan's book Criminal Law, fifth edition. This declared that the courts went too far when they said that the defendant had to demonstrate a desire not to fight. It was not consistent with the rule that a person can use force, not merely to counter an attack, but also to ward off an attack honestly and reasonably believed to be imminent. It was felt that the defendant's demonstration that he did not want to fight was the best evidence that he was acting reasonably and in good faith in self defence; but was no more than evidence to this effect.

The objective element

It has just been noted that the defendant's belief that he has to act in self defence need not be a reasonable belief. The test is subjective. With regard to the actual force used, however, the courts have now made it very plain that only reasonable force can be used to counter the threat and that this is an objective test. This had been felt to be the law but some doubt was cast upon this view in the case of *Scarlett 1993*. A pub landlord had forcibly ejected a drunken customer who had fallen down the steps and was killed. The judgment seemed to imply that the test for deciding whether the force used was excessive was also subjective. This was firmly denied by the Court of Appeal in *Owino 1996*. The court gave its view of the judge's words. 'What he was not saying, in our view (and indeed if he had said it, it would be contrary to authority) was that the belief, however ill-founded, of the defendant that the degree of force he was using was reasonable, will enable him to do what he did'. The court said that if such a view were taken, it would allow a person who was merely threatened with a punch to shoot the other and plead self defence. The court concluded 'That clearly is not, and cannot be, the law'.

In *Owino*, the defendant's claim that the jury should have been directed in this way because he was of the belief that he was only using reasonable force was therefore rejected.

The use of excessive force

It has now been made abundantly clear that an objective view is taken when assessing whether the defendant has used reasonable or excessive force. Should the force be found to be excessive by this standard, the defence will fail and the defendant will be guilty of whatever crime has been committed. This is shown clearly in the case of *Clegg 1995*, where the response of the soldier to a perceived threat was held to be excessive and he was convicted of murder.

The defendant had been on a night patrol in West Belfast, where 15 men were deployed in order to catch joy riders. His team was moving towards Belfast just beyond a checkpoint at a bridge. Clegg was not informed of the reason for the patrol but it was established at his trial that he did not believe the offenders were terrorists.

The car containing the victim was initially stopped at the checkpoint but then accelerated away in the centre of the road with its headlights full on. Someone in the checkpoint team shouted that it should be stopped and all four members of Clegg's team fired at it. Two others were with Clegg and another soldier, Private Ainbow, was on his own on the other side of the road. Clegg's evidence was that he fired four bullets into the windscreen and one into the side of the car as it passed. He claimed that he had believed that Ainbow had been struck by the speeding car and that his life had been in danger. Scientific evidence, on the other hand, showed that the last shot had been fired when the car had already passed and was over 50 feet further along the road. The victim, a passenger called Karen Reilly, had been hit in the back. It also emerged later that the speeding car had not

caused Private Ainbow's injuries. Instead, the soldiers were alleged to have deliberately stamped on his leg to make it look as though this had happened. Ainbow was later convicted of conspiring to pervert the course of justice.

There are no juries in such cases in Northern Ireland in view of the political situation; therefore it was the judge who found the defendant guilty of murder. He found that there was insufficient evidence for Clegg to use s.3 Criminal Law Act in his defence. The Court of Appeal disagreed. It decided that evidence existed that Clegg was acting in the prevention of crime or to arrest offenders and therefore the defence should have been considered. Despite this fault in the judgment, however, the court went on to hold that there had been no miscarriage of justice because the force used by Clegg with regard to the fourth shot had not been reasonable. This shot had been fired with the intention to kill or seriously injure the victim and was 'so grossly disproportionate to the mischief to be averted' that any tribunal of fact properly directed would have come to the same conclusion. Consequently, Clegg's conviction was upheld.

Nevertheless, the Court of Appeal had called on Parliament to consider making a change in the law and, meanwhile, put a point of law to the House of Lords. This was whether a killing by a police officer or soldier in the course of his duty should be manslaughter rather than murder where the force used is excessive and unreasonable.

The House of Lords first looked at the different defences of s.3 and the common law defence of self defence. It was decided that it would be impractical to make a distinction between excessive force used in trying to prevent a crime or apprehend a suspect and any excessive force used in self defence, particularly as the two often overlap. Their Lordships then reviewed authorities such as *Palmer 1971*, a Privy Council decision, *McInnes*, a Court of Appeal decision in the same year, and *Zecevic* v *DPP (Victoria) 1987*, an Australian case, and also decided that, in relation to both s.3 and self defence:

there is no half-way house. There is no rule that a defendant who has used a greater degree of force than was necessary in the circumstances should be found guilty of manslaughter rather than murder. . . . The defence either succeeds or it fails. If it succeeds the defendant is acquitted. If it fails, he is guilty of murder.

Lord Lloyd felt that there were persuasive arguments for changing the law but was influenced by the fact that Parliament had not considered this when effecting other changes relating to defences. Clegg's conviction for murder, therefore, was upheld although after a concentrated campaign in the media and elsewhere, he was released on licence after serving four years. He is now seeking to prove his innocence. Other soldiers have also been involved in similar serious errors in judgement leading to the imposition of life sentences. Fisher and Wright, for example served six years of their sentence for killing an 18 year old boy on the streets of Belfast before being released on licence.

COMMENT

The highest court in the land had a good opportunity in this case to change what many consider to be an unjust rule. If their Lordships had decided that a manslaughter verdict was sustainable in such circumstances, they could not have been accused of acting alone and against informed opinion. In *Howe 1958*, (not the same *Howe* as in duress), the Australian courts had decided that a killing by excessive force in self defence should be manslaughter, not murder, (although they later brought their law into line with the English courts). Our Criminal Law Revision Committee also favoured a more liberal defence and suggested a change in the law, as did a Select Committee of the House of Lords when its members looked into the question of murder and life imprisonment.

Whether such a change should only be effected in relation to the police and armed services or apply more universally is a much more contentious issue. Some would argue that a stronger case could be made out for the police and services because of the tense situations in which they might find themselves, where the need for a split-second decision is vital. The Home Secretary is carrying out a review of the defence in such cases. Others, however, strongly argue that any changes in the defence should apply equally to all and that it is dangerous to grant more leeway to certain sections of the community as this could be abused.

It is instructive to note at this point that English law does not recognise any defence of superior orders. A defendant is not permitted to claim that he only committed a crime because he was ordered to do so by a higher officer. Most people would agree that this is the correct attitude for the law to take, although, as the writer Dicey stated many years ago, it can result in injustice because a soldier might 'be liable to be shot by a court-martial if he disobeys an order and to be hanged by a judge if he obeys it'! In addition, the matter is not as clear-cut as it at first appears. The police cadets in the following article believed that if they did not participate in the horrific ill-treatment of their dogs, the animals would be destroyed. They have not been prosecuted alongside their superior officers but, if this had occurred, they could not have used the defence of duress of threats because these were not made to them or another person. Hopefully, the emergent defence of duress of circumstances would have been available. The men did have good cause to feel that death or serious injury would follow; it does not state in *Martin* that it has to be a human death!

PC tells court how dog died in his arms

A POLICE dog-handler told a court yesteday how he watched his German shepherd die in his arms after he kicked it repeatedly for growling and nipping him.

PC Mark Needham of Essex police accepted the disciplinary methods used were "barbaric" but said he had been ordered to inflict the punishment.

He was giving evidence yesterday on the third day of a trial at Chelmsford Magistrates' Court in which four police officers are accused of cruelty.

Inspector Graham Curtis, 43, who headed the Essex police dog unit in Sandon, Sergeant Andrew White, 37, who was in charge of instructors, and instructors PC Kenneth Boorman, 45, and PC Graham Hopkins, 42, all deny cruelty.

PC Needham, a policeman for 12 years, described how his dog Acer died last November.

He said that on the second day of the course he told PC Boorman that Acer had growled. He said he was ordered to string Acer up by his lead and kick the dog in the stomach with the side of his foot, which he did, six times, before being told to leave the dog suspended for 15 to 20 seconds.

Two days later the dog suffered similar punishment. PC Needham told the court that afterwards the dog appeared "very lethargic". He added: "He lay with his head across my lap. I sat with him, stroking him. I lifted up his lips. They were very blue. I knew he was very ill. And the next time I looked at him I knew that he had died."

Asked by the prosecutor Peter Wain what he thought of disciplining a dog by hanging it from a fence and kicking it, he replied: "It was barbaric."

He said he was in no doubt that refusal to obey instructions would mean his dog would be put down and that he would lose his post in the dog-handling unit.

The hearing continues today.

Taken from an article by Lewis Smith in *The Times*, 15 October 1998

activity

Fred had an argument with Wilma. He picked up some pebbles and made out he was going to throw them at her. Wilma could easily have deflected the blow but, instead, picked up a boulder and hit Fred with it, fracturing his skull in two places. Fred later died in hospital.

Advise Wilma on the issue of self defence.

11.7.3 POSSIBLE REFORM OF THE DEFENCE OF SELF DEFENCE

Clause 27 of the Draft Criminal Law Bill states that a person may use force to protect himself or another from harm or from damage to their property or to prevent a crime or breach of the peace. The use of force must be 'such as is reasonable in the circumstances as he believes them to be', which largely restates the present position, with its objective and subjective elements.

KEY
FACTS

- Most of the law on this subject comes from two main sources. S.3 Criminal Law Act 1967 allows a party to use reasonable force to prevent a crime or to assist in the apprehension of offenders and the common law defence of self defence is available where a person uses reasonable force to protect himself or another or their property. In many cases, the two areas overlap, and can be used in conjunction with each other (*Cousins 1982*)

- In both areas, a defendant may use reasonable force to avert the danger, and the jury will decide the matter (*Renouf 1986*)

- The belief that an attack is imminent is decided on a subjective basis, so an honest but unreasonable belief will suffice (*Williams (Gladstone) 1987, Beckford 1988*), although this rule will not apply if the mistake is caused by intoxication (*O'Grady 1987*)

- There is no longer a need for the defendant to show that he has tried to retreat from the danger (*Julien 1969, Palmer 1971* and *Bird 1985*), nor need he now demonstrate that he has no desire to fight (*Bird 1985*)

- The question of whether the force used is reasonable is decided objectively (*Clegg 1995, Owino 1995*), and will apply equally to the police and armed services (*Clegg 1995*)

- If the defence is successful, it results in a full acquittal; there is no half-way house, such as allowing the crime of murder to be reduced to manslaughter (*Clegg 1995*)

- Similarly, English law does not recognise the defence of superior orders

FIGURE 11.3 *Key facts chart on public and private defence*

summary

In this chapter we have learned that other general defences are available, in addition to those looked at in Chapter 10.

We have noted that the defence of mistake is limited and is only available for mistakes of fact. We have discovered that the defences of necessity, duress and duress of circumstances are closely connected and allow help when a person feels that breaking the law is the lesser of two evils or where he fears that, if he does not take this step, physical injury or death will result.

We have noted that the defence of marital coercion, applying specifically to wives but only in limited circumstances, has almost disappeared. The defences of preventing crime and self defence are, however, alive and well, though their scope is currently under debate.

Lastly, it should be remembered that, should these defences be successfully pleaded, the accused will be entitled to a full acquittal, unlike the more limited defences mentioned elsewhere in this book.

CHAPTER 12

PARTIES TO A CRIME

12.1 INTRODUCTION

IN THIS CHAPTER, we shall be looking at the position of the various perpetrators of a crime and assessing their liability. For example, two or more people may decide to carry out an armed robbery on a bank or to break into a house in order to steal. If they commit the offence together, they are considered in law to be joint principals. If one party merely helps the other to commit the crime, however, he is not considered to be a principal offender. Instead, he is known by a variety of names. He is normally known as a secondary offender, but could also be called an accessory or an accomplice. In some of the older cases, he may have been classed, rather confusingly, as a principal in the second degree. By whatever name he is known, the law takes a very strict attitude towards him and he is treated in virtually the same way as the principal offender. The law is to be found in a very old statute, which was amended by the Criminal Law Act 1967. S.8 Accessories and Abettors Act 1861, as amended, states that:

> Whosoever shall aid, abet, counsel and procure the commission of any indictable offence ... shall be liable to be tried, indicted and punished as a principal offender.

S.44 Magistrates Courts Act 1980 ensures that the same approach is taken with regard to summary offences.

It can thus be seen that a secondary offender will not escape liability by arguing that he is less blameworthy than the principal. In an armed robbery for example, the driver of the getaway car plays a vital role in the commission of the offence and, if he is caught along with the principal offender, he, too, is likely to be charged with the crime of armed robbery. If a death has resulted, they could both be liable for murder and face life imprisonment. The distinction between principal and secondary offenders could, however, be important in the matter of sentencing in cases where the judge has some discretion over this, as would be the position in our robbery example.

For this reason, the courts will need to distinguish between the principal offender (the perpetrator of the act) and the accessory or secondary offender who assists him.

12.2 THE PRINCIPAL OFFENDER

It has been noted that the person who directly brings about the *actus reus* of the offence, i.e. the main perpetrator of the crime, is known as the principal.

It has also been seen in many cases throughout this book, that it is possible to have more than one principal.

The test to decide whether an offender is a principal or a secondary offender is to discover whether his act is the most immediate cause of the *actus reus* or whether he is merely helping that cause to be effected.

Innocent Agents

It is usually a simple matter to discover the principal but there are some difficult areas. One of these is where the apparent principal is unaware that he is involved in wrongdoing, another is where he is too young to be apprehended. In such cases, the perpetrator of the crime is known as an innocent agent and the person instigating the crime will be treated as the principal.

An example of the first type of innocent agent would be where a postman personally delivers a letter bomb to the victim, believing it to be a harmless parcel. It explodes and kills the recipient. Obviously, it would be very unjust to convict the postman of this crime; he is merely the innocent agent. The principal, therefore, would be the person sending the bomb. Similarly, in an unnamed case in 1665, a daughter was instructed to give her father a potion to cure his cold. In fact, it was poison with which his wife intended to kill him. The wife was held to be the principal and the daughter was the innocent agent. The second type of innocent agency would exist if a modern day Fagin co-opted several children under the age of ten to engage in shoplifting on his behalf and ordered them to deliver the goods to him. The children could not be charged as principals because they would be under the age of criminal liability, as noted in Chapter 10; Fagin, therefore, would be the principal.

12.3 THE DIFFERENT TYPES OF SECONDARY OFFENDER

It can be seen from the Accessories and Abettors Act 1861 that secondary offenders are those who aid, abet, counsel or procure the commission of a crime. It was stated in *AG's Reference (No. 1 of 1975) 1975* that these words should be given their ordinary meaning. This is rather an odd statement for the judges to make given that only two of the four words are in everyday use! In ordinary speech, we do not often encounter the words abetting or procuring. The judges of the Court of Appeal did, however, make it clear that Parliament must have intended each of the four terms to have its own, distinct meaning, otherwise one or two words would have sufficed. The four terms 'aiding', 'abetting', 'counselling' and 'procuring' need, therefore, to be examined in more detail.

To aid

The term 'to aid' has been interpreted as 'to give help, support or assistance'. Normally, such help will be given at the time the crime is committed, although the cases show that this is not always the position.

To abet

The meaning of the term 'to abet' is 'to encourage, incite or instigate'. Again, it is felt that such encouragement would normally be at or near the scene of the crime. In this way it can be distinguished from the term 'to counsel', which has been held to have a similar meaning to 'abet' but takes place before the crime is committed.

The terms 'aiding and abetting' imply some sort of action on the part of the secondary offender; a merely passive presence at the scene of the crime will not normally make a person liable. In *Bland 1988*, the defendant's conviction for of aiding and abetting a dealer in drugs was quashed. The court decided that merely living with such an offender and perhaps having knowledge of his activities was not enough to incur liability; a more active involvement was required.

In the much earlier case of *Coney 1882*, the defendant's conviction for abetting a battery had also been quashed. The judge had not made it clear to the jury that a simple attendance at an illegal prize-fight was only evidence that the spectator may have been involved and was not, in itself, conclusive. If the jury had not been misdirected on this point and there had been some evidence that he had actively participated in the event, as, for example, by cheering and clapping, the jury could have rightly convicted him.

In *Wilcox* v *Jefferey 1951*, a more active involvement was found by the Divisional Court. The defendant was the proprietor of a magazine called the *Jazz Illustrated*. He had attended a concert at which a celebrated American jazz musician had played his saxophone, in direct contravention of an Alien's Order that prevented him from him performing while in the UK. There was no direct evidence that the magazine owner had actively participated at the concert, but he had attended and had later written an article for his magazine, describing the performance in glowing terms. Taken together, these actions by the defendant were considered by Lord Goddard, the Lord Chief Justice, to be enough to constitute aiding and abetting the contravention of the Order. The judge, in one of the provocative statements for which he was famous, stated that it would have been a different matter if Wilcox had booed the performance, or had told the saxophone player that 'The musicians' union do not like you foreigners coming here and playing and you ought to get off the stage'! Needless to say, the defendent's appeal was not allowed. It will be seen later in this chapter that Lord Goddard was strongly criticised in the case of *Craig and Bentley* for his equally forthright comments.

A party could also be held to be an aider and abettor in cases where he is held to be under some sort of duty to control the other party, as in *Tuck* v *Robson 1970*. The defendant was a licensee of a public house called the Canterbury Arms, which was visited by the police after closing time. They discovered 12 people still drinking and three of these were charged and convicted with consuming intoxicating liquor out of hours. The licensee was charged with aiding and abetting the crime.

The Divisional Court decided that he had knowledge that the offence was being commit-

ted. A more difficult matter was whether he could be said to have assisted in its commission. The court decided that there was enough evidence that he had aided and abetted the offenders. He had failed to eject the customers or even to withdraw their permission to be on the premises, when he possessed the requisite authority to take such a course of action.

To counsel

This also involves the giving of advice and encouragement but usually takes place before the crime takes place.

An example of counselling can be seen in the case of *Calhaem 1985*. The defendant was infatuated with her solicitor and wished to remove his girlfriend from the scene. She therefore hired a private detective called Zajac to murder her. Zajac claimed that he had no intention of committing the crime but was going to pretend that he had attempted the murder but had been unsuccessful. He alleged that he had visited the girlfriend's house with this plan in mind but had then panicked and killed her because she had screamed after he had gained entry.

Despite this contention, Zajac was convicted of murder and Calhaem was found guilty of being a secondary offender. She appealed on the grounds that the judge had not directed the jury that her counselling of the contract killer had to be a substantial cause of the killing. She tried to argue that it was not her words or actions that had persuaded the killer to commit the crime.

The Court of Appeal agreed with the trial judge that the word 'counsel' merely meant to 'advise, solicit or something of that sort' and decided that there was no implication in this word that there had to be a causal connection between the counselling and the crime. It will be noted below that a different view is taken with regard to the word 'procure'.

To procure

In *AG's Reference No. 1 of 1975 (1975)*, this term was held to mean 'to produce by endeavour'. Lord Widgery gave a more detailed explanation of this when he added 'You procure a thing by setting out to see that it happens and taking the appropriate steps to produce that happening'. It was also decided in this case that procuring can take place even though the principal offender has no knowledge of this. In most cases of aiding, abetting and counselling there will have been some form of contact between the principal and secondary offenders, 'some meeting of the minds', as stated by Lord Widgery C J.

He decided that this was not necessary in the case of procuring. The judge stated 'there are plenty of instances in which a person may be said to procure the commission of a crime by another even though there is no sort of conspiracy between the two, even though there is no attempt at agreement or discussion as to the form which the offence should take. In our judgment the offence described in this reference is such a case'. What is felt to be necessary, however, is some sort of connection between the acts of the secondary offender and the actual crime committed.

In this case, the defendant had 'spiked' the drinks of his friend with spirits, knowing that the other would later be driving home. The friend was charged with a drink driving offence under the Road Traffic Act in force at that time and the defendant was charged as an aider, abettor, counsellor and procurer.

The friend was convicted but the judge decided that there was no case to answer in relation to the secondary offender. The *Attorney General's Reference* was a result of the disquiet felt about this decision. The Court of Appeal decided that a person acting in such a way should have faced trial for two reasons. First, he had acted secretly in lacing the drinks of his friend. The latter was therefore unaware of the alcohol consumed and was unable to take precautions to avoid committing an offence. Secondly, as a direct consequence of the added spirits, the friend had driven with the excess alcohol in his blood. This provided the causal link between the actions of the alleged secondary offender and the principal offender, which was felt to be essential in cases of procuring.

To sum up, therefore, a secondary offender can be charged with all four types of secondary participation, aiding abetting, counselling and procuring but can be found guilty if just one of these is satisfied. Normally, the accomplice will counsel and procure before a crime is committed and will aid and abet during the course of an offence. With aiding, abetting and counselling there is usually some contact between the principal and the accessory in relation to the crime to be committed but this is not necessary for procuring. What is required here is some sort of connection between the acts of the secondary offender and the eventual crime.

12.4 THE *ACTUS REUS* OF PARTICIPATION

It has to be proved that the alleged secondary has done something positive to assist or encourage the committing of the offence or has taken some steps to procure its commission. It was noted above that a passive presence at the scene of the crime would not, on its own, be enough to constitute liability. In *Clarkson 1971*, the conviction of two soldiers for abetting a rape was quashed because they had not participated in any way; they had merely been present at the time the crime took place. It is not necessary, however, to prove that the actions of the accomplices had any utility in the committing of the crime or even to prove that any incitement or encouragement was heeded, as was shown in the case of *Calhaem*, mentioned earlier.

A point that needs consideration is whether accomplices may withdraw from the events in which they have played a part, without incurring liability. The very early authority of *Saunders and Archer 1573* suggests that this is possible. It appears, however, that a mere show of repentance will not be sufficient and the offenders will need to take positive steps to indicate that their assistance is at an end. It was stated in *Whitehouse 1941* that they will need to:

> serve unequivocal notice upon the other party to the common unlawful cause that if he proceeds upon it he does so without the further aid and assistance of those who withdraw.

In some cases, the accomplice will need to go further and neutralise the effect of any aid he has given, such as taking back the car he has stolen or making the other surrender the weapon that was supplied. He will find it more difficult to avoid liability if his change of heart comes about at the scene of the crime. In *Becerra and Cooper 1975*, the defendants and another man broke into the house of an elderly woman and attacked her, after hearing that she kept large sums of money there. Becerra had not been engaged in the cowardly attack on the defenceless woman but had used a knife to cut the telephone wires. Cooper later took control of this knife and moved towards the kitchen to look for the money. The men were then disturbed by the arrival of the tenant of the first floor flat who had heard the commotion and come to investigate. Becerra called to the others 'Come on, let's go!' and he and the third man escaped through a window. Cooper was unable to get away and, in the ensuing struggle, the tenant was fatally stabbed.

Becerra tried to argue that his withdrawal from the scene of the crime meant that he was not liable for this murder. The Court of Appeal refused to accept this and his conviction was upheld.

12.5 THE *MENS REA* OF SECONDARY OFFENDERS

For the *mens rea* of secondary liability to exist, the prosecution must show two things:

1 That the accomplice had knowledge of the type of crime to be committed.
2 That he had the intention to aid, abet, counsel. or procure the principal offender.

These two points require elaboration.

Knowledge that a crime is to be committed

It was stated in *Johnson* v *Youden and Others 1950* that, before a person can be convicted of aiding and abetting the commission of an offence 'he must at least know the essential matters which constitute that offence'. In *Bainbridge 1960* it was decided that the defendant need not know of the precise crime that is to be committed, provided that he possesses, not mere suspicion 'but knowledge that a crime of the type in question was intended'.

Six weeks before any criminal activity took place Bainbridge used a false name and address to purchase oxygen cutting equipment. This was used later by the principal offenders to cut through the windows, the doors, and the safe of the Midland Bank in Stoke Newington. Bainbridge was charged with being an accessory to the burglary but tried to argue that he did not know the purpose for which the equipment was being used. He claimed that while he had suspected that something illegal was going on, he had believed that his purchases were merely being used for the breaking up of stolen goods or something similar.

The Court of Appeal held that while it was not enough merely to show that the defendant knew that some sort of illegal activity was planned, it was not necessary to show that he knew the exact time and place of the intended crime. The court decided that the judge had explained the matter well to the jurors, who had obviously not believed the defendant's story. His conviction, therefore, was upheld.

The House of Lords took the matter a little further in the case of *DPP for Northern Ireland* v *Maxwell 1978*. The defendant was a member of a prohibited terrorist organisation, the Ulster Volunteer Force and, being a local man had guided other terrorists to a public house called the Crosskeys, which was owned by a Catholic. There a bomb was planted and the fuse ignited. The defendant was not involved in that activity and had not, at any time, had the bomb in his possession. Despite this, he was convicted. He appealed on the grounds that it had not been proved that he knew the type of crime that was going to be committed. The House of Lords was called upon to decide whether an accomplice could be convicted if 'the crime committed by the principal, and actually assisted by the accused, was one of a number of offences, one of which the accused knew the principal would probably commit.' Their Lordships firmly held that the answer was 'yes'.

Viscount Dilhorne explained their decision in the following way:

> An accessory who leaves it to his principal to choose is liable, provided always the choice is made from the range of offences from which the accessory contemplates the choice will be made.

He acknowledged that the lower court had gone further than earlier cases but added that 'it is a sound development of the law and in no way inconsistent with them. I accept it as good judge-made law in a field where there is no statute to offer guidance'.

The law seems to be undecided as to whether the accomplice's knowledge that an offence is probable is enough to make him liable, i.e. it is unclear whether he can be found guilty when he is merely reckless about whether a crime is committed.

In *Blakely, Sutton* v *DPP 1991*, there was a clear statement by the Divisional Court that objective or inadvertent recklessness is not sufficient to constitute liability but less certainty as to whether subjective recklessness would suffice. In this case, the two women defendants had 'spiked' the drink of the first defendant's lover to stop him returning home to his wife. They had intended to tell him what they had done but he had left before they could do so. He was convicted of a drink driving offence and the defendants were found guilty as accessories. The women had obviously intended that the defendant should drink the alcohol but, equally obviously, did not intend that the man should drive and thereby commit the offence. The court had to decide whether their convictions should be upheld on the grounds that they should have contemplated that the man's actions in leaving and driving were probable.

The Divisional Court quashed their conviction because the magistrates had used the *Caldwell* test of recklessness. The court was definite that this type of recklessness was insufficient to create liability. The judges were less clear with regard to *Cunningham*-type recklessness, although they did suggest that it was best to avoid the word 'reckless' altogether when deciding upon the *mens rea* of secondary offenders.

While the position with regard to subjective recklessness may be in doubt, mere negligence on the part of the alleged secondary offender is obviously insufficient to incur liability. In *Callow* v *Tillstone 1900*, a vet was negligent in his examination of a carcass of meat and declared it to be sound. The meat was later offered for sale and the owner was convicted of the strict liability offence of selling unfit food. The vet's conviction as an accessory, however, was quashed. He had not intended to be an accomplice and, as noted below, this point must also be shown for a secondary offender, even when the offence in question is a strict liability one.

The intention to aid, abet, counsel or procure

In addition to the knowledge that a crime will be committed, the prosecution must also prove that the accomplice had the intention to do the acts that assisted or encouraged the commission of the crime.

In *National Coal Board* v *Gamble 1959*, the Coal Board, via the actions of one of its employees, was found guilty of aiding and abetting because the intention to assist the principal offender was apparent, even though there was no benefit to the accomplices. The employee of the Coal Board operated a weighbridge and informed a lorry driver that his load was nearly four tons overweight. The driver decided to take the risk and the operator supplied him with a ticket permitting him to leave the premises. The driver's employers were later found guilty of contravening the Motor Vehicles (Construction and Use) Regulations 1955 and the National Coal Board was convicted as a secondary offender.

An equally strict line was taken in *Garrett* v *Arthur Churchill (Glass) Ltd 1970*, where the defendant's conviction for knowingly being involved in the exportation of goods without a licence was upheld, even though he was merely an agent and the goods actually belonged to the other party. The Lord Chief Justice dealt with the problem that it could be argued that the defendant was under a legal duty to deal with the goods in the way dictated by the owner. He argued that a civil action by the owner would be unlikely to succeed if the handing over of the goods in the way prescribed amounted to a criminal offence.

It was noted in Chapter 2 that, provided that an intention to commit the crime is proved, the offender's motive is irrelevant. This position does not appear to have been followed in *Gillick* v *West Norfolk Area Health Authority 1986*. Victoria Gillick, the campaigner for support of family values, sought a declaration that doctors would be acting illegally if they prescribed contraceptives to girls under the age of 16 without obtaining the consent of their parents. It was contended that, by such an action, the doctors were aiding and abetting the commission of unlawful sexual intercourse.

The House of Lords decided that the doctors would not have the intention to commit such a crime if they followed the guidelines that had been laid down, limiting such provision to exceptional cases. Lord Scarman stated:

> The bona fide exercise by a doctor of his clinical judgment must be a complete negation of the guilty mind which is an essential ingredient of the criminal offence of aiding and abetting the commission of unlawful sexual intercourse.

This was clearly a policy decision and he did go on to say that if a doctor gave the contraceptive treatment merely to facilitate the girl's unlawful sexual intercourse he may well be guilty of secondary liability.

12.6 PROBLEM AREAS

12.6.1 IF THE PRINCIPAL OFFENDER IS ACQUITTED

Before we leave the subject of the liability required for a secondary offender, it is necessary to examine whether the accomplice can still be held liable if the principal is acquitted.

The answer to this is that it is possible as long as the *actus reus* of the main offence has been committed and the secondary offender has the requisite *mens rea*. The courts are then prepared to combine the two elements and convict him. This complicated principle is best understood by looking at the appalling behaviour of the two husbands in the cases described below and the obvious desire of the courts to convict them.

In the case of *Bourne 1952*, a man forced his wife to have sexual intercourse with a dog. This is illegal but mercifully the wife was not charged. If she had been brought to court, she would have been able to plead the defences of marital coercion or duress and, hopefully, would have been acquitted. Because the *actus reus* of the crime was held to exist, however, the court was able to convict the husband for aiding and abetting the illegal act.

The decision in *Cogan and Leak 1976* is perhaps less easy to justify, although it is clear why the Court of Appeal was reluctant to quash the conviction. Leak wished to punish and humiliate his wife after she had refused him money so, on his return from a drinking session he forced her to have sexual intercourse, first with him and then with his drinking partner, Cogan, while the husband looked on. The unfortunate woman was said to be sobbing quietly throughout the ordeal. Later, Cogan was charged with rape and Leak with procuring this offence. Leak could not be charged with his own rape of his wife because, at that time, it was not an offence for a husband within a marriage to have sexual intercourse without his wife's consent.

Both men were convicted at first instance but appealed. Cogan's appeal was successful, following the questionable decision of the House of Lords in *Morgan 1976* in the interim period, which held that an honest belief that the other had consented could be a defence to a charge of rape; the belief did not have to be a reasonable one. Leach tried to argue that, as the principal had been acquitted, his conviction as an accomplice could not then stand and, brutal though his behaviour was, there could be said to be some merit in this argument. If Cogan's conviction had been quashed, it was arguable whether the crime of rape still existed.

The Court of Appeal, however, refused to quash Leak's conviction. Lawton L J took a robust approach to this problem, roundly declaring that an acquittal would be 'an affront to justice and to the common sense of ordinary folk'. He found that a rape had, indeed, been committed and confirmed that Leach had procured this offence. He rejected the appellant's arguments and stated 'Here one fact was clear – the wife had been raped...: The fact that Cogan was innocent of rape because he believed she was consenting does not affect the position ... In the language of the law the act of sexual intercourse without the wife's consent was the *actus reus*; it had been procured by Leak who had the appropriate *mens rea*, namely his intention that Cogan should have sexual intercourse with her without her consent'.

This possible expansion of the law was followed in the case of *Millward 1994*. The defendant was charged with aiding, abetting, counselling and procuring his employee to commit the offence of causing death by reckless driving. The vehicle in question was a tractor, with a trailer attached. The hitch on the tractor was defective and during the journey, the trailer became detached from the tractor and hit another vehicle. The driver of this car was killed. Both employer and employee were originally convicted but the employee's conviction was quashed on appeal. Millward tried to argue that the acquittal of the principal meant that the *actus reus* of the offence had not been committed because the recklessness of the employee had not been made out.

The Court of Appeal decided that the *actus reus* did still exist; it consisted of the taking of the vehicle onto the road in a defective condition so as to cause the death. It was stressed that procuring does not require a joint intention between the accessory and the principal, thus allowing the accessory to be convicted even when the principal is acquitted.

The court approved of the reasoning in *Cogan and Leak* and distinguished the earlier case of *Thornton* v *Mitchell 1940*, where the facts were somewhat similar to those in Millward. In the earlier case, a conductor had given inadequate signals to the driver of a bus who was trying to reverse and this had resulted in a fatal injury to a pedestrian. The conductor's conviction for aiding and abetting the careless driving of the principal was quashed on appeal because the driver of the bus had been acquitted. The Divisional Court clearly decided that, as the *actus reus* of careless driving no longer existed, there was no crime for the secondary offender to aid and abet.

▼ **COMMENT**

Some would argue that this case and *Millward* are so similar that the same principles should apply to both cases. Be that as it may, *Millward* is a Court of Appeal decision and represents the state of the current law.

12.6.2 IF THE LIABILITY OF THE SECONDARY OFFENDER IS DIFFERENT

Liability of the secondary offender for a different offence to that of the principal is possible, provided that both offences share the same *actus reus*. This was not held to be the case in *Dunbar 1988*, although it is submitted that the defendant was very lucky to escape serious punishment after the death of her former, female lover. It was alleged that Dunbar had expressed a wish to see her lover dead but she claimed that this comment had been made while she was intoxicated. It was shown that she had suspected that the co-defendants might break into the flat of her lover and, in the course of the burglary, might inflict some harm upon the woman. Dunbar argued strongly, however, that she had not envisaged that death or grievous bodily harm might result. The Court of Appeal quashed her conviction for manslaughter. The decision was arrived at because the trial judge had not made it clear to the jury that, if the defendant had not contemplated the possibility that death or grievous bodily harm might occur and had only suspected that some lesser harm might be inflicted, she could not be found guilty of manslaughter because the crime that she had contemplated was different to the one committed.

KEY FACTS

- The main perpetrator of a crime is called the principal offender; in some cases, there may be more than one principal
- If an innocent agent is involved, a person may be convicted as a principal even though he is not at the scene of the crime. Innocent agents are those without knowledge of the crime or those who lack capacity
- People with less involvement are called secondary offenders. They may also be known as accomplices or accessories
- Secondary offenders are liable to be tried and punished in the same way as principal offenders (s.8 Accessories and Abettors Act 1861, as amended and s.44 Magistrates Courts' Act 1980)
- They will fulfil this role if they have aided, abetted, counselled or procured the offence. In *AG's Reference (No. 1 of 1975) 1975*, it was stated that these words should be given their ordinary meaning
- All four terms may appear on the indictment but the secondary offender can be convicted if just one of these forms of assistance is proved
- Aiding and abetting usually takes place at the scene of the crime. Aiding means giving help, support or assistance; abetting means encouraging, inciting or instigating the crime. A purely passive presence at the scene of the crime will not incur liability, unless the person is involved in other ways or has the authority to control the others (see *Coney 1882*, *Clarkson 1971* and *Bland 1988*, and contrast with *Wilcox* v *Jeffrey 1951* and *Tuck* v *Robson 1970*)
- Counselling means inciting or encouraging, or 'to advise or solicit or something of that sort' (*Calhaem 1985*). This will take place before the crime takes place. Liability may still be incurred even where the principal offender does not heed the advice (*Calhaem 1985*)
- The term 'to procure' means 'to produce by endeavour', i.e. to set out to see that the crime happens, but there is no requirement that the principal has to know of these actions. There must, however, be some causal connection between the steps taken by the alleged accomplice and the actual crime committed (*AG's Reference (No. 1 of 1975) 1975*)

- The *actus reus* of participation requires the activities of aiding, abetting, counselling or procuring, i.e. something active to assist the commission of the crime, although it is not necessary for the help to have been of any use
- Accomplices may be able to withdraw from their criminal activity without incurring liability, but must take steps to make this position clear to the others involved in the crime (*Whitehouse 1941*). In many cases, they will need to go even further and will need to neutralise the effects of any help they have already given, such as taking back the weapons supplied. The later the withdrawal, the less likely it is that the courts will believe it is genuine (*Beccara 1975*)
- Two points have to be established before the *mens rea* of participation is satisfied. First, there must be knowledge that the crime is to be committed (*Johnson v Youden & Others 1950*) or, at the very least, *Cunningham*-style recklessness that an offence might happen (*Blakely, Sutton v DPP 1991*)
- It appears from the cases of *Bainbridge 1960* and *DPP for N.I. v Maxwell 1978*, that it is enough for the accused to be aware that a particular type of crime might be committed or one from a range of crimes. The accomplice is not required to know the exact details
- Secondly, there must be an intention to assist the principal (*NCB v Gamble 1959*, *Garrett v Arthur Churchill Glass Ltd 1970*)
- He has to have the *mens rea* of intending to do the assisting, even where the offence committed is a strict liability one, as in *Callow v Tillstone 1900*. He need not, however, intend that the actual crime should be committed
- *Gillick* appears to have been decided on its own particular facts
- A secondary offender may still be liable even when the principal offender has been acquitted, so long as the *actus reus* of the crime is still held to exist. This will then be merged with the *mens rea* of the accomplice (*Bourne 1957*, *Cogan and Leak 1976* and *Millward 1994*). This will not be the case if he contemplated a different offence (*Dunbar 1988*)

FIGURE 12.1 *Key facts chart on principal and secondary offenders*

12.6.3 WHEN THE PRINCIPAL OFFENDER IS A VICTIM

It was established in the early case of *Tyrrell 1894*, that the alleged accomplice cannot be found guilty of aiding and abetting if the offence in question was actually created to protect him or other. This is best illustrated by the facts of *Tyrrell*. An under-age girl was charged with aiding and abetting a man to have incestuous sexual intercourse with her but was acquitted. The court felt it to be wrong that she should face criminal proceedings when the act had been designed to protect young women in similar circumstances.

activity

1. Isaac recruited two children to steal mobile phones for him from a local store. Cain was aged 15, Abel was 9.

Assess the possible liability of Isaac, Cain and Abel.

2. Ruth is jealous of her friend Rachel, who has just passed her advanced motoring test. She secretly laces Rachel's orange juice with vodka, knowing that the latter will be driving home. Rachel is later charged with driving a motor vehicle with excess alcohol in the blood.

Discuss Ruth's involvement.

3 In *Rook 1993*, the defendant was convicted of being a secondary offender to the crime of murder. The case involved a contract killing in which the taxi driver, Afsar, arranged for three men to kill his wife. The men had at least two meetings in which they discussed the ways of carrying out the crime and Rook had asked for money 'up front' to help pay for the new clothes they would need after the event. He then had second thoughts about being involved and did not turn up at the pre-arranged murder spot. The other two men dragged the unfortunate woman from the car in which she was travelling with her husband and brutally murdered her. Rook was convicted with the others but appealed. He argued that he had never intended the woman to be killed and that he had merely tagged along to see how far the others would go. He then claimed that he had tried to stall them and had believed that if he did not turn up at the appointed place, the others would not go ahead with the crime.

Imagine that you are a judge of the Court of Appeal and decide whether Rook's appeal should succeed. Give clear reasons for your answer.

12.7 JOINT ENTERPRISES

In the situations mentioned earlier, the decision as to who will fulfil the role as principal offender and who will be classed as a mere accessory has usually been obvious. In some instances, however, the position is not so clear, especially where two or more parties embark on what it known in law as a joint enterprise. Professor John Smith would argue that there is little difficulty with such cases and that the ordinary rules of primary and secondary liability should be applied. In cases where the joint criminal enterprise fails and one party is alleging that he is less at fault than the other, all

that then needs to be worked out is whether he is, in truth, a secondary participator or whether he should be classed as a joint principal.

In the case of *Stewart and Schofield 1995*, however, the Court of Appeal refused to support this view and decided that the law should take a stricter approach in cases where the parties involved have set out together on a criminal escapade. Hobhouse L J stated:

> The allegation that a defendant took part in the execution of a crime as a joint enterprise is not the same as an allegation that he aided, abetted, counselled or procured the commission of that crime. A person who is a mere aider or abettor is truly a secondary party to the commission of whatever crime it is that the principal has committed . . . In contrast, where the allegation is joint enterprise, the allegation is that one defendant participated in the criminal act of another. This is a different principle. It renders each of the parties to a joint enterprise criminally liable for the acts done in the course of carrying out that joint enterprise.

The facts of this case are depressingly all too common. Heather Stewart bought some cigarettes from a corner shop and noted the shopkeeper removing a wad of money from the till and putting it in his pocket. She then met up with two men, Lambert and Schofield, and suggested that they should steal this money. They took with them an iron bar and a knife and returned to the shop. Schofield acted as a lookout and the other two went into the shop, where the Pakistani shopkeeper was beaten so badly with the iron bar by Lambert that he died a few days later. The attackers left with less than £100. When the offenders were later charged, Stewart and Schofield tried to argue that they had not imagined that the shopkeeper would be more than threatened and that they had not known that Lambert was so full of racial hatred that he would use excessive force. They therefore claimed that the attack had not formed part of the joint enterprise on which they had embarked. Despite this claim, they were found guilty of manslaughter.

The trial judge had relied on the statements made in *Reid 1975* that where the parties are engaged on a joint plan and carry offensive weapons, there was always a likelihood that one of them would use them and cause death or serious injury. In such a case, if the injury had not been one that the others intended, they could not be found guilty of murder, but they could, instead, be convicted of manslaughter.

The appellants tried to argue that this decision no longer represented the law, as it did not stand with other later Court of Appeal decisions. The judges reviewed these but decided that there was no conflict. Hobhouse L J concluded

> The question whether the relevant act was committed in the course of carrying out the joint enterprise in which the defendant was a participant is a question of fact not law. If the act was not so committed then the joint enterprise ceases to provide a basis for a finding of guilt against such a defendant. He ceases to be responsible for the act. This is the fundamental point illustrated by *R v Anderson and Morris* and *R v Lovesey, R v Peterson*. But it does not follow that a variation in the intent of some of the participants at the time the critical act is done precludes the act from having been done in the course of carrying out the joint enterprise, as is illustrated by *R v Betty* and *R v Reid*.

The appeals against the convictions therefore failed.

Uncertainty remains, however, as to how much variation of the plan can take place before it is considered to be outside the scope of the joint enterprise. It appears that the party in the joint enterprise who did not commit the final act will not escape liability if he knew that the other might commit such an act. This principle was laid down by the Privy Council in *Chan Wing-Siu 1985*.

The victim was the husband of a prostitute, Madam Lam, who, with her husband's consent advertised for clients in the Chinese newspapers. She therefore believed that one of the defendants was a client but when she opened the door to him, two other men also rushed in. She was made to kneel and they then went into the kitchen, where her husband was fatally stabbed. Madam Lam was also stabbed before the men left but survived. The defendants argued that they were merely collecting a debt and had themselves been attacked by the husband who had picked up a chopper after hearing his wife shout 'robbery!'. The defendants claimed that they had only carried the knives with them for protection. The jury had obviously preferred Madam Lam's version of events and all three men were found guilty of murder. The trial judge had told the jury that the defendants could be convicted even if they had not struck the final blow if they had contemplated that one of the other people involved might use a knife. They appealed on the grounds that this state of mind was insufficient and that they should only be found guilty if they had contemplated that death or serious injury was probable, not just possible. Sir Robin Cooke stated that the law was as follows:

> Where a man lends himself to a criminal enterprise knowing that potentially murderous weapons are to be carried, and in the event they are in fact used by his partner with an intent sufficient for murder, he should not escape the consequences. . .

He went on to say, however, that the test of *mens rea* is subjective, i.e. what the accused contemplated, but added that this could be inferred from his conduct and any other evidence throwing light on the matter. He made it clear that liability would not be incurred unless the defendant thought the risk was a real or substantial one, but preferred not to use just one term to describe it. In the event, the convictions were upheld.

In *Hyde & Others 1991*, the Court of Appeal approved of the statements in the above case and stated:

> If B realises (without agreeing to such conduct being used) that A may kill or intentionally inflict serious injury, but nevertheless continues to participate with A in the venture, that will amount to a sufficient mental element for B to be guilty of murder if A, with the requisite intent, kills in the scope of the venture.

In this case, the convictions for murder of the three defendants, who had kicked and punched another person outside a pub, were upheld, despite the fact it was impossible to say who had inflicted the fatal blow.

In *Mahmood 1994*, however, the Court of Appeal decided that the 15-year-old defendant could not have contemplated the actions of the other, even younger offender. The two boys were joy-riders, and were chased by the police after their erratic driving was noted. The driver jumped out of the car while it was still moving and Mahmood was believed to have followed. The empty car, still in gear, mounted a pavement and struck a child's pram, killing the ten-month-old baby inside.

The Court of Appeal thought that it may well have been in the contemplation of the passenger that someone may have been killed or injured by the other's dangerous driving but not that the car would have been abandoned in such a way. The conviction for manslaughter was therefore quashed.

In *Uddin 1998* the defendant's conviction for murder was quashed and a retrial ordered because the jury's attention had not been drawn to the use of a knife by the party inflicting the fatal blow, and the need to ascertain whether the others in the group enterprise were aware of this. It was stressed that the the fact that each partici-

pant had a shared intention to inflict serious harm wasn't in itself enough to make them responsible for the victim's death, although if they continued to attack after an unforeseen weapon was produced, they could be guilty of murder. *Powell, 1997*, a House of Lord's decision which appeared to limit the liability of those engaged in a joint enterprise, even though the actual appeals failed, was quoted with approval.

For the above principles to apply, a joint enterprise must be established. It was confirmed in *Petters and Parfitt 1995*, that if the parties act independently of each other but wish to achieve the same result, and it cannot be proved that they intended to assist or encourage the other, then they are not liable for the acts of the other. If a killing takes place in such circumstances, and it is impossible to prove who did this, both of the parties must be acquitted. This can lead to the distressing result that a crime goes unpunished, as sometimes occurs where a child has been killed, but it is impossible to prove which of the parents was responsible.

12.8 SUGGESTED REFORM ON SECONDARY OFFENDERS

The Law Commission has studied the law relating to accessories on several occasions. The most recent proposals are in their Consultation Paper No. 131, entitled *Assisting and Encouraging Crime*. The Commission invites comments on their proposals for radical changes in this area. It is suggested that two new offences should be created, one of assisting crime and the second on encouraging crime and to make them inchoate offences. This would mean that they are not dependent on the main crime having to take place.

To put matters simply, a person would be guilty of assisting crime if he knows or believes that another party is doing an act (or will do one) which will involve the commission of a crime and he does any act to assist this. To widen liability, the clause states that assistance includes the giving of advice about how to

KEY FACTS

- When two or more people embark upon a joint criminal venture, this is known in law as a joint enterprise
- Despite the misgivings of Professor John Smith, the Court of Appeal has firmly upheld the view that such cases are to be treated differently to those of ordinary secondary liability
- In cases of joint enterprise one party is held to participate in the criminal acts of another and will be criminally liable for the acts done in the course of carrying out the joint enterprise (*Stewart and Schofield 1995*)
- The participator in the joint enterprise will still be liable, even where the acts of the other vary from what was originally planned, provided that they are in the range of acts contemplated by him (*Stewart and Schofield 1995, Chan Wing-Siu v R 1985, Hyde 1991, Bamborough 1996*)
- The test, however, is subjective. The defendant must believe that the risk of the harm occurring is a substantial one but this can be inferred from the conduct of the defendant and any evidence throwing light on the matter (*Chan Wing-Siu v R 1985*)
- If the act is outside the contemplation of the defendant he cannot be found liable (*Mahmood 1996, Uddin 1998*)
- If no joint enterprise is found, and it cannot be established who inflicted the injury, the parties must be acquitted (*Petters and Parfitt 1995*)

FIGURE 12.2 *Key facts chart on joint enterprise*

commit the offence and advice on how to avoid detection or arrest.

The person will also be liable if he assists a principal and knows or believes that the latter intends to commit one of a number of offences (i.e. the *Bainbridge* situation).

The offence of encouraging crime will arise if the offender solicits, commands or encourages the principal to do acts which would involve the commission of an offence by the principal and he intends that such acts should be done.

The help should be brought to the attention of the principal but the latter does not need to be influenced by it. It is also not necessary that the offender should know the identity of the principal, nor even have any particular group in mind, provided that he intends that his communication will be acted upon by any person to whose attention it comes.

If effected, these changes would mean the abolition of aiding, abetting and counselling and also the abolition of the common law offence of incitement, which is dealt with in Chapter 13. The Commission believed that there may be a need for another new offence to cover procuring, in cases where there is no communication about this with the principal. It remains to be seen whether any of these far-reaching proposals will be acted upon.

12.9 ASSISTANCE AFTER THE CRIME

Only assistance before or during a crime can render a person liable as an accomplice. There is no longer such a concept as an 'accessory after the fact'; this was abolished in 1967.

There are, however, specific crimes that may be committed if help is given after a crime has been committed.

activity

Read the following article and answer the following questions:

1 Which crime were the offenders Craig and Bentley said to have committed and why

did Bentley's conviction arouse such controversy?

2 Describe three ways in which the trial judge, Lord Goddard, was said to have misdirected the jury.

3 What was the latest decision of the Court of Appeal in respect of Bentley?

Bentley trial unfair through flawed summing-up

Before Lord Bingham of Cornhill, Lord Chief Justice, Lord Justice Kennedy and Mr Justice Collins [Judgment July 30]

Having regard to the evidence adduced at trial the jury, if properly directed, would have been entitled to convict Derek Bentley of murder as the offence was then constituted, before the abolition of constructive malice and the introduction of the defence of diminished responsibilty.

However, since the trial judge in his summing-up failed to direct the jury on the standard and burden of proof, to give sufficient direction on the law of joint enterprise, or adequately to summarise the defence case, made prejudicial comments about the defendants and their defences and indicated that the police officers' evidence, because of their bravery on the night in question, was more worthy of belief then that of the defendants, Bentley was denied the fair trial to which he was entitled and his conviction was in consequence unsafe.

The Court of Appeal, Criminal Division, so held, when, on a reference by the Criminal Cases Review Commission under section 9 of the Criminal Appeal Act 1995, it allowed an appeal on behalf of Derek Bentley by his niece, Maria Bentley-Dingwall, and quashed his conviction for murder following a trial before Lord Goddard, Lord Chief Justice, and a jury at the Central Criminal Court on December 11, 1952.

On November 2, 1952, Christopher Craig, aged 16, armed with a knife, a revolver and ammunition, and Bentley, aged 19, who had knife and a knuckle-duster, went on a warehouse-breaking expedition. At about 9.15pm they were observed climbing into a warehouse premises in Croydon and the police were called, arriving at the site at about 9.25pm.

DC Fairfax and PC Harrison, finding that the defendants had climbed on to the roof pursued them there and a third officer followed. DC Fairfax arrested Bentley who was then, on the three officers' evidence, heard to shout: "Let him have it, Chris". Craig fired at DC Fairfax, slightly injuring him. Bentley broke away, but that officer grabbed him and removed the knife and knuckle-duster which he found in Bentleys pockets.

Thereafter, Bentley remained wholly docile beside the officer, offering no incitement and, on the police evidence, making various remarks which showed concern for his and their safety. Craig continued firing, and shot dead a fourth officer, PC Miles, as that officer reached the roof, probably a little before 9.57pm.

On the way to the police station Bentley was alleged to have said "I knew he had a gun but I didn't think he'd use it" and his statement under caution recorded: "I did not know Chris had one until he shot".

Following a two day trial, he was convicted with the jury's recommendation to mercy. He was sentenced to death, the only sentence then permitted, his appeal was dismissed on January 13, 1953 and he was executed on January 28. On July 29, 1993 he was granted a royal pardon in respect of the death sentence and execution.

Taken from a Law Report published in *The Times*, 31 July 1998

summary

In this chapter we have discovered that the participants in a crime may be principal or secondary offenders and that the latter are those who aid, abet, counsel or procure the offence.

We have learned that secondary offenders will normally be charged with the same offence as the principal and may be punished in the same way. We should also have noted that there are an increasing number of appeals on the subject of joint enterprises and that special rules apply in these cases.

CHAPTER 13

INCHOATE OFFENCES

13.1 INTRODUCTION

IF YOU LOOK in a dictionary to find out the meaning of the word 'inchoate', you will see that it is defined variously as 'just begun', 'in an initial or early stage' or 'not yet fully developed'. Inchoate offences, therefore, are incomplete offences. The parties involved may well have desired that a crime should go ahead, but circumstances beyond their control may have prevented this. For example, an offender may have planned to murder another, he may have raised the gun to shoot him, taken careful aim but then, for some reason, the gun does not fire. In another case, an armed robbery may have been plotted but the sudden re-routing of the security van may have prevented the planned ambush. In yet another scenario, a person may have been pressurising his friend to blackmail a business acquaintance, but this friend may have had 'cold feet' and might have decided to pull out of the venture. Not unnaturally, even though the main crimes did not go ahead, the law still takes the view that the people involved in these activities should be punished. In the first instance, therefore, the offender would be charged with attempted murder. In the second case, the wrongdoers might also be charged with attempt or might, instead, be charged with conspiracy. In our last example, the party exerting the pressure on his friend might be guilty of incitement. These three offences,

therefore, are the subject of this chapter and will be dealt with alphabetically.

13.2 ATTEMPT

The law of attempts is now governed by the Criminal Attempts Act 1981, which came into force on 27 August 1981. Before the passing of this act, the rules had been formulated at common law.

S.1(1) Criminal Attempts Act 1981 states that a person will be guilty of attempt if:

> with intent to commit an offence to which this section applies, a person does an act which is more than merely preparatory to the commission of the offence.

S.4(1) lays down the punishment and it will be noted that this may be severe. The subsection states that 'the attempt is punishable to the same extent as the substantive offence'.

13.2.1 THE ACTUS REUS OF ATTEMPT

The *actus reus* of attempt will exist where the party 'does an act which is more than merely preparatory to the commission of the offence'.

The law makes a clear distinction, therefore, between acts which are undertaken merely to prepare for the crime in question and acts done after this time which will then amount, in law, to an attempt to commit the actual offence. With regard to earlier acts, the party may be guilty of other, less serious offences, as, for example, obtaining a gun and ammunition unlawfully or stealing a car, but he will not, at this stage be guilty of the attempt to commit the main crime. For this to occur, he must do something more substantial and with a closer connection to the crime in question. Before the Criminal Attempts Act codified the law on attempts, the Court of Appeal in *Davey* v *Lee 1968* took the view that it had to be 'a step towards the commission of the specific crime, which is immediately and not merely remotely connected with the commission of it and the doing of it which cannot reasonably be regarded as having any other purpose than the commission of the specific crime'. In *DPP* v *Stonehouse 1978*, the House of Lords approved of the early description in *Eagleton 1855* that 'Acts remotely leading towards the commission of the offence are not to be considered as attempts to commit it; but acts immediately connected with it are'. Their Lordships therefore decided that 'the offender must have crossed the Rubicon and burnt his boats'. The Law Commission, when formulating the changes in the law of attempt, was not prepared to be so definite. The Commissioners decided that there was 'no magic formula' to work out when enough has been done to amount to an attempt and decided to concentrate instead on where the preparation has ended. With the benefit of the statement 'more than merely preparatory', as a guide, it was felt that the question of whether the offender had done enough to be charged with attempt could then be left to the jury's good sense.

In *Jones 1990* the defendant had been unable to accept that his ex mistress had a serious relationship with another man, Michael Foreman. Jones had purchased four guns and had shortened the barrel of one of them. On the day of the crime, he had driven to the school where Foreman was dropping off his child and had jumped into the victim's car. He had then pointed the loaded gun at Foreman and stated 'You are not going to like this'. The victim managed to grab the gun and throw it out of the window and then escaped himself, despite a cord pulling him back. The police later arrested the defendant who also had a knife with him. They also recovered his holdall, which contained a hatchet, some ammunition and a length of cord and his car, in which they found was a large quantity of English, French and Spanish money.

Jones claimed that he had only intended to kill himself and appealed against his subsequent conviction. He argued that he had at least three more acts to do before he could be said to be ready to kill anyone; i.e. he had to remove the safety catch on the gun, to put his finger on the trigger and thirdly, he had to pull that trigger.

The Court of Appeal decided that the acts of obtaining the gun, shortening it, loading it, putting on a disguise and going to the school were merely preparatory to the commission of the offence. The judges added, however, that 'once he had got into the car, taken out the loaded gun and pointed it at the victim with the intention of killing him there was sufficient evidence for the consideration of the jury on the charge of attempted murder'. The appeal, therefore, was dismissed.

In other cases, the matter is less clear-cut. In *Gullefer 1990*, the defendant had placed a bet of £18 at a greyhound stadium in Romford. The dog was not performing well so, in the final stages of the race, the defendant climbed over the fence and onto the track and tried to distract the dogs. He hoped that this action would result in the race being declared null and void and the eventual return of his stake money from the bookmaker. Unfortunately for Gullefer, he was no more successful in this plan than he was with his gambling and he was charged with attempted theft. His luck changed for the better, however, when his appeal was heard and his conviction was quashed. The former Lord Chief Justice, Lord Lane, decided that the attempt could not be said to begin until the defendant embarked upon 'the crime proper'. Gullefer's actions when he jumped onto the track, therefore, were merely acts in preparation for the later crime of theft and, at that time, he could not be said to be guilty of an attempt.

The decisions in the case of *Campbell 1991* and *Geddes 1996* are rather more disquieting. In the first case, the defendant was arrested within yards of a post office, armed with an imitation gun and was convicted of attempted armed robbery. In the second case, Geddes had been discovered by a teacher in the boys' lavatory block at a school in Brighton. He had no authority to be there and left when challenged, discarding his rucksack as he went. This was found to contain a large kitchen knife, ropes and a roll of masking tape. He was later convicted of attempted false imprisonment.

Both convictions, however, were quashed on appeal on the finding that the acts were not more than merely preparatory. While the appeal court appeared to be convinced in both cases that the defendants had the necessary intention to commit the crimes in question, they nevertheless felt bound to conclude that the actions were not advanced enough to merit a conviction.

The Court of Appeal took a more robust approach in *Attorney General's Reference (No 1 of 1992) 1993* and decided that a defendant could be found guilty of rape without the need to show that he had tried to penetrate the woman's vagina, provided that there was enough other evidence of attack.

13.2.2 THE *MENS REA* OF ATTEMPT

It will be noted when looking at the definition of attempt in s.1(1) that the mental element required for the crime of attempt is an intention to bring about the offence. The section states that a person will be guilty of attempt if 'with intent to commit an offence', he does an act which is more than merely preparatory to the commission of the offence. In relation to the attempt to commit the actual crime, therefore, recklessness behaviour is not sufficient to incur liability.

This was clearly affirmed by the Court of Appeal in *Millard and Vernon 1987*. The defendants were football supporters who were charged with attempted criminal damage. They had systematically pushed against a wooden wall at the ground. The prosecution alleged that they had done this in conjunction with each other in order to damage the line of planking, whereas the defendants strongly denied that they were acting with intent to damage the stand, or that they were acting in cohort. Despite this, they were convicted so they appealed on the ground that the judge had misdirected the jury about the need to establish intention. It was contended that recklessness was not enough, even though this state of mind would suffice for the full crime of criminal damage.

The Court of Appeal agreed with this reasoning and quashed their convictions. The same view would be taken if the defendant was charged with attempted grievous bodily harm under s.20 Offences Against the Person Act 1861. If the offence had been carried out, the offender could be convicted if he either intended to inflict grievous bodily harm or was reckless about this. For the charge of attempt to inflict grievous bodily harm to succeed, however, only intention will suffice. With the crime of murder, the defendant can be found guilty if it is proved that he intended to kill or to cause grievous bodily harm. For the crime of attempted murder, the wrongdoer must be shown to have had the intention to kill; the intention to cause grievous bodily harm is not enough and, if this is all that can be proved, the defendant must be acquitted. The following newspaper cutting illustrates this.

We now need to see how this intention to commit the crime can be established. It is primarily a jury matter. In *Mohan 1976*, passed

Husband cleared of trying to kill rival

THE husband of a British Airways stewardess was cleared at the Old Bailey today of attempting to murder her lover — and left court hand in hand with his wife.

Father-of-two Jose Jardin had struck his Italian rival seven times in the head and back after catching him in bed with his wife Zadia, 34, who had told Mr Jardin she was flying to Zurich.

But he told the jury he had just reacted to being rugby-tackled in the bedroom by designer Gianfranco Bertaggia and had hit out without realising he had a knife in his hand. Bertaggia, 40, from Harrow, spent six weeks in hospital.

Bus driver Jardin, 33, wept as he was found not guilty of attempted murder and wounding with intent. Now the couple plan to patch up their differences.

Taken from an article by Paul Cheston in the *Evening Standard*, 17 September 1998

---

before the Criminal Attempts Act 1981, the Court of Appeal said that intention meant:

> a decision to bring about, in so far as it lies within the accused's power, the commission of the offence which it is alleged the accused attempted to commit, no matter whether the accused desired the consequence or not.

In attempted murder, therefore, the fact that the defendant foresaw that his actions might cause the death of the victim would not be enough. As in the full crime of murder, however, if the defendant foresaw that death was a virtually certain consequence of his actions, this would be strong evidence from which the jury would be entitled to infer, that the wrongdoer had the necessary intention. In *Walker and Hayles 1990*, discussed earlier in Chapter 2, the Court of Appeal was prepared to accept a direction of the trial judge that the jury could infer that the defendant had the necessary intention if he foresaw that there was a very high degree of probability that death would result, although it was made clear that the court preferred the words 'virtually certain'.

In this case, the convictions for attempted murder were upheld. The appellants had thrown the victim from a third floor block of flats because it was believed that he had ill-treated Walker's sister. The Court of Appeal confirmed that it was necessary to show that the appellants had intended to kill the victim and that the intention to cause really serious harm was insufficient for attempted murder. The court found, however, that this had been proved and that the statements made by the trial judge did not amount to a misdirection.

Hopefully, so far the position is clear; for an attempt to commit a crime, the *mens rea* required is intention, and intention only; recklessness or negligence will not suffice, even if these lesser degrees of *mens rea* will be sufficient to create liability for the completed offence. The *mens rea* of intention will therefore be required for attempted murder, attempted grievous bodily harm, attempted actual bodily harm, attempted common assault, attempted theft and attempted basic criminal damage. It is also clear from the Law Commission's report that it was envisaged that intention had to be proved in all criminal attempts and with regard to all aspects of the offence. Unfortunately for the law student, however, the position is not as simple as this in a limited number of crimes, such as attempted rape and attempted arson.

Crimes where intention is not required for all the aspects of the offence

With certain offences, intention still has to be proved with regard to the actual conduct, but a lesser degree of blameworthiness, i.e. recklessness, may suffice in relation to the circumstances in which the crime was committed. In the offence of attempted rape, for example, the prosecution still has to prove that the defendant intended to have sexual intercourse with the victim. In relation to the issue of whether this was against her wishes, however, the courts have decided that it is enough for the prosecution to prove that the defendant was reckless as to whether the victim consented or not. Similarly, with the crime of attempted arson, it needs to be proved that the defendant intended to cause criminal damage by fire but, once this has been established, he can be found guilty if he was merely reckless as to whether life would be endangered. It does not have to be shown that he intended to endanger life. These exceptions are best explained by looking at the cases of *Khan 1990* and *AG's Reference (No. 3 of 1992) 1993*.

In *Khan & Others 1990*, a 16-year-old girl had gone to a house with five boys after a visit to a disco and other boys had joined them. It was alleged that three of the boys had raped the girl and that four others, the defendants in this case, had attempted to do so.

The defendants had been convicted of attempted rape but claimed that the judge had misdirected the jury on the *mens rea* required for this offence. They said that it had not been proved that they had intended to commit all aspects of the offence. They agreed that they had intended to have intercourse with the victim, but argued that they thought that the girl was consenting.

The Court of Appeal decided that the *mens rea* necessary for attempted rape was the same for the complete offence:

> namely an intention to have intercourse plus knowledge of or recklessness as to the woman's absence of consent. No question of attempting to achieve a reckless state of mind arises; the attempt relates to the physical activity; the mental state of the defendant is the same.

The court believed that this interpretation of the law was desirable because it 'did not require the jury to be burdened with different directions as to the accused's state of mind, dependant on whether the individual achieved or failed to achieve sexual intercourse'.

The same approach was taken and expanded upon in *AG's Reference (No. 3 of 1992) 1994*. The offence in question was attempted arson, being reckless whether life be endangered under s.1(2) Criminal Damage Act 1971. The defendants had been acquitted because the judge had ruled that, on a charge of attempt, intent to endanger life was required; recklessness was not sufficient. The Court of Appeal, however, decided that this was wrong and said that it was enough for the defendants to be in one of the states of mind required for the commission of the full offence.

To sum up, therefore, the *mens rea* of attempt is intention in relation to committing the actual crime but, in certain limited circumstances, recklessness will suffice with regard to the circumstances in which the crime is committed, provided that the full offence allows this lesser degree of *mens rea*.

Attempting to commit the impossible

Before leaving the subject of *mens rea*, it has to be decided whether a person can be guilty of an attempt to commit a crime, even though the crime itself is, for some reason, impossible to commit. Examples of this could occur where a gang member attempts to shoot and kill an informer while he is asleep in his bed but, unbeknown to him, another gang member has already strangled the man. Alternatively, a wrongdoer might be attempting to smuggle 50 crates of whisky into the country but the plan has been discovered and the bottles now contain cold tea. The question that needs to be asked is whether such people could be convicted with attempting to commit a crime because, as has been noted, the crime itself is now impossible. The House of Lords has made it clear that the answer to this question is 'yes' but, over the last two decades, the decisions of

COMMENT

One can see why the Court of Appeal was reluctant to see the offenders go unpunished in the situations described in the previous two cases. It has to be admitted, however, that the two decisions have 'muddied the waters' considerably and made the law very uncertain regarding the *mens rea* of attempt. In respect of the offences of rape and aggravated arson at least, the court appears to have changed that which has been clearly laid down by Parliament. With regard to other crimes, the courts have been definite in their opinion that intention only will suffice so, at present, a two-tier system operates which is extremely difficult for juries (and students!) to understand and will surely lead to further appeals.

One solution would be for Parliament to make it clear that the *mens rea* required for an attempt should be the same as for the full offence. Another would be for the House of Lords to overrule the decisions in *Khan* and the *Reference* and state that intention is needed for all aspects of every offence. This, however, is unlikely to happen. After the appeal in *Khan* was dismissed, the Appeal Committee of the House of Lords rejected the defendants' application to appeal to that House, thereby tacitly agreeing with the decision of the lower court. The third way is to accept the different treatment for these crimes. The Law Commission was originally in favour of demanding intention for all the aspects of a crime but came to believe that this approach was too narrow and now agrees with the changes effected by case law.

that court have swung alarmingly from one view to the other on this subject.

In *Haughton* v *Smith 1975*, which was decided before the law on attempts was put into statutory form, the police seized a quantity of stolen corned beef but allowed the lorry to continue on its journey under the control of a disguised policeman. At the end of its route, the people unloading the consignment were arrested and later convicted of attempting to handle stolen goods. The case reached the highest appeal court where their Lordships decided that the conviction for attempt could not be sustained if the crime itself was not possible.

The Criminal Attempts Act 1981 clearly intended to reverse such decisions. S.1(2) states that

A person may be guilty of attempting to commit an offence to which this section applies even though the facts are such that the commission of the offence is impossible.

Despite this plain wording, however, the House of Lords again quashed a conviction, this time in the case of *Anderton* v *Ryan 1985*.

Mrs Ryan had confessed that she had bought a video cassette recorder for £110 in the belief that it was a stolen one and was charged with both handling and attempted handling of stolen goods. In the event, the prosecution did not believe that it would be able to establish that the goods had been stolen, so the first charge was dropped and only the attempted handling charge pursued. The magistrates refused to convict but the Divisional Court supported the prosecution's appeal on the point of law. The House of Lords quashed the conviction, obviously believing that it would be unjust to find liability in a case such as this, despite what was laid down in s.1(3).

In *Shivpuri 1987*, the House of Lords overruled this decision, made less than two years earlier. The defendant had been arrested by customs officials on his return from a visit to India. While there, he had been approached by a dealer in drugs who had offered him £1000 to take control of a suitcase in Cambridge, the contents of which he was later to distribute to others. He believed that the drugs were either heroin or cannabis. He was later arrested in Southall, London, as he handed over a packet to a third party. This packet and the others in the lining of his suitcase were found to contain a harmless vegetable matter like snuff, not harmful drugs. The defendant argued, therefore, that his conviction for attempting to be knowingly concerned in dealing with a prohibited drug should be quashed on the grounds that the complete offence was impossible.

The case reached the House of Lords. The point of law on which that body was asked to decide was stated in the following, lengthy way: 'Does a person commit an offence under s.1 Criminal Attempts Act 1981 where, if the facts were as that person believed them to be, the full offence would have been committed by him, but where on the true facts of the offence which that person set out to commit was in law impossible, e.g. because the substance imported and believed to be heroin was not heroin but a harmless substance?'

The House of Lords decided that the answer was 'yes'.

Lord Bridge felt it was necessary to start with the Act itself (although he did not really explain why he had not taken that approach in Anderton!). He said it had to be decided whether the defendant had intended to receive, store and pass on to others packages of cannabis or heroin, to which the answer was clearly yes. It then had to be established whether he had done an act which was more than merely preparatory to the commission of the offence and, again, the answer was yes. Lastly, it had to be examined whether this act required anything further than this? S.1(2) indicates that the answer to this is no; the defendant, therefore, must be found guilty.

The learned judge then questioned whether this result could stand with the earlier decision in *Anderton* v *Ryan* and decided that it could not. His conclusion, therefore, was that *Anderton* v *Ryan* was wrongly decided and that he and his fellow judges 'fell into error' in their desire to avoid convicting Mrs Ryan and others in her situation. He was obviously influenced by the strong criticism of this ruling given by Professor Glanville Williams in the Criminal Law Journal in 1986. Lord Bridge stated ruefully 'The language in which he criticises the decision in *Anderton* v *Ryan* is not conspicuous for its mod-

KEY FACTS

- The law on attempts is in the Criminal Attempts Act 1981; the maximum punishment is the same as for the complete offence

- The *actus reus* exists where a party does an act which is more than merely preparatory. The jury will decide this issue but the conviction may be quashed if that body has not been directed properly on the matter or the acts cannot be said to be directly connected to the crime (*Gullefer 1990, Campbell 1991, Geddes 1996*)

- The mental element needed for the attempt is intention, which was said in *Mohan 1976* to mean a decision to bring about the commission of the offence whether or not it was desired

- With the crime of attempted murder, the word intention has the same meaning as in the complete offence (*Walker and Hayles 1990*)

- Recklessness about the actual commission of the offence is not normally enough (*Millard and Vernon 1987*)

- In attempted rape and attempted arson, however, although the offender must intend to commit the sexual intercourse or criminal damage, he may still be convicted if he is reckless about the woman's consent in the first instance or reckless about endangering life in the second situation (*Khan 1990, AG's Reference (No. 3 of 1992) 1994*)

- The House of Lords in *Shivpuri 1987* clearly affirmed s.1(2) Criminal Attempts Act and upheld that it is possible to be convicted of attempting to commit a crime, even though the actual offence may not have been possible

- It is not possible to attempt to conspire, to aid, abet counsel or procure or to attempt to assist an offender after the commission of a crime

FIGURE 13.1 *Key facts chart on attempts*

eration, but it would be foolish, on that account, not to recognise the force of the criticism and churlish not to acknowledge the assistance I have derived from it'. Their Lordships unanimously decided to overrule *Anderton* v *Ryan*, using the rights given under the Practice Statement of 1966 to do so and dismissed the appeal in *Shivpuri*. The position is, at last, crystal clear; a person can be found guilty of attempt, even though the actual crime is impossible.

Before leaving the question of attempts, it is important to note that certain crimes cannot be attempted. These are attempting to conspire, attempting to aid, abet, counsel or procure and attempting to assist an offender after the commission of a crime.

13.3 CONSPIRACY

A conspiracy can be said to be an agreement between two or more people to do an unlawful act. Until the passing of the Criminal Law Act 1977, conspiracy was a common law offence and covered a wide range of activities, including a conspiracy to commit a tort such as trespass. The Law Commission believed that the offence should be confined to agreements to commit crimes but felt that certain areas of the law needed to be discussed more fully. When the Criminal Law Act was passed, therefore, two forms of common law conspiracy were retained for what was supposed to be an interim period. Over 20 years later, this position remains so the law on conspiracy is an uncomfortable mix of statute law and common law.

Three main forms of conspiracy need to be looked at. These are:

1 Conspiracy to commit a crime, an offence defined in the Criminal Law Act 1977.
2 Conspiracy to defraud, a common law offence.
3 Conspiracy to corrupt public morals or outrage public decency, also created at common law.

These offences need closer examination.

13.3.1 CONSPIRACY TO COMMIT A CRIME

As stated, this offence is to be found in the Criminal Law Act 1977, as amended by the Criminal Attempts Act 1981 and the Criminal Justice Act 1987.

The wording of the sections, together with the later insertions, is very complicated so a summary of their main effect is given instead of reproducing them. S.1 states that the offence of conspiracy to commit a crime will take place when a person agrees with another person or persons to pursue a course of conduct which, if carried out, will amount to or involve the commission of an offence, or would do so if something had not happened making the offence impossible to commit.

Conspiracies to commit a crime are often known as s.1 conspiracies. The punishment is laid down in s.3 but this, too is complicated. In cases of murder and other very serious crimes, the maximum is life imprisonment; in other cases punishable by imprisonment, the maximum sentence should not exceed the maximum for the main offence.

The *actus reus* of conspiracy to commit a crime is satisfied if the party agrees with another or several others to pursue a course of conduct which, if carried out will amount to or involve the commission of an offence. There must, therefore, be some form of agreement about the course of conduct to be pursued, although, if several people are involved it is only necessary for the offender to have agreed with one of them, provided that this is not a spouse or a child or the intended victim. In *Chrastny 1991*, the defendant tried to argue that she had only discussed the matter of supplying Class A drugs with her husband. The Court of Appeal, however, rejected her appeal, as she had known that other conspirators were involved in the plan. It would have been different if she had been completely unaware of the involvement of others.

When looking at the position relating to the *mens rea* required for conspiracy, the Law Commission made it clear that there should only be liability if the defendant intended to commit the offence. The Bill introduced into Parliament originally stated that the defendant and his fellow conspirators 'must intend to bring about any consequence which is an element of the offence'. Unfortunately, this clause was deleted from the statute because the whole phrase, of which this was only a part, was felt to be too complicated. Instead, intention can be implied from the wording of s.1(1), when it states that a person must agree with another to pursue a course of conduct. S.1(2) also states that, in cases where the full offence can be committed without the offender having knowledge of any particular fact or circumstance necessary for the commission of the offence, such a person cannot be found guilty of conspiracy unless 'he and at least one other party to the agreement intend or know that the fact or circumstance shall or will exist at the time when the conduct constituting the offence is to take place'. This means that even in cases where recklessness, negligence or strict liability suffices for the complete offence or a part of it, this is not enough for conspiracy to commit such crimes; here, an intention must be proved. Situations like *Khan*, where recklessness about the girl's consent was sufficient for liability under the law of attempts, are not permitted where the crime of conspiracy is involved.

Given these statements of the law, therefore, it is very surprising to note the comments of the House of Lords in *Anderson 1986*. There must be something about these similar-sounding names which stimulates that House to change the accepted law, as the cases of *Morris*, *Anderton* v *Burnside 1984*, *Anderton* v *Ryan 1985* and now *Anderson 1986* illustrate!

In *Anderson 1986*, the defendant, while in Lewes prison, had agreed, in return for payment, to help a temporary cellmate, who faced very serious charges, to effect an escape from prison. The prisoner's brother and another man were also involved. After his release, therefore, Anderson had provided some diamond wire but was then involved in a car accident and took no further part in the plan. He tried to argue that he did not possess the *mens rea* for conspiracy. He claimed that he had never intended for the agreement to go ahead and had never believed that it could succeed. He stated that, instead of giving any additional help, he was going to go abroad with the money paid up-front. The House of Lords dismissed his appeal against conviction but the reasoning of Lord Bridge when reaching such a decision has been seriously questioned.

The point of law for their Lordships to consider was whether a person who agreed with others to pursue a course of conduct which they intended to carry through and he did not, could be found guilty of conspiracy. Lord Bridge decided firmly that he could and that he need not intend that the agreed plan should be carried out. He agreed that:

> an essential ingredient in the crime of conspiracy . . . under s.1(1) of the Act of 1977, is that the accused should agree that a course of conduct be pursued which he knows must involve the commission by one or more of parties to the agreement of that offence. [He went on to reject, however] any construction of the statutory language which would require the prosecution to prove an intention on the part of each conspirator that the criminal offence . . . should in fact be committed.

This view of the law ensured that Anderson's conviction could be upheld. It also makes it easier for the prosecution to convict those who only play a subordinate role in the planning of a crime and who do not really care whether or not the offence is carried out, so long as they are paid for their part in the proceedings. It has, however, been sharply criticised by academics. The wording of s.1(1) seems to imply that the defendant must have an intention to pursue the course of conduct which, if carried out would amount to or involve the commission of an offence. In addition, s.1(2) specifically demands that the offender must be shown to have knowledge or intention, before being convicted of conspiracy to commit certain crimes, such as strict liability offences and ones for which recklessness might suffice for the full offence. It would, therefore, be extremely odd if intention were required for these offences but not for all the others where a higher degree of *mens rea* is needed for the complete offence.

Anderson was distinguished on this point by the Court of Appeal in Northern Ireland, in the case of *McPhillips 1990*, where the defendant was found not guilty of conspiracy to murder. His conviction was quashed because it was believed that he had intended to give a warning that a bomb was primed to go off at a disco at 1am, the busiest part of the night, while the other conspirators had not.

If the statements mentioned above in *Anderson* had been followed, it would have been immaterial that McPhillips did not intend the crime to go ahead. The court, however, seized on another part of Lord Bridge's judgment, where he suggested that special consideration should be given to honest citizens who might find themselves caught up in a conspiracy and feel obliged, for a time, to go along with the plot. The court conveniently overlooked the fact that McPhillips was far from innocent in other respects and had definitely been involved in the criminal activities.

Lord Bridge's *dicta* that a conspirator may still be found guilty when he does not intend that the crime should be committed, was also ignored in *Edwards 1991*. There was a conspiracy to supply amphetamine, an illegal drug, but there was some doubt as to whether the defendant intended to supply another drug instead, which was not illegal. The Court of Appeal held that a direction by the trial judge that the defendant could only be convicted if he intended to supply amphetamines was held to be correct. If *Anderson* had been followed, a different answer would have been given.

Another part of Lord Bridge's judgment that has also given rise to problems was his contention that the defendant is only guilty of conspiracy if he intended to play some part in the proceedings.

Professor John Smith calls this 'a novel dictum' and notes that it is unsupported by authority. It also creates a loophole through which many offenders could escape, especially ringleaders, and others in a similar position, who organise events and then leave it to others to carry out the 'dirty work'. In *Siracusa 1990*, the Court of Appeal decided to address the issue, even though it was not directly pertinent to the appeal the court was hearing. The court decided in this drug smuggling case that participation in a conspiracy may be passive as well as active. The judges also stated that Lord Bridge could not have meant what he said! O'Connell L J remarked 'We think it obvious that Lord Bridge cannot have been intending that the organiser of a crime who recruited others to carry it out would not himself be guilty of conspiracy unless it could be proved that he intended to play some part himself'. Be that as it may, there is no getting away from the fact that he did clearly state that the necessary *mens rea* would only be established if 'the accused, when he entered into the agreement, intended to play some part in the agreed course of conduct in furtherance of the criminal purpose ...'. The appeal court did, however, make it clear that, to secure a conviction, the right charge must be brought. If an offender is alleged to have conspired to import heroin,

▼ COMMENT

It can be seen that the Court of Appeal has been making valiant efforts to limit the effect of these two statements by Lord Bridge and, that, so far, their attempts to do this have gone unchallenged and may be said to represent the law as it currently stands. It might have been clearer if the Court of Appeal had stated that Lord Bridge's second statement was merely *obiter* and that the court did not feel able to follow it. This might have lessened the likelihood of further appeals on this subject in the future.

then that is what must be proved, not that he imported cannabis; if another drug is involved, this should be stated instead or as an additional charge.

13.3.2 CONSPIRACY AT COMMON LAW

The first point to note is that s.5 Criminal Law Act 1977 states that, subject to certain listed exceptions, the offence of common law conspiracy is abolished.

The exceptions laid down are conspiracy to defraud, (s.5(2)) and conspiracy to corrupt public morals or outrage public decency, (s.5(3)).

Conspiracy to defraud

Reforms of this area of law has been promised for decades. The Criminal Law Act specifically retained it as a common law offence, while abolishing most other forms of common law conspiracy, in anticipation of fairly early reform. This never materialised; instead, in 1994, the Law Commission decided that a comprehensive review of the whole law of dishonesty was necessary. This will, of course, include the offence of conspiracy to defraud. In the meantime, however, it remains as a common law offence, along with conspiracy to corrupt public morals and outrage public decency.

Conspiracy to defraud acts as a safety net to ensure that certain offenders do not escape punishment, which, as seen in s.12 Criminal Law Act 1977, can be up to a maximum of ten years imprisonment. If there is a conspiracy to commit a substantive offence, the common law offence of conspiracy to defraud will not be normally be needed because conspiracy under s.1 of the Criminal Law Act 1977 can be charged. Common law conspiracy is, however, useful in the following situations: where the prosecution finds it difficult to establish any deception, where the fraud is not directly inflicted and in cases where no loss has been caused to the party defrauded.

In *Scott* v *MPC 1975*, the defendants had persuaded employees of a cinema to make copies of films without the permission of the owners which they then intended to show for a profit. The House of Lords upheld the conviction for conspiracy to defraud, claiming that it was enough that dishonesty and injury to the interests of another had been established. Their Lordships made it clear that there was no additional requirement to show that a deception had been practised.

The House of Lords was again involved in the case of *Hollinshead 1985*. The defendants manufactured devices which, when fitted, caused electricity meters to under record the amount of electricity used. They tried to argue that they were not guilty of conspiracy to defraud because they had not been involved in any agreement to use the boxes; they had merely sold them to a middle-man.

The House of Lords upheld the convictions, stating that it was enough that the defendants had arranged to put the boxes into circulation for the sole purpose of causing loss to the electricity boards.

In both the cases mentioned above, actual loss would have resulted from the conspiracy. The House of Lords had, however, already made it clear in *Welham* v *DPP 1961* that it is not always necessary, in the offence of conspiracy to defraud, to show that another party has suffered loss, so long as an intention to defraud is apparent. Examples cited included cases where the conspiracy to defraud was against a public authority or the holder of a public office and where a drug addict forged a doctor's certificate to obtain drugs from a chemist.

In *Moses and Ansbro 1991*, the defendants had unlawfully helped immigrants to obtain work permits to which they were not entitled. The Court of Appeal decided that there was a clear conspiracy to defraud; the defendants were acting dishonestly and contrary to their public duty. There was no additional need to show that economic loss had been caused by their actions.

Similarly, in *Wai Yu-Tsang 1992*, the Privy Council upheld a conviction for conspiracy where the defendant had agreed with others not to enter certain dishonoured cheques in the records of a bank in order to help safeguard the bank's reputation. The judges decided that the term 'conspiracy to defraud' should be given a wide meaning; it was enough if there was 'simply an intention to practise fraud on another or an intention to act to the prejudice of another man's right'.

The *actus reus* of conspiracy to defraud could be said to be an agreement between two or more people to bring about an unlawful object. The *mens rea* would be satisfied if this was done intentionally, even if this was for a benign purpose, as confirmed in the above case.

S.5 Criminal Law Act 1977, as amended, provides that either statutory conspiracy or conspiracy to defraud can be charged if there is any overlap between the two.

Conspiracy to corrupt public morals or outrage public decency

The re-emergence of this type of common law conspiracy caused disquiet among some academics. This was mainly due to certain comments uttered by the House of Lords in the case of *Shaw v DPP 1962*, which seemed to suggest that these top judges had the power to watch over the nation's morals and adapt the law for this purpose. When one looks at the material currently available in magazines, on late-night television and on the Internet, one can see that they were largely unsuccessful in holding back the tide of change.

The defendant had been convicted of the crime of conspiracy to corrupt public morals after he had published a magazine called the *Ladies' Directory*, in which the names and addresses of prostitutes were listed. He had fallen foul of the law because, in some instances, the names were accompanied by photographs of the women, together with the details of the sexual perversions they practised.

The House of Lords upheld the view of the Court of Criminal Appeal that a substantive offence of corrupting public morals did, in fact, exist and affirmed that it was therefore possible to conspire to commit this offence. Shaw's conviction was upheld.

It was the speech of Lord Simons that caused the furore. He suggested that the courts not only had the duty to uphold the law but also the power to conserve the moral welfare of the State. He claimed that it was their duty 'to guard it against attacks which may be the more insidious because they are novel and unprepared for'.

In *Knuller v DPP 1973*, the House of Lords was invited to overrule its decision in *Shaw*. Not only did their Lordships refuse to do this, they confirmed that there was also a common law offence of outraging public decency and that therefore it was possible to conspire with others to commit this crime.

The defendant in *Knuller* had been involved in the publication of a magazine alleged to be of interest to those holding 'progressive views'. The offending advertisements contained details of homosexual men who were obviously hoping to attract responses from like-minded people. The charge claimed that this material encouraged the readers 'to indulge in such practices, with intent thereby to debauch and corrupt' their morals.

Lord Simon denied that the judges have the right to create new criminal offences; that, he said, was a matter for Parliament. He decided that what they could do was to ascertain whether there were any existing offences that might cover the matter in question. If this were the case, they could then apply that law to the new circumstances. After reviewing the authorities, he decided that there was indeed an existing offence of outraging public decency and a corresponding one of conspiring to do this. He believed, however, that the latter offence should only be invoked in exceptional circumstances. He stated that the word 'outrage' was a very strong word and 'goes considerably beyond offending the susceptibilities of, or even shocking, reasonable people'. He acknowledged that standards are constantly changing and said that the jury should be reminded that we live in a multi-faceted society with a good record of tolerance for minority views.

In this particular case, therefore, although the existing offences relating to outraging public decency were recognised and upheld, the actual conviction was quashed because the behaviour in question did not satisfy the definition of the word 'outrage'.

The Court of Appeal decided that there was sufficient outrage in the case of *Gibson 1990* and upheld the conviction of an artist for the substantive offence of outraging public decency.

Gibson had displayed examples of his work in a gallery to which the public had free access. One of the exhibits was a pair of earrings, each of which had been made from a freeze-dried human foetus of three or four months. The court obviously believed that most members of the public would find such material offensive. It was also decided that the prosecution did not have to prove that the defendant intended to outrage public decency; all that was necessary was to prove that the publication or display was deliberate.

13.3.3 CONSPIRING TO COMMIT THE IMPOSSIBLE

S.1 Criminal Law Act 1977 makes it clear that a statutory conspiracy can take place even though the full offence is impossible. It is believed that, after the case of *Shivpuri*, relating to attempts, similar rules would also be applied to common law conspiracies if the matter came up.

13.3.4 CONSPIRACIES WHERE A FOREIGN ELEMENT IS INVOLVED

The last point to be considered relating to conspiracies is the position where the conspiring is done abroad but the crime is to be committed in England. It will obviously be of great advantage if the enforcers of law and order can act as soon as possible to prevent the crime taking place. The courts have done their best to help this process.

In *DPP* v *Doot 1973*, the House of Lords held that a conspiracy may, in some circumstances, be a continuing process. Where, there-

fore, an unlawful arrangement was made abroad to import cannabis into the UK, it was decided that the all the conspirators could be charged with the offence when one of their group landed in England. Their Lordships stated that:

> A conspiracy does not end with the making of the agreement. It will continue so long as there are two or more parties to it intending to carry out the design.

This very useful interpretation enabled the conspiracy to be thwarted and the crime prevented.

In *Liangsiriprasert* v *Government of the USA 1991*, the Privy Council took this reasoning a stage further and decided that even if an overt act like the above could not be proved, it was still possible to decide that a conspiracy existed. The court argued that:

> The only purpose of looking for an overt act in England in the case of a conspiracy entered into abroad, can be to establish the link between the conspiracy and England or possibly to show that the conspiracy is continuing. But if this can be established by other evidence, for example the taping of conversations between the conspirators showing a firm agreement to commit the crime at some future date, it defeats the preventative purpose of the crime of conspiracy to have to wait until some overt act is performed.

The Court of Appeal approved of this extension in *Samson 1991*.

In the cases just mentioned, the arrangement made abroad had to involve conduct which amounts to a crime in this country, otherwise no liability existed. S.1(4) Criminal Law Act 1977 makes this very clear. Amendments to the Act, however, also allow a person to be charged with conspiracy if acts are done in this country in preparation for a crime to be committed abroad. S.1A refers. In addition, the Sexual Offences (Conspiracy and Incitement) Act 1996 extends liability for conspiracy to paedophiles who conspire in this country to commit unlawful sexual acts outside the UK.

13.4 INCITEMENT

This is the last of the inchoate offences and is mainly a common law offence, although there are some specific offences of incitement which have been put in statutory form. Examples are inciting a person to commit murder, inciting others to mutiny or inciting racial hatred. The following newspaper article shows that a provocative adver-

---

KEY FACTS

- The rules relating to conspiracy to commit a crime are laid down in the Criminal Law Act 1977. S.1(1) defines the offence
- The *actus reus* is agreeing with another or others that a course of conduct will be pursued, which if carried out in accordance with their instructions, will necessarily amount to the commission of an offence (or would do so if the crime was not impossible)
- From the rather obscure wording of the statute, it appears that the defendant must intend that the offence should be carried out, but the House of Lords in *Anderson 1986* decided that the defendant was guilty even when this was not established. The Court of Appeal, however, did not follow this reasoning, in either *McPhillips 1990* or *Edwards 1991* so the law on this point is far from clear
- In *Anderson*, the House of Lords also stated, *obiter*, that the alleged conspirator must have intended to play some part in the commission of the offence. The Court of Appeal in *Siracusa 1990* decided that the House of Lords did not really mean to state this! The law on this point also remains uncertain. Academics appear to favour the view of the Court of Appeal on these issues
- The common law offences of conspiracy to defraud, and conspiracy to corrupt public morals and outrage public decency, have been specifically retained by s.5 Criminal Law Act 1977, although all other common law conspiracies were abolished by that act
- The term 'conspiracy to defraud' is given a broad meaning. The offence may be committed even when the motives of the perpetrators of the fraud are not necessarily bad (*Wai Yu-Tsang* v *The Queen 1992*). It may also arise in cases where there is no deception (*Scott 1975*), or no financial loss (*Welham 1961, Moses and Ansbro 1991*), or even where there is no direct link with the person who might commit the crime (*Hollinshead 1985*)
- The maximum punishment is ten years imprisonment
- The House of Lords has confirmed that the common law offences of corrupting public morals and outraging public decency do still exist and, therefore, so do the corresponding offences of conspiring to do these things (*Shaw* v *DPP 1962, Knuller 1973*)
- It was made clear by the Lords, however, that it has no residuary power to create new criminal offences and also that the offences of outraging public decency and conspiring to do this should be reserved for really offensive cases. The Court of Appeal in *Gibson 1990* felt that the display of a freeze-dried foetus made into an earring was such an example
- The Court of Appeal decided in the same case that it is unnecessary to prove that the defendant had the intention to outrage public decency, so long as his publication of the material was deliberate

FIGURE 13.2 *Key facts chart on conspiracy*

Shock posters send police on the trail of race commission

THE Commission for Racial Equality is being investigated by police for inciting racial hatred after a deliberately provocative advertising campaign depicting black people as rapists and orang-utans spectacularly backfired.

The blatantly offensive advertisements, part of new CRE "shock tactics" to highlight racism in society, were posted on 192 billboards across the country on Wednesday and Thursday of last week.

They gave no clue of the body's involvement and were intended as a "tease" to provoke complaints and test the strength of anti-racist feelings in society.

But the ruse rebounded on the commission when Avon and Somerset Police threatened the organisation with prosecution under the Race Relations Act — the same legislation used to create it in 1976.

Officers on duty in Bristol on Friday complained to their superiors after seeing the adverts in the city centre.

The force ordered the company responsible for the billboards to cover the adverts with blank paper. A file is to be sent to the Crown Prosecution Service. Explanatory adverts intended to replace the originals have also been banned in the constabulary's area.

The Advertising Standards Authority, which had received more than 30 complaints by yesterday, has begun its own inquiry.

The CRE could have the embarrassment of being the first body to have its adverts vetted under new agreements with the poster industry.

The posters were purporting to promote companies and products. One, for the TDX-5 rape alarm, shows a white woman sitting on the top deck of a bus anxiously eyeing a young black man in the foreground. The accompanying slogan reads: "Because it's a jungle out there."

Another, for a sports footwear manufacturer, shows a black man jumping to "slam-dunk" a basketball through a hoop. Next to him is an orang-utan in the same pose reaching for a branch. The caption reads: "Born to be agile".

The third poster, for a recruitment company, depicts two businessmen climbing a ladder, one black and one white. The white man is treading on the hand of the black man with the caption reading: 'Dominate the Race."

The CRE received 52 complaints, while the Advertising Standards Authority received more than 30. People who called the phone number on the adverts were met with a recorded message that gave no indication that they were dealing with the CRE.

Yesterday, the commission remained unapologetic about the campaign and said it would continue with the second "reveal" phase with the caption: "What was worse? This advert or your failure to complain?" beside smaller versions of the originals.

Taken from an article by Neil Tweedie in the *Daily Telegraph*, 22 September 1998. © Telegraph Group Limited, London, 1998.

tisement by the Commission for Racial Equality itself backfired on the Commission and could result in charges being brought.

The remaining part of this chapter will examine common law incitement. The current position is that incitement to commit a summary offence is only triable summarily, whereas an incitement to commit an indictable offence is triable on indictment. This might seem obvious but it was not always the law. An odd feature of the law which does remain is that, while the punishment for an incitement to commit a summary offence cannot exceed that given for the full offence, the courts have the discretion to set the punishment when the offence is tried on incitement. This means that, theoretically at least, the inciter could receive a higher sentence than the person committing the offence.

13.4.1 THE MEANING OF INCITEMENT

Incitement occurs when a person urges another to commit a crime or 'reaches or seeks to influence the mind of another'. The courts have decided that incitement can be effected by suggestion, argument, persuasion and, as stated in *Race Relations Board* v *Applin 1973*, even by threats or other pressure. Incitement will often be verbal but it is possible to put the words in writing and thereby incite members of the public. In the early case of *Most 1881*, the incitement seemed obvious when the defendants urged certain members of the community to rise up and assassinate the heads of state. In *Invicta Plastics Ltd* v *Clare 1976*, however, the conviction of the defendant company was also upheld when they merely put an advertisement in a motoring magazine drawing attention to their product called Radatec, an instrument which could be used to help evade police speed traps.

The Divisional Court held that, when looking at the advertisement as a whole, there was clear evidence of incitement.

The incitement does not have to be successful but it must be shown that there was incitement to commit an actual offence known to law. In *Whitehouse 1977*, a loophole was disclosed when a man was accused of inciting a young girl of 15 to have incestuous intercourse with him. S.11 Sexual Offences Act 1956 states that it is an offence for a woman of 16 or over to permit her father and other close relatives to have sexual intercourse with her but under-age girls are not included. Therefore, Whitehouse could not be found guilty because he was being charged with inciting a girl to commit a crime which, under statute, she was incapable of committing. The court also held that he could not be liable for inciting his daughter to aid and abet him to have sexual intercourse with her! The judges were understandably reluctant to decide that young girls in these appalling situations should be tainted with the suggestion that they, also, have done wrong. The case of *Tyrrell 1894*, which decided that victims like this should not be held liable for aiding and abetting the commission of a criminal offence, was cited with approval. The defendant, therefore, was found not guilty in the current case but the judges suggested that Parliament should step in and plug this loophole in the law. This was effected very speedily and s.54 Criminal Law Act 1977 lays down that it is an offence for a man to incite to have sexual intercourse with him a girl under the age of 16 whom he knows to be his grand-daughter, daughter or sister.

Another offender who escaped liability when he was obviously guilty of wrongdoing was *Curr*, a case decided in 1968. The defendant ran a highly lucrative business of advancing money to women with large families and in return taking their Family Allowance books to cover the debt, plus a large sum in interest. He handled between 40 and 80 such books a week and made a profit of around 800 per cent on the deals. He employed a team of women to cash the signed vouchers for him and was charged with inciting them to commit offences under the Family Allowances Act 1945. The crime that he was alleged to have incited was committed when a person received family allowance knowing that it was not properly payable or receivable by him or her. The Court of Appeal quashed the man's conviction, arguing that while it was obvious that the defendant knew that he was acting illegally, the prosecution also needed to establish that the women agents knew that they were committing a crime. This matter had not been properly put before the jury so the court felt obliged to quash the defendant's conviction for incitement of such an offence. He must have been laughing all the way back to the Post Office!

The team drafting the Criminal Code strongly criticised this decision, arguing that it was not necessary to prove that the person who was being incited had to know that an offence was being committed. It was felt to be enough that the defendant had such a belief. *Curr*, however, is a Court of Appeal decision that has not been overruled. It must, therefore, reflect the state of the law at the present time.

13.4.2 THE *MENS REA* OF INCITEMENT

It is necessary for the prosecution to prove that the defendant intended to bring about the criminal result and used persuasion or pressure to do this, although the offence incited need not actually take place. The early decision in *Higgins 1801* makes this position clear and the judges affirmed this in *Whitehouse 1977*. From the decision in *Curr 1968*, discussed above, the defendant must also believe that the person incited will have the necessary *mens rea* to commit the crime in question or, at least, another crime requiring the same *mens rea*. If he does not believe this, they could be in the position of innocent agents and he could be the principal offender, provided that he was charged correctly.

13.4.3 INCITEMENT OF CRIMES WHICH ARE IMPOSSIBLE TO COMMIT

The law on the subject of whether a person can be found guilty of incitement when the crime in question is impossible to commit is rather confused. Since the case of *Fitzmaurice 1983*, it is also out of line with the statutory position taken for the crimes of attempts and conspiracy to commit a crime.

In *McDonough 1962*, the defendant's conviction for inciting a number of butchers to handle stolen meat carcasses which he believed were in a cold store, was upheld. He tried to argue that his conviction should be quashed because, at that time, the carcasses were not, in fact, in that place and there was some doubt as to whether they had ever existed. The Court of Appeal held that the essence of the offence lay in his suggestion to the other parties that they should receive the meat that he believed was stolen.

The Law Commission felt that this was a sensible line to take and, with regard to attempts and conspiracy, Parliament made it clear when it passed the Criminal Attempts Act 1981 that the defendant may still be liable even if the actual offence is impossible.

The position with incitement, however, is now confused because of the later decision in *Fitzmaurice 1983*, which limited the cases where liability could still exist. The defendant was convicted of inciting three men to commit a 'wages snatch'. At his father's request, he had recruited the men allegedly to rob a woman walking from her workplace to the National Westminster Bank. In fact, the defendant's father had hatched a complicated plot to recover reward money by informing the authorities that there was an impending raid on a security van. He had therefore dissuaded his son from taking part but had arranged for him to assemble the gang. He then intended that they would be discovered outside the bank, wearing masks and carrying imitation firearms. The son was completely unaware of his father's plot but after it was discovered, he was charged with incitement.

He tried to argue that he could not be guilty of inciting the other men to commit a crime that could not, in fact, be committed. The Court of Appeal held that it was immaterial that the defendant's father was not planning a real offence at all because the defendant obviously believed that he was arranging for the men to commit a robbery in Bow and such an offence was not impossible to perform. The conviction, therefore, was upheld.

It can be seen therefore that, despite the upholding of the conviction, the judges have not decided that an offender can still be guilty of incitement even though the crime is impossible, as is now the case with attempts and statutory conspiracy. A far more limited rule has been laid down in relation to incitement. If the incitement is a specific one, such as inciting another to kill a third party when, in fact, that person is already dead, the inciter cannot be found guilty. If, however, the incitement is a more general one, as, for example, that the other wrongdoers should rob a woman carrying wages outside a bank in Bow, as was the case in *Fitzmaurice*, then the defence of impossibility would not prevail.

▼ **COMMENT**

It is difficult to understand why the Court of Appeal did not take this chance to put the law on incitement, in respect of crimes that are impossible to commit, on the same footing as attempts and conspiracy. It was clearly the intention of both the Law Commission and Parliament that the defence should not be available for any of the inchoate offences.

▼ **KEY FACTS**

- Incitement is a common law offence. If tried on indictment, the courts have the discretion to set the punishment
- The *actus reus* is committed when the offender suggests, urges, persuades, threatens or pressurises the other to commit a crime (*Race Relations Board* v *Applin 1973*). Incitement can be effected orally or in writing (*Most 1881*, *Invicta Plastics* v *Clare 1976*)
- The offender must be inciting the other to commit a crime known to law; if there is no such offence he cannot be found guilty (*Whitehouse 1977*). If the crime does exist, then it does not matter if the inciter is unsuccessful in his attempts to persuade the other to commit it
- The *mens rea* of incitement is an intention to bring about the required result, plus persuasion or pressure on the person targeted (*Hendrickson and Tichner 1977*)
- The controversial case of *Curr 1968* also decided that the person incited must have the *mens rea* to commit the offence in question. While this decision has been criticised, it has not been overruled
- *Fitzmaurice 1983* appears to have limited the previously wide interpretation of liability for incitement when the actual crime has been impossible to commit, as laid down in *McDonough 1962*. It now appears to be the law that the offender will only be guilty if the offence is a general crime that it might have been possible to commit. It is important to realise that this approach is at odds with the other inchoate offences where the Criminal Attempts Act 1981 specifically states that there can be liability to attempt to commit a crime that is impossible, or to conspire to do so

FIGURE 13.3 *Key facts chart on incitement*

13.5 SUGGESTED REFORM OF INCHOATE OFFENCES

It has been seen that a measure of reform of the law on conspiracy to commit a crime was effected by the Criminal Law Act 1977 and changes made to the law on attempts made in the Criminal Attempts Act 1981. Reform of the law of deception is under review and, within this, the law on conspiracy to defraud. The offence of incitement has not been subjected to such a degree of scrutiny. The Draft Code team did investigate whether to change the name of the offence but at that time, decided to retain it. Clause 47 of the Draft Code defines incitement. This states that a person will be guilty of incitement if: (a) he incites another to do or cause to be done an act or acts which if done, will involve the commission of the offence or offences by the other; and (b) he intends or believes that the other, if he acts as incited, shall or will do so with the fault required for the offence or offences.

Clause 50 of the Code, if ever enacted, provides for a common approach to be taken with regard to impossibility. It states that: a person may be guilty of incitement, conspiracy or attempt to commit an offence although the commission of the offence is impossible, if it would be possible in the circumstances which he believes or hopes exist or will exist at the relevant time.

As noted under Chapter 11, however, the Law Commission is now in favour of abolishing the crime of incitement altogether and is, instead, in favour of creating two new inchoate offences of assisting and encouraging crime.

activity

Decide whether the following wrongdoers may be charged with an inchoate offence, giving full reasons for your answers:

Pablo, Gustav and Salvador met to enjoy their weekly drink together and discussed the possibility of stealing the Crown Jewels. Salvador, a glass merchant, promised to provide the equipment to cut the glass behind which the jewels are kept. Unbeknown to the friends, their conversation was taped and they were arrested. Salvador claimed that he had never intended to take part in the crime itself and had never really believed that it was going to take place.

Vincent decided that shock tactics were needed if ever his work was to attract the attention of art critics. He therefore created a sculpture made up of dead hedgehogs which had been killed by passing motorists! He then displayed this in the centre of his free one-man exhibition at the local Town Hall.

Claude was at a racing track. The horse he had backed, called Monet's Folly, was trailing at the back of the field. Claude fired an air

pistol close to the track, trying to distract the leading horses. He was hoping to get the race called off and thereby retrieve his stake money. His plan failed miserably and he was later charged with attempted theft.

Jacques is a student activist, who fiercely opposes the contraction of art courses at Chagall University. He placed an advertisement in the *Student Quarterly Review* urging students to rise up and kill the Chancellor. The Chancellor, however, is aware of the strength of feeling that his reforms have engendered and has employed a team of bodyguards to keep a 24-hour watch over him.

summary

We have learned that, in cases where the full crime has not taken place or where the prosecution could experience difficulties in proving it, it might be possible for the offender to be charged, instead, with an inchoate offence. These offences are attempt, conspiracy and incitement.

We have discovered that the law on attempts and on conspiracy to commit a crime is in statutory form, whereas the offences of incitement, conspiracy to defraud and conspiracy to corrupt public morals or outrage public decency are still common law crimes.

We have seen that there is a lack of consistency between the two areas, particularly with regard to crimes that are impossible to commit.

It should also have been noted that the Law Commission has suggested that the offence of incitement should be abolished, along with liability for aiding, abetting, counselling and procuring and that at least two new inchoate offences, those of assisting and encouraging crime, should be created in their place, plus, perhaps, a more limited offence of procuring. At present, however, the rather unsatisfactory state of the law in this area remains.

CHAPTER 14

VICARIOUS AND CORPORATE LIABILITY

14.1 INTRODUCTION

THIS CHAPTER BEGINS by looking at the principle of vicarious liability and explains how this operates under criminal law; it then moves on to discuss the liability of corporations. It will be seen that there have been calls to extend the criminal liability of companies in the light of several well-publicised disasters and we need to see whether the proposals to do this are workable and fair.

14.2 VICARIOUS LIABILITY

Under the principle of vicarious liability a person or company may be held liable for the criminal acts of another. The principle is far more common in civil law under the law of tort, where one of the most notable examples is the liability of an employer for the acts of his employees, provided that these are committed in the course of his employment. Such liability can be found to exist, even where the employee is doing something to which the employer would obviously not agree. An illustration of this can be seen in the case of *Lloyd* v *Grace Smith and Co 1912*, where a fraudulent solicitor's clerk induced a widow to convey her property to him and he disposed of it for his own benefit. The employer was found to be liable.

Under criminal law, however, liability for the acts of another is naturally more strictly contained. The firm of solicitors mentioned above was not prosecuted; it was only sued under civil law principles for compensation and most people would feel that this is a best way to deal with such a matter. The same restrictive view was taken in the early case of *Huggins 1730*. The defendant was the warden of the Fleet prison in London and had been charged with the murder of a prisoner. The prisoner had died after being imprisoned in an unhealthy cell. Huggins was held to be unaware of this fact so therefore escaped liability, even though his employee was found guilty. The judge made it clear that there were important differences in the way the principle should be used in civil law and criminal law. In the latter instance, he stated that the parties 'must each answer for their own acts, and stand or fall by their own behaviour'. Over the years, however, the strength of this statement has been diluted and, in limited circumstances, it has been felt to be right to impose criminal liability on a party even though the acts in question have been committed by someone else. In this chapter we shall discover when such action is deemed appropriate but, before this is examined, the differences between vicarious liability and strict liability need to be stressed.

14.2.1 THE DIFFERENCES BETWEEN STRICT AND VICARIOUS LIABILITY

It was noted in Chapter 2 that many statutes

impose strict liability on a party. The offender may well be liable, even though he had no intention to commit the crime of which he is accused, was not reckless as to whether it was committed and may even have taken all possible care to ensure that it was not committed. The liability in such a case is imposed on the offender, often a company, for something that body is alleged to have done, i.e. liability is imposed for its own acts or omissions. Under the principle of vicarious liability, the offender is liable, not for his own acts, but for the criminal acts of another. In practice, there may be little difference in the effect. For example a company may be prosecuted for polluting a river because a statute makes the company strictly liable if such pollution takes place. Under the principle of vicarious liability, the company may also be found guilty along with an employee, if the latter has been charged personally with the crime. For one of the reasons described below, it may be felt that the company should also stand trial along with the employee for that person's acts. It will be seen that, under the principle of vicarious liability, the company could be liable in some circumstances even where *mens rea* has to be shown for the offence in question, although these instances are restricted. Again, these will be described below.

14.2.2 THE OPERATION OF VICARIOUS LIABILITY IN CRIMINAL LAW

As stated, the principle of vicarious liability under criminal law is more restrictive in its operation than in the law of tort. Under criminal law, such liability is only imposed in specific instances. These occur if a statute expressly lays down such liability, where the acts of an agent are held to be the acts of another, or where the delegation principle is held to apply. These three situations need to be looked in turn although it should be noted that there is a large measure of overlap between the first two.

Where a statute lays this down

Such statutes are usually of a regulatory nature. If they impose a legal duty on a person or, more often, a company, that body will be liable along with the person charged if the company has failed to ensure that the duty has been performed or obeyed in the way required. In *Mousell Bros Ltd* v *London and North Western Railway Co. 1917*, the court stated:

> while *prima facie* a principal is not to be made criminally responsible for the acts of his servants, yet the legislature may prohibit an act or enforce a duty in such words as to make the prohibition or the duty absolute; in which case the principal is liable if the act is in fact done by his servants.

Where the acts of the agent are held to be the acts of another

The case of the *Duke of Leinster 1924* illustrates this point well. The Duke was an undisclosed bankrupt who was convicted of obtaining credit without disclosing his true financial status. In fact it was his agent who had arranged for the credit, despite being instructed not to. The Duke was still held to be liable.

In many cases under this head, an employer is held liable for the actions of his employees. An example of this is the case of *Coppen* v *Moore (No. 2) 1898*, where the employer owned six shops and in one of them, a sales assistant had sold a ham, which she had described as 'a Scotch ham'. The employer had given clear instructions that the hams in his stores were to be described more generally as 'breakfast hams' but, despite this, he was convicted of selling goods to which a false trade description was applied. The court stated why he was liable 'It cannot be doubted that the appellant sold the ham in question, although the transaction was carried out by his servants. In other words he was the seller, although not the actual salesman'.

This approach is often used where the relevant statute uses the word 'sells' or 'keeps' or when the party is charged with 'presenting' a play even if he is far away at the time. The reasoning behind such a seemingly hard approach is to gain the conviction of the person thought to be the real culprit, even if this is only caused by his failure to employ suitable staff or to take sufficient care in the running of his business. In appropriate cases, therefore, the courts are prepared to extend the meaning of the statute in order to achieve this purpose.

The words of Morland J in *National Rivers Authority* v *Alfred McAlpine Homes (East) Ltd. 1994* help to illustrate why this approach was taken in one emotive area. The company was convicted after an appeal by the prosecution, of polluting a river, after employees of the company, who were constructing a water feature on the site, had discharged wet cement into it. The judge stated that:

> to make an offence an effective weapon in the defence of environmental protection, a company must by necessary implication be criminally liable for the acts or omissions of its servants or agents during activities being done for the company. I do not find that this affects our concept of a just or fair criminal justice system, having regard to the magnitude of environmental pollution.

There is obviously a limit to the lengths to which the courts will go when stretching the meaning of the words in the relevant statute in this way. The approach is obviously inappropriate where the wording denotes some activity by the offender that cannot realistically be imputed to the employer, such as the word 'drive'. In addition, it is felt that it should not be used where the statute uses words like 'knowingly'. It might be considered to be too great an extension to import the *mens rea* of the employee to the employer in these circumstances, although, as will be seen below, this is done under the

delegation principle. Under this head, however, it has been argued that the principle should be confined to offences of strict liability.

Where the delegation principle is said to apply

Use of such a principle can, on occasion, make a party liable even in cases where some form of *mens rea* is necessary for the commission of the offence. He will be liable even though he has delegated the duty to someone else, as in *Allen* v *Whitehead 1930*. The defendant, a licensee of a café, left the management of it to another and just visited it once a week. He was convicted under the quaintly worded section of the Metropolitan Police Act 1839 of 'knowingly permitting prostitutes or persons of notoriously bad character to meet on the premises'. He was found liable despite the fact that he had instructed his manager not to allow prostitutes to visit the café and had displayed notices to that effect!

The Divisional Court adopted such a rigid stance because it was felt that otherwise the statute would be completely ineffective, or 'rendered nugatory' as one judge put it. He went on to say 'This seems to me to be a case where the proprietor, the keeper to the house, had delegated his position to a manager so far as the conduct of the house was concerned; he had transferred to the manager the exercise of discretion in the conduct of the business, and it seems to me the only reasonable conclusion is, regard being had to the purpose of this Act, that knowledge in the manager was knowledge in the keeper of the house. I think, therefore, that this case ought to go back to the learned magistrate, with a direction to convict'.

This decision had its critics but was accepted in *Linnett* v *Metropolitan Police Commissioner 1946*, where a co-licensee was liable for permitting disorderly conduct on the premises even though he had delegated control to another. It came to be decided, however, that the principle only applied where there was a complete delegation by the owner or occupier. This appears, at first glance, to be an odd decision; one might assume that the opposite approach would have be taken and that the more the person remained in control, the more likely it would be that he was liable. When looked at more carefully, however, this interpretation ensures that an owner or occupier is not able to escape liability just because he absents himself from the premises. The principle can be used in cases where it might be difficult or non-productive to charge the actual offender. Be that as it may, this approach meant that owners were able to deny liability if they had not delegated the whole of their authority to another and the person committing the offence had acted without authority, like an employee in another part of the building.

The strangeness of this common law rule was examined by the House of Lords in the case of *Vane* v *Yiannopoullos 1964*, and reluctantly accepted as the correct view of the law. The owner of a restaurant had been charged with 'knowingly' supplying liquor to people who had not eaten in the restaurant, which contravened the terms of his licence. He was on one floor of the building and the waitress who had unlawfully sold the alcohol was on another. The owner argued that he was unaware of the actions of the waitress so could not be said to have committed the offence 'knowingly'. The first instance court agreed that he did not have the necessary *mens rea* and the charge was dismissed. The prosecutor appealed and the case eventually reached the House of Lords, which dismissed the appeal.

Lord Reid admitted that the argument that it would be difficult on occasions to enforce such statutes without the delegation principle was a strong one. He added, however, that if it had not been so firmly established for over half a century, he would be very tempted to challenge such a rule, which made a person liable even though the *mens rea* of the crime said that he had to commit the offence 'knowingly'. Because of the well-established authorities, he concluded that it was now 'too late to upset so long-standing a practice'.

He admitted that the distinction that had developed between full delegation where the owner was liable, and partial delegation where he might not be, was 'hard to justify'. Despite this, Lord Reid was not prepared to abolish it and by such a move make the defendant liable, which was what the prosecution was requesting in the appeal.

While this point was 'tidied up' in *Vane*, two of the Law Lords believed that the delegation principle was not applicable in relation to the Licensing Act 1961, while two others clearly thought it was. It was therefore inevitable that the matter would come up again.

In *Winson 1969*, the Court of Appeal accepted that the doctrine of delegation still formed part of English law and held that it did apply to the licensing laws.

The whole matter was thrown into confusion again in *Howker* v *Robinson 1973*, where the Divisional Court applied the doctrine of delegation in a case where there was only partial delegation.

The landlord had been serving in the public bar, while his barman had served drinks illegally in the lounge bar. The appeal court used *Winson* as a precedent to show that the doctrine still existed and simply accepted it as a fact that the magistrates had found that delegation had taken place. In fact, it was clear that only partial delegation existed in this case and that therefore, under this principle at least, the licensee should not have been convicted. It has been persuasively argued that this case was wrongly decided.

14.2.3 ARGUMENTS FOR AND AGAINST VICARIOUS LIABILITY

Views of those favouring the retention of the principle

The judges have stated on more than one occasion that, without the principle of vicarious liability, it would be very hard on occasion to obtain a conviction. The comments of the judges in *Mousell Ltd* v *London and North Western Railway Co. 1917* and in *Vane* v *Yiannopoullos 1965* illustrate this.

It has been argued that the principle helps to keep standards high and ensures that employers choose their staff with care.

Allied to this, the knowledge that they might become criminally liable may prevent employers from 'cutting corners' to reap greater profits.

Without the delegation principle, licensees and other employers could successfully argue that they were unaware of any violation of the law, because they were not on the premises at the relevant time.

In addition, this same principle helps to ensure that a licensee or other person in charge continues to retain proper control over his business even when he is not present. If he wishes to renounce such responsibility, he knows that it will be necessary to delegate this to someone who is capable of understanding and obeying the law. It has been argued that it is not too onerous to impose liability in this way, as the offences are only of a quasi-criminal status.

Adverse criticisms of the principle of vicarious liability

Probably the most important one is that it is unjust to penalise a party for the wrong of another, particularly in cases where he cannot possibly know of the wrong doing. It offends against the principle that criminal liability should only be imposed on the person concerned.

It is felt to be even more unjust when the offence requires *mens rea* and the *mens rea* of another is imputed to the person vicariously liable, as happens under the delegation principle.

A person or company can be made liable even where he has taken steps to see that the offence is not committed, as in *Coppen v Moore (No. 2) 1898*, the *Duke of Leinster 1924* and *Allen v Whitehead 1930*.

Allied to the last point, it has not been proved that the principle really does have the effect of raising standards. As noted above, in many cases the person charged has tried to ensure that the law is obeyed. In other cases, he may be completely unaware of the infringement.

The principles of vicarious liability in criminal law have not been laid down by Parliament; instead they are judge-made and, as can be seen under the delegation principle, often move completely away from the intention of Parliament. This can be seen when a person is found vicariously liable, but knows nothing about the infringement and the statute provides that the offence has to be committed 'knowingly'.

A criminal conviction is still seen as a serious matter, despite the fact that the offence is only a regulatory one. It might well have serious implications for future business activities.

14.2.4 POSSIBLE REFORM OF VICARIOUS LIABILITY

The Draft Criminal Code of 1989 would, if enacted, reform this area of law. It would drastically restrict the scope of vicarious liability. Probably the most important change would be to abolish the situations where the *mens rea* of the actual offender is also attributed to the employer or other person, so the delegation principle would no longer apply. Under Clause 29, such a person would only be liable if this is specified in the offence. In addition, an employer would only be liable in cases where the wrongdoer was acting within the scope of his employment, or as an independent contractor.

activity

1 Discuss whether the principle of vicarious liability in criminal law has any part to play in a just society.

2 Enrico owns a very successful restaurant called The Tenors. He has put Mario in charge of the establishment while he concentrates on his singing and just visits on a Sunday to check the books and count the profits! He is outraged to find that he has been charged with contravening the terms of his drinking licence. He has discovered that Mario has been serving drinks without meals to the impoverished students studying at the Figaro School of Music, close to the restaurant.

Advise Enrico. How would your answer to question 2 differ if Enrico maintained control of the ground floor restaurant and left Mario to deal with the first floor patrons?

14.3 CORPORATE LIABILITY

This subject is connected to the above, in that a corporation may sometimes be found vicariously liable for the acts of its employees. In addition, a corporation may well be liable in its own right under one of the ways mentioned below. In such a situation, the company itself will be charged as the principal offender, rather than being charged along with another offender, as in the case of vicarious liability.

The first point to establish is what is meant by the term 'corporation'. The word comes from the Latin '*corpus*', which means 'body'. A corporation therefore is a legal body, an artificially created organisation with directors managing the business and, in theory at least, the shareholders controlling it. The most common example of a corporation is the private or public limited company, a type of organisation which became widely recognised in the middle of the last century.

In the distant past, a corporation could not be found criminally liable because a personal appearance was needed in court. That problem was solved by using a complicated procedure which enabled an attorney to appear on the corporation's behalf in the Court of King's Bench but such a tortuous route became unnecessary with the passing of the Criminal Justice Act 1925. A corporation may now appear in court through a representative and we need to examine the circumstances under which it will

become liable. It is convenient to discuss this under three headings.

When the principle of vicarious liability is invoked

A company may be held vicariously liable in the same way as a natural person, and the same principles, discussed above, will apply to that body. In the cases of *Mousell Ltd* v *London and North Western Railway Co. 1917* and *National Rivers Authority* v *Alfred McAlpine Homes East Ltd 1994*, mentioned earlier, the respective companies were found guilty of an offence through the acts of their employees and were charged alongside them. In the first case, the company was liable for evading freight charges, in the second situation for being involved in the pollution of a river.

Where the statute expressly makes a corporation liable

Some statutes will expressly make a corporation liable and often such liability will be absolute. In such cases there will no problems with having to prove that the company possessed *mens rea*, as necessary in the cases mentioned below. It should also be noted that the word 'corporation' or 'company' does not have to be expressly stated. The Interpretation Act 1978 states that the word 'person' includes a body of persons corporate or unincorporate (the latter phrase includes clubs, societies and partnerships), unless otherwise stated.

There are obviously some offences that a company cannot commit as, for example, the crime of murder. The general rule is that a company cannot be convicted of a crime for which it cannot be sentenced, so it can only be convicted of offences where a fine can be imposed. With murder, the only sentence is one of life imprisonment. Over the years, the courts have also added the crimes of incest, perjury and rape. In an important ruling, however, in *P & O European Ferries (Dover) Ltd 1991*, it was decided that a company could be held liable for manslaughter. The defendants had tried to argue that an old definition existed, identified by Coke in the seventeenth century and applied in the USA and New Zealand, stating that a killing had to be 'of a human being by a human being'. Therefore, it was argued, a company could not be liable. Turner J disagreed, but made it clear that liability will not be easy to establish. He stated:

> A company may be vicariously liable for the negligent acts or omissions of its servants and agents, but for a company to be criminally liable for manslaughter – on the assumption I am making that such a crime exists – it is required that the *mens rea* and *actus reus* of manslaughter should be established not only against those who acted for or in the name of the company but against those who were identified as the embodiment of the company itself.

Where the doctrine of identification is used

Where an offence requires *mens rea*, therefore, there has to be some way of finding this within a company structure because an inanimate body obviously has no mind. The courts have done this by developing the doctrine of identification. This is done by looking for the personnel in the company who are said to be 'the directing mind and will' of the organisation. The phrase was first used back in 1915 in *Lennard's Carrying Co. Ltd* v *Asiatic Petroleum.*

The identification principle was taken further in three cases in 1944. In *DPP* v *Kent and Sussex Contractors Ltd 1944*, it was held that the intention and belief of a responsible agent of the company could be imputed to the company itself. This case was quoted with approval in *ICR Haulage 1944* where, again, the company tried to argue that, not being a natural person, it could not have a mind, honest or otherwise and so could not be indicted, in this instance with conspiracy to defraud. The Court of Appeal decided that knowledge and intention of the agent involved in the conspiracy could be imputed to the company. Lastly, in *Moore* v *Bresler 1944*, matters were taken even further and the company involved was found guilty of making false tax returns, via the company secretary and a branch sales manager even though this action on their part was designed to defraud the company itself. This decision has been criticised and the provisions of the Draft Code, if ever enacted, would not make a company liable in cases where the acts of the controlling officers, as they are known in the Code, were done with the intention of causing harm to the company.

In *Robert Millar (Contractors) Ltd and Millar 1970*, the courts went further still and found the managing director of a company liable for counselling and procuring causing death by dangerous driving. He had allowed a heavy lorry and trailer to be taken out on the road, laden with 18 tons of bricks, knowing that the front offside tyre was badly worn. The tyre had blown, the driver had lost control and the lorry had crashed into a car travelling the other way, killing all the occupants, a family of six. The driver, who had also known of the dangerous state of the vehicle and had complained about it many times, was found guilty of dangerous driving but treated leniently by the judge, with a modest fine and a disqualification. The company, however, was fined £750 and the managing director was sent to prison for nine months. The appeal was dismissed, the Court of Appeal affirming that 'at the moment this accident happened ... the appellants were still counselling and procuring the dangerous driving'.

In *HL Bolton (Engineering) Co Ltd* v *TJ Graham and Sons Ltd 1957*, Lord Denning delivered his interpretation of the doctrine of identification in his own inimitable style. He likened a company to a human body and went on to say:

It has a brain and nerve centre which controls what it does. It also has hands which hold the tools and act in accordance with directions from the centre. Some of the people in the company are mere servants and agents who are nothing more than hands to do the work and cannot be said to represent the mind or will. Others are directors and managers who represent the directing mind and will of the company and control what it does. The state of mind of these managers is the state of mind of the company and is treated by the law as such.

This statement was quoted with approval by the House of Lords in *Tesco Ltd* v *Natrass 1972*, the leading case on the doctrine of identification. The facts were very simple. An old age pensioner had tried to buy a packet of washing powder at a price that had appeared in advertisements and in Tesco's shop window but was told that the only packets left were at the normal price. A sales assistant had put out the full price packets, after discovering the special offer packets had all been sold, but had failed to inform the manager that more should be ordered.

The pensioner complained and the company was prosecuted and convicted under the Trade Descriptions Act 1968. Tesco relied on a defence in the Act. This states that liability will not arise if the person charged can prove that he has taken all reasonable precautions and exercised all due diligence to avoid the commission of the offence and show that the offence was committed by 'another person'. The branch manager was duly named as that person but the magistrates took the view that he was part of the company and convicted Tesco. The House of Lords disagreed. Their Lordships decided that the branch manager was too far down in the scale of command to be part of the 'directing mind or will' of the company. To be in such a position, Lord Reid felt that the company member needed to be part of the board of directors, the managing director or perhaps be one of the other superior officers. Viscount Dilhorne included a person in actual control of the operations of a company and who is not answerable to anyone else.

Similarly in *Boal 1992*, an assistant general manager at a large bookstore was not held to be in such a position and so escaped liability under the Fire Precautions Act 1971 for the company's breaches of its fire certificate. If he had been classed as a director, manager, company secretary or other similar officer both he, and the company could have been liable.

These decisions make it apparent that it is not easy to gain a conviction in this way, although in *Redfern 1993* the Court of Appeal stressed that the important factor was whether the person committing the crime had true powers of management. In the civil cases concerning the *Ready Mixed Concrete Co. 1995* and *Meridian Global Funds Management Asia Ltd 1995*, the House of Lords and Privy Council respectively did not attempt to rely on such a doctrine and managed to find the companies liable under a construction of the relevant acts.

The difficulties of gaining a conviction against a company for a serious charge were highlighted after the sinking of the *Herald of Free Enterprise* in Zeebrugge harbour in March 1987, when the charges of manslaughter against seven individuals and against P & O European Ferries itself all collapsed. There appeared to be a high degree of mismanagement within the company but it was difficult to apportion the blame. The Sheen Report in 1987 came to the conclusion that the company was 'infected with the disease of sloppiness' but, because of the state of the law at that time, several separate errors could not be combined to make the company liable for what was then reckless manslaughter. Even today, when gross negligence manslaughter has replaced reckless manslaughter, the negligence must be gross and this, again, is hard to establish.

In *Seaboard Offshore* v *Secretary of State for Transport 1994*, the company was convicted of failing to take all reasonable steps to ensure that the ship in question operated in a safe manner, as required under the Merchant Shipping Act 1988. The ship had put to sea within three hours of a new chief engineer joining it. Because he had no time to study the workings of the ship, he had flooded the engines, although no one's life had been endangered.

The magistrates decided that the company could be found liable if anyone had allowed the ship to leave in these conditions and it was convicted. The Divisional Court allowed the company's appeal that the question of the structure of the company had not been properly reviewed. The prosecutor then appealed. The House of Lords dismissed this, although for different reasons than those given by the lower court. Their Lordships decided that the Act imposed a duty on the actual owner of the vessel but, provided that he had taken all reasonable steps, he could not be made criminally liable for the faults of his employees.

14.3.1 POSSIBLE REFORM OF CORPORATE LIABILITY

The Law Commission has specifically addressed this issue after noting the depth of feeling on the subject and recognising that some sort of reform is essential.

The Commission recommends the creation of a new offence of corporate killing. This would arise where a management failure of the company was the cause, or one of the causes, of the person's death and the failure constitutes

Police send Southall train crash dossier for prosecution decision

POLICE have presented their evidence to the Crown Prosecution Service over the Southall rail crash in which seven died and 13 were seriously injured.

A decision is expected shortly on whether charges of corporate manslaughter will be levied against Railtrack and Greater Western, the company whose express crashed at 100mph into a freight train crossing at a junction last September.

It could be made before the express driver, Larry Harrison, 50, appears in court at the end of this month.

He has already been charged with manslaughter.

Sources connected with the crash, however, say that Railtrack will not face action though CPS solicitors could still recommend a corporate manslaughter charge against Great Western. A Crown Prosecution Service spokeswoman said that files compiled by the British Transport Police had now been received and were "currently under consideration".

The spokeswoman said a decision had not yet been made and was unable to say when it would be. A spokesman for the British Transport Police said: "There is a continuing inquiry into aspects of corporate liability. We are trying to finalise it as soon as possible."

In addition to corporate manslaughter charges the CPS could also instigate proceedings through the Health and Safety at Work Act which relates to passenger safety. The Southall crash has been dogged by accusations that safety equipment on the express was not working and had previously been reported to be out of action.

Colleagues of Mr Harrison said that the train's Automatic Warning System (AWS) had been logged in the train's repair book as non-operational when he took charge of the Swansea to London service at Cardiff.

As the driver approaches a red signal, or yellow or double yellow, a buzzer or hooter sounds in the cab along with a visual indicator.

This system, however, was out of action and will form a major part of the defence case.

Taken from an article by Dick Murray in the *Evening Standard*, 5 August 1998

- A person or company may be liable under the principle of vicarious liability for the criminal acts of another, although such liability is much more restricted than in civil law
- Such liability will arise in three main ways: first where a statute states this (*Mousell Ltd* v *London and North West Railway Co. 1917*), secondly where the acts of an agent can be imputed to the other (*Coppen* v *Moore (No. 2) 1898, Duke of Leinster 1924* and *National Rivers Authority* v *Alfred McAlpine Homes East 1994*), and thirdly, where the delegation principle applies (*Allen* v *Whitehead 1930, Linnett* v *MPC 1946, Vane* v *Yiannopoullos 1965, Winson 1969*)
- The second head is confined to offences of strict liability but, under the third head, the *mens rea* of the party committing the offence can be imputed to the person delegating the authority
- The delegation principle only applies where the whole of the authority has been delegated (*Vane* v *Yiannopoullos 1964*). *Howker* v *Robinson 1973*, a Divisional Court decision, is felt to be wrong on this point; it certainly conflicts with the House of Lords' decision in *Vane*
- The principle of vicarious liability can apply to a company in the same way as to an individual (*Mousell Ltd* v *London and North West Railway Co. 1917, National Rivers Authority* v *Alfred McAlpine Homes East 1994*)
- A company may also be liable on its own account in two ways: first, where a statute expressly states this and secondly where the doctrine of identification is used
- This applies if those with the 'directing mind and will' of the company have committed the offence (*Lennards Carrying Co.* v *Asiatic Petroleum 1915, DPP* v *Kent and Sussex Contractors 1944, ICR Haulage 1944, Moore* v *Bresler 1944, HL Bolton* v *TJ Graham 1957, Robert Millar (Contractors) and Millar 1970, Tesco* v *Natrass 1972*)
- Lord Denning talked of those at the brain and nerve centre, for whose actions the company would be liable and the mere 'hands' of the business, where the company was not liable under this doctrine (*HL Bolton* v *TJ Graham 1957*). The Court of Appeal found the company liable where the employee had 'true powers of management' (*Redfern 1993*)
- The employees were not held to be part of the 'directing mind and will' in *Tesco* v *Natrass 1972*, or *Boal 1992*
- Under this doctrine, a company may still be liable even if the offence has been committed to defraud it (*Moore* v *Bresler 1944*)
- In a dangerous driving case, the company may be liable for counselling and procuring (*Robert Millar (Contractors) and Millar 1970*)
- A company may be liable for most offences, except murder, bigamy, rape and incest. It can be liable for manslaughter (*P & O European Ferries 1991, OLL 1994*), but convictions are rare and reform has been called for

FIGURE 14.1 *Key facts chart on vicarious and corporate liability*

It can be seen that there appears to be a real need to change the law in this area to deal with the disquiet caused when companies evade responsibility, especially for death and really serious injuries, caused wholly or partly by their own failures. No corporate liability was found after the Kings Cross fire, the Zeebrugge disaster or the Clapham rail crash. Following the Zeebrugge tragedy, the courts did at least recognise that a company can be liable for manslaughter, even though no convictions ensued. In addition, the change from reckless to gross negligence manslaughter may well help in some cases. In *OLL Ltd 1994*, a company was successfully prosecuted for the Lyme Bay canoe disaster, although it was seen in Chapter 5 that the company director's prison sentence was reduced on appeal. A similar thing happened in the case of *O'Connor*, concerning the sinking of the *Pescado*, also noted in that chapter.

conduct falling far below what can reasonably be expected of the corporation in the circumstances.

Such failure on the part of a company would arise: 'if the way in which its activities are managed or organised fails to ensure the health and safety of persons employed in or affected by those activities: and such a failure may be regarded as a cause of a person's death notwithstanding that the immediate cause is the act or omission of an individual.'

The offence would be an indictable one, with an unlimited fine as punishment. The courts are also showing an increasing willingness to impose large fines as evidenced by the seven figure fine imposed on a company recently for failing to control an oil spill.

It will be noted that the offence is carefully worded to try to ensure that the company cannot pass the liability on to another. The new offence will run parallel to the existing offence of gross negligence manslaughter and would also co-exist with the proposed new offence of reckless killing, should this change be effected.

activity

Discuss the following statement:

❝ The current rules relating to the liability of a corporation are weighted too much in favour of the company, at the expense of the employees and the general public. ❞

summary

In this chapter, we have discovered that an individual or company may, in some instances, be criminally liable for the acts of another, under the principle of vicarious liability. Such liability is kept within narrow limits and will only operate where a statute lays this down, where the acts are by an agent or where the delegation principle applies. We have also learned that a corporation, usually in the form of a public or private limited company, may be liable in its own right for criminal acts committed by the officers of the company and may even be charged with manslaughter.

We have noted, however, that the success rate for such prosecutions is poor and that this has caused widespread concern. We have seen that the matter has been taken up by the Law Commission, which has suggested the creation of a new offence, called corporate killing, which might be easier to sustain.

CHAPTER 15

BRINGING IT ALL TOGETHER

15.1 INTRODUCTION

WELL, YOU'VE MADE it! Hopefully, you will have enjoyed studying criminal law and should by now have a good knowledge of the key topics. In this chapter, it is intended to go through each preceding chapter and highlight the important areas that could come up on your examination paper as either essays or problems. This will be followed by a brief discussion on a workable revision plan and conclude with advice on examination technique.

Remember that the chapters are set out in a distinctive way to help you in your study. Apart from the law on general defences, all the law on a particular topic will be found in one chapter. The key facts charts summarise the law, with an inclusion of the cases and statutes laying this down. These are vital for your revision. Various aspects of the law are discussed in 'Comment' sections. This should provide a good foundation for answering essay questions, where the law needs to be evaluated and discussed on a wider basis. You are also strongly advised to tackle the activities; they consist of a mix of discussion topics and problem questions, and are valuable practice for the exam.

15.2 HIGHLIGHTS OF CHAPTERS 1 TO 14

The following are only my suggestions on the important points; those setting the papers for the various boards may have different ideas. They might be of help, however, in your revision plan.

Chapter 1

Chapter 1 should be carefully read. It contains important information on the layout of the book, the appeal courts and a reminder of the importance of precedent in English law.

It is very important to understand the workings of the appeal system when studying criminal law. Many of the cases concern 'grey' areas that these courts have helped to solve. The Divisional Court hears appeals from the magistrates' court or the Crown Court where there has already been an appeal there from the lower court. You will not find points of law on indictable offences there. If there is an important question of law, there may be a further appeal from the Divisional Court straight to the House of Lords. The vast majority of appeals concerning indictable offences and triable either way offences where the case is dealt with in the Crown Court, are dealt with by the Court of Appeal. Remember that, on the criminal side of the law, the House of Lords will only deal with points of law of general public importance. The normal stopping place is the Court of Appeal.

Remember the importance of the doctrine of precedent. If a precedent is laid down by a sufficiently high court, that decision will be binding on the lower court unless it can be distinguished. The Court of Appeal is often bound by decisions of the House of Lords, which it might, on occasion, prefer not to follow. It can choose not to follow the Privy Council, as can be seen under provocation and, in a more limited way, it may also choose not to follow its own earlier rulings, as noted under actual bodily harm.

Chapter 2

There are several important areas in Chapter 2. When looking at the *actus reus* of a crime, you should note the 'state of affairs' cases, like *Larsonneur*, and, particularly, the area on omissions. There could be an essay on the lines of whether there should be liability for failing to act or a problem situation on assuming a duty or failing to put right a dangerous situation. When studying *mens rea*, remember that the question of intention is to be decided by the jury and that *Moloney* has established that in most cases no extra help on the meaning of intention will be given. What has caused problems is where the defendant is claiming that it was not his intention to kill, i.e. where an oblique intent has to be established. Here the problem is the wording of the judge's direction. Remember that the judge's ruling that the defendant must have foreseen that death or serious injury was virtually certain (or highly probable), is only evidence from which the jury is entitled to infer that he did intend to kill; it is the jury's decision. Foresight of death or serious harm is not the same as intention. Know the cases on this up to *Woollin 1998*. The most important so far are *Hancock* and *Nedrick*. This will usually be an essay question topic.

Remember that two types of recklessness exist in English law, *Cunningham* and *Caldwell* recklessness and remember that the first type is needed for all assault cases. The latter is now reserved for criminal damage alone. Know how

this came about. Be able to discuss the strictness of *Caldwell* in cases like *Elliott* and also know that the House of Lords is only prepared to recognise a lacuna, or loophole, in very limited circumstances. This will probably come up as an essay question or be combined with a problem on assault of some sort or with a problem on criminal damage. Questions on negligence will normally be confined to gross negligence manslaughter, as described in Chapter 5.

Questions on strict liability often take the form of an essay but remember to answer the question set and not give a mere list of advantages and disadvantages.

Chapter 3

In Chapter 3 it is vital to learn the definition of murder, so that you can identify when it is not established and manslaughter can be pleaded. The subject of causation, often in the form of a problem, is a popular area. One of the most important points to remember is that it will take a very special event to break the chain of causation. Know the cases on this.

With regard to murder, know that it is a common law offence, there is no statutory definition. Know also that the year and a day rule has been abolished and note the difficulties of establishing birth and death. Note also the importance of the *AG's Reference (No. 3 of 1994) 1996*. It may be manslaughter or murder when a foetus is injured, is then born alive and then dies.

Chapter 4

Note that Chapter 4 deals with voluntary manslaughter and is a fertile ground for both problems and essays. Know that the law is mainly in the Homicide Act 1957. The limited defence of diminished responsibility, reducing the crime to manslaughter, could be linked to the general defence of insanity, which is available for all crimes but has a stigma attached. Know the definitions of both diminished responsibility and insanity and the criticisms of the M'Naghten Rules.

Know the three elements of provocation and

be able to apply them in a clear way to a problem situation. Be aware that the concept of the reasonable man continues to give trouble and note the latest cases on this. Currently, the Court of Appeal is seeking to extend the characteristics that may be attributed to this mythical figure, while the Privy Council wants to curtail them. Watch out for a House of Lords ruling on this. Meanwhile *Camplin* is still the main authority but has been extended by the Court of Appeal.

Chapter 5

As mentioned earlier, gross negligence is back, so study this carefully. Note also the elements that have to be established for constructive manslaughter and the Law Commission's view on this offence. This could be an area for an essay or it could make a good problem with having to establish an unlawful and dangerous act.

Chapter 6

Chapter 6 is a very large chapter containing all the non-fatal offences against the person. You need to know the *actus reus* and *mens rea* of each one, from assault and battery up to grievous bodily harm with intent. Note that abh can be established with the *mens rea* of a common assault and that the *mens rea* for a s.20 offence is merely 'some harm' but for liability under s.18, there must be an intention to cause gbh. Be able to pinpoint the other differences between s.18 and s.20. Note the restrictions on the defence of consent, after the decisions of the House of Lords and the European Court in *Brown*, but note *Wilson*, which has opened matters up again! Note that the courts have been prepared to accept psychiatric harm (*Constanza, Ireland*), but note that the Protection from Harassment Act lessens the need for such help.

Chapter 7

Chapter 7 is another huge chapter. There is nearly always a question on theft in the exam. It is important to understand the *actus reus* and *mens rea* and be able to apply ss.2–6 to problem situations. There are several problems for you to tackle in this chapter, which should help with this. Know the specific defences laid down in the Act. Appropriation of property is still a favourite area so know the case of *Gomez* and the cases after this. You should also be able to decide when someone is or is not dishonest under the Act.

Know that the definition of theft must first be satisfied for robbery and burglary. The latter may come up in a problem situation but the largest part of your time should be explaining the elements of theft. Blackmail again, is likely to be included in a problem, rather than having its own treatment.

Chapter 8

Chapter 8 concerns the deception offences. It is should be remembered that, after *Gomez*, anyone satisfying the definition of s.15 will also be guilty of theft. Know the differences between the elements for theft and deception. The two often come up together. You need to memorise the *actus reus* and *mens rea* of the other deception offences and s.3 Theft Act 1978. If you know the elements of each offence, you will do really well in this area.

Chapter 9

Chapter 9 gives detail on basic criminal damage and the aggravated offences under s.1(2) and s.1(3). Know what is meant by the terms damage and destruction and be aware of the defence of lawful excuse under s.5. Note the difference between the basic and aggravated offences. Under s.1(2), the property need not belong to another but know that the life must be endangered by the damaging or destroying of property. Note that the defence of lawful excuse does not apply to the more serious offences. Remember that *Caldwell* concerned criminal damage in both the basic and aggravated forms, and *Shimmen* relates to the basic offence. Be able to discuss both the damage and the *mens rea* needed for the offences. Remember that damage by the use of fire is arson under s.1(3).

Chapter 10

Chapter 10 concerns the first four of the ten general defences. Note that the presumption that no liability exists for 10–14-year-olds has been removed by Parliament. We looked at the defence of insanity earlier. The defence may not be well used but examiners like this area! It could also be combined with automatism, which is a complete defence; note the cases on hypoglycaemia and compare with hyperglycaemia, which could be insanity. Examiners also like intoxication! Remember that the rules differ for basic intent crimes, for which intoxication is no defence, and specific intent crimes, where it may be, although it will usually only reduce the crime, apart from cases of theft. Note the important ruling in *Kingston*, however, that a drunken intent is still an intent. Watch out for involuntary intoxication.

Chapter 11

Chapter 11 concerns the other general defences. The defence of mistake may not come up alone but could be combined with others. The defences of necessity, duress of circumstances which is an extension of this, and duress of threats should all be learned together and the elements of each known well. Duress of circumstances is a developing defence so it is a popular area. Know that the restrictions on the defences of duress of circumstances and duress of threats are the same, so the defendant must be a sober man of reasonable firmness. The courts are still deciding which of the characteristics of the defendant can be attributed to him. Neither defence, nor the defence of necessity can be used for murder, either as a principal or as an accomplice, nor can it be used for attempted murder. Self defence and the prevention of crime are also popular areas and may well be the subject of a problem question, in which too much force is used and a death results. At present, this is still murder.

Chapter 12

Chapter 12 concerns parties to a crime and you need to learn the differences between aiders, abettors, counsellors and procurers. This may well come up as a problem question. You also need to know how the *mens rea* for participation is established. Note also that the law is hard on those who embark on a joint enterprise. They will be liable along with the other unless the latter does something completely unexpected. Know the latest cases on this fertile area.

Chapter 13

Chapter 13 describes the different types of inchoate offences, attempt, conspiracy and incitement. You need to be able to identify each type of offence and know the *mens rea* required. It could come up as a problem question, along with a substantive offence, or you might be asked to compare them or be asked whether common law conspiracy should remain. Remember that you can be found guilty of incitement, attempt and statutory conspiracy, even though the main crime is impossible.

Chapter 14

Chapter 14 concerns the area of vicarious and corporate liability and the latter could be a popular area with the promise of reforms in this area. The first part of the chapter nearly always arises as an essay question and is easy to learn, but it is possible that corporate liability could be combined with manslaughter by gross negligence.

15.3 A REVISION PLAN

You are probably inundated with the advice on revision so this is only intended as a brief guide. Your lecturers will give you valuable help with this. The most important point is try to enjoy your revision and you can do this if you don't leave it all until the last minute. Most successful revision entails careful planning to avoid last minute panics and attendant loss of confidence.

I have known a few students who have managed to learn the whole of the course in just three or four weeks but one of them was a policeman. Such a course is not to be recommended if you wish to keep your health, looks and sanity!

If you are answering the problem questions as you learn each area and discussing the other topics, you will be pleasantly surprised when you start your formal revision to discover just how much you know already. I would suggest that, before you begin your concentrated revision, you should re-read as much of your work as possible, not with the object of learning it all but just to get the whole picture. It is important to start with a general view of the subject before zooming in on particular topics. At this stage, it is advisable to write down all the areas you need to learn, to know from the start the revision route that you are going to take. You can then condense down and down and, by examination day, just have cards of the main points, to trigger your memory. It is important, when dividing up your work, not to set yourself impossible tasks; take a small area at a time, read the information, take notes and ask yourself what you have learned. Have periodic breaks and give yourselves treats. The diet can be reactivated after the exam! It is often a good plan to work with friends. One excellent way to revise is to teach the subject to another. Your positions can then be reversed and you can take notes as your friend explains the matter to you. Remember, you are not in competition; you are all going to obtain high grades. A word of warning, though! Don't talk with your friends on the day of the exam. They might start to discuss an area with which you are not familiar.

15.4 EXAMINATION TECHNIQUE

Again, this is only intended to give a very brief guide to supplement the fuller advice given by your lecturers. In those first tense moments when you are waiting to start, jot down the various topic areas; use the chapters of this book as a guide. When the examination gets under way, don't start writing immediately, however great the temptation. It is advisable to spend several minutes reading the paper, remembering to turn over the page if appropriate. There may well be a 'doddle' of a question lurking there! Remember, too, that both essays and problems require some planning before you start. The examiner may be marking hundreds of scripts so you need to make an impact with your first words. A brief explanation of the course your answer is to take works wonders, as it puts the examiner on the same track as you immediately. Remember also that the examiner is looking for your knowledge of the law, so remember that it is vital to back up your answer with appropriate case law or relevant Acts of Parliament. Don't spend valuable time writing out all the facts of a case, a brief explanation to convince the examiner that you know your stuff will suffice; it is the principle of law that is the most important part. If you can't remember the name of the case, don't panic; put in brief facts and quote the principle coming from it. If you can't even remember that, put in general information and you may pick up some marks. You cannot get any from a blank page. Should you run short of time, be ruthless. Stop one question and continue with the next and finish with notes if you are completely out of time at the end. It is surprising how much information you can put down in this way in roughly the same time as writing one complete sentence. The latter will only give you minimal marks, whereas examiners are sympathetic if there appears to be a genuine time problem, especially if you have written a lot before this. Leave some space after each question so that you can return to it at a later time if you have something extra to add.

A good essay will have an introduction, a middle and an effective conclusion, hopefully bringing in the title or indicating in some other way that you have answered the question set by the examiner and not what you were hoping he would ask. In problem questions, it is important to realise that several issues may be involved. If there is little guidance from the question, it is better to deal with the substantive offences first and then see if there are any specific or general defences. There may be more than one party involved and you might need to see if the others are joint principals or secondary offenders or, alternatively, whether any inchoate offences exist.

If you get the time, it is a good idea to read through and correct your answers. You'll be surprised sometimes with the odd things you may have written in the stress of the moment. Finally, after having done your best, put it all behind you until result time. The very best of luck to all of you!

TABLE OF CASES

Table of statutes and statutory instruments

INDEX